THE RESPONSIBLE PERSON Second Edition

Essays · Short Stories · Poems

Titled in its first edition *The Responsible Man*

Edited by

C. Jeriel Howard *and* Richard Francis Tracz

Bishop College   Southern Methodist University

Canfield Press   ⨍   *San Francisco*
A Department of Harper & Row, Publishers, Inc.
New York   Evanston   London

The Responsible Person, Second Edition

75   76   77   78   10 9 8 7 6 5 4 3 2 1

Library of Congress Cataloging in Publication Data

Howard, C   Jeriel, 1939–   comp.
    The responsible person.

    1.   College readers.   I.   Tracz, Richard Francis,
joint comp.   II.   Title.
PE1122.H69   1975   808'.04275   74–23953

ISBN 0-06-383901-6

Preface

Responsibility, *irresponsibility*, and their various synonyms were frequently used—and very important words they were—when we wrote the preface to the first edition of this anthology in 1970; today these words are even more important. Changing family structures, continuing instability on many college campuses, drastic changes within organized religious bodies, and scandals within virtually every level of government make a proper understanding of personal responsibility essential to the development and maturity of every individual. The present generation of college students is unwilling to accept for ideas of responsibility those lukewarm, emotional, or secondhand arguments offered them by their elders. They feel a commitment to test their own ideas of individual and group responsibility in an effort to define their own standards. Although their actions may momentarily suggest instability, their quest for universal truth is, we believe, sincere; and we further believe that they have a right to discuss and evaluate any idea in their quest for truth. No area of life should be regarded so sacred as to prohibit exploration.

This book is designed to open for discussion many of the most important questions of personal and social responsibility. We have established our organization, made our selections, and written our questions for discussion and topics for writing with a distinct focus on selected problems of responsibility to oneself and to the world in which one lives.

The organization of the text is simple. We have grouped problems for discussion into six broad areas: responsibility to oneself, to family, and to peers; responsibility to church, to school, and to government. Although many of the problems presented for discussion do overlap, we feel that they can best be discussed when isolated into these broad divisions.

In each of our six sections we have included selections of essays, short stories, and poems. We have based our selections on the problems that we wished to emphasize, but we have also been aware of literary quality as a basis for selection. Our personal bias has been toward the literature of this century, for we feel that contemporary students can best find their own feelings and problems mirrored in literature of their age. In each section we have included one or two selections from an earlier period in an effort to show that humanity's thinking has not greatly changed with the passing of time.

The second edition contains many selections not found in the first; also, some of the original selections have been moved to different units where we and other users of the book found them more useful. Unfortunately, some publishers and agents have virtually priced their client–authors out of anthologies. Several selections that we would have wished to use were eliminated by unusually high fee requests. But we feel that we have captured the feeling of the decade of the seventies with this edition, whose new entries include a large representation from minority and women writers. In light of the current interest in language as a reinforcer of prejudice, the book's title has been changed to eliminate an apparent masculine bias. Responsibility is not a function of sex. Each individual faces the same problems and conflicts in developing values.

We have assumed that this book will be used in freshman and sophomore courses where the course format demands more discussion than lecture; therefore we have attempted to select short works that lend themselves to discussion. In some instances we have rejected selections that might well have suited our thematic development because we felt that they were too long to fit the total plan for the text. The selections in later sections of the text are generally longer and more complicated than those in the earlier sections.

We have been committed to the idea that if we cannot ask pertinent questions about an entry it does not belong in the text. Therefore, each entry is followed by questions for discussion, topics for comparison, and suggestions for writing. The questions for discussion open for careful exploration many sensitive areas relative to responsibility. We purposely have not prepared an instructor's manual with an answer for each question because we feel that there is no one correct answer. Rather, there are many answers. Fundamental to the philosophy of this book is the idea that individuals must work out for themselves their own answers to these questions and then learn to live with whatever responsibilities their answers place upon them. The topics for comparison seek to bring together related or conflicting opinions as they are found in the selections within one division. These topics may be discussed after both selections have been read, or all the topics for comparison may be used as a means to review the entire section after it has been completed. Suggestions for writing are designed to be used for short paragraphs or entire essays, depending on the structure of the course. Some instructors may wish to have students keep a notebook with short responses to each selection. Other instructors may wish to assign themes on only certain selections.

None of the introductory material mentions literary form or history. We believe that students must first learn that literature has something to say to them about their problems before they can become interested in how or why it develops its message. Also, we are aware that every instructor has a favorite method of developing this subject. At any time during the course an instructor may pause to add whatever comments he or she wishes to make about the style of a particular selection.

Our work on this second edition was made easier by the many helpful suggestions from instructors and students who used the first. To these individuals we extend our appreciation. Continued appreciation goes to James P. Campbell who, along with us, understands and recalls the genesis of this project. And, finally, we must thank Mabel Buggherz for the consistently good humor she shared with us during our long evenings of work.

C. J. H.
R. F. T.

Contents

Part Two   INDIVIDUAL – FAMILY

Part Three   INDIVIDUAL—PEERS

Part Four   INDIVIDUAL—SCHOOL

Part Five   INDIVIDUAL—RELIGION

stories:

poems:

Part Six   INDIVIDUAL—STATE

essays:

stories:

poems:

photo by **Kate Kline May**

Part One

INDIVIDUAL–SELF

Philosophers ancient and modern agree that the most important development in one's life is the coming to a true understanding of oneself. An individual must learn what he or she really believes, must recognize personal strengths and weaknesses, and must be true to his or her own ideas and ideals. The happy, successful individual is usually a person who has properly adjusted to himself or herself and has learned to live within self-created boundaries.

In the process of learning to live with oneself, it becomes impossible to separate self-respect from self-responsibility. One who violates the obligations to oneself ultimately will lose self-respect. However, being true to one's own sense of responsibility is not always easy. The individual must be confident without appearing cocky, self-interested without being selfish. One must learn to relate to oneself as a means of relating to others.

In the following selections, you will find posed for you many of the problems closely related to self-responsibility. You will search for answers to such questions as: How responsible is a person for the way he or she is? Is it possible for an individual to change? Must human beings believe in something beyond themselves? Why is decision making so important and so frightening? Does everyone need a momentary escape from responsibilities?

CHARLES MORRIS

from THE OPEN SELF

New Selves for Old

Our crisis is a strange one. We are as children playing with high explosives. And we know this. But since we know it we are unlike children. We are afraid of ourselves, afraid that we will be inadequate, afraid to assume the responsibilities that might give us back the joy of innocence. If an "implacable opponent" is destroying man, that opponent is man himself. We sense acutely the dark powers in ourselves.

We are equally aware that we have great reserves of inner strength. The feeling that a new age is beginning is as insistent as the realization that an old one ends. We have already called it the atomic age. But we do not yet know how to unlock our human resources. We have not yet devised a psychological bomb more powerful than the atomic bomb. We can release gigantic physical power by atomic fission. How can we produce a fission within the locked forces of ourselves that will release correspondingly great human power?

This is our problem. We have new engines, new fabrics, new buildings, new headaches. *We need new selves. And new relationships between selves.* We must bring ourselves up to date. We can subordinate impersonal forces to human ends only if we recover the standpoint of the personal. We must become person-centered in order to construct a person-centered society. Men and women must again become the focus of our attention and our concern. We have made over the material environment, and now we cannot evade remaking ourselves. If the bogeyman gets us, it will be our own fault, for the bogeyman is in us. Our crisis is a human crisis.

To shock ourselves into creativity we must know ourselves. We need to know the sources of our motivations and our frustrations. We need to know the techniques of self-making, and its pitfalls. Contemporary students of man have much to tell us about ourselves. We shall endeavor to tap this knowledge for our purposes, even to add to it. But our purpose remains personal. Our task is to decide what we want to do with our lives while we still have them. Our hope is to unlock energies in ourselves sufficient to blast apart our stalemates and our frustrations. "The experience of each new age requires a new confession." We must dare this new confession. "Safer the center of peril," Melville tells us, "than the circumference."

Reprinted from *The Open Self* by permission of the author.

What is man now to make of man? What are we going to make of ourselves? Such is our theme and our problem.

But these are dawn words that set work for the day.

Stocktaking

Fortunately the day is sober. A proper day to think about ourselves. It occasions neither the somber moodiness of rain nor the outgoing praisefulness of the sun. It is a sturdy day for honest thought. The night is too large and the dawn too expectant for the hard work that must be done. The most difficult task we face is to be honest about ourselves, honest with ourselves. It is easier for man to praise himself than to condemn himself, and easier for him to condemn himself than to know himself. A sober day makes for honest thought.

In this mood we at once find ourselves in doubt concerning the night's delivery that man is the maker of himself.

Man makes many things, to be sure, but does he really make himself? Did we not give the case away when we said that a sober day makes for honest thought? For this suggests that our thoughts are influenced even by the physical environment. And this doubt which our own words awaken is reinforced by doctrines widely current among us, doctrines that our physiques determine what we are, or that the society in which we live molds us into the personalities which we are. Environment, physique, society—are not these the clothes which make the man?

They are indeed mighty agencies. And the doctrines which celebrate their might have almost become the major dogmas of our time. It is not dogma to recognize that the human personality has as its core a biological organism whose growth and fruition takes place only within a society inhabiting a physical environment. It is not dogma to recognize that the human personality carries with it into every future its entire past. The emerging science of man has established these matters beyond legitimate doubt. The recognition of the role of physical environment, physique, and society in the making of man becomes questionable only when their power is made all-inclusive, when they are used to deny that man is unique among all living beings in the degree to which he makes himself and his history.

It is obvious enough that man has greatly modified his physical environment, controlling temperature and humidity in his homes, planting crops and raising cattle, closing and opening the access of the seas and rivers to chosen spots of land. It is less obvious but no less true that man has worked on his body and will in the future work much more. In his capacity as physician he doctors himself into something at least a little different from what he otherwise would have been; his choice of mates

determines to some degree the kinds of bodies future men and women
will have; he can, if he wishes, consciously select and breed the persons
who are to inhabit the earth. And, finally, it is now recognized by some
anthropologists that man himself has built through his own choices the
various patterns of channeled activity which are the cultures. The cultures of the world are human creations, patterns for living together which
persons have constructed, and will continue to construct in unforeseeable
ways. Geography, heredity, society set the conditions for human creativity, supply it with the materials upon which it must work, hinder it
or enhance it. But to admit that life-making works always within specific
conditions cannot be twisted into a denial that man is a major agency in
the making of himself.

At this point sober reflection becomes uneasy at so much talk of man.
Instead of discourse about man it suggests that we talk of individual
men and women, and justly. For it is individual men and women, each
unique, each different, who are making their lives. And the history of
man is the history of their many specific and diverse careers. In this
history different individuals play different roles of hero, villain, minor
character, chorus. The richness of the human play resides in this multiplicity of different players. We are only now beginning to see how different various persons really are. To understand these differences will be
one of our central tasks. Here merely the fact of difference is under-
scored, and its importance. For it allows us to recognize that self-
making is a matter of degree. There are persons who flow along through
life like a river in a meadow, following effortlessly the contours and the
channels marked out by the things and people in the social countryside.
There are other persons whose lives resemble a rushing waterfall which
breaks barriers and carves into new forms the mountain of social history.
It is only a few individuals who affect in a momentous manner the course
of mankind. Most persons play a humbler role, adopting the ideas, the
inventions, the manners of life which others have constructed. Yet the
difference remains one of degree, for even to adopt as one's own something built by others is to choose to admit it into one's self; and such
admission involves at least some minimum of scrutiny and appraisal,
some element, in short, of the self determining what it is to be. Without
such acceptance the innovations of those who have more largely made
themselves remain only personal achievements. The history of mankind
is a history of all men's self-makings, small and great.

The day's sober thoughts impose a third caution. Is not "making" too
strong a word and too strenuous a theme? Does it not suggest that all
men and women are or should be athletic mountain climbers, continually
daring strenuous ascents of the self's Himalayas, extroverted and restless
doers? If it does, this suggestion should immediately be erased. For a

life with such emphasis is inappropriate for many persons, inappropriate and frustrating. The ways of self-making must be many to answer to human differences. We must champion the right to be different. The current stress in our culture on power has, for instance, devastating effects on many individuals; it destroys their confidence in themselves, and drives them in large numbers through the gates of our asylums. To the list of the many kinds of minorities which we must protect we need to add a new item: the protection of psychological minorities.

The ways of self-making must be many if human potentialities and human differences are to be respected. There are demands in the self for receptivity and enjoyment, for affection and support, for meditation and truth seeking, for dependence and for detachment, as well as for power and domination. These demands differ in their strength in individuals and all are legitimate. Our theme is the technique of self-making, to be sure, but the stress is on its varieties. In the matter of life-making each of us must remain faithful to our needs and our resources. We wish, in the words of Louis MacNiece, a world of persons "equal in difference, interchangeably sovereign."

With these daytime restrictions and amplifications, the doctrine that man is uniquely the maker of himself loses the grandiose character which the meditations of large night imposed. But not its grandeur. Men live in a physical world mightier than themselves and in societies that channel and transform in various ways their biological urgencies. The artisan must always work where he is and on the materials at hand. These materials are obdurate and set conditions which his work must respect. Not everything can be made with all materials, and what can be made takes skill and time. Creation is nowhere unconditioned. And it does not always reach fruition. The artisan may bungle, may turn in rage against the obdurate stuff on which he works.

For Discussion

1. What does Morris mean by "bringing ourselves up to date"? By "new selves"?
2. Who or what, according to Morris, makes man? Do you agree with his ideas? How much responsibility for what he is lies with the individual man?
3. What is man's relationship to society? Isn't society after all a collection of individual men? Is a part of man's individuality necessarily lost when he becomes a part of society?

For Comparison

1. How does the philosophy expressed by Morris compare with that in Henley's poem "Invictus"?
2. Would Morris agree that the narrator in Shepherd's essay has become an open person?

For Composition

1. How I changed something about myself.
2. We can't always change.
3. The individual versus society.

JAMES WELDON JOHNSON

from THE AUTOBIOGRAPHY OF AN EX-COLOURED MAN

I Discover I Am a Negro

My school-days ran along very pleasantly. I stood well in my studies, not always so well with regard to my behaviour. I was never guilty of any serious misconduct, but my love of fun sometimes got me into trouble. I remember, however, that my sense of humour was so sly that most of the trouble usually fell on the head of the other fellow. My ability to play on the piano at school exercises was looked upon as little short of marvellous in a boy of my age. I was not chummy with many of my mates, but, on the whole, was about as popular as it is good for a boy to be.

One day near the end of my second term at school the principal came into our room and, after talking to the teacher, for some reason said: "I wish all of the white scholars to stand for a moment." I rose with the others. The teacher looked at me and, calling my name, said: "You sit down for the present, and rise with the others." I did not quite understand her, and questioned: "Ma'm?" She repeated, with a softer tone in her voice: "You sit down now, and rise with the others." I sat down dazed. I saw and heard nothing. When the others were asked to rise, I did not know it. When school was dismissed, I went out in a kind of stupor.

A few of the white boys jeered me, saying: "Oh, you're a nigger too." I heard some black children say: "We knew he was coloured." "Shiny" said to them: "Come along, don't tease him," and thereby won my undying gratitude.

I hurried on as fast as I could, and had gone some distance before I perceived that "Red Head" was walking by my side. After a while he said to me: "Le' me carry your books." I gave him my strap without being able to answer. When we got to my gate, he said as he handed me my books: "Say, you know my big red agate? I can't shoot with it any more. I'm going to bring it to school for you tomorrow." I took my books and ran into the house. As I passed through the hallway, I saw that my mother was busy with one of her customers; I rushed up into my own little room, shut the door, and went quickly to where my looking-glass hung on the wall. For an instant I was afraid to look, but when I did, I looked long and earnestly. I had often heard people say to my mother: "What a pretty boy you have!" I was accustomed to hear remarks about my beauty; but now, for the first time, I became conscious of it and recognized it. I noticed the ivory whiteness of my skin, the beauty of my mouth, the size and liquid darkness of my eyes, and how the long, black lashes that fringed and shaded them produced an effect that was strangely fascinating even to me. I noticed the softness and glossiness of my dark hair that fell in waves over my temples, making my forehead appear whiter than it really was. How long I stood there gazing at my image I do not know. When I came out and reached the head of the stairs, I heard the lady who had been with my mother going out. I ran downstairs and rushed to where my mother was sitting, with a piece of work in her hands. I buried my head in her lap and blurted out: "Mother, mother, tell me, am I a nigger?" I could not see her face, but I knew the piece of work dropped to the floor and I felt her hands on my head. I looked up into her face and repeated: "Tell me, mother, am I a nigger?" There were tears in her eyes and I could see that she was suffering for me. And then it was that I looked at her critically for the first time. I had thought of her in a childish way only as the most beautiful woman in the world; now I looked at her searching for defects. I could see that her skin was almost brown, that her hair was not so soft as mine, and that she did differ in some way from the other ladies who came to the house; yet, even so, I could see that she was very beautiful, more beautiful than any of them. She must have felt that I was examining her, for she hid her face in my hair and said with difficulty: "No, my darling, you are not a nigger." She went on: "You are as good as anybody; if anyone calls you a nigger, don't notice them." But the more she talked, the less was I reassured, and I stopped her by asking: "Well, mother, am I white? Are you white?" She answered tremblingly: "No, I am not white, but you—

your father is one of the greatest men in the country—the best blood of the South is in you ——" This suddenly opened up in my heart a fresh chasm of misgiving and fear, and I almost fiercely demanded: "Who is my father? Where is he?" She stroked my hair and said: "I'll tell you about him some day." I sobbed: "I want to know now." She answered: "No, not now."

Perhaps it had to be done, but I have never forgiven the woman who did it so cruelly. It may be that she never knew that she gave me a sword-thrust that day in school which was years in healing.

Since I have grown older I have often gone back and tried to analyse the change that came into my life after that fateful day in school. There did come a radical change, and, young as I was, I felt fully conscious of it, though I did not fully comprehend it. Like my first spanking, it is one of the few incidents in my life that I can remember clearly. In the life of everyone there is a limited number of unhappy experiences which are not written upon the memory, but stamped there with a die; and in long years after, they can be called up in detail, and every emotion that was stirred by them can be lived through anew; these are the tragedies of life. We may grow to include some of them among the trivial incidents of childhood—a broken toy, a promise made to us which was not kept, a harsh, heart-piercing word—but these, too, as well as the bitter experiences and disappointments of mature years, are the tragedies of life.

And so I have often lived through that hour, that day, that week, in which was wrought the miracle of my transition from one world into another; for I did indeed pass into another world. From that time I looked out through other eyes, my thoughts were coloured, my words dictated, my actions limited by one dominating, all-pervading idea which constantly increased in force and weight until I finally realized in it a great, tangible fact.

And this is the dwarfing, warping, distorting influence which operates upon each and every coloured man in the United States. He is forced to take his outlook on all things, not from the view-point of a citizen, or a man, or even a human being, but from the view-point of a *coloured* man. It is wonderful to me that the race has progressed so broadly as it has, since most of its thought and all of its activity must run through the narrow neck of this one funnel.

And it is this, too, which makes the coloured people of this country, in reality, a mystery to the whites. It is a difficult thing for a white man to learn what a coloured man really thinks; because, generally, with the latter an additional and different light must be brought to bear on what he thinks; and his thoughts are often influenced by considerations so delicate and subtle that it would be impossible for him to confess or explain them to one of the opposite race. This gives to every coloured man, in proportion to his intellectuality, a sort of dual personality; there is one phase of him which is disclosed only in the freemasonry of his own race. I have often watched with interest and sometimes with amazement even ignorant coloured men under cover of broad grins and minstrel antics maintain this dualism in the presence of white men.

I believe it to be a fact that the coloured people of this country know and understand the white people better than the white people know and understand them.

I now think that this change which came into my life was at first more subjective than objective. I do not think my friends at school changed so much toward me as I did toward them. I grew reserved, I might say suspicious. I grew constantly more and more afraid of laying myself open to some injury to my feelings or my pride. I frequently saw or fancied some slight where, I am sure, none was intended. On the other hand, my friends and teachers were, if anything different, more considerate of me; but I can remember that it was against this very attitude in particular that my sensitiveness revolted. "Red" was the only one who did not so wound me; up to this day I recall with a swelling heart his clumsy efforts to make me understand that nothing could change his love for me.

I am sure that at this time the majority of my white school-mates did not understand or appreciate any differences between me and themselves; but there were a few who had evidently received instructions at home on the matter, and more than once they displayed their knowledge in word and action. As the years passed, I noticed that the most innocent and ignorant among the others grew in wisdom.

I myself would not have so clearly understood this difference had it not been for the presence of the other coloured children at school; I had learned what their status was, and now I learned that theirs was mine. I had had no particular like or dislike for these black and brown boys and girls; in fact, with the exception of "Shiny," they had occupied very little of my thought; but I do know that when the blow fell, I had a very strong aversion to being classed with them. So I became something of a solitary. "Red" and I remained inseparable, and there was between "Shiny" and me a sort of sympathetic bond, but my intercourse with the others was never entirely free from a feeling of constraint. I must add, however, that this feeling was confined almost entirely to my intercourse with boys and girls of about my own age; I did not experience it with my seniors. And when I grew to manhood, I found myself freer with elderly white people than with those near my own age.

For Discussion

1. How, in a sense, does every man make a similar discovery about his personal differences?
2. Why does man owe it to himself to "discover himself"? How many of us really know ourselves?
3. Johnson dwells upon the negative aspects of his discovery. Do you see a positive side to the discovery of personal differences?
4. What particular responsibility is placed upon you by a knowledge of one or more of your personal differences?

For Comparison

1. Compare the discovery made in this story with those experienced by the narrator in Sherwood Anderson's "I'm a Fool." Are the effects in any way similar?
2. How would Johnson's attitude differ if he totally embraced the philosophy expressed by Morris in "The Open Self"?

For Composition

1. A discovery I made about myself.
2. Differences can be rewarding.
3. Self-knowledge brings responsibility.

JEAN SHEPHERD

THE ENDLESS STREETCAR RIDE INTO THE NIGHT, AND THE TINFOIL NOOSE

Mewling, puking babes. That's the way we all start. Damply clinging to someone's shoulder, burping weakly, clawing our way into life. *All* of us. Then gradually, surely, we begin to divide into two streams, all marching together up that long yellow brick road of life, but on opposite sides of the street. One crowd goes on to become the Official people, peering out at us from television screens, magazine covers. They are forever appearing in newsreels, carrying attaché cases, surrounded by banks of microphones while the world waits for their decisions and statements. And the rest of us go on to become . . . just us.

They are the Prime Ministers, the Presidents, Cabinet members, Stars, dynamic molders of the Universe, while we remain forever the onlookers, the applauders of their real lives.

Forever down in the dark dungeons of our souls we ask ourselves:

"How did they get away from me? When did I make that first misstep that took me forever to the wrong side of the street, to become eternally part of the accursed, anonymous Audience?"

It seems like one minute we're all playing around back of the garage, kicking tin cans and yelling at girls, and the next instant you find yourself doomed to exist as an office boy in the Mail Room of Life, while another ex-mewling, puking babe sends down Dicta, says "No comment" to the Press, and lives a real, geniune *Life* on the screen of the world.

Countless sufferers at this hour are spending billions of dollars and endless man hours lying on analysts' couches, trying to pinpoint the exact moment that they stepped off the track and into the bushes forever.

It all hinges on one sinister reality that is rarely mentioned, no doubt due to its implacable, irreversible inevitability. These decisions cannot be changed, no matter how many brightly cheerful, buoyantly optimistic books on HOW TO ACHIEVE A RICHER, FULLER, MORE BOUNTIFUL LIFE or SEVEN MAGIC GOLDEN KEYS TO INSTANT DYNAMIC SUCCESS or THE SECRET OF HOW TO BECOME A BILLIONAIRE we read, or how many classes are attended for instruction in handshaking, back-slapping, grinning, and making After-Dinner speeches. Joseph Stalin was not a Dale Carnegie graduate. He went all the way. It is an unpleasant truth that is swallowed, if at all, like a rancid, bitter pill. A star is a star; a numberless cipher is a numberless cipher.

Even more eerie a fact is that the Great Divide is rarely a matter of talent or personality. Or even luck. Adolph Hitler had a notoriously weak handshake. His smile was, if anything, a vapid mockery. But inevitably his star zoomed higher and higher. Cinema luminaries of the first order are rarely blessed with even the modicum of Talent, and often their physical beauty leaves much to be desired. What is the difference between Us and Them, We and They, the Big Ones and the great, teeming rabble?

There are about four times in a man's life, or a woman's, too, for that matter, when unexpectedly, from out of the darkness, the blazing carbon lamp, the cosmic searchlight of Truth shines full upon them. It is how we react to those moments that forever seals our fate. One crowd simply puts on its sunglasses, lights another cigar, and heads for the nearest plush French restaurant in the jazziest section of town, sits down and orders a drink, and ignores the whole thing. While we, the Doomed, caught in the brilliant glare of illumination, see ourselves inescapably for what we are, and from that day on skulk in the weeds, hoping no one else will spot us.

Those moments happen when we are least able to fend them off. I caught the first one full in the face when I was fourteen. The fourteenth summer is a magic one for all kids. You have just slid out of the pupa stage, leaving your old baby skin behind, and have not yet become a grizzled, hardened, tax-paying beetle. At fourteen you are made of cellophane. You curl easily and everyone can see through you.

When I was fourteen, Life was flowing through me in a deep, rich torrent of Castoria. How did I know that the first rocks were just ahead, and I was about to have my keel ripped out on the reef? Sometimes you feel as though you are alone in a rented rowboat, bailing like mad in the darkness with a leaky bailing can. It is important to know that there are at least two billion other ciphers in the same boat, bailing with the same leaky can. They all think they are alone and are crossed with an evil star. They are right.

I'm fourteen years old, in my sophomore year at high school. One day Schwartz, my purported best friend, sidled up to me edgily outside of school while we were waiting on the steps to come in after lunch. He proceeded to outline his plan:

"Helen's old man won't let me take her out on a date Saturday night unless I get a date for her girlfriend. A double date. The old coot figures, I guess, that if there are four of us there won't be no monkey business. Well, how about it? Do you want to go on a blind date with this chick? I never seen her."

Well. For years I had this principle—absolutely *no* blind dates. I was a man of perception and taste, and life was short. But there is a time in your life when you have to stop taking and begin to give just a little. For the first time the warmth of sweet Human Charity brought the roses to my cheeks. After all, Schwartz was my friend. It was little enough to do, have a blind date with some no doubt skinny, pimply girl for your best friend. I would do it for Schwartz. He would do as much for me.

"Okay. Okay, Schwartz."

Then followed the usual ribald remarks, reckless boasting, and dirty jokes about dates in general and girls in particular. It was decided that next Saturday we would go all the way. I had a morning paper route at the time, and my life savings stood at about $1.80. I was all set to blow it on one big night.

I will never forget that particular Saturday as long as I live. The air was as soft as the finest of spun silk. The scent of lilacs hung heavy. The catalpa trees rustled in the early evening breeze from off the Lake. The inner Me itched in that nameless way, that indescribable way that only the fourteen-year-old Male fully knows.

All that afternoon I had carefully gone over my wardrobe to select the proper symphony of sartorial brilliance. That night I set out wearing my magnificent electric blue sport coat, whose shoulders were so wide that they hung out over my frame like vast, drooping eaves, so wide I had difficulty going through an ordinary door head-on. The electric blue sport coat that draped voluminously almost to my knees, its wide lapels flapping soundlessly in the slightest breeze. My pleated gray flannel slacks began just below my breastbone and indeed chafed my armpits. High-belted, cascading down finally to grasp my ankles in a vise-like grip. My tie, indeed one of my most prized possessions, had been a gift from my Aunt Glenn upon the state occasion of graduation from eighth grade. It was of a beautiful silky fabric, silvery pearly colored, four inches wide at the fulcrum, and of such a length to endanger occasionally my zipper in moments of haste. Hand-painted upon it was a magnificent blood-red snail.

I had spent fully two hours carefully arranging and rearranging my great mop of wavy hair, into which I had rubbed fully a pound and a half of Greasy Kid Stuff.

Helen and Schwartz waited on the corner under the streetlight at the streetcar stop near Junie Jo's home. Her name was Junie Jo Prewitt. I won't forget it quickly, although she has, no doubt, forgotten mine. I walked down the dark street alone, past houses set back off the street, through the darkness, past privet hedges, under elm trees, through air rich and ripe with promise. Her house stood back from the street even farther than the others. It sort of crouched in the darkness, looking out at me, kneeling. Pregnant with Girldom. A real Girlfriend house.

The first faint touch of nervousness filtered through the marrow of my skullbone as I knocked on the door of the screen-enclosed porch. No answer. I knocked again, louder. Through the murky screens I could see faint lights in the house itself. Still no answer. Then I found a small door-bell button buried in the sash. I pressed. From far off in the bowels of the house I heard two chimes "Bong" politely. It sure didn't sound like our doorbell. We had a real ripper that went off like a broken buzz saw, more of a BRRRAAAAKKK than a muffled Bong. This was a rich people's doorbell.

The door opened and there stood a real, geniune, gold-plated Father: potbelly, underwear shirt, suspenders, and all.

"Well?" he asked.

For one blinding moment of embarassment I couldn't remember her name. After all, she was a blind date. I couldn't just say:

"I'm here to pick up some girl."
He turned back into the house and hollered:
"JUNIE JO! SOME KID'S HERE!"
"Heh, heh. . . ." I countered.

He led me into the living room. It was an itchy house, sticky stucco walls of a dull orange color, and all over the floor this Oriental rug with the design crawling around, making loops and sworls. I sat on an over-stuffed chair covered in stiff green mohair that scratched even through my slacks. Little twisty bridge lamps stood everywhere. I instantly began to sweat down the back of my clean white shirt. Like I said, it was a very itchy house. It had little lamps sticking out of the walls that looked like phony candles, with phony glass orange flames. The rug started moaning to itself.

I sat on the edge of the chair and tried to talk to this Father. He was a Cub fan. We struggled under water for what seemed like an hour and a half, when suddenly I heard someone coming down the stairs. First the feet; then those legs, and there she was. She was magnificent! The greatest-looking girl I ever saw in my life! I have hit the double jackpot! And on a blind date! Great Scot!

My senses actually reeled as I clutched the arm of that bilge-green chair for support. Junie Jo Prewitt made Cleopatra look like a Girl Scout!

Five minutes later we are sitting in the streetcar, heading toward the bowling alley. I am sitting next to the most fantastic creation in the Feminine department known to Western man. There are the four of us in that long, yellow-lit streetcar. No one else was aboard; just us four. I, naturally, being a trained gentleman, sat on the aisle to protect her from candy wrappers and cigar butts and such. Directly ahead of me, also on the aisle, sat Schwartz, his arm already flung affectionately in a death grip around Helen's neck as we boomed and rattled through the night.

I casually flung my right foot up onto my left knee so that she could see my crepe-soled, perforated, wing-toed, Scotch bluchers with the two-toned lace. I started to work my famous charm on her. Casually, with my practiced offhand, cynical, cutting, sardonic humor I told her about how my Old Man had cracked the block in the Oldsmobile, how the White Sox were going to have a good year this year, how my kid brother wet his pants when he saw a snake, how I figured it was going to rain, what a great guy Schwartz was, what a good second baseman I was, how I figured I might go out for football. On and on I rolled, like Old Man River, pausing significantly for her to pick up the conversation. Nothing.

Ahead of us Schwartz and Helen were almost indistinguishable one from the other. They giggled, bit each other's ears, whispered, clasped hands, and in general made me itch even more.

From time to time Junie Jo would bend forward stiffly from the waist and say something I could never quite catch into Helen's right ear.

I told her my great story of the time that Uncle Carl lost his false teeth down the airshaft. Still nothing. Out of the corner of my eye I could see that she had her coat collar turned up, hiding most of her face as she sat silently, looking forward past Helen Weathers into nothingness.

I told her about this old lady on my paper route who chews tobacco, and roller skates in the backyard every morning. I still couldn't get through to her. Casually I inched my right arm up over the back of the seat behind her shoulders. The acid test. She leaned forward, avoiding my arm, and stayed that way.

"Heh, heh, heh. . . ."

As nonchalantly as I could, I retrieved it, battling a giant cramp in my right shoulder blade. I sat in silence for a few seconds, sweating heavily as ahead Schwartz and Helen are going at it hot and heavy.

It was then that I became aware of someone saying something to me. It was an empty car. There was no one else but us. I glanced around, and there it was. Above us a line of car cards looked down on the empty streetcar. One was speaking directly to me, to me alone.

DO YOU OFFEND?

Do I *offend?!*

With no warning, from up near the front of the car where the motorman is steering, I see this thing coming down the aisle directly toward *me*. It's coming closer and closer. I can't escape it. It's this blinding, fantastic, brilliant, screaming blue light. I am spread-eagled in it. There's a pin sticking through my thorax. I see it all now.

I AM THE BLIND DATE!

ME!!

I'M the one they're being nice to!

I'm suddenly getting fatter, more itchy. My new shoes are like bowling balls with laces; thick, rubber-crepe bowling balls. My great tie that Aunt Glenn gave me is two feet wide, hanging down to the floor like some crinkly tinfoil noose. My beautiful hand-painted snail is seven feet high, sitting up on my shoulder, burping. Great Scot! It is all clear to me in the searing white light of Truth. My friend Schwartz, I can see him saying to Junie Jo:

"I got this crummy fat friend who never has a date. Let's give him a break and. . . ."

I AM THE BLIND DATE!

They are being nice to *me!* She is the one who is out on a Blind Date. A Blind Date that didn't make it.

In the seat ahead, the merriment rose to a crescendo. Helen tittered; Schwartz cackled. The marble statue next to me stared gloomily out into the darkness as our streetcar rattled on. The ride went on and on.

I AM THE BLIND DATE!

I didn't say much the rest of the night. There wasn't much to be said.

For Discussion

1. Discuss each of the negative images in the first paragraph of this essay.
2. What is meant by stepping off the track and into the bushes?
3. Shepherd says that people experience perhaps four truly important moments in their lives. Do you agree? What makes these moments significant? Can you identify any of those times in your own life?
4. How does the living room of his date's home contribute to the narrator's discomfort? How does the father, as described, contribute to this feeling?
5. What is the significance of the title? Why is it important that the streetcar is empty except for the four characters?
6. What was your attitude toward the narrator at the end of the story? Were you prepared for this type of self-realization? What major truths about yourself have you discovered in a similar manner?

For Comparison

1. What if anything does this narrator have in common with the narrator in "I'm a Fool"?
2. In which of the worlds described by Carl Sandburg is this individual now living?

For Composition

1. From the tracks to the bushes.
2. A blind date I had once.
3. My most startling self-realization.

KATHERINE MANSFIELD

A DILL PICKLE

And then, after six years, she saw him again. He was seated at one of those little bamboo tables decorated with a Japanese vase of paper daffodils. There was a tall plate of fruit in front of him, and very carefully, in a way she recognized immediately as his "special" way, he was peeling an orange.

He must have felt that shock of recognition in her for he looked up and met her eyes. Incredible! He didn't know her! She smiled; he frowned. She came towards him. He closed his eyes an instant, but opening them his face lit up as though he had struck a match in a dark room. He laid down the orange and pushed back his chair, and she took her little warm hand out of her muff and gave it to him.

"Vera!" he exclaimed. "How strange. Really, for a moment I didn't know you. Won't you sit down? You've had lunch? Won't you have some coffee?"

She hesitated, but of course she meant to.

"Yes, I'd like some coffee." And she sat down opposite him.

"You've changed. You've changed very much," he said, staring at her with that eager, lighted look. "You look so well. I've never seen you look so well before."

"Really?" She raised her veil and unbuttoned her high fur collar. "I don't feel very well. I can't bear this weather, you know."

"Ah, no. You hate the cold . . ."

"Loathe it." She shuddered. "And the worst of it is that the older one grows . . ."

He interrupted her. "Excuse me," and tapped on the table for the waitress. "Please bring some coffee and cream." To her: "You are sure you won't eat anything? Some fruit, perhaps. The fruit here is very good."

"No thanks. Nothing."

"Then that's settled." And smiling just a hint too broadly he took up the orange again. "You were saying—the older one grows—"

"The colder," she laughed. But she was thinking how well she remembered that trick of his—the trick of interrupting her—and of how it used to exasperate her six years ago. She used to feel then as though he, quite suddenly, in the middle of what she was saying, put his hand over her lips, turned from her, attended to something different, and then took his hand away, and with just the same slightly too broad smile, gave her his attention again . . . Now we are ready. That is settled.

"The colder!" He echoed her words, laughing too. "Ah, ah. You still say the same things. And there is another thing about you that is not changed at all—your beautiful voice—your beautiful way of speaking." Now he was very grave; he leaned towards her, and she smelled the warm, stinging scent of the orange peel. "You have only to say one word and I would know your voice among all other voices. I don't know what it is— I've often wondered—that makes your voice such a—haunting memory . . . Do you remember that first afternoon we spent together at Kew Gardens? You were so surprised because I did not know the names of any flowers. I am still just as ignorant for all your telling me. But whenever it is very fine and warm, and I see some bright colors—it's awfully strange —I hear your voice saying: 'Geranium, marigold and verbena.' And I feel those three words are all I recall of some forgotten, heavenly language . . . You remember that afternoon?"

"Oh, yes, very well." She drew a long, soft breath, as though the paper daffodils between them were almost too sweet to bear. Yet what had remained in her mind of that particular afternoon was an absurd scene over the tea table. A great many people taking tea in a Chinese pagoda, and he behaving like a maniac about the wasps—waving them away, flapping at them with his straw hat, serious and infuriated out of all proportion to the occasion. How delighted the sniggering tea drinkers had been. And how she had suffered.

But now, as he spoke, that memory faded. His was the truer. Yes, it had been a wonderful afternoon, full of geranium and marigold and verbena, and—warm sunshine. Her thoughts lingered over the last two words as though she sang them.

In the warmth, as it were, another memory unfolded. She saw herself sitting on a lawn. He lay beside her, and suddenly, after a long silence, he rolled over and put his head in her lap.

"I wish," he said, in a low, troubled voice, "I wish that I had taken poison and were about to die—here now!"

At that moment a little girl in a white dress, holding a long, dripping water lily, dodged from behind a bush, stared at them, and dodged back again. But he did not see. She leaned over him.

"Ah, why do you say that? I could not say that."

But he gave a kind of soft moan, and taking her hand he held it to his cheek.

"Because I know I am going to love you too much—far too much. And I shall suffer so terribly, Vera, because you never, never will love me."

He was certainly far better looking now than he had been then. He had lost all that dreamy vagueness and indecision. Now he had the air of a man who has found his place in life, and fills it with a confidence and an assurance which was, to say the least, impressive. He must have made money, too. His clothes were admirable, and at that moment he pulled a Russian cigarette case out of his pocket.

"Won't you smoke?"

"Yes, I will." She hovered over them. "They look very good."

"I think they are. I get them made for me by a little man in St. James's Street. I don't smoke very much. I'm not like you—but when I do, they must be delicious, very fresh cigarettes. Smoking isn't a habit with me; it's a luxury—like perfume. Are you still so fond of perfumes? Ah, when I was in Russia . . ."

She broke in: "You've really been to Russia?"

"Oh, yes. I was there for over a year. Have you forgotten how we used to talk of going there?"

"No, I've not forgotten."

He gave a strange half laugh and leaned back in his chair. "Isn't it curious. I have really carried out all those journeys that we planned. Yes, I have been to all those places that we talked of, and stayed in them long enough to—as you used to say, 'air oneself' in them. In fact, I have spent the last three years of my life traveling all the time. Spain, Corsica, Siberia, Russia, Egypt. The only country left is China, and I mean to go there, too, when the war is over."

As he spoke, so lightly, tapping the end of his cigarette against the ashtray, she felt the strange beast that had slumbered so long within her bosom, stir, stretch itself, yawn, prick up its ears, and suddenly bound to its feet, and fix its longing, hungry stare upon those far away places. But all she said was, smiling gently: "How I envy you."

He accepted that. "It has been," he said, "very wonderful—especially Russia. Russia was all that we had imagined, and far, far more. I even spent some days on a river boat on the Volga. Do you remember that boatman's song that you used to play?"

"Yes." It began to play in her mind as she spoke.

"Do you ever play it now?"

"No, I've no piano."

He was amazed at that. "But what has become of your beautiful piano?"

She made a little grimace. "Sold. Ages ago."

"But you were so fond of music," he wondered.

"I've no time for it now," said she.

He let it go at that. "That river life," he went on, "is something quite special. After a day or two you cannot realize that you have ever known another. And it is not necessary to know the language—the life of the boat creates a bond between you and the people that's more than sufficient. You eat with them, pass the day with them, and in the evening there is that endless singing."

She shivered, hearing the boatman's song break out again loud and tragic, and seeing the boat floating on the darkening river with melancholy trees on either side . . . "Yes, I should like that," she said, stroking her muff.

"You'd like almost everything about Russian life," he said warmly. "It's so informal, so impulsive, so free without question. And then the peasants are so splendid. They are such human beings—yes, that is it. Even the man who drives your carriage has—has some real part in what is happening. I remember the evening a party of us, two friends of mine and the wife of one of them, went for a picnic by the Black Sea. We took supper and champagne and ate and drank on the grass. And while we were eating the coachman came up. 'Have a dill pickle,' he said. He wanted to share with us. That seemed to me so right, so—you know what I mean?"

And she seemed at that moment to be sitting on the grass beside the mysteriously Black Sea, black as velvet, and rippling against the banks in silent, velvet waves. She saw the carriage drawn up to one side of the road, and the little group on the grass, their faces and hands white in the moonlight. She saw the pale dress of the woman outspread and her folded parasol, lying on the grass like a huge pearl crochet hook. Apart from them, with his supper in a cloth on his knees, sat the coachman. "Have a dill pickle," said he, and although she was not certain what a dill pickle was, she saw the greenish glass jar with a red chili like a parrot's beak glimmering through. She sucked in her cheeks; the dill pickle was terribly sour . . .

"Yes, I know perfectly what you mean," she said.

In the pause that followed they looked at each other. In the past when they had looked at each other like that they had felt such a boundless understanding between them that their souls had, as it were, put their arms round each other and dropped into the same sea, content to be drowned, like mournful lovers. But now, the surprising thing was that it was he who held back. He who said:

"What a marvelous listener you are. When you look at me with those wild eyes I feel that I could tell you things that I would never breathe to another human being."

Was there just a hint of mockery in his voice or was it her fancy? She could not be sure.

"Before I met you," he said, "I had never spoken of myself to anybody. How well I remember one night, the night that I brought you the little Christmas tree, telling you all about my childhood. And of how I was so miserable that I ran away and lived under a cart in our yard for two days without being discovered. And you listened, and your eyes shone, and I felt that you had even made the little Christmas tree listen too, as in a fairy story."

But of that evening she had remembered a little pot of caviare. It had cost seven and sixpence. He could not get over it. Think of it—a tiny jar like that costing seven and sixpence. While she ate it he watched her, delighted and shocked.

"No, really, that is eating money. You could not get seven shillings into a little pot that size. Only think of the profit they must make . . ." And he had begun some immensely complicated calculations . . . But now good-by to the caviare. The Christmas tree was on the table, and the little boy lay under the cart with his head pillowed on the yard dog.

"The dog was called Bosun," she cried delightedly.

But he did not follow. "Which dog? Had you a dog? I don't remember a dog at all."

"No, no. I mean the yard dog when you were a little boy." He laughed and snapped the cigarette case to.

"Was he? Do you know I had forgotten that. It seems such ages ago. I cannot believe that it is only six years. After I had recognized you today—I had to take such a leap—I had to take a leap over my whole life to get back to that time. I was such a kid then." He drummed on the table. "I've often thought how I must have bored you. And now I understand so perfectly why you wrote to me as you did—although at the time that letter nearly finished my life. I found it again the other day, and I couldn't help laughing as I read it. It was so clever—such a true picture of me." He glanced up. "You're not going?"

She had buttoned her collar again and drawn down her veil.

"Yes, I am afraid I must," she said, and managed a smile. Now she knew that he had been mocking.

"Ah, no, please," he pleaded. "Don't go just for a moment," and he caught up one of her gloves from the table and clutched at it as if that would hold her. "I see so few people to talk to nowadays, that I have turned into a sort of barbarian," he said. "Have I said something to hurt you?"

"Not a bit," she lied. But as she watched him draw her glove through his fingers, gently, gently, her anger really did die down, and besides, at the moment he looked more like himself of six years ago . . .

"What I really wanted then," he said softly, "was to be a sort of carpet—to make myself into a sort of carpet for you to walk on so that you need not be hurt by the sharp stones and the mud that you hated so. It was nothing more positive than that—nothing more selfish. Only I did desire, eventually, to turn into a magic carpet and carry you away to all those lands you longed to see."

As he spoke she lifted her head as though she drank something; the strange beast in her bosom began to purr . . .

"I felt that you were more lonely than anybody else in the world," he went on, "and yet, perhaps, that you were the only person in the world who was really, truly alive. Born out of your time," he murmured, stroking the glove, "fated."

Ah, God! What had she done! How had she dared to throw away her happiness like this. This was the only man who had ever understood her. Was it too late? Could it be too late? *She* was the glove that he held in his fingers . . .

"And then the fact that you had no friends and never had made friends with people. How I understood that, for neither had I. Is it just the same now?"

"Yes," she breathed. "Just the same. I am as alone as ever."

"So am I," he laughed gently, "just the same."

Suddenly with a quick gesture he handed her back the glove and scraped his chair on the floor. "But what seemed to me so mysterious then is perfectly plain to me now. And to you, too, of course . . . It simply was that we were such egoists, so self-engrossed, so wrapped up in ourselves that we hadn't a corner in our hearts for anybody else. Do you know," he cried, naive and hearty, and dreadfully like another side of that old self again, "I began studying a Mind System when I was in Russia, and I found that we were not peculiar at all. It's quite a well-known form of . . ."

She had gone. He sat there, thunder-struck, astounded beyond words. . . . And then he asked the waitress for his bill.

"But the cream has not been touched," he said. "Please do not charge me for it."

For Discussion

1. Why is the story entitled "A Dill Pickle"? What is the significance of the dill pickle?
2. Vera's name comes from a Latin word meaning "truth." Does she live up to her name? Is she truthful to her former sweetheart? To herself?
3. Who is responsible for the breakdown that exists between the two characters? What is Mansfield saying about the nature of love?
4. Does Vera have a right to impose her feelings and attitudes on her former sweetheart? Does she have a responsibility to give him freedom and to accept things as they are?
5. He suggests that Vera is "more lonely than anybody else in the world." Is she lonely because she is basically selfish? Is she lonely because she does not personally accept the responsibilities of friendship? What are some of these responsibilities?

For Comparison

1. In which of the worlds described by Carl Sandburg ("Between Worlds") does Vera spend most of her time?
2. Compare Vera with the woman in "Theft." How is Vera's lying to herself a form of theft? Why are both women lonely? Is their loneliness a product of their theft? Is such lying to oneself a denial of personal responsibility?

For Composition

1. Vera will (will never) become a responsible person.
2. Being truthful is a sign of responsibility.
3. A lonely, selfish person I have known.

———

KATHERINE ANNE PORTER

THEFT

She had the purse in her hand when she came in. Standing in the middle of the floor, holding her bathrobe around her and trailing a damp towel in one hand, she surveyed the immediate past and remembered everything clearly. Yes, she had opened the flap and spread it out on the bench after she had dried the purse with her handkerchief.

She had intended to take the Elevated, and naturally she looked in her purse to make certain she had the fare, and was pleased to find forty cents in the coin envelope. She was going to pay her own fare, too, even if Camilo did have the habit of seeing her up the steps and dropping a nickel in the machine before he gave the turnstile a little push and sent her through it with a bow. Camilo by a series of compromises had managed to make effective a fairly complete set of smaller courtesies, ignoring the larger and more troublesome ones. She had walked with him to the station in a pouring rain, because she knew he was almost as poor as she was, and when he insisted on a taxi, she was firm and said, "You know it simply will not do." He was wearing a new hat of a pretty biscuit shade, for it never occurred to him to buy anything of a practical color; he had put it on for the first time and the rain was spoiling it. She kept thinking,

"But this is dreadful, where will he get another?" She compared it with Eddie's hats that always seemed to be precisely seven years old and as if they had been quite purposely left out in the rain, and yet they sat with a careless and incidental rightness on Eddie. But Camilo was far different; if he wore a shabby hat it would be merely shabby on him, and he would lose his spirits over it. If she had not feared Camilo would take it badly, for he insisted on the practice of his little ceremonies up to the point he had fixed for them, she would have said to him as they left Thora's house, "Do go home. I can surely reach the station by myself."

"It is written that we must be rained upon tonight," said Camilo, "so let it be together."

At the foot of the platform stairway she staggered slightly—they were both nicely set up on Thora's cocktails—and said: "At least, Camilo, do me the favor not to climb these stairs in your present state, since for you it is only a matter of coming down again at once, and you'll certainly break your neck."

He made three quick bows, he was Spanish, and leaped off through the rainy darkness. She stood watching him, for he was a very graceful young man, thinking that tomorrow morning he would gaze soberly at his spoiled hat and soggy shoes and possibly associate her with his misery. As she watched, he stopped at the far corner and took off his hat and hid it under his overcoat. She felt she had betrayed him by seeing, because he would have been humiliated if he thought he even suspected him of trying to save his hat.

Roger's voice sounded over her shoulder above the clang of the rain falling on the stairway shed, wanting to know what she was doing out in the rain at this time of night, and did she take herself for a duck? His long, imperturbable face was streaming with water, and he tapped a bulging spot on the breast of his buttoned-up overcoat: "Hat," he said. "Come on, let's take a taxi."

She settled back against Roger's arm which he laid around her shoulders, and with the gesture they exchanged a glance full of long amiable associations, then she looked through the window at the rain changing the shapes of everything, and the colors. The taxi dodged in and out between the pillars of the Elevated, skidding slightly on every curve, and she said: "The more it skids the calmer I feel, so I really must be drunk."

"You must be," said Roger. "This bird is a homicidal maniac, and I could do with a cocktail myself this minute."

They waited on the traffic at Fortieth Street and Sixth Avenue, and three boys walked before the nose of the taxi. Under the globes of light they were cheerful scarecrows, all very thin and all wearing very seedy snappy-cut suits and gay neckties. They were not very sober either, and they stood for a moment wobbling in front of the car, and there was an argument going on among them. They leaned toward each other as if they were getting ready to sing, and the first one said: "When I get married it won't be jus' for getting married, I'm gonna marry for *love*, see?" and the second one said, "Aw, gwan and tell that stuff to *her*, why n't yuh?" and the third one gave a kind of hoot, and said, "Hell, dis guy? Wot the hell's he got?" and the first one said: "Aaah, shurrup yuh mush, I got plenty." Then they all squealed and scrambled across the street beating the first one on the back and pushing him around.

"Nuts," commented Roger, "pure nuts."

Two girls went skittering by in short transparent raincoats, one green, one red, their heads tucked against the drive of the rain. One of them was saying to the other, "Yes, I know all about *that*. But what about me? You're always so sorry for *him* . . ." and they ran on with their little pelican legs flashing back and forth.

The taxi backed up suddenly and leaped forward again, and after a while Roger said: "I had a letter from Stella today, and she'll be home on the twenty-sixth, so I suppose she's made up her mind and it's all settled."

"I had a sort of letter today too," she said, "making up my mind for me. I think it is time you and Stella do something definite."

When the taxi stopped on the corner of West Fifty-third Street, Roger said, "I've just enough if you'll add ten cents," so she opened her purse and gave him a dime, and he said, "That's beautiful, that purse."

"It's a birthday present," she told him, "and I like it. How's your show coming?"

"Oh, still hanging on, I guess. I don't go near the place. Nothing sold yet. I mean to keep right on the way I'm going and they can take it or leave it. I'm through with the argument."

"It's absolutely a matter of holding out, isn't it?"

"Holding out's the tough part."

"Good night, Roger."

"Good night, you should take aspirin and push yourself into a tub of hot water, you look as though you're catching cold."

"I will."

With the purse under her arm she went upstairs, and on the first landing Bill heard her step and poked his head out with his hair tumbled and his eyes red, and he said: "For Christ's sake, come in and have a drink with me. I've had some bad news."

"You're perfectly sopping," said Bill, looking at her drenched feet. They had two drinks, while Bill told how the director had thrown his play out after the cast had been picked over twice, and had gone through three rehearsals. "I said to him, 'I didn't say it was a masterpiece, I said it would make a good show.' And he said, 'It just doesn't *play*, do you see? It needs a doctor.' So I'm stuck, absolutely stuck," said Bill, on the edge of weeping again. "I've been crying," he told her, "in my cups." And he went on to ask her if she realized his wife was ruining him with her extravagance. "I send her ten dollars every week of my unhappy life, and I don't really have to. She threatens to jail me if I don't, but she can't do it. God, let her try it after the way she treated me! She's no right to alimony and she knows it. She keeps on saying she's got to have it for the baby and I keep on sending it because I can't bear to see anybody suffer. So I'm way behind on the piano and the victrola, both—"

"Well, this is a pretty rug, anyhow," she said.

Bill stared at it and blew his nose. "I got it at Ricci's for ninety-five dollars," he said. "Ricci told me it once belonged to Marie Dressler, and cost fifteen hundred dollars, but there's a burnt place on it, under the divan. Can you beat that?"

"No," she said. She was thinking about her empty purse and that she could not possibly expect a check for her latest review for another three days, and her arrangement with the basement restaurant could not last much longer if she did not pay something on account. "It's no time to speak of it," she said, "but I've been hoping you would have by now that fifty dollars you promised for my scene in the third act. Even if it doesn't play. You were to pay me for the work anyhow out of your advance."

"Weeping Jesus," said Bill, "you, too?" He gave a loud sob, or hiccough, in his moist handkerchief. "Your stuff was no better than mine, after all. Think of that."

"But you got something for it," she said. "Seven hundred dollars."

Bill said, "Do me a favor, will you? Have another drink and forget about it. I can't, you know I can't, I would if I could, but you know the fix I'm in."

"Let it go, then," she found herself saying almost in spite of herself. She had meant to be quite firm about it. They drank again without speaking, and she went to her apartment on the floor above.

There, she now remembered distinctly, she had taken the letter out of the purse before she spread the purse out to dry.

She had sat down and read the letter over again: but there were phrases that insisted on being read many times, they had a life of their own separate from the others, and when she tried to read past and around them, they moved with the movement of her eyes, and she could not escape them . . . "thinking about you more than I mean to . . . yes, I even talk about you . . . why were you so anxious to destroy . . . even if I could see you now I would not . . . not worth all this abominable . . . the end . . ."

Carefully she tore the letter into narrow strips and touched a lighted match to them in the coal grate.

Early the next morning she was in the bathtub when the janitress knocked and then came in, calling out that she wished to examine the radiators before she started the furnace going for the winter. After moving about the room for a few minutes, the janitress went out, closing the door very sharply.

She came out of the bathroom to get a cigarette from the package in the purse. The purse was gone. She dressed and made coffee, and sat by the window while she drank it. Certainly the janitress had taken the purse, and certainly it would be impossible to get it back without a great deal of ridiculous excitement. Then let it go. With this decision of her mind, there rose coincidentally in her blood a deep almost murderous anger. She set the cup carefully in the center of the table, and walked steadily downstairs, three long flights and a short hall and a steep short flight into the basement, where the janitress, her face streaked with coal dust, was shaking up the furnace. "Will you please give me back my purse? There isn't any money in it. It was a present, and I don't want to lose it."

The janitress turned without straightening up and peered at her with hot flickering eyes, a red light from the furnace reflected in them. "What do you mean, your purse?"

"The gold cloth purse you took from the wooden bench in my room," she said. "I must have it back."

"Before God I never laid eyes on your purse, and that's the holy truth," said the janitress.

"Oh, well then, keep it," she said, but in a very bitter voice; "keep it if you want it so much." And she walked away.

She remembered how she had never locked a door in her life, on some principle of rejection in her that made her uncomfortable in the ownership of things, and her paradoxical boast before the warnings of her friends, that she had never lost a penny by theft; and she had been pleased with the bleak humility of this concrete example designed to illustrate and justify a certain fixed, otherwise baseless and general faith which ordered the movements of her life without regard to her will in the matter.

In this moment she felt that she had been robbed of an enormous number of valuable things, whether material or intangible: things lost or broken by her own fault, things she had forgotten and left in houses when she moved: books borrowed from her and not returned, journeys she had planned and had not made, words she had waited to hear spoken to her and had not heard, and the words she had meant to answer with; bitter alternatives and intolerable substitutes worse than nothing, and yet inescapable: the long patient suffering of dying friendships and the dark inexplicable death of love—all that she had had, and all that she had missed, were lost together, and were twice lost in this landslide of re-membered losses.

The janitress was following her upstairs with the purse in her hand and the same deep red fire flickering in her eyes. The janitress thrust the purse towards her while they were still a half dozen steps apart, and said: "Don't never tell on me. I musta been crazy. I get crazy in the head sometimes, I swear I do. My son can tell you."

She took the purse after a moment, and the janitress went on: "I got a niece who is going on seventeen, and she's a nice girl and I thought I'd give it to her. She needs a pretty purse. I musta been crazy; I thought maybe you wouldn't mind, you leave things around and don't seem to notice much."

She said: "I missed this because it was a present to me from some-one . . ."

The janitress said: "He'd get you another if you lost this one. My niece is young and needs pretty things, we oughta give the young ones a chance. She's got young men after her maybe will want to marry her. She oughta have nice things. She needs them bad right now. You're a grown woman, you've had your chance, you ought to know how it is!"

She held the purse out to the janitress saying: "You don't know what you're talking about. Here, take it, I've changed my mind. I really don't want it."

The janitress looked up at her with hatred and said: "I don't want it either now. My niece is young and pretty, she don't need fixin' up to be pretty, she's young and pretty anyhow! I guess you need it worse than she does!"

"It wasn't really yours in the first place," she said, turning away. "You mustn't talk as if I had stolen it from you."

"It's not from me, it's from her you're stealing it," said the janitress, and went back downstairs.

She laid the purse on the table and sat down with the cup of chilled coffee, and thought: I was right not to be afraid of any thief but myself, who will end by leaving me nothing.

For Discussion

1. Why does the woman call herself a thief? How has she committed theft? From others? From herself?
2. Is it possible for one to be a thief and not steal anything material? If so, who has committed the greater crime, the woman or the janitress?

3. Do you feel that the woman is using the various men in a way that permits her to escape some of her personal responsibilities? Is such use of another person a form of theft?
4. What truth do you see in the old adage "to thine own self be true"?

For Comparison

1. In "The Open Self," Morris suggests that a person may change his character by conscious effort. Now that the woman in this story has discovered she is a thief, do you think that she will make any changes in her character? Do you agree with Morris that she is capable if she really wants to?
2. Which of the woman's actions can be explained by the "self unsatisfied" concept expressed in Schwartz's poem?

For Composition

1. A time when I stole from myself.
2. I used a friend to escape my responsibility.
3. Liars are thieves.

SHERWOOD ANDERSON

I'M A FOOL

It was a hard jolt for me, one of the most bitterest I ever had to face. And it all came about through my own foolishness too. Even yet, sometimes, I want to cry or swear or kick myself. Perhaps even now, after all this time, there will be a kind of satisfaction in making myself look cheap by telling of it.

It began at three o'clock one October afternoon as I sat in the grandstand at the fall trotting and pacing meet at Sandusky, Ohio.

To tell the truth, I felt a little foolish that I should be sitting in the grandstand at all. During the summer before I had left my home town with Harry Whitehead and, with a nigger named Burt, had taken a job as swipe with one of the two horses. Harry was campaigning through the fall race meets that year. Mother cried and my sister Mildred, who wanted to get a job as school teacher in our town that fall, stormed and

Reprinted by permission of Harold Ober Associates Incorporated. Copyright 1922 by Dial Publishing Company, Inc. Renewed 1949 by Eleanor Copenhaver Anderson.

scolded about the house all during the week before I left. They both thought it something disgraceful that one of our family should take a place as a swipe with race horses. I've an idea Mildred thought my taking the place would stand in the way of her getting the job she'd been working so long for.

But after all I had to work and there was no other work to be got. A big lumbering fellow of nineteen couldn't just hang around the house and I had got too big to mow people's lawns and sell newspapers. Little chaps who could get next to people's sympathies by their sizes were always getting jobs away from me. There was one fellow who kept saying to everyone who wanted a lawn mowed or a cistern cleaned that he was saving money to work his way through college, and I used to lie awake nights thinking up ways to injure him without being found out. I kept thinking of wagons running over him and bricks falling on his head as he walked along the street. But never mind him.

I got the place with Harry and I liked Burt fine. We got along splendid together. He was a big nigger with a lazy sprawling body and soft kind eyes, and when it came to a fight he could hit like Jack Johnson. He had Bucephalus, a big black pacing stallion that could do 2.09 or 2.10 if he had to, and I had a little gelding named Doctor Fritz that never lost a race all fall when Harry wanted him to win.

We set out from home late in July in a boxcar with the two horses, and after that, until late November, we kept moving along to the race meets and the fairs. It was a peachy time for me, I'll say that. Sometimes, now, I think that boys who are raised regular in houses, and never have a fine nigger like Burt for best friend, and go to high schools and college, and never steal anything or get drunk a little, or learn to swear from fellows who know how, or come walking up in front of a grandstand in their shirt sleeves and with dirty horsey pants on when the races are going on and the grandstand is full of people all dressed up—What's the use talking about it? Such fellows don't know nothing at all. They've never had no opportunity.

But I did. Burt taught me how to rub down a horse and put the bandages on after a race and steam a horse out and a lot of valuable things for any man to know. He could wrap a bandage on a horse's leg so smooth that if it had been the same color you would think it was his skin, and I guess he'd have been a big driver, too, and got to the top like Murphy and Walter Cox and the others if he hadn't been black.

Gee whizz, it was fun. You got to a county-seat town maybe, say, on a Saturday or Sunday, and the fair began the next Tuesday and lasted until Friday afternoon. Doctor Fritz would be, say, in the 2.25 trot on Tuesday afternoon and on Thursday afternoon Bucephalus would knock 'em cold in the "free-for-all" pace. It left you a lot of time to hang around and listen to horse talk, and see Burt knock some yap cold that got too gay, and you'd find out about horses and men and pick up a lot of stuff you could use all the rest of your life if you had some sense and salted down what you heard and felt and saw.

And then at the end of the week when the race meet was over, and Harry had run home to tend up to his livery-stable business, you and Burt hitched the two horses to carts and drove slow and steady across country to the place for the next meeting so as not to overheat the horses, etc., etc., you know.

Gee whizz, gosh amighty, the nice hickory nut and beechnut and oaks and other kinds of trees along the roads, all brown and red, and the good smells, and Burt singing a song that was called *Deep River*, and the country girls at the windows of houses and everything. You can stick your colleges up your nose for all me. I guess I know where I got my education.

Why, one of those little burgs of towns you come to on the way, say now, on a Saturday afternoon, and Burt says, "Let's lay up here." And you did.

And you took the horses to a livery stable and fed them and you got your good clothes out of a box and put them on.

And the town was full of farmers gaping, because they could see you were race-horse people, and the kids maybe never seen a nigger before and was afraid and run away when the two of us walked down their main street.

And that was before prohibition and all that foolishness, and so you went into a saloon, the two of you, and all the yaps come and stood around, and there was always someone pretended he was horsey and knew things and spoke up and began asking questions, and all you did was to lie and lie all you could about what horses you had, and I said I owned them, and then some fellow said, "Will you have a drink of whisky?" and Burt knocked his eye out the way he could say, offhand like, "Oh, well, all, all right, I'm agreeable to a little nip. I'll split a quart with you." Gee whizz.

But that isn't what I want to tell my story about. We got home late in November and I promised Mother I'd quit the race horses for good. There's a lot of things you've got to promise a mother because she don't know any better.

And so, there not being any work in our town any more than when I left there to go to the races, I went off to Sandusky and got a pretty good place taking care of the horses for a man who owned a teaming and delivery and storage business there. It was a pretty good place with good eats and a day off each week and sleeping on a cot in the big barn, and mostly just shoveling in hay and oats to a lot of big good enough skates of horses that couldn't have trotted a race with a toad. I wasn't dissatisfied and I could send money home.

And then, as I started to tell you, the fall races come to Sandusky and I got the day off and I went. I left the job at noon and had on my good clothes and my new brown derby hat I'd just bought the Saturday before, and a stand-up collar.

First of all I went downtown and walked about with the dudes. I've always thought to myself, "put up a good front," and so I did it. I had forty dollars in my pocket and so I went into the West House, a big hotel, and walked up to the cigar stand. "Give me three twenty-five-cent cigars," I said. There was a lot of horse men and strangers and dressed-up people from other towns standing around in the lobby and in the bar, and I mingled amongst them. In the bar there was a fellow with a cane and a Windsor tie on, that it made me sick to look at him. I like a man to be a man and dress up, but not to go put on that kind of airs. So I pushed him aside, kind of rough, and had me a drink of whisky. And then he looked at me as though he thought he'd get gay, but he changed his mind and didn't say anything. And then I had another drink of whisky, just to show him something, and went out and had a hack out to the races all to myself, and when I got there I bought myself the best seat I could get up in the grandstand, but didn't go in for any of these boxes. That's putting on too many airs.

And so there I was, sitting up in the grandstand as gay as you please and looking down on the swipes coming out with their horses and with their dirty horsey pants on and the horse blankets swung over their shoulders same as I had been doing all the year before. I liked one thing about the same as the other, sitting up there and feeling grand and being down there and looking up at the yaps and feeling grander and more important too. One thing's about as good as another if you take it just right. I've often said that.

Well, right in front of me, in the grandstand that day, there was a fellow with a couple of girls and they was about my age. The young fellow was a nice guy all right. He was the kind maybe that goes to college and then comes to be a lawyer or maybe a newspaper editor or something like that, but he wasn't stuck on himself. There are some of that kind are all right and he was one of the ones.

He had his sister with him and another girl and the sister looked around over his shoulder, accidental at first, not intending to start anything—she wasn't that kind—and her eyes and mine happened to meet. You know how it is. Gee, she was a peach. She had on a soft dress, kind of blue stuff, and it looked carelessly made, but was well sewed and made and everything. I knew that much. I blushed when she looked right at me and so did she. She was the nicest girl I've ever seen in my life. She wasn't stuck on herself and she could talk proper grammar without being like a schoolteacher or something like that. What I mean is, she was O.K. I think maybe her father was well to do, but not rich to make her chesty because she was his daughter, as some are. Maybe he owned a drugstore or a drygoods store in their home town, or something like that. She never told me and I never asked.

My own people are all O.K. too, when you come to that. My grandfather was Welsh and over in the old country, in Wales, he was—but never mind that.

The first heat of the first race come off and the young fellow setting there with the two girls left them and went down to make a bet. I knew what he was up to, but he didn't talk big and noisy and let everyone around know he was a sport, as some do. He wasn't that kind. Well, he come back and I heard him tell the two girls what horse he'd bet on, and when the heat was trotted they all half got to their feet and acted in the excited, sweaty way people do when they've got money down on a race, and the horse they bet on is up there pretty close at the end, and they think maybe he'll come on with a rush, but he never does because he hasn't got the old juice in him, come right down to it.

And, then, pretty soon, the horses came out for the 2.18 pace and there was a horse in it I knew. He was a horse Bob French had in his string, but Bob didn't own him. He was a horse owned by a Mr. Mathers down at Marietta, Ohio.

This Mr. Mathers had a lot of money and owned a coal mine or something, and he had a swell place out in the country, and he was stuck on race horses, but was a Presbyterian or something, and I think more than likely his wife was one, too, maybe a stiffer one than himself. So he never raced his horses hisself, and the story round the Ohio race tracks was that when one of his horses got ready to go to the races he turned him over to Bob French and pretended to his wife he was sold.

So Bob had the horses and he did pretty much as he pleased and you can't blame Bob; at least, I never did. Sometimes he was out to win and sometimes he wasn't. I never cared much about that when I was swiping a horse. What I did want to know was that my horse had the speed and could go out in front if you wanted him to.

And, as I'm telling you, there was Bob in this race with one of Mr. Mathers' horses, was named "About Ben Ahem" or something like that, and was fast as a streak. He was a gelding and had a mark of 2.21, but could step in .08 or .09.

Because when Burt and I were out, as I've told you, the year before, there was a nigger Burt knew, worked for Mr. Mathers, and we went out there one day when we didn't have no race on at the Marietta Fair and our boss Harry had gone home.

And so everyone was gone to the fair but just this one nigger, and he took us all through Mr. Mathers' swell house and he and Burt tapped a bottle of wine Mr. Mathers had hid in his bedroom, back in a closet, without his wife knowing, and he showed us this Ahem horse. Burt was always stuck on being a driver, but didn't have much chance to get to the top, being a nigger, and he and the other nigger gulped that whole bottle of wine and Burt got a little lit up.

So this nigger let Burt take this About Ben Ahem and step him a mile in a track Mr. Mathers had all to himself, right there on the farm. And Mr. Mathers had one child, a daughter, kinda sick and not very good-looking, and she came home and we had to hustle and get About Ben Ahem stuck back in the barn.

I'm only telling you to get everything straight. At Sandusky, that afternoon I was at the fair, this young fellow with the two girls was fussed, being with the girls and losing his bet. You know how a fellow is that way. One of them was his girl and the other his sister. I had figured that out.

"Gee whizz," I says to myself, "I'm going to give him the dope." He was mighty nice when I touched him on the shoulder. He and the girls were nice to me right from the start and clear to the end. I'm not blaming them.

And so he leaned back and I gave him the dope on About Ben Ahem. "Don't bet a cent on this first heat because he'll go like an oxen hitched to a plow, but when the first heat is over go right down and lay on your pile." That's what I told him.

Well, I never saw a fellow treat anyone sweller. There was a fat man sitting beside the little girl that had looked at me twice by this time, and I at her, and both blushing, and what did he do but have the nerve to turn and ask the fat man to get up and change places with me so I could set with his crowd.

Gee whizz, amighty. There I was. What a chump I was to go and get gay up there in the West House bar, and just because that dude was standing there with a cane and that kind of a necktie on, to go and get all balled up and drink that whisky, just to show off.

Of course, she would know, me setting right beside her and letting her smell of my breath. I could have kicked myself right down out of that grandstand and all around that race track and made a faster record than most of the skates of horses they had there that year.

Because that girl wasn't any mutt of a girl. What wouldn't I have given right then for a stick of chewing gum to chew, or a lozenger, or some licorice, or most anything. I was glad I had those twenty-five-cent cigars in my pocket, and right away I give that fellow one and lit one myself. Then that fat man got up and we changed places and there I was plunked down beside her.

They introduced themselves, and the fellow's best girl he had with him was named Miss Elinor Woodbury, and her father was a manufacturer of barrels from a place called Tiffin, Ohio. And the fellow himself was named Wilbur Wessen and his sister was Miss Lucy Wessen.

I suppose it was their having such swell names got me off my trolley. A fellow, just because he has been a swipe with a race horse, and works taking care of horses for a man in the teaming, delivery and storage business, isn't any better or worse than anyone else. I've often thought that, and said it, too.

But you know how a fellow is. There's something in that kind of nice clothes, and the kind of nice eyes she had, and the way she looked at me, awhile before, over her brother's shoulder, and me looking back at her, and both of us blushing.

I couldn't show her up for a boob, could I?

I made a fool of myself, that's what I did. I said my name was Walter Mathers from Marietta, Ohio, and then I told all three of them the smashingest lie you ever heard. What I said was that my father owned the horse About Ben Ahem, and that he had let him out to this Bob French for racing purposes, because our family was proud and had never gone into racing that way, in our own name, I mean. Then I had got started, and they were all leaning over and listening, and Miss Lucy Wessen's eyes were shining, and I went the whole hog.

I told her about our place down at Marietta, and about the big stables and the grand brick house we had on a hill, up above the Ohio River, but I knew enough not to do it in no bragging way. What I did was to start things and then let them drag the rest out of me. I acted just as reluctant to tell as I could. Our family hasn't got any barrel factory, and, since I've known us, we've always been pretty poor, but not asking anything of anyone at that, and my grandfather, over in Wales—but never mind that.

We set there talking like we had known each other for years and years, and I went and told them that my father had been expecting maybe this Bob French wasn't on the square, and had sent me up to Sandusky on the sly to find out what I could.

And I bluffed it through I had found out all about the 2.18 pace in which About Ben Ahem was to start.

I said he would lose the first heat by pacing like a lame cow and then he would come back and skin 'em alive after that. And to back up what I said I took thirty dollars out of my pocket and handed it to Mr. Wilbur Wessen and asked him would he mind, after the first heat, to go down and place it on About Ben Ahem for whatever odds he could get. What I said was that I didn't want Bob French to see me and none of the swipes.

Sure enough the first heat came off and About Ben Ahem went off his stride, up the back stretch, and looked like a wooden horse or a sick one, and come in to be last. Then this Wilbur Wessen went down to the betting place under the grandstand and there I was with the two girls, and when that Miss Woodbury was looking the other way once, Lucy Wessen kinda, with her shoulder you know, kinda touched me. You know how a woman can do. They get close, but not getting gay either. You know what they do. Gee whizz.

And then they give me a jolt. What they had done when I didn't know was to get together, and they had decided Wilbur Wessen would bet fifty dollars, and the two girls had gone and put in ten dollars each of their own money, too. I was sick then, but I was sicker later.

About the gelding, About Ben Ahem, and their winning their money I wasn't worried a lot about that. It come out O.K. Ahem stepped the next three heats like a bushel of spoiled eggs going to market before they could be found out, and Wilbur Wessen had got nine to two for the money. There was something else eating at me.

Because Wilbur come back after he had bet the money, and after that he spent most of his time talking to that Miss Woodbury, and Lucy Wessen and I was left alone together like on a desert island. Gee, if I'd only been on the square or if there had been any way of getting myself on the square. There ain't any Walter Mathers, like I said to her and them, and there hasn't ever been one, but if there was, I bet I'd go to Marietta, Ohio, and shoot him tomorrow.

There I was, big boob that I am. Pretty soon the race was over, and Wilbur had gone down and collected our money, and we had a hack downtown, and he stood us a swell dinner at the West House, and a bottle of champagne beside.

And I was with that girl and she wasn't saying much, and I wasn't saying much either. One thing I know. She wasn't stuck on me because of the lie about my father being rich and all that. There's a way you know. . . . Craps amighty. There's a kind of girl you see just once in your life, and if you don't get busy and make hay then you're gone for good and all and might as well go jump off a bridge. They give you a look from inside of them somewhere, and it ain't no vamping, and what it means is—you want that girl to be your wife, and you want nice things around her like flowers and swell clothes, and you want her to have the kids you're going to have, and you want good music played and no ragtime. Gee whizz.

There's a place over near Sandusky, across a kind of bay, and it's called Cedar Point. And when we had had that dinner we went over to it in a launch, all by ourselves. Wilbur and Miss Lucy and that Miss

Woodbury had to catch a ten-o'clock train back to Tiffin, Ohio, because when you're out with girls like that you can't get careless and miss any trains and stay out all night like you can with some kinds of Janes.

And Wilbur blowed himself to the launch and it cost him fifteen cold plunks, but I wouldn't ever have knew it if I hadn't listened. He wasn't no tin horn kind of a sport.

Over at the Cedar Point place we didn't stay around where there was a gang of common kind of cattle at all.

There was big dance halls and dining places for yaps, and there was a beach you could walk along and get where it was dark, and we went there.

She didn't talk hardly at all and neither did I, and I was thinking how glad I was my mother was all right, and always made us kids learn to eat with a fork at table and not swill soup and not be noisy and rough like a gang you see around a race track that way.

Then Wilbur and his girl went away up the beach and Lucy and I set down in a dark place where there was some roots of old trees the water had washed up, and after that, the time, till we had to go back in the launch and they had to catch their trains, wasn't nothing at all. It went like winking your eye.

Here's how it was. The place we were setting in was dark, like I said, and there was roots from that old stump sticking up like arms, and there was a watery smell, and the night was like—as if you could put your hand out and feel it—so warm and soft and dark and sweet like an orange.

I most cried and I most swore and I most jumped up and danced, I was so mad and happy and sad.

When Wilbur come back from being alone with his girl and she saw him coming, Lucy she says, "We got to go to the train now," and she was most crying, too, but she never knew nothing I knew, and she couldn't be so all busted up. And then, before Wilbur and Miss Woodbury got up to where she was, she put her face up and kissed me quick and put her head up against me and she was all quivering and—Gee whizz.

Sometimes I hope I have cancer and die. I guess you know what I mean. We went in the launch across the bay to the train like that, and it was dark too. She whispered and said it was like she and I could get out of the boat and walk on the water, and it sounded foolish, but I knew what she meant.

And then quick, we were right at the depot, and there was a big gang of yaps, the kind that goes to the fairs, and crowded and milling around like cattle, and how could I tell her? "It won't be long because you'll write and I'll write to you." That's all she said.

I got a chance like a hay barn afire. A swell chance I got.

And maybe she would write me, down at Marietta that way, and the letter would come back, and stamped on the front of it by the U.S.A. "there ain't any such guy," or something like that, whatever they stamp on a letter that way.

And me trying to pass myself off for a bigbug and a swell—to her, as decent a little body as God ever made. Craps amighty. A swell chance I got.

And then the train come in and she got on, and Wilbur Wesson come and shook hands with me, and that Miss Woodbury was nice too, and bowed to me and I at her and the train went and I busted out and cried like a kid.

Gee, I could have run after that train and made Dan Patch look like a freight train after a wreck, but socks amighty, what was the use? Did you ever see such a fool?

I'll bet you what—if I had an arm broke right now or a train had run over my foot—I wouldn't go to no doctor at all. I'd go set down and let her hurt and hurt—that's what I'd do.

I'll bet you what—if I hadn't a drunk that booze I'd a never been such a boob as to go tell such a lie—that couldn't never be made straight to a lady like her.

And if I'm not another you just go find me one and I'll quit working and be a bum and give him my job. I don't care nothing for working and earning money and saving it for no such boob as myself.

For Discussion

1. As precisely as you can, define what it means to be a fool.
2. Why does the boy feel that he is a fool? Does he fit your definition of fool?
3. Why has the incident had such a profound effect upon him? Do you feel that he is making too much of a relatively small matter?
4. What does the boy in the end learn about the nature of responsibility? To himself? To others? What would have happened if he had been truly responsible to himself?

For Comparison

1. Using Anderson's idea of a fool, show how the narrator in Housman's "Is My Team Ploughing" might also be considered a fool.
2. Is the character in this story the same type of thief as the young woman in Porter's story "Theft"? Which of the two major characters is the more responsible?

For Composition

1. Bragging got me into trouble.
2. A time I wish I had not lied.
3. Big shots fall hard.

E. B. WHITE

THE DOOR

Everything (he kept saying) is something it isn't. And everybody is always somewhere else. Maybe it was the city, being in the city, that made him feel how queer everything was and that it was something else. Maybe (he kept thinking) it was the names of the things. The names were tex and frequently koid. Or they were flex and oid or they were duroid (sani) or flexsan (duro), but everything was glass (but not quite glass) and the thing that you touched (the surface, washable, crease-resistant) was rubber, only it wasn't quite rubber and you didn't quite touch it but almost. The wall, which was glass but thrutex, turned out on being approached not to be a wall, it was something else, it was an opening or doorway— and the doorway (through which he saw himself approaching) turned out to be something else, it was a wall. And what he had eaten not having agreed with him.

He was in a washable house, but he wasn't sure. Now about those rats, he kept saying to himself. He meant the rats that the Professor had driven crazy by forcing them to deal with problems which were beyond the scope of rats, the insoluble problems. He meant the rats that had been trained to jump at the square card with the circle in the middle, and the card (because it was something it wasn't) would give way and let the rat into a place where the food was, but then one day it would be a trick played on the rat, and the card would be changed, and the rat would jump but the card wouldn't give way, and it was an impossible situation (for a rat) and the rat would go insane and into its eyes would come the unspeakably bright imploring look of the frustrated, and after the convulsions were over and the frantic racing around, then the passive stage would set in and the willingness to let anything be done to it, even if it was something else.

He didn't know which door (or wall) or opening in the house to jump at, to get through, because one was an opening that wasn't a door (it was a void, or koid) and the other was a wall that wasn't an opening, it was a sanitary cupboard of the same color. He caught a glimpse of his eyes staring into his eyes, in the thrutex, and in them was the expression he had seen in the picture of the rats—weary after convulsions and the frantic racing around, when they were willing and did not mind having anything done to them. More and more (he kept saying) I am confronted by a problem which is incapable of solution (for this time even if he chose the right door, there would be no food behind it) and that is what madness is, and things seeming different from what they are. He heard, in the house where he was, in the city to which he had gone (as toward a door which might, or might not, give way), a noise—not a loud noise but more of a low prefabricated humming. It came from a place in the base of the wall (or stat) where the flue carrying the filterable air was, and not far from the Minipiano, which was made of the same material nailbrushes are made of, and which was under the stairs. "This, too, has been tested," she said, pointing, but not at it, "and found viable." It wasn't a loud noise, he kept thinking, sorry that he had seen his eyes, even though it was through his own eyes that he had seen them.

First will come the convulsions (he said), then the exhaustion, then the willingness to let anything be done. "And you better believe it *will* be."

All his life he had been confronted by situations which were incapable of being solved, and there was a deliberateness behind all this, behind this changing of the card (or door), because they would always wait till you had learned to jump at the certain card (or door)—the one with the circle—and then they would change it on you. There have been so many doors changed on me, he said, in the last twenty years, but it is now becoming clear that it is an impossible situation, and the question is whether to jump again, even though they ruffle you in the rump with a blast of air—to make you jump. He wished he wasn't standing by the Minipiano. First they would teach you the prayers and the Psalms, and that would be the right door (the one with the circle), and the long sweet words with the holy sound, and that would be the one to jump at to get where the food was. Then one day you jumped and it didn't give way, so that all you got was the bump on the nose, and the first bewilderment, the first young bewilderment.

I don't know whether to tell her about the door they substituted or not, he said, the one with the equation on it and the picture of the amoeba reproducing itself by division. Or the one with the photostatic copy of the check for thirty-two dollars and fifty cents. But the jumping was so long ago, although the bump is . . . how those old wounds hurt! Being crazy this way wouldn't be so bad if only, if only. If only when you put your foot forward to take a step, the ground wouldn't come up to meet your foot the way it does. And the same way in the street (only I may never get back to the street unless I jump at the right door), the curb coming up to meet your foot, anticipating ever so delicately the weight of the body, which is somewhere else. "We could take your name," she said, "and send it to you." And it wouldn't be so bad if only you could read a sentence all the way through without jumping (your eye) to something else on the same page; and then (he kept thinking) there was that man out in Jersey, the one who started to chop his trees down, one by one, the man who began talking about how he would take his house to pieces, brick by brick, because he faced a problem incapable of solution, probably, so he began to hack at the trees in the yard, began to pluck with trembling fingers at the bricks in the house. Even if a house is not washable, it is worth taking down. It is not till later that the exhaustion sets in.

But it is inevitable that they will keep changing the doors on you, he said, because that is what they are for; and the thing is to get used to it and not let it unsettle the mind. But that would mean not jumping, and you can't. Nobody can not jump. There will be no not-jumping. Among rats, perhaps, but among people never. Everybody has to keep jumping at a door (the one with the circle on it) because that is the way everybody is, specially some people. You wouldn't want me, standing here, to tell you, would you, about my friend the poet (deceased) who said, "My heart has followed all my days something I cannot name"? (It had the circle on it.) And like many poets, although few so beloved, he is gone. It killed him, the jumping. First, of course, there were the preliminary bouts, the convulsions, and the calm and the willingness.

I remember the door with the picture of the girl on it (only it was spring), her arms outstretched in loveliness, her dress (it was the one with the circle on it) uncaught, beginning the slow, clear, blinding cascade—and I guess we would all like to try that door again, for it seemed like the way and for a while it was the way, the door would open and you would go through winged and exalted (like any rat) and the food would be there, the way the Professor had it arranged, everything O.K., and you had chosen the right door for the world was young. The time they changed that door on me, my nose bled for a hundred hours—how do you like that, Madam? Or would you prefer to show me further through this so strange house, or you could take my name and send it to me, for although my heart has followed all my days something I cannot name, I am tired of the jumping and I do not know which way to go, Madam, and I am not even sure that I am not tried beyond the endurance of man (rat, if you will) and have taken leave of sanity. What are you following these days, old friend, after your recovery from the last bump? What is the name, or is it something you cannot name? The rats have a name for it by this time, perhaps, but I don't know what they call it. I call it plexikoid and it comes in sheets, something like insulating board, unattainable and ugliproof.

And there was the man out in Jersey, because I keep thinking about his terrible necessity and the passion and trouble he had gone to all those years in the indescribable abundance of a householder's detail, building the estate and the planting of the trees and in spring the lawn-dressing and in fall the bulbs for the spring burgeoning, and the watering of the grass on the long light evenings in summer and the gravel for the driveway (all had to be thought out, planned) and the decorative borders, probably, the perennials and the bug spray, and the building of the house from plans of the architect, first the sills, then the studs, then the full corn in the ear, the floors laid on the floor timbers, smoothed, and then the carpets upon the smooth floors and the curtains and the rods therefor. And then, almost without warning, he would be jumping at the same old door and it wouldn't give: they had changed it on him, making life no longer supportable under the elms in the elm shade, under the maples in the maple shade.

"Here you have the maximum of openness in a small room."

It was impossible to say (maybe it was the city) what made him feel the way he did, and I am not the only one either, he kept thinking—ask any doctor if I am. The doctors, they know how many there are, they even know where the trouble is only they don't like to tell you about the prefrontal lobe because that means making a hole in your skull and removing the work of centuries. It took so long coming, this lobe, so many, many years. (Is it something you read in the paper, perhaps?) And now, the strain being so great, the door having been changed by the Professor once too often . . . but it only means a whiff of ether, a few deft strokes, and the higher animal becomes a little easier in his mind and more like the lower one. From now on, you see, that's the way it will be, the ones with the small prefrontal lobes will win because the other ones are hurt too much by this incessant bumping. They can stand just so much, eh, Doctor? (And what is that, pray, that you have in your hand?) Still, you never can tell, eh, Madam?

He crossed (carefully) the room, the thick carpet under him softly, and went toward the door carefully, which was glass and he could see himself in it, and which, at his approach, opened to allow him to pass through; and beyond he half expected to find one of the old doors that he had known, perhaps the one with the circle, the one with the girl her arms outstretched in loveliness and beauty before him. But he saw instead a moving stairway, and descended in light (he kept thinking) to the street below and to the other people. As he stepped off, the ground came up slightly, to meet his foot.

For Discussion

1. What do the doors represent? Think of specific meanings for each of the four doors referred to in the story.
2. How is man like the rat? If man is the one who changes things behind the rat's door, who or what changes things behind man's? Is it fair to blame situations on this force, or must man assume responsibility because he alone selects the door?
3. Why is selecting doors in life's experiences a frightening challenge?
4. The author suggests that man's tensions can be relieved by a brain operation. Is such a move a denial of responsibility? What is meant by the statement, "Nobody can not jump"?

For Comparison

1. Is the philosophy expressed by this short story at odds with that expressed by William Henley in "Invictus"?
2. If a person could have such an operation as described by the narrator in this story, would he be creating a "new self" as described by Morris in "The Open Self"? According to the definition used by Morris, would he be bringing himself "up to date"?

For Composition

1. Frightening doors I have faced.
2. Being frustrated can be healthy.
3. I can't blame anyone but myself.

WILLIAM HENLEY

INVICTUS

Out of the night that covers me,
    Black as the Pit from pole to pole,
I thank whatever gods may be
    For my unconquerable soul.

In the fell clutch of circumstance
    I have not winced nor cried aloud.
Under the bludgeonings of chance
    My head is bloody, but unbowed.

Beyond this place of wrath and tears
    Looms but the horror of the shade,
And yet the menace of the years
    Finds, and shall find me, unafraid.

It matters not how strait the gate,
    How charged with punishments the scroll,
I am the master of my fate:
    I am the captain of my soul.

For Discussion

1. What does it mean to be the captain of one's soul?
2. Is Henley's view of the world around him optimistic or pessimistic? How do you know?
3. Is it possible for a person to be the master of his fate and to be a responsible citizen at the same time? Does pressure from society sometimes prohibit a person from being his own captain?

For Comparison

1. Compare Henley's idea of an afterlife with that suggested by Sandburg in "Between Worlds."
2. How would the narrator of this poem relate to the narrator in Wright's poem? If you are master of your fate, do you then have the right to waste your life if you wish?

From *Poems* by William Henley. Charles Scribner's Sons.

For Composition

1. A person can (cannot) be responsible and free at the same time.
2. An important decision I made against the grain of society.

ROBERT FROST

THE ROAD NOT TAKEN

Two roads diverged in a yellow wood,
And sorry I could not travel both
And be one traveler, long I stood
And looked down one as far as I could
To where it bent in the undergrowth;

Then took the other, as just as fair,
And having perhaps the better claim,
Because it was grassy and wanted wear;
Though as for that the passing there
Had worn them really about the same,

And both that morning equally lay
In leaves no step had trodden black.
Oh, I kept the first for another day!
Yet knowing how way leads on to way,
I doubted if I should ever come back.

I shall be telling this with a sigh
Somewhere ages and ages hence:
Two roads diverged in a wood, and I –
I took the one less traveled by,
And that has made all the difference.

For Discussion

1. Is Frost writing only about a walk in a forest?
2. Why couldn't the narrator go back some day to the other road?
3. Do you feel that he has any regret about his first choice?
4. How completely might his first choice affect later choices?
5. Who is responsible for the narrator's actions? Himself? Fate?

From *Complete Poems of Robert Frost.* Copyright 1916, 1930, 1939 by Holt, Rinehart and Winston, Inc. Copyright 1944, © 1958 by Robert Frost. Copyright © 1967 by Lesley Frost Ballantine. Reprinted by permission of Holt, Rinehart and Winston, Inc.

For Comparison

1. Frost's narrator selected a path that would later be impossible to retrace. Show how the narrator in Sherwood Anderson's "I'm a Fool"
   has also chosen a path which he cannot retrace.
2. What comparisons do you see between Frost's paths and the doors described in E. B. White's story?

For Composition

1. The joys and pains of making a decision.
2. A decision I wish I could change.
3. How an early decision in my life still affects me.

CARL SANDBURG

BETWEEN WORLDS

And he said to himself
in a sunken morning moon
between two pines,
between lost gold and lingering green:

I believe I will count up my worlds.
There seem to me to be three.
There is a world I came from which is Number One.
There is a world I am in now, which is Number Two.
There is a world I go to next, which is Number Three.

There was the seed pouch, the place I lay dark in, nursed and shaped in a
    warm, red, wet cuddling place; if I tugged at a latchstring or doubled a
    dimpled fist or twitched a leg or a foot, only the Mother knew.

There is the place I am in now, where I look back and look ahead,
    and dream and wonder.

There is the next place —
And he took a look out of a window
at a sunken morning moon
between two pines,
between lost gold and lingering green.

For Discussion

1. Do you personally feel that this life is simply a stopping off place between "two worlds"?
2. What does Sandburg mean when he describes the present world as being "between lost gold and lingering green"?
3. Do you think that some events from world Number One are responsible for your present character? Is it necessary for the self-responsible person to escape hereditary forces?
4. The poet ends the poem by dreaming about the future. Is there a danger in looking forward to the future so much that you become irresponsible to the present?

For Comparison

1. How does Sandburg's picture of world Number Three compare with that found in A. E. Housman's poem "Is My Team Ploughing"?
2. Trace the importance of Sandburg's worlds one and two in James Weldon Johnson's autobiographic essay. Show how world one affected developments in world two.

For Composition

1. This world is (is not) all that matters.
2. A bad trait that I inherited.
3. Looking for the ideal can be dangerous.

A. E. HOUSMAN

IS MY TEAM PLOUGHING

"Is my team ploughing,
That I was used to drive
And hear the harness jingle
When I was man alive?"

Aye, the horses trample,
  The harness jingles now;
No change though you lie under
  The land you used to plough.

"Is football playing
  Along the river shore,
With lads to chase the leather,
  Now I stand up no more?"

Aye, the ball is flying,
  The lads play heart and soul;
The goal stands up, the keeper
  Stands up to keep the goal.

"Is my girl happy,
  That I thought hard to leave,
And has she tired of weeping
  As she lies down at eve?"

Aye, she lies down lightly,
  She lies not down to weep:
Your girl is well contented.
  Be still, my lad, and sleep.

"Is my friend hearty,
  Now I am thin and pine;
And has he found to sleep in
  A better bed than mine?"

Yes, lad, I lie easy,
  I lie as lads would choose;
I cheer a dead man's sweatheart,
  Never ask me whose.

For Discussion

1. Housman is obviously concerned with more than just ploughing, playing football, etc. What is the speaker from the grave really asking?
2. Is the speaker's interest in the live world, his girl friend's happiness,
   for instance, sincere or merely selfish?
3. What responsibility do our lovers or our friends have to us after our
   death?

4. We like to think all life stops when we do and all nature mourns our death. How does Housman's poem suggest that the death of one individual does little or nothing to affect the total world?

For Comparison

1. The narrator in this poem is concerned that life goes on for everyone else after his death. Do you think that he would agree with the idea expressed by James Wright in "Lying in a Hammock at William Duffy's Farm in Pine Island, Minnesota"?
2. The narrator wants to feel that life cannot go on without him and that he is vitally important to every part of it. Show how this same attitude is held by the principal character in "Theft."

For Composition

1. What life owes me.
2. What would happen to any favorite person (or possession) if I should die today.

LANGSTON HUGHES

AS I GREW OLDER

It was a long time ago.
I have almost forgotten my dream.
But it was there then,
In front of me,
Bright like a sun—
My dream.

And then the wall rose,
Rose slowly,
Slowly,
Between me and my dream.
Rose slowly, slowly,
Dimming,
Hiding,
The light of my dream.
Rose until it touched the sky—
The wall.

Shadow.
I am black.

I lie down in the shadow.
No longer the light of my dream before me,
Above me.
Only the thick wall.
Only the shadow.

My hands!
My dark hands!
Break through the wall!
Find my dream!
Help me to shatter this darkness,
To smash this night,
To break this shadow
Into a thousand lights of sun,
Into a thousand whirling dreams
Of sun!

For Discussion

1. When is the "then" spoken of by Hughes in line 3?
2. What might have been the "wall" that separated the poet from his dream? What other symbols can you find in the poem? What, for instance, is suggested by the sky?
3. What implications are in the final stanza? Is Hughes suggesting that his hands will break through the wall with violence? What are the responsible alternatives?

For Comparison

1. On what matters would Hughes and James Weldon Johnson agree? On what specific matters of racial significance would they disagree?
2. What attitude would Hughes take toward the narrator in Schwartz's poem "The Self Unsatisfied Runs Everywhere"?

For Composition

1. A dream that kept me going.
2. Langston Hughes was right.
3. Racial prejudices build walls.

ARCHIBALD MacLEISH

SPEECH TO A CROWD

Tell me, my patient friends—awaiters of messages—
From what other shore: from what stranger:
Whence was the word to come? Who was to lesson you?

Listeners under a child's crib in a manger—
Listeners once by the oracles; now by the transoms—
Whom are you waiting for? Who do you think will explain?

Listeners thousands of years and still no answer—
Writers at night to Miss Lonely-Hearts: awkward spellers—
Open your eyes! There is only earth and the man!

There is only you: there is no one else on the telephone:
No one else is on the air to whisper:
No one else but you will push the bell.

No one knows if you don't: neither ships
Nor landing-fields decode the dark between:
You have your eyes and what your eyes see *is*.

The earth you see is really the earth you are seeing;
The sun is truly excellent: truly warm:
Women are beautiful as you have seen them—

Their breasts (believe it) like cooing of doves in a portico:
They bear at their breasts tenderness softly. Look at them!
Look at yourselves. You are strong. You are well formed.

Look at the world—the world you never took!
It is really true you may live in the world heedlessly:
Why do you wait to read it in a book then?

Write it yourselves! Write to yourselves if you need to!
Tell yourselves there is sun and the sun will rise:
Tell yourselves the earth has food to feed you:—

Let the dead men say that men must die!
Who better than you can know what death is?
How can a bone or a broken body surmise it?

Let the dead shriek with their whispering breath:
Laugh at them! Say the murdered gods may wake
But we who work have end of work together:

Tell yourselves the earth is yours to take!

Waiting for messages out of the dark you were poor.
The world was always yours: you will not take it.

For Discussion

1. What kind of messages do men await in the dark?
2. What advice is MacLeish really giving to the writers to Miss Lonely-Hearts?
3. Is his advice to take life by force and to live it the way you see it realistic? What would happen to society if everyone lived according to this theory?
4. MacLeish suggests that the living should only be involved with the living and that the dead should take care of the dead. Does this suggestion represent a rejection of some of the responsibilities of life?
5. What in the poem suggests that it is more than a commitment to fulfill an individual's selfish desires?

For Comparison

1. This poem seems closely related to "Invictus," but there are differences. What are some of the differences?
2. How might the last two lines of this poem be especially significant to Langston Hughes? Where in "As I Grew Older" do you find a similar idea suggested?

For Composition

1. There is only earth and the man.
2. I agree (disagree) with MacLeish.
3. Acceptance of others begins with acceptance of self.

JAMES WRIGHT

LYING IN A HAMMOCK AT WILLIAM DUFFY'S FARM IN PINE ISLAND, MINNESOTA

Over my head, I see the bronze butterfly,
Asleep on the black trunk,
Blowing like a leaf in green shadow.
Down the ravine behind the empty house,
The cowbells follow one another
Into the distances of the afternoon.
To my right,
In a field of sunlight between two pines,
The droppings of last year's horses
Blaze up into golden stones.
I lean back, as the evening darkens and comes on,
A chicken hawk floats over, looking for home.
I have wasted my life.

For Discussion

1. How is the title of this poem important to an understanding of its meaning? Is there a special effect created by the rather long title for the relatively short poem?
2. What specific importance do you attach to the nature images used throughout the poem? In what way do you think the speaker is like the butterfly, the leaf, the chicken hawk, etc.?
3. Why does the speaker think that he has wasted his life? Does a person have the right to waste his life if he wants to? What do you think it means to waste your life?

For Comparison

1. How have the characters in "Theft" and "A Dill Pickle" wasted their lives?
2. Explain whether or not you can visualize the narrator in Jean Shepherd's essay becoming this kind of individual now that he has seen something very important about himself.

For Composition

1. A time for goofing off.
2. The most wasted life I know.
3. My favorite escape from responsibility.

DELMORE SCHWARTZ

THE SELF UNSATISFIED RUNS EVERYWHERE

Sunday and sunlight ashen on the Square,
Hard wind, high blue, and clouded pennant sky,
Fifth Avenue empty in the autumn air,
As if a clear photograph of a dead day.
It was the Lord's day once, solemn and full
—Now I in an aftermath, desire spent,
Move with a will appeased and see a gull,
Then gulls drop from an arch—scythes of descent—

Having, I think, no wish beyond the foam
Toppling to them at each fresh exercise,
Knowing success like fountains, perhaps more wise
Than one who hesitantly writes a poem
—But who, being human, wishes to be a gull,
Knows nothing much, though birds are beautiful.

For Discussion

1. What does the title of this poem mean to you?
2. What images of "self unsatisfied" are in the poem itself?
3. Why is a gull used as the bird? If the gull has no wish beyond the foam, what might be the equivalent statement for the narrator?
4. Why might the narrator be tempted for a moment to change places with the gull?

From Delmore Schwartz, *Vaudeville for a Princess*. Copyright 1950 by New Directions. Reprinted by permission of New Directions Publishing Corporation.

For Comparison

1. Might the narrator of this poem be a part of the crowd addressed by MacLeish? If he were indeed in that crowd, how would he react to what MacLeish says?
2. At least on the surface the ideas in this poem compare with those in James Wright's poem. Are there any differences in the two narrators? Which of the two seems the more responsible individual?

For Composition

1. My dissatisfaction with myself.
2. Being bored, being lonely.
3. An animal I would trade places with.

photo by Nacio Jan Brown/BBM Associates

Part Two

INDIVIDUAL–FAMILY

Learning self-responsibility is only one step toward becoming a totally responsible individual. The second level of responsibility is that which is found within the family structure. The mature, responsible individual has a definite understanding of his or her relationship to the family and recognizes the responsibilities that relationship demands.

The problems of family responsibility are complex because a person's relationship to the family structure constantly changes. One's first family responsibility is directed toward one's parents. But the boundaries of that responsibility change constantly as a person becomes older. One's second family responsibility begins at that time when one plans for and begins a new family. But that responsibility, too, changes as time progresses and children are added to the family structure.

Modern society is now re-evaluating traditional concepts of family life and of male and female roles. Although some of the contemporary attitudes emerging directly challenge established codes of behavior, they do not abolish responsibility: they add to it a totally new dimension.

Questions to be answered as you read the selections in this section are more complex than those in the previous chapter because you must constantly weigh your self-responsibility against your family responsibility. Typical questions include: Who is responsible for happiness in the home? What responsibilities exist between husband and wife? Between parents and children? Between children and parents? Between children and their brothers and sisters? Who is responsible for divorce? How do responsibilities change as children become older? Can you blame your family structure for faults in your character and personality?

ALFRED ADLER

THE FAMILY CONSTELLATION

We have often drawn attention to the fact that before we can judge a human being we must know the situation in which he grew up. An important moment is the position which a child occupied in his family constellation. Frequently we can catalogue human beings according to this view point after we have gained sufficient expertness, and can recognize whether an individual is a first-born, an only child, the youngest child, or the like.

People seem to have known for a long time that the youngest child is usually a peculiar type. This is evidenced by the countless fairy tales, legends, Biblical stories, in which the youngest always appears in the same light. As a matter of fact he does grow up in a situation quite different from that of all other people, for to parents he represents a particular child, and as the youngest he experiences an especially solicitous treatment. Not only is he the youngest, but also usually the smallest, and by consequence, the most in need of help. His other brothers and sisters have already acquired some degree of independence and growth during the time of his weakness, and for this reason he usually grows up in an atmosphere warmer than that which the others have experienced.

Hence there arise a number of characteristics which influence his attitude toward life in a remarkable way, and cause him to be a remarkable personality. One circumstance which seemingly is a contradiction for our theory must be noted. No child likes to be the smallest, the one whom one does not trust, the one in whom one has no confidence, all the time. Such knowledge stimulates a child to prove that he can do everything. His striving for power becomes markedly accentuated and we find the youngest very usually a man who has developed a desire to overcome all others, satisfied only with the very best.

This type is not uncommon. One group of these youngest children excels every other member of the family, and becomes the family's most capable member. But there is another more unfortunate group of these same youngest children; they also have a desire to excel, but lack the necessary activity and self-confidence, as a result of their relationships to their older brothers and sisters. If the older children are not to be excelled, the youngest frequently shies from his tasks, becomes cowardly, a chronic plaintiff forever seeking an excuse to evade his duties. He does not become less ambitious, but he assumes that type of ambition which forces him to wriggle out of situations, and satisfy his ambition in activity out-

From *Understanding Human Nature*, copyright 1946, Greenberg: Publisher. Reprinted by permission of Mrs. Florence T. Wolfe.

side of the necessary problems of life, to the end that he may avoid the danger of an actual test of ability, so far as possible.

It will undoubtedly have occurred to many readers that the youngest child acts as though he were neglected and carried a feeling of inferiority within him. In our investigations we have always been able to find this feeling of inferiority and have been able also to deduce the quality and fashion of his psychic development from the presence of this torturing sentiment. In this sense a youngest child is like a child who has come into the world with weak organs. What the child *feels* need not actually be the case. It does not matter what really has happened, whether an individual is really inferior or not. What is important is his *interpretation* of his situation. We know very well that mistakes are easily made in childhood. At that time a child is faced with a great number of questions, of possibilities, and consequences.

What shall an educator do? Shall he impose additional stimuli by spurring on the vanity of this child? Should he constantly push him into the limelight so that he is always the first? This would be a feeble response to the challenge of life. Experience teaches us that it makes very little difference whether one is first or not. It would be better to exaggerate in the other direction, and maintain that being first, or the best, is unimportant. We are really tired of having nothing but the first and best people. History as well as experience demonstrates that happiness does not consist in being the first or best. To teach a child such a principle makes him one-sided; above all it robs him of his chance of being a good fellow-man.

The first consequence of such doctrines is that a child thinks only of himself and occupies himself in wondering whether someone will overtake him. Envy and hate of his fellows and anxiety for his own position, develop in his soul. His very place in life makes a speeder trying to beat out all others, of the youngest. The racer, the marathon runner in his soul, is betrayed by his whole behavior, especially in little gestures which are not obvious to those who have not learned to judge his psychic life in all his relationships. These are the children, for instance, who always march at the head of the procession and cannot bear to have anyone in front of them. Some such race-course attitude is characteristic of a large number of children.

This type of the youngest child is occasionally to be found as a clear cut type example although variations are common. Among the youngest we find active and capable individuals who have gone so far that they have become the saviors of their whole family. Consider the Biblical story of Joseph! Here is a wonderful exposition of the situation of the youngest son. It is as though the past had told us about it with a purpose and a clarity arising in the full possession of the evidence which we acquire so laboriously today. In the course of the centuries much valuable material has been lost which we must attempt to find again.

Another type, which grows secondarily from the first, is often found. Consider our marathon runner who suddenly comes to an obstacle which he does not trust himself to hurdle. He attempts to avoid the difficulty by going around it. When a youngest child of this type loses his courage he becomes the most arrant coward that we can well imagine. We find him far from the front, every labor seems too much for him, and he becomes a veritable "alibi artist" who attempts nothing useful, but spends his whole energy wasting time. In any actual conflict he always fails. Usually he is to be found carefully seeking a field of activity in which every chance of competition has been excluded. He will always find excuses for his failures. He may contend that he was too weak or petted, or that his brothers and sisters did not allow him to develop. His fate becomes more bitter if he actually has a physical defect, in which case he is certain to make capital out of his weakness to justify him in his desertion.

Both these types are hardly ever good fellow human beings. The first type fares better in a world where competition is valued for itself. A man of this type will maintain his spiritual equilibrium only at the cost of others, whereas individuals of the second remain under the oppressive feeling of their inferiority and suffer from their lack of reconciliation with life as long as they live.

The oldest child also has well defined characteristics. For one thing he has the advantage of an excellent position for the development of his psychic life. History recognizes that the oldest son has had a particularly favorable position. Among many peoples, in many classes, this advantageous status has become traditional. There is no question for instance that among the European farmers the first born knows his position from his early childhood and realizes that some day he will take over the farm, and therefore he finds himself in a much better position than the other children who know that they must leave their father's farm at some time; in other strata of society it is frequently held that the oldest son will some day be the head of the house. Even where this tradition has not actually become crystallized, as in simple bourgeois or proletarian families, the oldest child is usually the one whom one accredits with enough power and common sense to be the helper or foreman of his parents. One can imagine how valuable it is to a child to be constantly entrusted with responsibilities by his environment. We can imagine that his thought processes are somewhat like this: "You are the larger, the stronger, the older, and therefore you must also be cleverer than the others."

If his development in this direction goes on without disturbance then we shall find him with the traits of a guardian of law and order. Such persons have an especially high evaluation of power. This extends not only to their own personal power, but affects their evaluation of the concepts of power in general. Power is something which is quite self-understood for the oldest child, something which has weight and must be honored. It is not surprising that such individuals are markedly conservative.

The striving for power in the case of a second born child also has its especial nuance. Second born children are constantly under steam, striving for superiority under pressure: the race course attitude which determines their activity in life is very evident in their actions. The fact that there is someone ahead of him who has already gained power is a strong stimulus for the second born. If he is enabled to develop his powers and takes up the battle with the first born he will usually move forward with a great deal of élan, while the first born, possessing power, feels himself relatively secure until the second threatens to surpass him.

This situation has also been described in a very lively fashion in the Biblical legend of Esau and Jacob. In this story the battle goes on relentlessly, not so much for actual power, but for the semblance of power; in cases like this it continues with a certain compulsion until the goal is reached and the first born is overcome, or the battle is lost, and the retreat, which often evinces itself in nervous diseases, begins. The attitude of the second born is similar to the envy of the poor classes. There is a dominant note of being slighted, neglected, in it. The second born may place his goal so high that he suffers from it his whole life, annihilates his inner harmony in following, not the veritable facts of life, but an evanescent fiction and the valueless semblance of things.

The only child of course finds himself in a very particular situation. He is at the utter mercy of the educational methods of his environment. His parents, so to speak, have no choice in the matter. They place their whole educational zeal upon their only child. He becomes dependent to a high degree, waits constantly for someone to show him the way, and searches for support at all times. Pampered throughout his life, he is accustomed to no difficulties, because one has always removed difficulties from his way. Being constantly the center of attention he very easily acquires the feeling that he really counts for something of great value. His position is so difficult that mistaken attitudes are almost inevitable in his case. If the parents understand the dangers of his situation, to be sure, there is a possibility of preventing many of them, but at best it remains a difficult problem.

Parents of "only" children are frequently exceptionally cautious, people who have themselves experienced life as a great danger, and therefore approach their child with an inordinate solicitude. The child in turn interprets their attentions and admonitions as a source of additional pressure. Constant attention to health and well being finally stimulate him to conceive of the world as a very hostile place. An eternal fear of difficulties arises in him and he approaches them in an unpractised and clumsy manner because he has tested only the pleasant things in life. Such children have difficulties with every independent activity and sooner or latter they become useless for life. Shipwrecks in their life's activity are to be expected. Their life approaches that of a parasite who does nothing, but enjoys life while the rest of the world cares for his wants.

Various combinations are possible in which several brothers and sisters of the same or opposite sexes compete with each other. The evaluation of any one case therefore becomes exceedingly difficult. The situation of an only boy among several girls is a case in point. A feminine influence dominates such a household and the boy is pushed into the background, particularly if he is the youngest, and sees himself opposed by a closed phalanx of women. His striving for recognition encounters great difficulties. Threatened on all sides, he never senses with certainty the privilege which in our retarded masculine civilization is given to every male. A lasting insecurity, an inability to evaluate himself as a human being, is his most characteristic trait. He may become so intimidated by his womenfolk that he feels that to be a man is equivalent to occupying a position of lesser honor. On the one hand his courage and self-confidence may easily be eclipsed, or on the other the stimulus may be so drastic that the young boy forces himself to great achievements. Both cases arise from the same situation. What becomes of such boys in the end is determined by other concomitant and closely related phenomena.

We see therefore that the very position of the child in the family may lend shape and color to all the instincts, tropisms, faculties and the like, which he brings with him into the world. The affirmation robs of all value the theories of the inheritance of especial traits or talents, which are so harmful to all educational effort. There are doubtless occasions and cases in which the effect of hereditary influences can be shown, as for instance, in a child who grows up removed entirely from his parents, yet develops certain similar "familial" traits. This becomes much more comprehensible if one remembers how closely certain types of mistaken development in a child are related to inherited defects of the body. Take a given child who comes into the world with a weak body which results, in turn, in his greater tension toward the demands of life and his environment. If his father came into the world with similarly defective organs and approached the world with a similar tension, it is not to be wondered at that similar mistakes and character traits should result. Viewed from this standpoint it would seem to us that the theory of inheritance of acquired characteristics is based upon very weak evidence.

From our previous descriptions we may assume that whatever the errors to which a child is exposed in his development, the most serious consequences arise from his desire to elevate himself over all his fellows, to seek more personal power which will give him advantages over his fellow man. In our culture he is practically compelled to develop according to a fixed pattern. If we wish to prevent such a pernicious development we must know the difficulties he has to meet and understand them. There is one single and essential point of view which helps us to overcome all these difficulties; it is the view-point of the development of the social feeling. If this development succeeds, obstacles are insignificant, but since the opportunities for this development are relatively rare in our culture, the difficulties which a child encounters play an important rôle. Once this is recognized we shall not be surprised to find many people who spend their whole life fighting for their lives and others to whom life is a vale of sorrows. We must understand that they are the victims of a mistaken development whose unfortunate consequence is that their attitude toward life also is mistaken.

Let us be very modest then, in our judgment of our fellows, and above all, let us never allow ourselves to make any *moral* judgments, judgments concerning the moral worth of a human being! On the contrary we must make our knowledge of these facts socially valuable. We must approach such a mistaken and misled human being sympathetically, because we are in a position to have a much better idea of what is going on within him than he is himself. This gives rise to important new points of view in the matter of education. The very recognition of the source of error puts a great many influential instruments for betterment into our hands. By analysing the psychic structure and development of any human being we understand not only his past, but may deduce further what his future probably will be. Thus our science gives us some conception of what a human being really is. He becomes a living being for us, not merely a flat silhouette. And as a consequence we can have a richer and more meaningful sense of his value as a fellow human than is usual in our day.

For Discussion

1. How accurate are Adler's descriptions of traits peculiar to family positions? Suggest persons you know who evidence some of the basic traits named in the essay.
2. What effect has your position in your family constellation had upon you?
3. In what manner might a person overcome traits usually associated with his family position? Have you tried successfully or unsuccessfully to overcome any such traits? Explain.

4. Near the end of the essay, Adler cites a case of an only boy in a family of several girls. What might be the effect on an only girl in a family of several boys?
5. How is the responsibility of parents different to each child in the family? Do you feel that your own parents have distinguished the different needs of their children?

For Comparison

1. How are Adler's traits of family positions evidenced by the children in Van Doren's "Nobody Say a Word"?
2. Adler feels that the attitude with which a person faces the obstacles in life is at least partially responsible for his success or his failure. Cadwallader's essay suggests that marriage is filled with far too many obstacles. According to Adler, how might the presence of these obstacles be used in a positive way to ensure success?

For Composition

1. How I fit (do not fit) Adler's description.
2. My parents' different children.
3. The opportunities (disadvantages) of the only child.

MERVYN CADWALLADER

MARRIAGE AS A WRETCHED INSTITUTION

Our society expects us all to get married. With only rare exceptions we all do just that. Getting married is a rather complicated business. It involves mastering certain complex hustling and courtship games, the rituals and the ceremonies that celebrate the act of marriage, and finally the difficult requirements of domestic life with a husband or wife. It is an enormously elaborate round of activity, much more so than finding a job, and yet while many resolutely remain unemployed, few remain unmarried.

Now all this would not be particularly remarkable if there were no question about the advantages, the joys, and the rewards of married life, but most Americans, even young Americans, know or have heard that marriage is a hazardous affair. Of course, for all the increase in divorce, there are still young marriages that work, unions made by young men and women intelligent or fortunate enough to find the kind of mates they want, who know that they want children and how to love them when they come, or who find the artful blend between giving and receiving. It is not these marriages that concern us here, and that is not the trend in America today. We are concerned with the increasing number of others who, with mixed intentions and varied illusions, grope or fling themselves into marital disaster. They talk solemnly and sincerely about working to make their marriage succeed, but they are very aware of the countless marriages they have seen fail. But young people in particular do not seem to be able to relate the awesome divorce statistics to the probability of failure of their own marriage. And they rush into it, in increasing numbers, without any clear idea of the reality that underlies the myth.

Parents, teachers, and concerned adults all counsel against premature marriage. But they rarely speak the truth about marriage as it really is in modern middle-class America. The truth as I see it is that contemporary marriage is a wretched institution. It spells the end of voluntary affection, of love freely given and joyously received. Beautiful romances are transmuted into dull marriages, and eventually the relationship becomes constricting, corrosive, grinding, and destructive. The beautiful love affair becomes a bitter contract.

The basic reason for this sad state of affairs is that marriage was not designed to bear the burdens now being asked of it by the urban American middle class. It is an institution that evolved over centuries to meet some very specific functional needs of a nonindustrial society. Romantic love was viewed as tragic, or merely irrelevant. Today it is the titillating prelude to domestic tragedy, or, perhaps more frequently, to domestic grotesqueries that are only pathetic.

Marriage was not designed as a mechanism for providing friendship, erotic experience, romantic love, personal fulfillment, continuous lay psychotherapy, or recreation. The Western European family was not designed to carry a lifelong load of highly emotional romantic freight. Given its present structure, it simply has to fail when asked to do so. The very idea of an irrevocable contract obligating the parties concerned to a lifetime of romantic effort is utterly absurd.

Other pressures of the present era have tended to overburden marriage with expectations it cannot fulfill. Industrialized, urbanized America is a society which has lost the sense of community. Our ties to our society, to the bustling multitudes that make up this dazzling kaleidoscope of contemporary America, are as formal and superficial as they are numerous. We all search for community, and yet we know that the search is futile. Cut off from the support and satisfactions that flow from community, the confused and searching young American can do little but place all of his bets on creating a community in microcosm, his own marriage.

And so the ideal we struggle to reach in our love relationship is that of complete candor, total honesty. Out there all is phony, but within the romantic family there are to be no dishonest games, no hypocrisy, no misunderstanding. Here we have a painful paradox, for I submit that total exposure is probably always mutually destructive in the long run. What starts out as a tender coming together to share one's whole person with the beloved is transmuted by too much togetherness into attack and counterattack, doubt, disillusionment, and ambivalence. The moment the once-upon-a-time lover catches a glimpse of his own hatred, something precious and fragile is shattered. And soon another brave marriage will end.

The purposes of marriage have changed radically, yet we cling desperately to the outmoded structures of the past. Adult Americans behave as though the more obvious the contradiction between the old and the new, the more sentimental and irrational should be their advice to young people who are going steady or are engaged. Our schools, both high schools and colleges, teach sentimental rubbish in their marriage and family courses. The texts make much of a posture of hard-nosed objectivity that is neither objective nor hard-nosed. The basic structure of Western marriage is never questioned, alternatives are not proposed or discussed. Instead, the prospective young bride and bridegroom are offered housekeeping advice and told to work hard at making their marriage succeed. The chapter on sex, complete with ugly diagrams of the male and female genitals, is probably wedged in between a chapter on budgets and life insurance. The message is that if your marriage fails, you have been weighed in the domestic balance and found wanting. Perhaps you did not master the fifth position for sexual intercourse, or maybe you bought cheap term life rather than a preferred policy with income protection and retirement benefits. If taught honestly, these courses would alert the teenager and young adult to the realities of matrimonial life in the United States and try to advise them on how to survive marriage if they insist on that hazardous venture.

But teen-agers and young adults do insist upon it in greater and greater numbers with each passing year. And one of the reasons they do get married with such astonishing certainty is because they find themselves immersed in a culture that is preoccupied with and schizophrenic about sex. Advertising, entertainment, and fashion are all designed to produce and then to exploit sexual tension. Sexually aroused at an early age and asked to postpone marriage until they become adults, they have no recourse but to fill the intervening years with courtship rituals and games that are supposed to be sexy but sexless. Dating is expected to culminate in going steady, and that is the beginning of the end. The dating game hinges on an important exchange. The male wants sexual intimacy, and the female wants social commitment. The game involves bartering sex for security amid the sweet and heady agitations of a romantic entanglement. Once the game reaches the going-steady stage, marriage is virtually inevitable. The teen-ager finds himself driven into a corner, and the one way to legitimize his sex play and assuage the guilt is to plan marriage.

Another reason for the upsurge in young marriages is the real cultural break between teen-agers and adults in our society. This is a recent phenomenon. In my generation there was no teen culture. Adolescents wanted to become adults as soon as possible. The teen-age years were a time of impatient waiting, as teen-age boys tried to dress and act like little men. Adolescents sang the adults' songs ("South of the Border," "The Music Goes Round and Round," "Mairzy Doats"—notice I didn't say anything about the quality of the music), saw their movies, listened to their radios, and waited confidently to be allowed in. We had no money, and so there was no teen-age market. There was nothing to do then but get it over with. The boundary line was sharp, and you crossed it when you took your first serious job, when you passed the employment test.

Now there is a very definite adolescent culture, which is in many ways hostile to the dreary culture of the adult world. In its most extreme form it borrows from the beats and turns the middle-class value system inside out. The hip teen-ager on Macdougal Street or Telegraph Avenue can buy a costume and go to a freak show. It's fun to be an Indian, a prankster, a beat, or a swinging troubadour. He can get stoned. That particular trip leads to instant mysticism.

Even in less extreme forms, teen culture is weighted against the adult world of responsibility. I recently asked a roomful of eighteen-year-olds to tell me what an adult is. Their deliberate answer, after hours of discussion, was that an adult is someone who no longer plays, who is no longer playful. Is Bob Dylan an adult? No, never! Of course they did not want to remain children, or teens, or adolescents; but they did want to remain youthful, playful, free of squares, and free of responsibilty. The teen-ager wants to be old enough to drive, drink, screw, and travel. He does not want to get pushed into square maturity. He wants to drag the main, be a surf bum, a ski bum, or dream of being a bum. He doesn't want to go to Vietnam, or to IBM, or to buy a split-level house in Knotty Pines Estates.

This swing away from responsibility quite predictably produces friction between the adolescent and his parents. The clash of cultures is likely to drive the adolescent from the home, to persuade him to leave the dead world of his parents and strike out on his own. And here we find the central paradox of young marriages. For the only way the young person can escape from his parents is to assume many of the responsibilities that he so reviles in the life-style of his parents. He needs a job and an apartment. And he needs some kind of emotional substitute, some means of filling the emotional vacuum that leaving home has caused. And so he goes steady, and sooner rather than later, gets married to a girl with similar inclinations.

When he does this, he crosses the dividing line between the cultures. Though he seldom realizes it at the time, he has taken the first step to adulthood. Our society does not have a conventional "rite of passage." In Africa the Masai adolescent takes a lion test. He becomes an adult the first time he kills a lion with a spear. Our adolescents take the domesticity test. When they get married they have to come to terms with the system in one way or another. Some brave individuals continue to fight it. But most simply capitulate.

The cool adolescent finishing high school or starting college has a skeptical view of virtually every institutional sector of his society. He knows that government is corrupt, the military dehumanizing, the corporations rapacious, the churches organized hypocrisy, and the schools dishonest. But the one area that seems to be exempt from his cynicism is romantic love and marriage. When I talk to teen-agers about marriage, that cool skepticism turns to sentimental dreams right out of *Ladies' Home Journal* or the hard-hitting pages of *Reader's Digest*. They all mouth the same vapid platitudes about finding happiness through sharing and personal fulfillment through giving (each is to give 51 percent). They have all heard about divorce, and most of them have been touched by it in some way or another. Yet they insist that their marriage will be different.

So, clutching their illusions, young girls with ecstatic screams of joy lead their awkward brooding boys through the portals of the church into the land of the Mustang, Apartment 24, Macy's, Sears, and the ubiquitous drive-in. They have become members in good standing of the adult world.

The end of most of these sentimental marriages is quite predictable. They progress, in most cases, to varying stages of marital ennui, depending on the ability of the couple to adjust to reality; most common are (1) a lackluster standoff, (2) a bitter business carried on for the children, church, or neighbors, or (3) separation and divorce, followed by another search to find the right person.

Divorce rates have been rising in all Western countries. In many countries the rates are rising even faster than in the United States. In 1910 the divorce rate for the United States was 87 per 1000 marriages. In 1965 the rate had risen to an estimated figure of well over 300 per 1000 in many parts of the country. At the present time some 40 percent of all brides are between the ages of fifteen and eighteen; half of these marriages break up within five years. As our population becomes younger and the age of marriage continues to drop, the divorce rate will rise to significantly higher levels.

What do we do, what can we do, about this wretched and disappointing institution? In terms of the immediate generation, the answer probably is, not much. Even when subjected to the enormous strains I have described, the habits, customs, traditions, and taboos that make up our courtship and marriage cycle are uncommonly resistant to change. Here and there creative and courageous individuals can and do work out their own unique solutions to the problem of marriage. Most of us simply suffer without understanding and thrash around blindly in an attempt to reduce the acute pain of a romance gone sour. In time, all of these individual actions will show up as a trend away from the old and toward the new, and the bulk of sluggish moderates in the population will slowly come to accept this trend as part of social evolution. Clearly, in middle-class America, the trend is ever toward more romantic courtship and marriage, earlier premarital sexual intercourse, earlier first marriages, more extramarital affairs, earlier first divorces, more frequent divorces and remarriages. The trend is away from stable lifelong monogamous relationships toward some form of polygamous male-female relationship. Perhaps we should identify it as serial or consecutive polygamy, simply because Americans in significant numbers are going to have more than one husband or more than one wife. Attitudes and laws that make multiple marriages (in sequence, of course) difficult for the romantic and sentimental among us are archaic obstacles that one learns to circumvent with the aid of weary judges and clever attorneys.

Now, the absurdity of much of this lies in the fact that we pretend that marriages of short duration must be contracted for life. Why not permit a flexible contract perhaps for one to two or more years, with periodic options to renew? If a couple grew disenchanted with their life together, they would not feel trapped for life. They would not have to anticipate and then go through the destructive agonies of divorce. They would not have to carry about the stigma of marital failure, like the mark of Cain on their foreheads. Instead of a declaration of war, they could simply let their contract lapse, and while still friendly, be free to continue their romantic quest. Sexualized romanticism is now so fundamental to American life—and is bound to become even more so—that marriage will simply have to accommodate itself to it in one way or another. For a great proportion of us it already has.

What of the children in a society that is moving inexorably toward consecutive plural marriages? Under present arrangements in which marriages are ostensibly lifetime contracts and then are dissolved through hypocritical collusions or messy battles in court, the children do suffer. Marriage and divorce turn lovers into enemies, and the child is left to thread his way through the emotional wreckage of his parents' lives. Financial support of the children, mere subsistence, is not really a problem in a society as affluent as ours. Enduring emotional support of children by loving, healthy, and friendly adults is a serious problem in America, and it is a desperately urgent problem in many families where divorce is unthinkable. If the bitter and poisonous denouement of divorce could be avoided by a frank acceptance of short-term marriages, both adults and children would benefit. Any time husbands and wives and ex-husbands and ex-wives treat each other decently, generously, and respectfully, their children will benefit.

The braver and more critical among our teen-agers and youthful adults will still ask, But if the institution is so bad, why get married at all? This is a tough one to deal with. The social pressures pushing any couple who live together into marriage are difficult to ignore even by the most resolute rebel. It can be done, and many should be encouraged to carry out their own creative experiments in living together in a relationship that is wholly voluntary. If the demands of society to conform seem overwhelming, the couple should know that simply to be defined by others as married will elicit married-like behavior in themselves, and that is precisely what they want to avoid.

How do you marry and yet live like gentle lovers, or at least like friendly roommates? Quite frankly, I do not know the answer to that question.

For Discussion

1. Why does Cadwallader feel that marriage is a wretched institution?
2. Cadwallader states that couples marry for the wrong reasons. What are some of these reasons? In your opinion, why should a couple marry?
3. What does the author mean by the "adolescent culture"? How does this culture contribute to the problem as he sees it?
4. What is an adult? Cadwallader seems to associate adulthood with responsibility? Do you agree that the main difference between adults and adolescents is one of responsibility? Why or why not?
5. Who or what ultimately is responsible for the breakdown in today's marriages? Do you agree with Cadwallader's proposal for a revision of the marriage system?

For Comparison

1. What advice would Cadwallader give to Emily and Martin in "A Domestic Dilemma"?
2. What ideas from this essay are also stated in Corso's poem "Marriage"? Would Corso agree with everything that Cadwallader states in his essay? If not, on which points would the two differ?

For Composition

1. Marriage is (is not) a wretched institution.
2. The adolescent culture.
3. A teenager is a responsible person.

BETTY ROLLIN

MOTHERHOOD: WHO NEEDS IT?

Motherhood is in trouble, and it ought to be. A rude question is long overdue: Who needs it? The answer used to be 1) society and 2) women. But now, with the impending horrors of overpopulation, society desperately *doesn't* need it. And women don't need it either. Thanks to The Motherhood Myth—the idea of having babies is something that all normal women instinctively want and need and will enjoy doing—they just *think* they do.

The notion that the maternal wish and the activity of mothering are instinctive or biologically predestined is baloney. Try asking most sociologists, psychologists, psychoanalysts, biologists—many of whom are mothers—about motherhood being instinctive; it's like asking department-store presidents if their Santa Clauses are real. "Motherhood—instinctive?" shouts distinguished sociologist/author Dr. Jessie Bernard. "Biological destiny? Forget biology! If it were biology, people would die from not doing it."

"Women don't need to be mothers any more than they need spaghetti," says Dr. Richard Rabkin, a New York psychiatrist. "But if you're in a world where everyone is eating spaghetti, thinking they need it and want it, you will think so too. Romance has really contaminated science. So-called instincts have to do with stimulation. They are not things that well up inside of you."

"When a woman says with feeling that she craved her baby from within, she is putting into biological language what is psychological," says University of Michigan psychoanalyst and motherhood-researcher Dr. Frederick Wyatt. "There are no instincts," says Dr. William Goode, [president] of the American Sociological Association. "There are reflexes, like eye-blinking, and drives, like sex. There is no innate drive for children. Otherwise, the enormous cultural pressures that there are to reproduce wouldn't exist. There are no cultural pressures to sell you on getting your hand out of the fire."

There are, to be sure, biologists and others who go on about biological destiny, that is, the innate or instinctive goal of motherhood. (At the turn of the century, even good old capitalism was explained by a theorist as "the *instinct* of acquisitiveness.") And many psychoanalysts still hold the Freudian view that women feel so rotten about not having a penis that they are necessarily propelled into the child-wish to replace the missing organ. Psychoanalysts also make much of the psychological need to repeat what one's parent of the same sex has done. Since every woman has a mother, it is considered normal to wish to imitate one's mother by being a mother.

There is, surely, a wish to pass on love if one has received it, but to insist women must pass it on in the same way is like insisting that every man whose father is a gardener has to be a gardener. One dissenting psychoanalyst says, simply, "There is a wish to comply with one's biology, yes, but we needn't and sometimes we shouldn't." (Interestingly, the woman who has been the greatest contributor to child therapy and who has probably given more to children than anyone alive is Dr. Anna Freud, Freud's magnificent daughter, who is not a mother.)

Anyway, what an expert cast of hundreds is telling us is, simply, that biological *possibility* and desire are not the same as biological *need*. Women have childbearing equipment. To choose not to use the equipment is no more blocking what is instinctive than it is for a man who, muscles or no, chooses not to be a weight lifter.

So much for the wish. What about the "instinctive" *activity* of mothering. One animal study shows that when a young member of a species is put in a cage, say, with an older member of the same species, the latter will act in a protective, "maternal" way. But that goes for both males and females who have been "mothered" themselves. And studies indicate that a human baby will also respond to whoever is around playing mother —even if it's father. Margaret Mead and many others frequently point out that mothering can be a fine occupation, if you want it, for either sex. Another experiment with monkeys who were brought up without mothers found them lacking in maternal behavior toward their own offspring. A similar study showed that monkeys brought up without other monkeys of the opposite sex had no interest in mating—all of which suggests that both mothering and mating behavior are learned, not instinctual. And, to turn the cart (or the baby carriage) around, baby ducks who lovingly follow their mothers seemed, in the mother's absence, to just as lovingly follow wooden ducks or even vacuum cleaners.

If motherhood isn't instinctive, when and why, then, was The Motherhood Myth born? Until recently, the entire question of maternal motivation was academic. Sex, like it or not, meant babies. Not that there haven't always been a lot of interesting contraceptive tries. But until the creation of the diaphragm in the 1880s, the birth of babies was largely unavoidable. And, generally speaking, nobody really seemed to mind. For one thing, people tend to be sort of good sports about what really seems to be inevitable. For another, in the past, the population needed beefing up. Mortality rates were high, and agricultural cultures, particularly, have always needed children to help out. So because it "just happened" and because it was needed, motherhood was assumed to be innate.

Originally, it was the word of God that got the ball rolling with "Be fruitful and multiply," a practical suggestion, since the only people around then were Adam and Eve. But in no time, super-moralists like St. Augustine changed the tone of the message: "Intercourse, even with one's legitimate wife is unlawful and wicked where the conception of the offspring is prevented," he, we assume, thundered. And the Roman Catholic position was thus cemented. So then and now, procreation took on a curious value among people who viewed (and view) the pleasures of sex as sinful. One could partake in the sinful pleasure, but feel vindicated by the ensuing birth. Motherhood cleaned up sex. Also, it cleaned up women, who have always been considered somewhat evil, because of Eve's transgression (". . . but the woman was deceived and became a transgressor. Yet woman will be saved through bearing children . . . ," I Timothy, 2:14-15) and somewhat dirty because of menstruation.

And so, based on need, inevitability and pragmatic fantasy—the Myth *worked*, from society's point of view—the Myth grew like corn in Kansas. And society reinforced it with both laws and propaganda—laws that made woman a chattel, denied her education and personal mobility, and madonna propaganda that said she was beautiful and wonderful doing it and it was all beautiful and wonderful to do. (One rarely sees a madonna washing dishes.)

In fact, the Myth persisted—breaking some kind of record for long-lasting fallacies—until something like yesterday. For as the truth about the Myth trickled in—as women's rights increased, as women gradually got the message that it was certainly possible for them to do most things that men did, that they live longer, that their brains were not tinier—

then, finally, when the really big news rolled in, that they could *choose* whether or not to be mothers—what happened? The Motherhood Myth soared higher than ever. As Betty Friedan made oh-so-clear in *The Feminine Mystique*, the '40's and '50's produced a group of ladies who not only had babies as if they were going out of style (maybe they were) but, as never before, they turned motherhood into a cult. First, they wallowed in the aesthetics of it all—natural childbirth and nursing became maternal musts. Like heavy-bellied ostriches, they grounded their heads in the sands of motherhood, only coming up for air to say how utterly happy and fulfilled they were. But, as Mrs. Friedan says only too plainly, they weren't. The Myth galloped on, moreover, long after making babies had turned from practical asset to liability for both individual parents *and* society. With the average cost of a middle-class child figured conservatively at $30,000 (not including college), any parent knows that the only people who benefit economically from children are manufacturers of consumer goods. Hence all those gooey motherhood commercials. And the Myth gathered momentum long after sheer numbers, while not yet extinguishing us, have made us intensely uncomfortable. Almost all of our societal problems, from minor discomforts like traffic to major ones like hunger, the population people keep reminding us, have to do with there being too many people. And who suffers most? The kids who have been so mindlessly brought into the world, that's who. They are the ones who have to cope with all of the difficult and dehumanizing conditions brought on by overpopulation. They are the ones who have to cope with the psychological nausea of feeling unneeded by society. That's not the only reason for drugs, but, surely, it's a leading contender.

Unfortunately, the population curbers are tripped up by a romantic, stubborn, ideological hurdle. How can birth-control programs really be effective as long as the concept of glorious motherhood remains unchanged? (Even poor old Planned Parenthood has to euphemize—why not Planned Unparenthood?) Particularly among the poor, motherhood is one of the few inherently positive institutions that are accessible. As Berkeley demographer Judith Blake points out, "Poverty-oriented birth control programs do not make sense as a welfare measure . . . as long as existing pronatalist policies . . . encourage mating, pregnancy and the care, support and rearing of children." Or, she might have added, as long as the less-than-idyllic childrearing part of motherhood remains "in small print."

Sure, motherhood gets dumped on sometimes: Philip Wylie's Momism got going in the '40's and Philip Roth's *Portnoy's Complaint* did its best to turn rancid the chicken-soup concept of Jewish motherhood. But these are viewed as the sour cries of a black humorist here, a malcontent there.

Everyone shudders, laughs, but it's like the mouse and the elephant joke. Still, the Myth persists. Last April, a Brooklyn woman was indicted on charges of manslaughter and negligent homicide—11 children died in a fire in a building she owned and criminally neglected—"But," sputtered her lawyer, "my client, Mrs. Breslow, is a mother, a grandmother and a great-grandmother!"

Most remarkably, The Motherhood Myth persists in the face of the most overwhelming maternal unhappiness and incompetence. If reproduction were merely superfluous and expensive, if the experience were as rich and rewarding as the cliché would have us believe, if it were a predominantly joyous trip for everyone riding—mother, father, child— then the going everybody-should-have-two-children plan would suffice. Certainly, there are a lot of joyous mothers, and their childern and (sometimes, not necessarily) their husbands reflect their joy. But a lot of evidence suggests that for more women than anyone wants to admit, motherhood can be miserable. ("If it weren't" says one psychiatrist wryly, "the world wouldn't be in the mess it's in.")

There is a remarkable statistical finding from a recent study of Dr. Bernard's, comparing the mental illness and unhappiness of married mothers and single women. The latter group, it turned out, was both markedly less sick and overtly more happy. Of course, it's not easy to measure slippery attitudes like happiness. "Many women have achieved a kind of reconciliation—a conformity," says Dr. Bernard, "that they interpret as happiness. Since feminine happiness is supposed to lie in devoting one's life to one's husband and children, they do that; so *ipso facto*, they assume they are happy. And for many women, untrained for independence and 'processed' for motherhood, they find their state far preferable to the alternatives, which don't really exist." Also, unhappy mothers are often loath to admit it. For one thing, if in society's view not to be a mother is to be a freak, not to be a *blissful* mother is to be a witch. Besides, unlike a disappointing marriage, disappointing motherhood cannot be terminated by divorce. Of course, none of that stops such a woman from expressing her dissatisfaction in a variety of ways. Again, it is not she who suffers but her husband and children as well. Enter the harridan housewife, the carping shrew. The realities of motherhod can turn women into terrible people. And, judging from the 50,000 cases of child abuse in the U.S. each year, some are worse than terrible.

In some cases, the unpleasing realities of motherhood begin even before the beginning. In *Her Infinite Variety*, Morton Hunt describes young married women pregnant for the first time as "very likely to be frightened and depressed, masking these feelings in order not to be considered contemptible. The arrival of pregnancy interrupts a pleasant dream of motherhood and awakens them to the realization that they have too little money, or not enough space, or unresolved marital problems. . . ."

The following are random quotes from interviews with some mothers in Ann Arbor, Mich., who described themselves as reasonably happy. They all had positive things to say about their children, although when asked about the best moment of their day, they *all* confessed it was when the children were in bed. Here is the rest:

"Suddenly I had to devote myself to the child totally. I was under the illusion that the baby was going to fit into my life, and I found that I had to switch my life and my schedule to fit *him*. You think, 'I'm in love, I'll get married, and we'll have a baby.' First there's two, then three, it's simple and romantic. You don't even think about the work." . . . "You never get away from the responsibility. Even when you leave the children with a sitter, you are not out from under the pressure of the responsibility." . . . "I hate ironing their pants and doing their underwear, and they never put their clothes in the laundry basket. . . . As they get older, they make less demands on your time because they're in school, but the demands are greater in forming their values. . . . Best moment of the day is when all the children are in bed. . . . The worst time of the day is 4 p.m., when you have to get dinner started, the kids are tired, hungry and crabby—everybody wants to talk to you about *their* day . . . your day is only half over."

"Once a mother, the responsibility and concern for my children became so encompassing. . . . It took a great deal of will to keep up other parts of my personality. . . . To me, motherhood gets harder as they get older because you have less control. . . . In an abstract sense, I'd have several. . . . In the non-abstract, I would not have any." . . . "I had anticipated that the baby would sleep and eat, sleep and eat. Instead, the experience was overwhelming. I really had not thought particularly about what motherhood would mean in a realistic sense. I want to do *other* things, like to become involved in things that are worthwhile—I don't mean women's clubs—but I don't have the physical energy to go out in the evenings. I feel like I'm missing something . . . the experience of being somewhere with people and having them talking about something—something that's going on in the world."

Every grown-up person expects to pay a price for his pleasures, but seldom is the price as vast as the one endured "however happily" by most mothers. We have mentioned the literal cost factor. But what does that mean? For middle-class American women, it means a lifestyle with severe and unusually unimagined limitations; i.e., life in the suburbs, because who can afford three bedrooms in the city? And what do suburbs mean? For women, suburbs mean other women and children and leftover peanut-butter sandwiches and car pools and seldom-seen husbands. Even the Feminine Mystiqueniks—the housewives who finally admitted that their lives behind brooms (OK, electric brooms) were driving them crazy—were loath to trace their predicament to their children. But it is simply a fact that a childless married woman has no child-work and little housework. She can live in a city, or, if she chooses the suburbs or the country, she can leave on the commuter train with her husband if she wants to. Even the most ardent job-seeking mother will find little in the way of great opportunities in Scarsdale. Besides, by the time she wakes up, she usually lacks both the preparation for the outside world and the self-confidence to get it. You will say there are plenty of city-dwelling working mothers. But most of those women do additional-funds-for-the-family kind of work, not the interesting career kind that takes plugging during "childbearing years."

Nor is it a bed of petunias for the mother who does make it profession-ally. Says writer/critic Marya Mannes: "If the creative woman has children, she must pay for this indulgence with a long burden of guilt, for her life will be split three ways between them and her husband and her work. . . . No woman with any heart can compose a paragraph when her child is in trouble. . . . The creative woman has no wife to protect her from intrusion. A man at his desk in a room with closed door is a man at work. A woman at a desk in any room is available."

Speaking of jobs, do remember that mothering, salary or not, is a job. Even those who can afford nurses to handle the nitty-gritty still need to put out emotionally. "Well-cared-for" neurotic rich kids are not exactly unknown in our society. One of the more absurd aspects of the Myth is the underlying assumption that, since most women are biologically equipped to bear children, they are psychologically, mentally, emotion-ally and technically equipped (or interested) to rear them. Never mind happiness. To assume that such an exacting, consuming and important task is something almost all women are equipped to do is far more dan-gerous and ridiculous than assuming that everyone with vocal chords should seek a career in the opera.

A major expectation of the Myth is that children make a not-so-hot marriage hotter, or a hot marriage, hotter still. Yet almost every available study indicates that childless marriages are far happier. One of the big-gest, of 850 couples, was conducted by Dr. Harold Feldman of Cornell University, who states his finding in no uncertain terms: "Those couples with children had a significantly lower level of marital satisfaction than did those without children." Some of the reasons are obvious. Even the most adorable children make for additional demands, complications and hardships in the lives of even the most loving parents. If a woman feels disappointed and trapped in her mother role, it is bound to affect her marriage in any number of ways: she may take out her frustrations directly on her husband, or she may count on him too heavily for what she feels she is missing in her daily life.

". . . You begin to grow away from your husband," says one of the Michigan ladies. "He's working on his career and you're working on your family. But you both must gear your lives to the children. You do things the children enjoy, more than things you might enjoy." More subtle and possibly more serious is what motherhood may do to a woman's sexuality. Often when the stork flies in, sexuality flies out. Both in the emotional minds of some women *and* in the minds of their husbands, when a woman becomes a mother, she stops being a woman. It's not only that motherhood may destroy her physical attractiveness, but its madonna concept may destroy her *feelings* of sexuality.

And what of the payoff? Usually, even the most self-sacrificing maternal self-sacrificers expect a little something back. Gratified parents are not unknown to the Western world, but there are probably at least just as many who feel, to put it crudely, shortchanged. The experiment mentioned earlier—where the baby ducks followed vacuum cleaners instead of their mothers—indicates that what passes for love from baby to mother is merely a rudimentary kind of object attachment. Without necessarily feeling like a Hoover, a lot of women become disheartened because babies and children are not only not interesting to talk to (not everyone thrills at the wonders of da-da-ma-ma talk) but they are generally not empathetic, considerate people. Even the nicest children are not capable of empathy, surely a major ingredient of love, until they are much older. Sometimes they're never capable of it. Dr. Wyatt says that often, in later years particularly, when most of the "returns" are in, it is the "good mother" who suffers most of all. It is then she must face a reality: The child—the appendage with her genes—is not an appendage, but a separate person. What's more, he or she may be a separate person who doesn't even like her—or whom she doesn't really like.

So if the music is lousy, how come everyone's dancing? Because the motherhood minuet is taught free from birth, and whether or not she has rhythm or likes the music, every woman is expected to do it. Indeed, she *wants* to do it. Little girls start learning what to want—and what to be— when they are still in their cribs. Dr. Miriam Keiffer, a young social psychologist at Bensalem, The Experimental College of Fordham University, points to studies showing that "at six months of age, mothers are already treating their baby girls and boys quite differently. For instance, mothers have been found to touch, comfort, and talk to their females more. If these differences can be found at such an early stage, it's not surprising that the end product is as different as it is. What is surprising is that men and women are, in so many ways, similar." Some people point to the way little girls play with dolls as proof of their "innate motherliness." But remember, little girls are *given* dolls. When Margaret Mead presented some dolls to New Guinea children, it was the boys, not the girls, who wanted to play with them, which they did by crooning lullabies and rocking them in the most maternal fashion.

By the time they reach adolescence, most girls, unconsciously or not, have learned enough about role definition to qualify for a master's degree. In general, the lesson has been that no matter what kind of career thoughts one may entertain, one must, first and foremost, be a wife and mother. A girl's mother is usually her first teacher. As Dr. Goode says, "A woman is not only taught by society to have a child; she is taught to have a child who will have a child." A woman who has hung her life on The Motherhood Myth will almost always reinforce her young married daughter's early training by pushing for grandchildren. Prospective grandmothers are not the only ones. Husbands, too, can be effective sellers. After all, they have The Fatherhood Myth to cope with. A married man is *supposed* to have children. Often, particularly among Latins, children are a sign of potency. They help him assure the world—and himself— that he is the big man he is supposed to be. Plus, children give him both immortality (whatever that means) and possibly the chance to become "more" in his lifetime through the accomplishments of his children, particularly his son. (Sometimes it's important, however, for the son to do better, but not *too* much better.)

Friends, too, can be counted on as myth-pushers. Naturally one wants to do what one's friends do. One study, by the way, found an absolute correlation between a woman's fertility and that of her three closest friends. The negative sell comes into play here, too. We have seen what the concept of non-mother means (cold, selfish, unwomanly, abnormal). In practice, particularly in the suburbs, it can mean, simply, exclusion— both from child-centered activities (that is, most activities) and child-centered conversations (that is, most conversations). It can also mean being the butt of a lot of unfunny jokes. ("Whaddya waiting for? An immaculate conception? Ha ha.") Worst of all, it can mean being an object of pity.

In case she's escaped all of those pressures (that is, if she was brought up in a cave), a young married woman often wants a baby just so that she'll 1) have something to do (motherhood is better than clerk/typist, which is often the only kind of job she can get, since little more has been expected of her and, besides, her boss also expects her to leave and be a mother); 2) have something to hug and possess, to be needed by and have power over; and 3) have something to be—e.g., a baby's mother. Motherhood affords an instant identity. First, through wifehood, you are somebody's wife; then you are somebody's mother. Both give not only identity and activity, but status and stardom of a kind. During pregnancy, a woman can look forward to the kind of attention and pampering she may not ever have gotten or may never otherwise get. Some women consider birth the biggest accomplishment of their lives, which may be interpreted as saying not much for the rest of their lives. As Dr. Goode says, "It's like the gambler who may know the roulette wheel is crooked, but it's the only game in town." Also, with motherhood, the feeling of accomplishment is immediate. It is really much faster and easier to make a baby than paint a painting, or write a book, or get to the point of accomplishment in a job. It is also easier in a way to shift focus from self-development to child development—particularly since, for women, self-development is considered selfish. Even unwed mothers may achieve a feeling of this kind. (As we have seen, little thought is given to the aftermath.) And, again, since so many women are underdeveloped as people, they feel that, besides children, they have little else to give—to themselves, their husbands, to their world.

You may ask why then, when the realities do start pouring in, does a woman want to have a second, third, even fourth child? OK, 1) Just because reality is pouring in doesn't mean she wants to *face* it. A new baby can help bring back some of the old illusions. Says psychoanalyst Dr. Natalie Shainess, "She may view each successive child as a knight in armor that will rescue her from being a 'bad/unhappy mother.' " 2) Next on the horror list of having no children, is having one. It suffices to say that only children are not only OK, they even have a high rate of exceptionality. 3) Both parents usually want at least one child of each sex. The husband, for reasons discussed earlier, probably wants a son. 4) The more children one has, the more of an excuse one has not to develop in any other way.

What's the point? A world without children? Of course not. Nothing could be worse or more unlikely. No matter what anyone says in *LOOK* or anywhere else, motherhood isn't about to go out like a blown bulb, and who says it should? Only the Myth must go out, and now it seems to be dimming.

The younger-generation females who have been reared on the Myth have not rejected it totally, but at least they recognize it can be more loving to children not to have them. And at least they speak of adopting children instead of bearing them. Moreover, since the new non-breeders are "less hung-up" on ownership, they seem to recognize that if you dig loving children, you don't necessarily have to own one. The end of The

Motherhood Myth might make available more loving women (and men!) for those children who already exist.

When motherhood is no longer culturally compulsory, there will, certainly, be less of it. Women are now beginning to think and do more about development of self, of their individual resources. Far from being selfish, such development is probably our only hope. That means more alternatives for women. And more alternatives mean more selective, better, happier, motherhood—and childhood and husbandhood (or manhood) and peoplehood. It is not a question of whether or not children are sweet and marvelous to have and rear; the question is, even if that's so, whether or not one wants to pay the price for it. It doesn't make sense any more to pretend that women need babies, when what they really need is themselves. If God were still speaking to us in a voice we could hear, even He would probably say, "Be fruitful. Don't multiply."

For Discussion

1. What exactly is meant by "The Motherhood Myth"? Do you agree or disagree with Rollin's criticism of this myth?
2. What are some specific words or phrases used by Rollin to create definite negative or positive reactions among her readers? Is this type of writing misleading? If so, explain why. If not, defend the style by relating it to the author's intentions.
3. To what extent do you feel mothers have bought the "motherhood myth" as security from their own frustrations?
4. Rollin cites evidence to suggest that mothers may be less happy than single women. Why might this be true? Carefully evaluate this idea in terms of responsibilities.
5. In your own opinion can children themselves help stabilize a marriage, or do they add a new dimension to the problem of instability?
6. Rollin is careful to say that motherhood must not disappear but that only the myth should. What exactly does she mean? Is this a trend that you see emerging in today's world? If so, evaluate the trend in terms of total responsibility.

For Comparison

1. To what extent has the "motherhood myth" affected the mother in D. H. Lawrence's "The Rocking-Horse Winner"?
2. Using your understanding of the "motherhood myth," discuss what Cadwallader might well have called the "marriage myth."

For Composition

1. I do (do not) believe in the "motherhood myth."
2. The liberated woman.
3. My mother and the myth.

———————————

JAMES AGEE

EMMA

I am fond of Emma, and very sorry for her, and I shall probably never see her again after a few hours from now. I want to tell you what I can about her.

She is a big girl, almost as big as her sister is wiry, though she is not at all fat: her build is rather that of a young queen of a child's magic story who throughout has been coarsened by peasant and earth living and work, and that of her eyes and her demeanor, too, kind, not fully formed, resolute, bewildered, and sad. Her soft abundant slightly curling brown hair is cut in a square bob which on her large fine head is particularly childish, and indeed Emma is rather a big child, sexual beyond propriety to its years, than a young woman; and this can be seen in a kind of dimness of definition in her features, her skin, and the shape of her body, which will be lost in a few more years. She wears a ten cent necklace and a sunday cotton print dress because she is visiting and is from town, but she took off her slippers as soon as she came, and worked with Annie Mae. According to her father she is the spitn image of her mother when her mother was young; Annie Mae favors her father and his people, who were all small and lightly built.

Emma is very fond of her father and very sorry for him, as his sister is, and neither of them can stand his second wife. I have an idea that his marrying her had a lot to do with Emma's own marriage, which her father so strongly advised her against. He married the second time when Emma was thirteen, and for a long while they lived almost insanely, as I will tell you of later, far back in a swamp: and when Emma was sixteen she married a man her father's age, a carpenter in Cherokee City. She has been married to him two years; they have no children. Emma loves good times, and towns, and people her own age, and he is jealous and mean to her and suspicious of her. He has given her no pretty dresses nor the money to buy cloth to make them. Every minute he is in the house he keeps his eye right on her as if she was up to something, and when he goes out, which is as seldom as he can, he locks her in: so that twice already she has left him and come home to stay, and then after a while he has come down begging, and crying, and swearing he'll treat her good, and give her anything she asks for, and that he'll take to drink or kill himself if she leaves him, and she has gone back: for it isn't any fun at home, hating that woman the way she does, and she can't have fun with anyone else because she is married and nobody will have fun with her that way: and now (and I think it may be not only through the depression but through staying in the house because of jealousy and through fear of living in a town with her, and so near a home she can return to), her husband can no longer get a living in Cherokee City; he has heard of a farm on a plantation over in the red hills in Mississippi and has already gone, and taken it, and he has sent word to Emma that she is to come in a truck in which a man he knows, who has business to drive out that way, is moving their furniture; and this truck is leaving tomorrow. She doesn't want to go at all, and during the past two days she has been withdrawing into rooms with her sister and crying a good deal, almost tearlessly and almost without voice, as if she knew no more how to cry than how to take care for her life; and Annie Mae is strong against her going, all that distance, to a man who leaves her behind and then just sends for her, saying, Come on along, now; and George too is as committal over it as he feels will appear any right or business of his to be, he a man, and married, to the wife of another man, who is no kin to him, but only the sister of his wife, and to whom he is himself unconcealably attracted: but she is going all the same, without at all understanding why. Annie Mae is sure she won't stay out there long, not all alone in the country away from her kinfolks with that man; that is what she keeps saying, to Emma, and to George, and even to me; but actually she is surer than not that she may never see her younger sister again, and she grieves for her, and for the loss of her to her own loneliness, for she loves her, both for herself and her dependence and for that softness of youth which already is drawn so deep into the trap, and in which Annie Mae can perceive herself as she was ten years past; and she gives no appearance of noticing the clumsy and shamefaced would-be-subtle demeanors of flirtation which George is stupid enough to believe she does not understand for what they are: for George would only be shocked should she give him open permission, and Emma could not be too well trusted either. So this sad comedy has been going on without comment from anyone, which will come to nothing: and another sort has been going on with us, of a kind fully as helpless. Each of us is attractive to Emma, both in sexual immediacy and as symbols or embodiments of a life she wants and knows she will never have; and each of us is fond of her, and attracted toward her. We are not only strangers to her, but we are strange, unexplainable, beyond what I can begin yet fully to realize. We have acted toward her with the greatest possible care and shyness and quiet, yet we have been open or 'clear' as well, so that she knows we understand her and like her and care for her almost intimately. She is puzzled by this and yet not at all troubled, but excited; there is nothing to do about it on either side. There is tenderness and sweetness and mutual pleasure in such a 'flirtation' which one would not for the world restrain or cancel, yet there is also an essential cruelty, about which nothing can be done, and strong possibility of cruelty through misunderstanding, and inhibition, and impossibly, which can be restrained, and which one would rather die than cause any of: but it is a cruel and ridiculous and restricted situation, and everyone to some extent realizes it. Everyone realizes it, I think, to such a degree even as this: supposing even that nothing can be helped about the marriage, supposing she is going away and on with it, which she shouldn't, then if only Emma could spend her last few days alive having a gigantic good time in bed, with George, a kind of man she is best used to, and with Walker and with me, whom she is curious about and attracted to, and who are at the same moment tangible and friendly and not at all to be feared, and on the other hand have for her the mystery or glamour almost of mythological creatures. This has a good many times in the past couple of days come very clearly through between all of us except the children, and without fear, in sudden and subtle but unmistakable expressions of the eyes, or ways of smiling; yet not one of us would be capable of trusting ourselves to it unless beyond any doubt each knew all the others to be thus capable: and even then how crazily the conditioned and inferior parts of each of our beings would rush in, and take revenge. But this is just a minute specialization of a general brutal pity; almost any person, no matter how damaged and poisoned and blinded, is infinitely more capable of intelligence and of joy than he can let himself be or than he usually knows; and even if he had no reason to fear his own poisons, he has those that are in others to fear, to assume and take care for, if he would not hurt both himself and that other person and the pure act itself beyond cure.

But here I am going to shift ahead of where I am writing, to a thing which is to happen, or which happened, the next morning (you mustn't be puzzled by this, I'm writing in a continuum), and say what came of it.

The next morning was full of the disorganized, half listless, yet very busy motions of ordinary life broken by an event: Emma's going away. I was going to take her and Annie Mae to her brother Gallatin's house near Cookstown, where she was to meet the man with his truck, and I was

waiting around on the front porch in the cool-hot increasing morning
sunlight, working out my notes, while the morning housework was done
up in special speed. (George was gone an hour or more ago, immediately
after the breakfast they had all sat through, not talking much. There had
been a sort of lingering in eating and in silences, and a little when the
food was done, broken by talk to keep the silences from becoming too
frightening; I had let the breakfast start late by telling him I would take
him in the car; then abruptly he got up saying, 'Well, Jimmy, if you—'
Whether he would kiss Emma goodbye, as a sort of relative, was on everybody's mind. He came clumsily near it: she half got from her chair, and
their bodies were suddenly and sharply drawn toward each other a few
inches: but he was much too shy, and did not even touch her with the
hand he reached out to shake hers. Annie Mae drawled, smiling, What's
wrong with ye George; she ain't agoin' to bite ye; and everyone laughed,
and Emma stood up and they embraced, laughing, and he kissed her on
her suddenly turned cheek, a little the way a father and an adolescent son
kiss, and told her goodbye and wished her good luck, and I took him to
work in the car, and came back. And now here I was, as I have said, on
the porch.) Here I was on the porch, diddling around in a notebook and
hearing the sounds of work and the changing patterns of voices inside,
and the unaccustomed noise of shoeleather on the floor, because someone
was dressed up for travel: and a hen thudded among dried watermelon
seeds on the oak floor, looking, as they usually do, like a nearsighted
professor; and down hill beyond the open field a little wind laid itself in
a wall against the glistening leaves of the high forest and lay through
with a long sweet granular noise of rustling water; and the hen dropped
from the ledge of the porch to the turded dirt with a sodden bounce; and
an involuntary cluck as her heaviness hit the ground on her sprung legs;
and the long lithe wind released the trees and was gone on, wandering the fringed earth in its affairs like a saturday schoolchild in the sun,
and the leaves hung troubling in the aftermath; and I heard footsteps in
the hall and Emma appeared, all dressed to go, looking somehow as if
she had come to report a decision that had been made in conference, for
which I, without knowing it, seemed to have been waiting. She spoke in
that same way, too, not wasting any roundabout time or waiting for an
appropriate rhythm, yet not in haste, looking me steadily and sweetly in
the eyes, and said, I want you and Mr. Walker to know how much we all
like you, because you make us feel easy with you; we don't have to act
any different from what it comes natural to act, and we don't have to
worry what you're thinking about us, it's just like you was our own people
and had always lived here with us, you all are so kind, and nice, and quiet,
and easygoing, and we wisht you wasn't never going to go away but stay

on here with us, and I just want to tell you how much we all keer about
you; Annie Mae says the same, and you please tell Mr. Walker, too, if I
don't see him afore I go. (I knew she could never say it over again, and
I swore I certainly would tell him.)

What's the use trying to say what I felt. It took her a long time to
say what she wanted so much to say, and it was hard for her, but there
she stood looking straight into my eyes, and I straight into hers, longer
than you'd think it would be possible to stand it. I would have done anything in the world for her (that's always characteristic, I guess, of the
seizure of the strongest love you can feel: pity, and the wish to die for
a person, because there isn't anything you can do for them that is at all
measurable to your love), and all I could do, the very most, for this girl
who was so soon going out of my existence into so hopeless a one of hers,
the very most I could do was not to show all I cared for her and for what
she was saying, and not to even try to do, or to indicate the good I wished
I might do her and was so utterly helpless to do. I had such tenderness
and such gratitude toward her that while she spoke I very strongly, as
something steadier than an 'impulse,' wanted in answer to take her large
body in my arms and smooth the damp hair back from her forehead and
to kiss and comfort and shelter her like a child, and I can swear that I
now as then almost believe that in that moment she would have so well
understood this, and so purely and quietly met it, that now and then I
only wish to God I had done it; but instead the most I did was to stand
facing her, and to keep looking into her eyes (doing her the honor at
least of knowing that she did not want relief from this), and, managing
to keep the tears from running down my face, to smile to her and say
that there was nothing in my whole life that I cared so much to be told,
and had been so grateful for (and I believe this is so); and that I wanted
her to know how much I liked them, too, and her herself, and that I certainly felt that they were my own people, and wanted them to be, more
than any other kind of people in the world, and that if they felt that of me,
and that I belonged with them, and we all felt right and easy with each
other and fond of each other, then there wasn't anything in the world I
could be happier over, or be more glad to know (and this is so, too); and
that I knew I could say all the same of Walker (and this, too, I know I
was true in saying). I had stood up, almost without realizing I was doing
it, the moment she appeared and began to speak, as though facing some
formal, or royal, or ritual action, and we stayed thus standing, not leaning
against or touching anything, about three feet apart, facing each other.
I went on to say that whatever might happen to her or that she might do
in all her life I wished her the best luck anyone could think of, and not
ever to forget it, that nobody has a right to be unhappy, or to live in a way

that makes them unhappy, for the sake of being afraid, or what people will think of them, or for the sake of anyone else, if there is any way they can possibly do better, that won't hurt other people too much. She slowly and lightly blushed while I spoke and her eyes became damp and bright, and said that she sure did wish me the same. Then we had nothing to say, unless we should invent something, and nothing to do, and quite suddenly and at the same instant we smiled, and she said well, she reckoned she'd better git on in and help Annie Mae, and I nodded, and she went, and a half-hour later I was driving her, and Annie Mae, and her father, and Louise, and Junior, and Burt, and the baby, to her brother's house near Cookstown. The children were silent and intent with the excitement of riding in the car, stacked on top of each other around their mother on the back seat and looking out of the windows like dogs, except Louise, whose terrible gray eyes met mine whenever I glanced for them in the car mirror. Emma rode between me and her father, her round sleeveless arms cramped a little in front of her. My own sleeves were rolled high, so that in the crowding our flesh touched. Each of us at the first few of these contacts drew quietly away, then later she relaxed her arms, and her body and thighs as well, and so did I, and perhaps for fifteen minutes we lay quietly and closely side by side, and intimately communicated also in our thoughts. Our bodies were very hot, and the car was packed with hot and sweating bodies, and with a fine salt and rank odor like that of crushed grass: and thus in a short while, though I knew speed was not in the mood of anyone and was going as slowly as I felt I could with propriety, we covered the short seven mileage of clay, then slag, to Cookstown, and slowly through the town (eyes, eyes on us, of men, from beneath hatbrims), and down the meandering now sandy road to where her brother lived. I had seen him once before, a man in his thirties with a bitter, intelligent, skull-formed face; and his sour wife, and their gold skinned children: and now here also was another man, forty or so, leathery-strong, blackshaven, black-hatted, booted, his thin mouth tightened round a stalk of grass showing gold stained teeth, his cold, mean eyes a nearly white blue; and he was sardonically waiting, and his truck, loaded with chairs and bed-iron, stood in the sun where the treeshade had slid beyond it. He was studying Emma coldly and almost without furtiveness, and she avoiding his eyes. It was impossible to go quite immediately. We all sat around a short while and had lemonade from a pressed-glass pitcher, from which he had already taken two propitiatory glasses. It had been made in some hope of helping the leavetaking pass off as a sort of party, from two lemons and spring water, without ice, and it was tepid, heavily sweetened (as if to compensate the lack of lemons), and scarcely tart; there was half a glass for each of us, out of five tumblers, and we all gave most of it to the children. The children of the two families stayed very quiet, shy of each other; the others, save the black-hatted man, tried to talk, without managing much; they tried especially hard when Emma got up, as suddenly as if she had to vomit, and went into the next room and shut the door, and Annie Mae followed her. Gallatin said it was mighty hard on a girl so young as that leaving her kinfolks so far behind. The man in the hat twisted his mouth on the grass and, without opening his teeth, said Yeah-ah, as if he had his own opinions about that. We were trying not to hear the voices in the next room, and that same helpless, frozen, creaky weeping I had heard before; and after a little it quieted; and after a little more they came out, Emma flourily powdered straight to the eyes, and the eyes as if she had cried sand instead of tears; and the man said—it was the first kind gesture I had seen in him and one of the few I suspect in his life, and I am sure it was kind by no intention of his: 'Well, we can't hang around here all day. Reckon you'd better come along, if you're coming.'

With that, Emma and her father kiss, shyly and awkwardly, children doing it before parents; so do she and her brother; she and Annie Mae embrace; she and I shake hands and say good-bye: all this in the sort of broken speed in which a family takes leave beside the black wall of a steaming train when the last crates have been loaded and it seems certain that at any instant the windows, and the leaned unpitying faces, will begin to slide past on iron. Emma's paper suitcase is lifted into the trunk beside the bedsprings which will sustain the years on years of her cold, hopeless nights; she is helped in upon the hard seat beside the driver above the hot and floorless engine, her slippered feet propped askew at the ledges of that pit into the road; the engine snaps and coughs and catches and levels on a hot white moistureless and thin metal roar, and with a dreadful rendering noise that brings up the mild heads of cattle a quarter of a mile away the truck rips itself loose from the flesh of the planed dirt of the yard and wrings into the road and chucks ahead, we waving, she waving, the black hat straight ahead, she turned away, not bearing it, our hands drooped, and we stand disconsolate and emptied in the sun; and all through these coming many hours while we slow move within the anchored rondures of our living, the hot, screaming, rattling, twenty-mile-an-hour traveling elongates steadily crawling, a lost, earnest, and frowning ant, westward on red roads and on white in the febrile sun above no support, suspended, sustained from falling by force alone of its outward growth, like that long and lithe incongruous slender runner a vine spends swiftly out on the vast blank wall of the earth, like snake's head and slim stream feeling its way, to fix, and anchor, so far, so wide of the strong and stationed stalk: and that is Emma.

For Discussion

1. According to the author's description of Emma, what kind of a person is she? What does this description do to shape your attitude toward her?
2. What is Annie Mae's role in the selection? Discuss how Emma and Annie Mae are similar and how they differ.
3. What is the role of the narrator? Through what means does he characterize himself?
4. The narrator expresses great sorrow for Emma. Does Emma feel sorry for herself? Why does she agree to go to such a remote place to live with her husband?
5. Is it possible that in his own way her husband loves Emma? What clues to his true feelings are given in the work itself?

For Comparison

1. Rollin's essay "Motherhood: Who Needs It?" discusses the myth of motherhood. What myth about the woman's role in life is evidenced in this selection by Agee?
2. Using ideas from "The Family Constellation," discuss how Emma and Annie Mae reflect their positions in their own family structure.

For Composition

1. Emma should (should not) have gone.
2. How I see Emma ten years from now.
3. I know someone like Emma.

CARSON MCCULLERS

A DOMESTIC DILEMMA

On Thursday Martin Meadows left the office early enough to make the first express bus home. It was the hour when the evening lilac glow was fading in the slushy streets, but by the time the bus had left the Midtown terminal the bright city night had come. On Thursdays the maid had a half-day off and Martin liked to get home as soon as possible, since for the past year his wife had not been—well. This Thursday he was very tired and, hoping that no regular commuter would single him out for conversation, he fastened his attention to the newspaper until the bus had crossed the George Washington Bridge. Once on 9-W Highway Martin always felt that the trip was halfway done, he breathed deeply, even in cold weather when only ribbons of draught cut through the smoky air of the bus, confident that he was breathing country air. It used to be that at this point he would relax and begin to think with pleasure of his home. But in this last year nearness brought only a sense of tension and he did not anticipate the journey's end. This evening Martin kept his face close to the window and watched the barren fields and lonely lights of passing townships. There was a moon, pale on the dark earth and areas of late, porous snow; to Martin the countryside seemed vast and somehow desolate that evening. He took his hat from the rack and put his folded newspaper in the pocket of his overcoat a few minutes before time to pull the cord.

The cottage was a block from the bus stop, near the river but not directly on the shore; from the living-room window you could look across the street and opposite yard and see the Hudson. The cottage was modern, almost too white and new on the narrow plot of yard. In summer the grass was soft and bright and Martin carefully tended a flower border and a rose trellis. But during the cold, fallow months the yard was bleak and the cottage seemed naked. Lights were on that evening in all the rooms in the little house and Martin hurried up the front walk. Before the steps he stopped to move a wagon out of the way.

The children were in the living room, so intent on play that the opening of the front door was at first unnoticed. Martin stood looking at his safe, lovely children. They had opened the bottom drawer of the secretary and taken out the Christmas decorations. Andy had managed to plug in the Christmas tree lights and the green and red bulbs glowed with out-of-season festivity on the rug of the living room. At the moment he was trying to trail the bright cord over Marianne's rocking horse. Marianne sat on the floor pulling off an angel's wings. The children wailed a startling welcome. Martin swung the fat little baby girl up to his shoulder and Andy threw himself against his father's legs.

"Daddy, Daddy, Daddy!"

Martin set down the little girl carefully and swung Andy a few times like a pendulum. Then he picked up the Christmas tree cord.

"What's all this stuff doing out? Help me put it back in the drawer. You're not to fool with the light socket. Remember I told you that before. I mean it, Andy."

The six-year-old child nodded and shut the secretary drawer. Martin stroked his fair soft hair and his hand lingered tenderly on the nape of the child's frail neck.

"Had supper yet, Bumpkin?"

"It hurt. The toast was hot."

The baby girl stumbled on the rug and, after the first surprise of the fall, began to cry; Martin picked her up and carried her in his arms back to the kitchen.

"See, Daddy," said Andy. "The toast—"

Emily had laid the children's supper on the uncovered porcelain table. There were two plates with the remains of cream-of-wheat and eggs and silver mugs that had held milk. There was also a platter of cinnamon toast, untouched, except for one tooth-marked bite. Martin sniffed the bitten piece and nibbled gingerly. Then he put the toast into the garbage pail.

"Hoo—phui—What on earth!"

Emily had mistaken the tin of cayenne for the cinnamon.

"I like to have burnt up," Andy said. "Drank water and ran outdoors and opened my mouth. Marianne didn't eat none."

"Any," corrected Martin. He stood helpless, looking around the walls of the kitchen. "Well, that's that, I guess," he said finally. "Where is your mother now?"

"She's up in you alls' room."

Martin left the children in the kitchen and went up to his wife. Outside the door he waited for a moment to still his anger. He did not knock and once inside the room he closed the door behind him.

Emily sat in the rocking chair by the window of the pleasant room. She had been drinking something from a tumbler and as he entered she put the glass hurriedly on the floor behind the chair. In her attitude there was confusion and guilt which she tried to hide by a show of spurious vivacity.

"Oh, Marty! You home already? The time slipped up on me. I was just going down—" She lurched to him and her kiss was strong with sherry. When he stood unresponsive she stepped back a pace and giggled nervously.

"What's the matter with you? Standing there like a barber pole. Is anything wrong with you?"

"Wrong with *me*?" Martin bent over the rocking chair and picked up the tumbler from the floor. "If you could only realize how sick I am—how bad it is for all of us."

Emily spoke in a false, airy voice that had become too familiar to him. Often at such times she affected a slight English accent copying perhaps some actress she admired. "I haven't the vaguest idea what you mean. Unless you are referring to the glass I used for a spot of sherry. I had a finger of sherry—maybe two. But what is the crime in that, pray tell me? I'm quite all right. Quite all right."

"So anyone can see."

As she went into the bathroom Emily walked with careful gravity. She turned on the cold water and dashed some on her face with her cupped hands, then patted herself dry with the corner of a bath towel. Her face was delicately featured and young, unblemished.

"I was just going down to make dinner." She tottered and balanced herself by holding to the door frame.

"I'll take care of dinner. You stay up here. I'll bring it up."

"I'll do nothing of the sort. Why, whoever heard of such a thing?"

"Please," Martin said.

"Leave me alone. I'm quite all right. I was just on the way down—"

"Mind what I say."

"Mind your grandmother."

She lurched toward the door, but Martin caught her by the arm. "I don't want the children to see you in this condition. Be reasonable."

"Condition!" Emily jerked her arm. Her voice rose angrily. "Why, because I drink a couple of sherries in the afternoon you're trying to make me out a drunkard. Condition! Why, I don't even touch whiskey. As well you know. *I* don't swill liquor at bars. And that's more than you can say. I don't even have a cocktail at dinnertime. I only sometimes have a glass of sherry. What, I ask you, is the disgrace of that? Condition!"

Martin sought words to calm his wife. "We'll have a quiet supper by ourselves up here. That's a good girl." Emily sat on the side of the bed and he opened the door for a quick departure.

"I'll be back in a jiffy."

As he busied himself with the dinner downstairs he was lost in the familiar question as to how this problem had come upon his home. He himself had always enjoyed a good drink. When they were still living in

Alabama they had served long drinks or cocktails as a matter of course. For years they had drunk one or two—possibly three drinks before dinner, and at bedtime a long nightcap. Evenings before holidays they might get a buzz on, might even become a little tight. But alcohol had never seemed a problem to him, only a bothersome expense that with the increase in the family they could scarcely afford. It was only after his company had transferred him to New York that Martin was aware that certainly his wife was drinking too much. She was tippling, he noticed, during the day.

The problem acknowledged, he tried to analyze the source. The change from Alabama to New York had somehow disturbed her; accustomed to the idle warmth of a small Southern town, the matrix of the family and cousinship and childhood friends, she had failed to accommodate herself to the stricter, lonelier mores of the North. The duties of motherhood and housekeeping were onerous to her. Homesick for Paris City, she had made no friends in the suburban town. She read only magazines and murder books. Her interior life was insufficient without the artifice of alcohol.

The revelations of incontinence insidiously undermined his previous conceptions of his wife. There were times of unexplainable malevolence, times when the alcoholic fuse caused an explosion of unseemly anger. He encountered a latent coarseness in Emily, inconsistent with her natural simplicity. She lied about drinking and deceived him with unsuspected stratagems.

Then there was an accident. Coming home from work one evening about a year ago, he was greeted with screams from the children's room. He found Emily holding the baby, wet and naked from her bath. The baby had been dropped, her frail, frail skull striking the table edge, so that a thread of blood was soaking into the gossamer hair. Emily was sobbing and intoxicated. As Martin cradled the hurt child, so infinitely precious at that moment, he had an affrighted vision of the future.

The next day Marianne was all right. Emily vowed that never again would she touch liquor, and for a few weeks she was sober, cold and downcast. Then gradually she began—not whiskey or gin—but quantities of beer, or sherry, or outlandish liqueurs; once he had come across a hatbox of empty crème de menthe bottles. Martin found a dependable maid who managed the household competently. Virgie was also from Alabama and Martin had never dared tell Emily the wage scale customary in New York. Emily's drinking was entirely secret now, done before he reached the house. Usually the effects were almost imperceptible—a looseness of movement or the heavy-lidded eyes. The times of irresponsibilities, such as the cayenne-pepper toast were rare, and Martin could dismiss his worries when Virgie was at the house. But, nevertheless, anxiety was always latent, a threat of undefined disaster that underlaid his days.

"Marianne!" Martin called, for even the recollection of that time brought the need for reassurance. The baby girl, no longer hurt, but no less precious to her father, came into the kitchen with her brother. Martin went on with the preparations for the meal. He opened a can of soup and put two chops in the frying pan. Then he sat down by the table and took Marianne on his knees for a pony ride. Andy watched them, his fingers wobbling the tooth that had been loose all that week.

"Andy-the-candyman!" Martin said. "Is that old critter still in your mouth? Come closer, let Daddy have a look."

"I got a string to pull it with." The child brought from his pocket a tangled thread. "Virgie said to tie it to the tooth and tie the other end to the doorknob and shut the door real suddenly."

Martin took out a clean handkerchief and felt the loose tooth carefully. "That tooth is coming out of my Andy's mouth tonight. Otherwise I'm awfully afraid we'll have a tooth tree in the family."

"A what?"

"A tooth tree," Martin said. "You'll bite into something and swallow that tooth. And the tooth will take root in poor Andy's stomach and grow into a tooth tree with sharp little teeth instead of leaves."

"Shoo, Daddy," Andy said. But he held the tooth firmly between his grimy little thumb and forefinger. "There ain't any tree like that. I never seen one."

"There *isn't* any tree like that and I never *saw* one."

Martin tensed suddenly. Emily was coming down the stairs. He listened to her fumbling footsteps, his arm embracing the little boy with dread. When Emily came into the room he saw from her movements and her sullen face that she had again been at the sherry bottle. She began to yank open drawers and set the table.

"Condition!" she said in a furry voice. "You talk to me like that. Don't think I'll forget. I remember every dirty lie you say to me. Don't you think for a minute that I forget."

"Emily!" he begged. "The children—"

"The children—yes! Don't think I don't see through your dirty plots and schemes. Down here trying to turn my own children against me. Don't think I don't see and understand."

"Emily! I beg you—please go upstairs."

"So you can turn my children—my very own children—" Two large tears coursed rapidly down her cheeks. "Trying to turn my little boy, my Andy, against his own mother."

With drunken impulsiveness Emily knelt on the floor before the startled child. Her hands on his shoulders balanced her. "Listen, my Andy—you wouldn't listen to any lies your father tells you? You wouldn't believe what he says? Listen, Andy, what was your father telling you before I came downstairs?" Uncertain, the child sought his father's face. "Tell me. Mama wants to know."

"About the tooth tree."

"What?"

The child repeated the words and she echoed them with unbelieving terror. "The tooth tree!" she swayed and renewed her grasp on the child's shoulder. "I don't know what you're talking about. But listen, Andy, Mama is all right, isn't she?" The tears were spilling down her face and Andy drew back from her, for he was afraid. Grasping the table edge, Emily stood up.

"See! You have turned my child against me."

Marianne began to cry, and Martin took her in his arms.

"That's all right, you can take *your* child. You have always shown partiality from the very first. I don't mind, but at least you can leave me my little boy."

Andy edged close to his father and touched his leg. "Daddy," he wailed.

Martin took the children to the foot of the stairs. "Andy, you take up Marianne and Daddy will follow you in a minute."

"But Mama?" the child asked, whispering.

"Mama will be all right. Don't worry."

Emily was sobbing at the kitchen table, her face buried in the crook of her arm. Martin poured a cup of soup and set it before her. Her rasping sobs unnerved him; the vehemence of her emotion, irrespective of the source, touched in him a strain of tenderness. Unwillingly he laid his hand on her dark hair. "Sit up and drink the soup." Her face as she looked up at him was chastened and imploring. The boy's withdrawal or the touch of Martin's hand had turned the tenor of her mood.

"Ma-Martin," she sobbed. "I'm so ashamed."

"Drink the soup."

Obeying him, she drank between gasping breaths. After a second cup she allowed him to lead her up to their room. She was docile now and more restrained. He laid her nightgown on the bed and was about to leave the room when a fresh round of grief, the alcoholic tumult, came again.

"He turned away. My Andy looked at me and turned away."

Impatience and fatigue hardened his voice, but he spoke warily. "You forget that Andy is still a little child—he can't comprehend the meaning of such scenes."

"Did I make a scene? Oh Martin, did I make a scene before the children?"

Her horrified face touched and amused him against his will. "Forget it. Put on your nightgown and go to sleep."

"My child turned away from me. Andy looked at his mother and turned away. The children—"

She was caught in the rhythmic sorrow of alcohol. Martin withdrew from the room, saying: "For God's sake go to sleep. The children will forget by tomorrow."

As he said this he wondered if it was true. Would the scene glide so easily from memory—or would it root in the unconscious to fester in the after-years? Martin did not know, and the last alternative sickened him. He thought of Emily, foresaw the morning-after humiliation: the shards of memory, the lucidities that glared from the obliterating darkness of shame. She would call the New York office twice—possibly three or four times. Martin anticipated his own embarrassment, wondering if the others at the office could possibly suspect. He felt that his secretary had divined the trouble long ago and that she pitied him. He suffered a moment of rebellion against his fate, he hated his wife.

Once in the children's room he closed the door and felt secure for the first time that evening. Marianne fell down on the floor, picked herself up and calling: "Daddy, watch me," fell again, got up, and continued the falling-calling routine. Andy sat in the child's low chair, wobbling the tooth. Martin ran the water in the tub, washed his own hands in the lavatory, and called the boy into the bathroom.

"Let's have another look at that tooth." Martin sat on the toilet, holding Andy between his knees. The child's mouth gaped and Martin grasped the tooth. A wobble, a quick twist and the nacreous milk tooth was free. Andy's face was for the first moment split between terror, astonishment, and delight. He mouthed a swallow of water, and spat into the lavatory.

"Look, Daddy! It's blood. Marianne!"

Martin loved to bathe his children, loved inexpressibly the tender, naked bodies as they stood in the water so exposed. It was not fair of Emily to say that he showed partiality. As Martin soaped the delicate boy-body of his son he felt that further love would be impossible. Yet he admitted the difference in the quality of his emotions for the two children. His love for his daughter was graver, touched with a strain of melancholy, a gentleness that was akin to pain. His pet names for the little boy were the absurdities of daily inspiration—he called the little girl always Marianne, and his voice as he spoke it was a caress. Martin patted dry the fat baby stomach and the sweet little genital fold. The washed child faces were radiant as flower petals, equally loved.

"I'm putting the tooth under my pillow. I'm supposed to get a quarter."

"What for?"

"*You* know, Daddy. Johnny got a quarter for his tooth."

"Who puts the quarter there?" asked Martin. "I used to think the fairies left it in the night. It was a dime in my day, though."

"That's what they say in kindergarten."

"Who does put it there?"

"Your parents," Andy said. "You!"

Martin was pinning the cover on Marianne's bed. His daughter was already asleep. Scarcely breathing, Martin bent over and kissed her forehead, kissed again the tiny hand that lay palm-upward, flung in slumber beside her head.

"Good night, Andy-man."

The answer was only a drowsy murmur. After a minute Martin took out his change and slid a quarter underneath the pillow. He left a night light in the room.

As Martin prowled about the kitchen making a late meal, it occurred to him that the children had not once mentioned their mother or the scene that must have seemed to them incomprehensible. Absorbed in the instant—the tooth, the bath, the quarter—the fluid passage of child-time had borne these weightless episodes like leaves in the swift current of a shallow stream while the adult enigma was beached and forgotten on the shore. Martin thanked the Lord for that.

But his own anger, repressed and lurking, rose again. His youth was being frittered by a drunkard's waste, his very manhood subtly undermined. And the children, once the immunity of incomprehension passed— what would it be like in a year or so? With his elbows on the table he ate his food brutishly, untasting. There was no hiding the truth—soon there would be gossip in the office and in the town; his wife was a dissolute woman. Dissolute. And he and his children were bound to a future of degradation and slow ruin.

Martin pushed away from the table and stalked into the living room. He followed the lines of a book with his eyes but his mind conjured miserable images: he saw his children drowned in the river, his wife a disgrace on the public street. By bedtime the dull, hard anger was like a weight upon his chest and his feet dragged as he climbed the stairs.

The room was dark except for the shafting light from the half-opened bathroom door. Martin undressed quietly. Little by little, mysteriously, there came in him a change. His wife was asleep, her peaceful respiration sounding gently in the room. Her high-heeled shoes with the carelessly dropped stockings made to him a mute appeal. Her underclothes were flung in disorder on the chair. Martin picked up the girdle and the soft, silk brassière and stood for a moment with them in his hands. For the first time that evening he looked at his wife. His eyes rested on the sweet forehead, the arch of the fine brow. The brow had descended to Marianne, and the tilt at the end of the delicate nose. In his son he could trace the high cheekbones and pointed chin. Her body was full-bosomed, slender and undulant. As Martin watched the tranquil slumber of his wife the ghost of the old anger vanished. All thoughts of blame or blemish were distant from him now. Martin put out the bathroom light and raised the window. Careful not to awaken Emily he slid into the bed. By moonlight he watched his wife for the last time. His hand sought the adjacent flesh and sorrow paralleled desire in the immense complexity of love.

For Discussion

1. At one point Martin feels he cannot love his wife anymore. Should he continue living with her or should he divorce her? Are his obligations different than they might be if the couple had no children?
2. Would Martin's wife stop drinking so much if they moved to a smaller city? Is Martin at least partially responsible for her drinking so much? Should he move to a smaller city even though it would upset his professional life?
3. Is Martin's responsibility greater to his wife or to his children? What decision would you make if you were Martin? If you were one of the children, what would you want your father to do?
4. Which of the children will suffer the more in later life by recalling scenes such as those described in the story?
5. Is Martin sincere at the end of the story? Is it possible to love and hate someone at almost the same time?

For Comparison

1. Both this story and Van Doren's "Nobody Say a Word" deal with the effect a bad experience may have on a child's later life. How quickly do children forget these experiences? Can a parent help to erase such a memory from a child's mind?
2. How is the sense of responsibility evidenced by Martin different from the attitude projected by the father in James Merrill's "The Broken Home"?

For Composition

1. Martin should (should not) divorce Emily.
2. The most important person in a family.
3. Loving and hating are related.

Mark Van Doren

NOBODY SAY A WORD

After the children stopped asking she told them.

"I don't know where your father is," she said quietly during supper on the sixth day. They were all at the table—neither of the girls had gone to the kitchen for anything, and their small brother hadn't bolted yet to resume his playing in the yard. They sat, paralyzed, and listened.

"I simply don't know." The strain of saying this was nothing to what it had been when Madie, the first evening he wasn't there, kept running to the door and reporting that he hadn't come in sight yet up the walk; or when Arthur, always a hard one to satisfy, had insisted every night when he went to bed: "Papa's on a business trip. He'll be back tomorrow." He would say it the next night as if he had never said it before, and Margaret learned soon enough to nod and say nothing, as if of course the child knew.

But the worst thing had been the anticipation of what Madie asked now. She was the directest of the three, though she wasn't the oldest. "What did he say, Mother, the last time he—what did he *say*?"

The worst thing was to have to answer "Nothing," for in a way it wasn't true. George hadn't ever said, "I'm going, and I'm not coming back," but she had always known he would leave her, and so he didn't need to say so. He knew she knew.

But here was Madie looking at her, accusing her of holding something back. And a deep, sudden blush was her way of admitting that she had; only, what was there to tell, and how could it be told to these three? To Sarah most of all, who never had really asked. Sarah was the serious one who didn't like things to go wrong or change. No child does, said Margaret to herself; but the others had talked and Sara hadn't—except, of course, with her strange large eyes. They had got larger every day, under the fine hair she insisted on combing straight back from her forehead. Young as she was, she knew the effect of that—knew it gave her authority, as if she weren't young after all; and in a sense she never had been.

"He didn't say anything," said Margaret, "about not—I mean, about not ever—"

"Not ever!" Madie was scowling in the odd way that made everybody love her. She looked nearsighted, though the doctor said she wasn't. She looked fierce; whereas she was the fondest of them all.

The words had given too much away. "Not ever" sounded—well, as fatal as the fact. And Margaret felt that she must have grown all at once very pale, for the children stared at her with a new intentness, and Arthur barely mumbled, "Papa's on a business trip—we know that," as if he had lost his confidence that this was so.

But Sarah's face had altered less, and her eyes not at all. Did Sarah understand that some men did what George had done? Some women, too? But the men. That father of five children, years ago when *she* was a child, that meek neighbor man, she forgot his name, who did so poorly and was so apologetic—"no force," her own father said—who disappeared one day and didn't come home for years. But he came home, and the town never knew how he made it up with his family: what he said to them, or they to him, or whether there was bitterness and quarreling. Not a sound or a sign from the house into which he walked one night and —well, what then? The next day he was in his leather shop as usual, and nobody had the nerve to ask him where he had been. He had so little nerve himself, it would have been torture on both sides.

Sarah had never heard of him, but she looked now as if she might have. Margaret was startled by the suspicion, yet there it was: Sarah's mind was on the same track as her own. She was even thinking—

Then she said it.

"When he does come"—Sarah closed her eyes a moment, imagining— "I know what we should do. Act just the same as if he never went anywhere. No talk, no questions. Not a word. I know."

Madie shook her brown hair out of her eyes. "I couldn't. I'd have to tell him I was glad."

Arthur merely stared down at his napkin.

They were all trying to help, they were all trying to seem undeserted, unafraid.

"You wouldn't have to tell him," Sarah said. "Wouldn't he know? *He'd* be glad. He'd like it best if none of us said a word."

At least, thought Margaret, motionless in her chair, it's confessed now. They realize he did desert me—and them. But me first of all. They are sorry for me. They are trying to be good children. And they are, they are.

Madie and Arthur, flying from their places across the table, reached her at the same moment. Neither one of them had ever seen her weep like this.

But Sarah didn't come.

What was the saying? She had been right—she really had except of course that George would never—

What was she saying? The two others were so close about, it was almost impossible to hear.

"Listen! Mother, Madie, Arthur—listen! Nobody say a word."

For there was George.

Sarah must have seen him out of the back of her head; the hall door was behind her. Margaret, facing him with Madie and Arthur, started to her feet, but the two children clutched her closer and she sat down again, trembling. They hadn't looked up yet. When they did—

"Madie!" she managed to whisper. "You and Arthur—don't say anything. Don't go to him—not yet. Your father's come. He's here."

Now she had to clutch at them, they were so wild in her two arms. They all had to wait till Sarah spoke. Sarah hadn't been wrong about *one* thing. George couldn't stay away. And her heart struggled with itself, not knowing how the whole of her should feel. It was bad, it was good. She was still hurt, yet she was happy—in a strange way, as if she were asleep; in a bitter way, as if this new sweet taste—it might be so, it might —were the taste of poison.

The two children were quieter than she would have believed possible. They were minding her, they were waiting for Sarah. Or was it because George looked so terribly tired? Standing in the door, his shoulders drooping, he must have shocked them too.

His eyes were the biggest thing about him. They seemed to want to look away; to close and stay closed; but they couldn't. They were for Margaret entirely, they saw no children there, no chairs, no table, no dishes, no clock.

"Hello," said Sarah, turning halfway round. "You're late. Was it a hard day at the shop?" It was scarcely her voice they heard. "Was Mr. Meeker mean, and kept you? Did somebody have an accident? You know, I was the one that set the table and I counted wrong. You go wash up, I'll fix a place." It was as if she were reciting from memory. "All of us helped get supper, even Arthur. He mashed the potatoes—partly."

But her father, if he listened to a single word, gave not a sign that he did. His dark eyes traveled for a moment, impartially, over the three young faces that separated him from Margaret, then returned to her where she sat, half guilty because of her silence, in her walnut armchair that matched his across the room. His stood against the wall, in shadow, as it had stood all week.

"Arthur," she said, "get Papa's chair for him." She spoke slowly, as if it were a deep wrong to mention only this. "Go on."

For the boy was staring at the man. A business trip, a business trip— he must be fighting the temptation to say those words and prove he had been right. A business trip. But he looked sidewise at Sarah and said nothing; then, embarrassed, ran to drag the armchair into place.

Madie's face burned with excitement, and her body shook all the way down; Margaret's arm felt the straight, strong back trembling as if in terror. But it wasn't terror. It was doubt that she ought to be where she was. It wasn't like Madie to keep this distance from someone she adored.

She only said: "Hello, Dad. We had a test in history today. I think I did all right. I'll tell you about it later. Miss Martingale—"

She stopped because he didn't seem to hear. He hadn't shifted a foot, he hadn't twitched a finger, since he came.

Margaret thought: He's a ghost, he isn't really there. It's like a game— all of us pretending to see him. It's like children who play family, and make up uncles and cousins. They're making up a father. That isn't him, that isn't George.

And suddenly she screamed—not loud, not long, but she knew she screamed. The sound was worse because it was so weak—she was ashamed and reached for Arthur who had jumped away.

But he was already at his father's knees, and Madie, her face streaming tears, had hold of one of George's arms, which she embraced as if it had once been wounded in a war. It was veritable flesh. She hung upon it with all her weight.

Sarah came around the table, defeated, and stood while Margaret kissed her pale forehead. "All right, dear," said her mother. "It was a good thing to try, even if I broke down. You go over there with them. Quick, now."

For still George had not said a word. His hands strayed over two young heads, then three; but even while they did this they seemed to be thinking of the wife they had not touched. Never had touched, maybe, or else might never touch again. As if *she* were the ghost.

Margaret settled it.

"All three of you," she said, standing straight up at last, "go somewhere else now. Outdoors, or anywhere. Don't stay long, I mean, but— oh, I don't need any help with Papa's supper. Madie—really—I don't need help."

"Are you sure?" asked Sarah. She was so responsible.

"Yes, dear. You take Arthur."

Sarah led them both out, never looking back, while Margaret waited for him to come close, to touch her flesh with his, to make one sound she could hear.

He didn't soon enough. He was still all eyes, mournful and ashamed. He was still a man come out of a new grave.

So she went close to him.

For Discussion

1. Did Margaret have a right or a duty to tell the children that their father might not return? Should she have told them that their father was on a business trip?

2. Who do you think was the most responsible for what happened? How much blame do you put on Margaret? How much on George?
3. Did the father have an obligation to tell the family about his disappearance? If you were in the place of the children, would you prefer that your father told you he was leaving? Should he give any reasons?
4. The story is told to us from Margaret's side. How might it be told differently if we could hear it from the father's point of view?

For Comparison

1. Both Margaret and Emma show evidence of strength in the face of of conflict. Which do you feel is the most responsible? Project Emma into a situation similar to Margaret's and explain how she might react.
2. Both this story and "A Domestic Dilemma" end with a gentle, somewhat positive scene. Will the basic situations described in the two stories be repeated? Which of the two marriages has the better chance of surviving?

For Composition

1. Margaret should (should not) have told the truth.
2. Children have a right to know parents' problems.
3. (Name one of the characters) will be the most hurt.

WILLIAM MELVIN KELLEY

A VISIT TO GRANDMOTHER

Chig knew something was wrong the instant his father kissed her. He had always known his father to be the warmest of men, a man so kind that when people ventured timidly into his office, it took only a few words from him to make them relax, and even laugh. Doctor Charles Dunford cared about people.

But when he had bent to kiss the old lady's black face, something new and almost ugly had come into his eyes: fear, uncertainty, sadness, and perhaps even hatred.

Ten days before in New York, Chig's father had decided suddenly he wanted to go to Nashville to attend his college class reunion, twenty years out. Both Chig's brother and sister, Peter and Connie, were packing for camp and besides were too young for such an affair. But Chig was seventeen, had nothing to do that summer, and his father asked if he would like to go along. His father had given him additioinal reasons: "All my running buddies got their diplomas and were snapped up by them crafty young gals, and had kids within a year—now all those kids, some of them gals, are your age."

The reunion had lasted a week. As they packed for home, his father, in a far too offhand way, had suggested they visit Chig's grandmother. "We this close. We might as well drop in on her and my brothers."

So, instead of going north, they had gone farther south, had just entered her house. And Chig had a suspicion now that the reunion had been only an excuse to drive south, that his father had been heading to this house all the time.

His father had never talked much about his family, with the exception of his brother, GL, who seemed part con man, part practical joker and part Don Juan; he had spoken of GL with the kind of indulgence he would have shown a cute, but ill-behaved and potentially dangerous, five-year-old.

Chig's father had left home when he was fifteen. When asked why, he would answer: "I wanted to go to school. They didn't have a Negro high school at home, so I went up to Knoxville and lived with a cousin and went to school."

They had been met at the door by Aunt Rose, GL's wife, and ushered into the living room. The old lady had looked up from her seat by the window. Aunt Rose stood between the visitors.

The old lady eyed his father. "Rose, who that? Rose?" She squinted. She looked like a doll, made of black straw, the wrinkles in her face running in one direction like the head of a broom. Her hair was white and course and grew out straight from her head.. Her eyes were brown—the whites, too, seemed light brown—and were hidden behind thick glasses, which remained somehow on a tiny nose. "That Hiram?" That was another of his father's brothers. "No, it ain't Hiram; too big for Hiram." She turned then to Chig. "Now that man, he look like Eleanor, Charles's wife, but Charles wouldn't never send my grandson to see me. I never even heard from Charles." She stopped again.

"It Charles, Mama. That who it is." Aunt Rose, between them, led them closer. "It Charles come all the way from New York to see you, and brung little Charles with him."

The old lady stared up at them. "Charles? Rose, that really Charles?" She turned away, and reached for a handkerchief in the pocket of her

clean, ironed, flowered housecoat, and wiped her eyes. "God have mercy.
Charles." She spread her arms up to him, and he bent down and kissed
her cheek. That was when Chig saw his face, grimacing. She hugged him;
Chig watched the muscles in her arms as they tightened around his father's neck. She half rose out of her chair. "How are you, son?"

Chig could not hear his father's answer.

She let him go, and fell back into her chair, grabbing the arms. Her
hands were as dark as the wood, and seemed to become part of it. "Now,
who that standing there? Who that man?"

"That's one of your grandsons, Mama." His father's voice cracked.
"Charles Dunford, junior. You saw him once, when he was a baby, in
Chicago. He's grown now."

"I can see that, boy!" She looked at Chig squarely. "Come here, son,
and kiss me once." He did. "What they call you? Charles too?"

"No, ma'am, they call me Chig."

She smiled. She had all her teeth, but they were too perfect to be her
own. "That's good. Can't have two boys answering to Charles in the
same house. Won't nobody at all come. So you that little boy. You don't
remember me, do you. I used to take you to church in Chicago, and you'd
get up and hop in time to the music. You studying to be a preacher?"

"No, ma'am. I don't think so. I might be a lawyer."

"You'll be an honest one, won't you?"

"I'll try."

"Trying ain't enough! You be honest, you hear? Promise me. You be
honest like your daddy."

"All right. I promise."

"Good. Rose, where's GL at? Where's that thief? He gone again?"

"I don't know, Mama." Aunt Rose looked embarrassed. "He say he
was going by his liquor store. He'll be back."

"Well, then where's Hiram? You call up those boys, and get them over
here—now! You got enough to eat? Let me see." She started to get up.
Chig reached out his hand. She shook him off. "What they tell you about
me, Chig? They tell you I'm all laid up? Don't believe it. They don't know
nothing about old ladies. When I want help, I'll let you know. Only time
I'll need help getting anywheres is when I dies and they lift me into the
ground."

She was standing now, her back and shoulders straight. She came only
to Chig's chest. She squinted up at him. "You eat much? Your daddy ate
like two men."

"Yes, ma'am."

"That's good. That means you ain't nervous. Your mama, she ain't nervous. I remember that. In Chicago, she'd sit down by a window all afternoon and never say nothing, just knit." She smiled. "Let me see what we got to eat."

"I'll do that, Mama." Aunt Rose spoke softly. "You haven't seen Charles in a long time. You sit and talk."

The old lady squinted at her. "You can do the cooking if you promise it ain't because you think I can't."

Aunt Rose chuckled. "I know you can do it, Mama."

"All right. I'll just sit and talk a spell." She sat again and arranged her skirt around her short legs.

Chig did most of the talking, told all about himself before she asked. His father only spoke when he was spoken to, and then, only one word at a time, as if by coming back home, he had become a small boy again, sitting in the parlor while his mother spoke with her guests.

When Uncle Hiram and Mae, his wife, came they sat down to eat. Chig did not have to ask about Uncle GL's absence; Aunt Rose volunteered an explanation: "Can't never tell where the man is at. One Thursday morning he left here and next thing we knew, he was calling from Chicago, saying he went up to see Joe Louis fight. He'll be here though; he ain't as young and foot-loose as he used to be." Chig's father had mentioned driving down that GL was five years older than he was, nearly fifty.

Uncle Hiram was somewhat smaller than Chig's father; his short-cropped kinky hair was half gray, half black. One spot, just off his forehead, was totally white. Later, Chig found out it had been that way since he was twenty. Mae (Chig could not bring himself to call her Aunt) was a good deal younger than Hiram, pretty enough so that Chig would have looked at her twice on the street. She was a honey-colored woman, with long eye lashes. She was wearing a white sheath.

At dinner, Chig and his father sat on one side, opposite Uncle Hiram and Mae; his grandmother and Aunt Rose sat at the ends. The food was good; there was a lot and Chig ate a lot. All through the meal, they talked about the family as it had been thirty years before, and particularly about the young GL. Mae and Chig asked questions; the old lady answered; Aunt Rose directed the discussion, steering the old lady onto the best stories; Chig's father laughed from time to time; Uncle Hiram ate.

"Why don't you tell them about the horse, Mama?" Aunt Rose, over Chig's weak protest, was spooning mashed potatoes onto his plate. "There now, Chig."

"I'm trying to think." The old lady was holding her fork halfway to her mouth, looking at them over her glasses. "Oh, you talking about that crazy horse GL brung home that time."

"That's right, Mama." Aunt Rose nodded and slid another slice of white meat on Chig's plate.

Mae started to giggle. "Oh, I've heard this. This is funny, Chig."

The old lady put down her fork and began: Well, GL went out of the house one day with an old, no-good chair I wanted him to take over to the church for a bazaar, and he met up with this man who'd just brung in some horses from out West. Now, I reckon you can expect one swindler to be in every town, but you don't rightly think there'll be two, and God forbid they should ever meet—but they did, GL and his chair, this man and his horses. Well, I wished I'd-a been there; there must-a been some mighty high-powered talking going on. That man with his horses, he told GL them horses was half-Arab, half-Indian, and GL told that man the chair was an antique he'd stole from some rich white folks. So they swapped. Well, I was a-looking out the window and seen GL dragging this animal to the house. It looked pretty gentle and its eyes was most closed and its feet was shuffling.

"GL, where'd you get that thing?" I says.

"I swapped him for that old chair, Mama," he says. "And made myself a bargain. This is even better than Papa's horse."

Well, I'm a-looking at this horse and noticing how he be looking more and more wide awake every minute, sort of warming up like a teakettle until, I swears to you, that horse is blowing steam out its nose.

"Come on, Mama," GL says, "come on and I'll take you for a ride." Now George, my husband, God rest his tired soul, he'd brung home this white folk's buggy which had a busted wheel and fixed it and was to take it back that day and GL says: "Come on, Mama, we'll use this fine buggy and take us a ride."

"GL," I says, "no, we ain't. Them white folks'll burn us alive if we use their buggy. You just take that horse right on back." You see, I was sure that boy'd come by that animal ungainly.

"Mama, I can't take him back," GL says.

"Why not?" I says.

"Because I don't rightly know where that man is at," GL says.

"Oh," I says. "Well, then I reckon we stuck with it." And I turned around to go back into the house because it was getting late, near dinner time, and I was cooking for ten.

"Mama," GL says to my back. "Mama, ain't you coming for a ride with me?"

"Go on, boy. You ain't gettin me inside kicking range of that animal." I was eyeing that beast and it was boiling hotter all the time. I reckon maybe that man had drugged it. "That horse is wild, GL," I says.

"No, he ain't. He ain't. That man say he is buggy and saddle broke and as sweet as the inside of a apple."

My oldest girl, Essie, had-a come out on the porch and she says: "Go on, Mama. I'll cook. You ain't been out the house in weeks."

"Sure, come on, Mama," GL says. "There ain't nothing to be fidgety about. This horse is gentle as a rose petal." And just then that animal snorts so hard it sets up a little dust storm around its feet.

"Yes, Mama," Essie says, "you can see he gentle." Well, I looked at Essie and then at that horse because I didn't think we could be looking at the same animal. I should-a figured how Essie's eyes ain't never been so good.

"Come on, Mama," GL says.

"All right," I says. So I stood on the porch and watched GL hitching that horse up to the white folks' buggy. For a while there, the animal was pretty quiet, pawing a little, but not much. And I was feeling a little better about riding with GL behind that crazy-looking horse. I could see how GL was happy I was going with him. He was scurrying around that animal buckling buckles and strapping straps, all the time smiling, and that made me feel good.

Then he was finished, and I must say, that horse looked mighty fine hitched to that buggy and I knew anybody what climbed up there would look pretty good too. GL came around and stood at the bottom of the steps, and took off his hat and bowed and said: "Madam," and reached out his hand to me and I was feeling real elegant like a fine lady. He helped me up to the seat and then got up beside me and we moved out down our alley. And I remember how colored folks come out on their porches and shook their heads, saying: "Lord now, will you look at Eva Dunford, the fine lady! Don't she look good sitting up there!" And I pretended not to hear and sat up straight and proud.

We rode on through the center of town, up Market Street, and all the way out where Hiram is living now, which in them days was all woods, there not being even a farm in sight and that's when that horse must-a first realized he weren't at all broke or tame or maybe thought he was back out West again, and started to gallop.

"GL," I says, "now you ain't joking with your mama, is you? Because if you is, I'll strap you purple if I live through this."

Well, GL was pulling on the reins with all his meager strength, and yelling, "Whoa, you. Say now, whoa!" He turned to me just long enough to say, "I ain't fooling with you, Mama. Honest!"

I reckon that animal weren't too satisfied with the road, because it made a sharp right turn just then, down into a gulley and struck out across a hilly meadow. "Mama," GL yells. "Mama, do something!"

I didn't know what to do, but I figured I had to do something so I stood up, hopped down onto the horse's back and pulled it to a stop. Don't ask me how I did that; I reckon it was that I was a mother and my baby asked me to do something, is all.

"Well, we walked that animal all the way home; sometimes I had to club it over the nose with my fist to make it come, but we made it, GL and me. You remember how tired we was, Charles?"

"I wasn't here at the time." Chig turned to his father and found his face completely blank, without even a trace of a smile or a laugh.

"Well, of course you was, son. That happened in . . . in . . . it was a hot summer that year and—"

"I left in June of that year. You wrote me about it."

The old lady stared past Chig at him. They all turned to him; Uncle Hiram looked up from his plate.

"Then you don't remember how we all laughed?"

"No, I don't, Mama. And I probably wouldn't have laughed. I don't think it was funny." They were staring into each other's eyes.

"Why not, Charles?"

"Because in the first place, the horse was gained by fraud. And in the second place, both of you might have been seriously injured or even killed." He broke off their stare and spoke to himself more than to any of them: "And if I'd done it, you would've beaten me good for it."

"Pardon?" The old lady had not heard him; only Chig had heard.

Chig's father sat up straight as if preparing to debate. "I said that if I had done it, if I had done just exactly what GL did, you would have beaten me good for it, Mama." He was looking at her again.

"Why did you say that, son?" She was leaning toward him.

"Don't you know? Tell the truth. It can't hurt me now." His voice cracked, but only once. "If GL and I did something wrong, you'd beat me first and then be too damn tired to beat him. At dinner, he'd always get seconds and I wouldn't. You'd do things with him, like ride in that buggy, but if I wanted you to do something for me, you were always too busy." He paused and considered whether to say what he finally did say: "I cried when I left here. Nobody loved me, Mama. I cried all the way up to Knoxville. That was the last time I ever cried in my life."

"Oh, Charles." She started to get up, to come around the table to him. He stopped her. "It's too late."

"But you don't understand."

"What don't I understand? I understood then; I understand now."

Tears now traveled down the lines of her face, but when she spoke, her voice was clear. "I thought you knew. I had ten children. I had to give all of them what they needed most." She nodded. "I paid more mind to

GL. I had to. GL could-a ended up swinging if I hadn't. But you was smarter. You was more growed up than GL when you was five and he was ten, and I tried to show you that by letting you do what you wanted to do."

"That's not true, Mama. You know it. GL was light-skinned and had good hair and looked almost white and you loved him for that."

"Charles, no. No, son. I didn't love any one of you more than any other."

"That can't be true." His father was standing now, his fists clenched tight. "Admit it, Mama . . . please!" Chig looked at him, shocked; the man was actually crying.

"It may not-a been right what I done, but I ain't no liar." Chig knew she did not really understand what had happened, what he wanted of her. "I'm not lying to you, Charles."

Chig's father had gone pale. He spoke very softly. "You're about thirty years too late, Mama." He bolted from the table. Silverware and dishes rang and jumped. Chig heard him hurrying up to their room.

They sat in silence for awhile and then heard a key in the front door. A man with a new, lacquered straw hat came in. He was wearing brown and white two-tone shoes with very pointed toes and a white summer suit. "Say now! Man! I heard my brother was in town. Where he at? Where that rascal?"

He stood in the doorway, smiling broadly, an engaging, open, friendly smile, the innocent smile of a five-year-old.

For Discussion

1. Why did the father really want to go back home anyway? Did he think things would be different? What was he trying to capture from his past?
2. Evaluate Chig's feelings for his father. Is his respect healthy? What facts about Chig's character are shown through his attitude toward persons and events in the story?
3. Why is so much of the story devoted to retelling the horse episode? What might be the symbolic meaning of Mama hitting the horse with her fist and forcing it home?
4. Why did the horse story so antagonize Charles? Is he sincere when he says, "It's too late"? Will he forgive his mother? Can their relationship improve?

5. Was the mother's position in treating the two sons differently a responsible one? Did she consciously treat them this way when they were young, or was her explanation a rationalization?
6. How did your attitude toward Charles and his mother change when you read the last two lines of the story?

For Comparison

1. Evaluate the characters in this story in terms of the roles described in "The Family Constellation."
2. The grandmother in this story and the mother in "The Rocking-Horse Winner" are both strong characters. Compare their actions and suggest who seems to you the most responsible.

For Composition

1. Charles should (should not) have returned home.
2. The grandmother was (was not) unfair.
3. My mother (father) plays favorites.

JAMES JOYCE

CLAY

The matron had given her leave to go out as soon as the women's tea was over and Maria looked forward to her evening out. The kitchen was spick and span: the cook said you could see yourself in the big copper boilers. The fire was nice and bright and on one of the side-tables were four very big barmbracks. These barmbracks seemed uncut; but if you went closer you would see that they had been cut into long thick even slices and were ready to be handed round at tea. Maria had cut them herself.

Maria was a very, very small person indeed but she had a very long nose and a very long chin. She talked a little through her nose, always soothingly: *"Yes, my dear,"* and *"No, my dear."* She was always sent for

From *Dubliners* by James Joyce. Originally published by B. W. Huebsch, Inc., in 1916, copyright © 1967 by the Estate of James Joyce. All rights reserved. Reprinted by permission of the Viking Press, Inc.

when the women quarreled over their tubs and always succeeded in making peace. One day the matron had said to her:

"Maria, you are a veritable peacemaker!"

And the sub-matron and two of the Board ladies had heard the compliment. And Ginger Mooney was always saying what she wouldn't do to the dummy who had charge of the irons if it wasn't for Maria. Everyone was so fond of Maria.

The women would have their tea at six o'clock and she would be able to get away before seven. From Ballsbridge to the Pillar, twenty minutes; from the Pillar to Drumcondra, twenty minutes; and twenty minutes to buy the things. She would be there before eight. She took out her purse with the silver clasps and read again the words *A Present from Belfast*. She was very fond of that purse because Joe had brought it to her five years before when he and Alphy had gone to Belfast on a Whit-Monday trip. In the purse were two half-crowns and some coppers. She would have five shillings clear after paying train fare. What a nice evening they would have, all the children singing! Only she hoped that Joe wouldn't come in drunk. He was so different when he took any drink.

Often he had wanted her to go and live with them; but she would have felt herself in the way (though Joe's wife was ever so nice with her) and she had become accustomed to the life of the laundry. Joe was a good fellow. She had nursed him and Alphy too; and Joe used often say:

"Mamma is mamma but Maria is my proper mother."

After the break-up at home the boys had got her that position in the *Dublin by Lamplight* laundry, and she liked it. She used to have such a bad opinion of Protestants but now she thought they were very nice people, a little quiet and serious, but still very nice people to live with. Then she had her plants in the conservatory and she liked looking after them. She had lovely ferns and wax-plants and, whenever anyone came to visit her, she always gave the visitor one or two slips from her conservatory. There was one thing she didn't like and that was the tracts on the walls; but the matron was such a nice person to deal with, so genteel.

When the cook told her everything was ready she went into the women's room and began to pull the big bell. In a few minutes the women began to come in by twos and threes, wiping their steaming hands in their petticoats and pulling down the sleeves of their blouses over their red steaming arms. They settled down before their huge mugs which the cook and the dummy filled up with hot tea, already mixed with milk and sugar in huge tin cans. Maria superintended the distribution of the barmbrack and saw that every woman got her four slices. There was a great deal of laughing and joking during the meal. Lizzie Fleming said Maria was sure to get the ring and, though Fleming had said that for so many Hallow

Eves, Maria had to laugh and say she didn't want any ring or man either; and when she laughed her gray-green eyes sparkled with disappointed shyness and the tip of her nose nearly met the tip of her chin. Then Ginger Mooney lifted up her mug of tea and proposed Maria's health while all the other women clattered with their mugs on the table, and said she was sorry she hadn't a sup of porter to drink it in. And Maria laughed again till the tip of her nose nearly met the tip of her chin and till her minute body nearly shook itself asunder because she knew that Mooney meant well though, of course, she had the notions of a common woman.

But wasn't Maria glad when the women had finished their tea and the cook and the dummy had begun to clear away the tea things! She went into her little bedroom and, remembering that the next morning was a mass morning, changed the hand of the alarm from seven to six. Then she took off her working skirt and her house-boots and laid her best skirt out on the bed and her tiny dress-boots beside the foot of the bed. She changed her blouse too and, as she stood before the mirror, she thought of how she used to dress for mass on Sunday morning when she was a young girl; and she looked with quaint affection at the diminutive body which she had so often adorned. In spite of its years she found it a nice tidy little body.

When she got outside the streets were shining with rain and she was glad of her old brown waterproof. The tram was full and she had to sit on the little stool at the end of the car, facing all the people, with her toes barely touching the floor. She arranged in her mind all she was going to do and thought how much better it was to be independent and to have your own money in your pocket. She hoped they would have a nice evening. She was sure they would but she could not help thinking what a pity it was Alphy and Joe were not speaking. They were always falling out now but when they were boys together they used to be the best of friends: but such was life.

She got out of her tram at the Pillar and ferreted her way quickly among the crowds. She went into Downes's cake-shop but the shop was so full of people that it was a long time before she could get herself attended to. She bought a dozen of mixed penny cakes, and at last came out of the shop laden with a big bag. Then she thought what else would she buy: she wanted to buy something really nice. They would be sure to have plenty of apples and nuts. It was hard to know what to buy and all she could think of was cake. She decided to buy some plumcake but Downes's plumcake had not enough almond icing on top of it so she went over to a shop in Henry Street. Here she was a long time in suiting herself and the stylish young lady behind the counter, who was evidently a little annoyed by her, asked her was it wedding cake she wanted to buy. That

made Maria blush and smile at the young lady; but the young lady took
it all very seriously and finally cut a thick slice of plumcake, parceled it up
and said:

"Two-and-four, please."

She thought she would have to stand in the Drumcondra tram because
none of the young men seemed to notice her but an elderly gentleman
made room for her. He was a stout gentleman and he wore a brown hard
hat; he had a square red face and a grayish mustache. Maria thought he
was a colonel-looking gentleman and she reflected how much more polite
he was than the young men who simply stared straight before them. The
gentleman began to chat with her about Hallow Eve and the rainy
weather. He supposed the bag was full of good things for the little ones
and said it was only right that the youngsters should enjoy themselves
while they were young. Maria agreed with him and favored him with
demure nods and hems. He was very nice with her, and when she was getting out at the Canal Bridge she thanked him and bowed, and he bowed
to her and raised his hat and smiled agreeably; and while she was going
up along the terrace, bending her tiny head under the rain, she thought
how easy it was to know a gentleman even when he has a drop taken.

Everybody said: *"O, here's Maria!"* when she came to Joe's house.
Joe was there, having come home from business, and all the children had
their Sunday dresses on. There were two big girls in from next door and
games were going on. Maria gave the bag of cakes to the eldest boy,
Alphy, to divide and Mrs. Donnelly said it was too good of her to bring
such a big bag of cakes and made all the children say:

"Thanks, Maria."

But Maria said she had brought something special for papa and
mamma, something they would be sure to like, and she began to look for
her plumcake. She tried in Downes's bag and then in the pockets of her
waterproof and then on the hallstand but nowhere could she find it. Then
she asked all the children had any of them eaten it—by mistake, of
course—but the children all said no and looked as if they did not like to
eat cakes if they were to be accused of stealing. Everybody had a solution
for the mystery and Mrs. Donnelly said it was plain that Maria had left it
behind her in the tram. Maria, remembering how confused the gentleman
with the grayish mustache had made her, colored with shame and vexa-
tion and disappointment. At the thought of the failure of her little surprise and of the two and four-pence she had thrown away for nothing she
nearly cried outright.

But Joe said it didn't matter and made her sit down by the fire. He
was very nice with her. He told her all that went on in his office, repeating
for her a smart answer which he had made to the manager. Maria did not

understand why Joe laughed so much over the answer he had made but she said that the manager must have been a very overbearing person to deal with. Joe said he wasn't so bad when you knew how to take him, that he was a decent sort so long as you didn't rub him the wrong way. Mrs. Donnelly played the piano for the children and they danced and sang. Then the two next-door girls handed round the nuts. Nobody could find the nutcrackers and Joe was nearly getting cross over it and asked how did they expect Maria to crack nuts without a nutcracker. But Maria said she didn't like nuts and that they weren't to bother about her. Then Joe asked would she take a bottle of stout and Mrs. Donnelly said there was port wine too in the house if she would prefer that. Maria said she would rather they didn't ask her to take anything: but Joe insisted.

So Maria let him have his way and they sat by the fire talking over old times and Maria thought she would put in a good word for Alphy. But Joe cried that God might strike him stone dead if ever he spoke a word to his brother again and Maria said she was sorry she had mentioned the matter. Mrs. Donnelly told her husband it was a great shame for him to speak that way of his own flesh and blood but Joe said that Alphy was no brother of his and there was nearly being a row on the head of it. But Joe said he would not lose his temper on account of the night it was and asked his wife to open some more stout. The two next-door girls had arranged some Hallow Eve games and soon everything was merry again. Maria was delighted to see the children so merry and Joe and his wife in such good spirits. The next-door girls put some saucers on the table and then led the children up to the table, blindfold. One got the prayer book and the other three got the water; and when one of the next-door girls got the ring Mrs. Donnelly shook her finger at the blushing girl as much as to say: *O, I know all about it!* They insisted then on blind-folding Maria and leading her up to the table to see what she would get; and, while they were putting on the bandage, Maria laughed and laughed again till the tip of her nose nearly met the tip of her chin.

They led her up to the table amid laughing and joking and she put her hand out in the air as she was told to do. She moved her hand about here and there in the air and descended on one of the saucers. She felt a soft wet substance with her fingers and was surprised that nobody spoke or took off her bandage. There was a pause for a few seconds; and then a great deal of scuffling and whispering. Somebody said something about the garden, and at last Mrs. Donnelly said something very cross to one of the next-door girls and told her to throw it out at once: that was no play. Maria understood that it was wrong that time and so she had to do it over again: and this time she got the prayer book.

After that Mrs. Donnelly played Miss McCloud's Reel for the children and Joe made Maria take a glass of wine. Soon they were all quite merry again and Mrs. Donnelly said Maria would enter a convent before the year was out because she had got the prayer book. Maria had never seen Joe so nice to her as he was that night, so full of pleasant talk and reminiscences. She said they were all very good to her.

At last the children grew tired and sleepy and Joe asked Maria would she not sing some little song before she went, one of the old songs. Mrs. Donnelly said: *"Do, please, Maria!"* and so Maria had to get up and stand beside the piano. Mrs. Donnelly bade the children be quiet and listen to Maria's song. Then she played the prelude and said *"Now, Maria!"* and Maria, blushing very much, began to sing in a tiny quavering voice. She sang *I Dreamt that I Dwelt,* and when she came to the second verse she sang again:

> *I dreamt that I dwelt in marble halls*
> *With vassals and serfs at my side,*
> *And of all who assembled within those walls*
> *That I was the hope and the pride.*
>
> *I had riches too great to count, could boast*
> *Of a high ancestral name,*
> *But I also dreamt, which pleased me most,*
> *That you loved me still the same.*

But no one tried to show her her mistake; and when she had ended her song Joe was very much moved. He said that there was no time like the long ago and no music for him like poor old Balfe, whatever other people might say; and his eyes filled up so much with tears that he could not find what he was looking for and in the end he had to ask his wife to tell him where the corkscrew was.

For Discussion

1. Are Joe and his wife trying to shirk their responsibility, or do you feel they even have a responsibility toward Maria? How long must you be your brother's keeper?
2. What kind of person is Joe? Is he a good husband? A good brother? Why does he cry at the end of the story?
3. How important are Joe and his family to Maria? How important is she to them?
4. What do you think about Maria as a person? Do you feel sorry for her or not? Why? Is she fully aware of what is happening?

For Comparison

1. What would be Joe's attitude toward Emma? What similarities exist between the character of Emma and Maria?
2. Joe and Emily ("A Domestic Dilemma") escape some of life's realities by drinking, but their basic philosophies of life are quite different. How are they different? How do their concepts of personal responsibility and integrity differ?

For Composition

1. Joe is (is not) responsible for Maria.
2. I am (am not) my brother's keeper.
3. Limits of family responsibility.

D. H. LAWRENCE

THE ROCKING-HORSE WINNER

There was a woman who was beautiful, who started with all the advantages, yet she had no luck. She married for love, and the love turned to dust. She had bonny children, yet she felt they had been thrust upon her, and she could not love them. They looked at her coldly, as if they were finding fault with her. And hurriedly she felt she must cover up some fault in herself. Yet what it was that she must cover up she never knew. Nevertheless, when her children were present, she always felt the centre of her heart go hard. This troubled her, and in her manner she was all the more gentle and anxious for her children, as if she loved them very much. Only she herself knew that at the centre of her heart was a hard little place that could not feel love, no, not for anybody. Everybody else said of her: "She is such a good mother. She adores her children." Only she herself, and her children themselves, knew it was not so. They read it in each other's eyes.

There were a boy and two little girls. They lived in a pleasant house, with a garden, and they had discreet servants, and felt themselves superior to anyone in the neighbourhood.

Although they lived in style, they felt always an anxiety in the house. There was never enough money. The mother had a small income, and the father had a small income, but not nearly enough for the social position which they had to keep up. The father went into town to some office. But though he had good prospects, these prospects never materialized. There was always the grinding sense of the shortage of money, though the style was always kept up.

At last the mother said: "I will see if I can't make something." But she did not know where to begin. She racked her brains, and tried this thing and the other, but could not find anything successful. The failure made deep lines come into her face. Her children were growing up, they would have to go to school. There must be more money, there must be more money. The father, who was always very handsome and expensive in his tastes, seemed as if he never would be able to do anything worth doing. And the mother, who had a great belief in herself, did not succeed any better, and her tastes were just as expensive.

And so the house came to be haunted by the unspoken phrase: There must be more money! There must be more money! The children could hear it all the time, though nobody said it aloud. They heard it at Christmas, when the expensive and splendid toys filled the nursery. Behind the shining modern rocking horse, behind the smart doll's-house, a voice would start whispering: "There must be more money! There must be more money!" And the children would stop playing, to listen for a moment. They would look into each other's eyes, to see if they had all heard. And each one saw in the eyes of the other two that they too had heard. "There must be more money! There must be more money!"

It came whispering from the springs of the still-swaying rocking horse, and even the horse, bending his wooden, champing head, heard it. The big doll, sitting so pink and smirking in her new pram, could hear it quite plainly, and seemed to be smirking all the more self-consciously because of it. The foolish puppy, too, that took the place of the Teddy bear, he was looking so extraordinarily foolish for no other reason but that he heard the secret whisper all over the house: "There must be more money!"

Yet nobody ever said it aloud. The whisper was everywhere, and therefore no one spoke it. Just as no one ever says: "We are breathing!" in spite of the fact that breath is coming and going all the time.

"Mother," said the boy Paul one day, "why don't we keep a car of our own? Why do we always use uncle's, or else a taxi?"

"Because we're the poor members of the family," said the mother.

"But why are we, mother?"

"Well—I suppose," she said slowly and bitterly, "it's because your father has no luck."

The boy was silent for some time.

"Is luck money, mother?" he asked, rather timidly.

"No, Paul. Not quite. It's what causes you to have money."

"Oh!" said Paul vaguely. "I thought when Uncle Oscar said filthy lucker, it meant money."

"Filthy lucre does mean money," said the mother. "But it's lucre, not luck."

"Oh!" said the boy. "Then what is luck, mother?"

"It's what causes you to have money. If you're lucky you have money. That's why it's better to be born lucky than rich. If you're rich, you may lose your money. But if you're lucky, you will always get more money."

"Oh! Will you? And is father not lucky?"

"Very unlucky, I should say," she said bitterly.

The boy watched her with unsure eyes.

"Why?" he asked.

"I don't know. Nobody ever knows why one person is lucky and another unlucky."

"Don't they? Nobody at all? Does nobody know?"

"Perhaps God. But He never tells."

"He ought to, then. And aren't you lucky either, mother?"

"I can't be, if I married an unlucky husband."

"But by yourself, aren't you?"

"I used to think I was, before I married. Now I think I am very unlucky indeed."

"Why?"

"Well—never mind! Perhaps I'm not really," she said.

The child looked at her, to see if she meant it. But he saw, by the lines of her mouth, that she was only trying to hide something from him.

"Well, anyhow," he said stoutly, "I'm a lucky person."

"Why?" said his mother, with a sudden laugh.

He stared at her. He didn't even know why he had said it.

"God told me," he asserted, brazening it out.

"I hope He did, dear!" she said, again with a laugh, but rather bitter.

"He did, mother!"

"Excellent!" said the mother, using one of her husband's exclamations.

The boy saw she did not believe him; or, rather, that she paid no attention to his assertion. This angered him somewhat, and made him want to compel her attention.

He went off by himself, vaguely, in a childish way, seeking for the clue to "luck." Absorbed, taking no heed of other people, he went about with a sort of stealth, seeking inwardly for luck. He wanted luck, he wanted it, he wanted it. When the two girls were playing dolls in the nursery, he would sit on his big rocking horse, charging madly into space, with a frenzy that made the little girls peer at him uneasily. Wildly the horse careered, the waving dark hair of the boy tossed, his eyes had a strange glare in them. The little girls dared not speak to him.

When he had ridden to the end of his mad little journey, he climbed down and stood in front of his rocking horse, staring fixedly into its lowered face. Its red mouth was slightly open, its big eye was wide and glassy-bright.

"Now!" he would silently command the snorting steed. "Now, take me to where there is luck! Now take me!"

And he would slash the horse on the neck with the little whip he had asked Uncle Oscar for. He knew the horse could take him to where there was luck, if only he forced it. So he would mount again, and start on his furious ride, hoping at last to get there. He knew he could get there.

"You'll break your horse, Paul!" said the nurse.

"He's always riding like that! I wish he'd leave off!" said his elder sister Joan.

But he only glared down on them in silence. Nurse gave him up. She could make nothing of him. Anyhow he was growing beyond her.

One day his mother and his Uncle Oscar came in when he was on one of his furious rides. He did not speak to them.

"Hallo, you young jockey! Riding a winner?" said his uncle.

"Aren't you growing too big for a rocking horse? You're not a very little boy any longer, you know," said his mother.

But Paul only gave a blue glare from his big, rather close-set eyes. He would speak to nobody when he was in full tilt. His mother watched him with an anxious expression on her face.

At last he suddenly stopped forcing his horse into the mechanical gallop, and slid down.

"Well, I got there!" he announced fiercely, his blue eyes still flaring, and his sturdy long legs straddling apart.

"Where did you get to?" asked his mother.

"Where I wanted to go," he flared back at her.

"That's right, son!" said Uncle Oscar. "Don't you stop till you get there. What's the horse's name?"

"He doesn't have a name," said the boy.

"Gets on without all right?" asked the uncle.

"Well, he has different names. He was called Sansovino last week."

"Sansovino, eh? Won the Ascot. How did you know his name?"

"He always talks about horse races with Bassett," said Joan.

The uncle was delighted to find that his small nephew was posted with all the racing news. Bassett, the young gardener, who had been wounded in the left foot in the war and had got his present job through Oscar Cresswell, whose batman he had been, was a perfect blade of the "turf." He lived in the racing events, and the small boy lived with him.

Oscar Cresswell got it all from Bassett.

"Master Paul comes and asks me, so I can't do more than tell him, sir," said Bassett, his face terribly serious, as if he were speaking of religious matters.

"And does he ever put anything on a horse he fancies?"

"Well—I don't want to give him away—he's a young sport, a fine sport, sir. Would you mind asking him yourself? He sort of takes a pleasure in it, and perhaps he'd feel I was giving him away, sir, if you don't mind."

Bassett was serious as a church.

The uncle went back to his nephew, and took him off for a ride in the car.

"Say, Paul, old man, do you ever put anything on a horse?" the uncle asked.

The boy watched the handsome man closely.

"Why, do you think I oughtn't to?" he parried.

"Not a bit of it! I thought perhaps you might give me a tip for the Lincoln."

The car sped on into the country, going down to Uncle Oscar's place in Hampshire.

"Honour bright?" said the nephew.

"Honour bright, son!" said the uncle.

"Well, then, Daffodil."

"Daffodil! I doubt it, sonny. What about Mirza?"

"I only know the winner," said the boy. "That's Daffodil."

"Daffodil, eh?"

There was a pause. Daffodil was an obscure horse comparatively.

"Uncle!"

"Yes, son?"

"You won't let it go any further, will you? I promised Bassett."

"Bassett be damned, old man! What's he got to do with it?"

"We're partners. We've been partners from the first. Uncle, he lent me my first five shillings, which I lost. I promised him, honour bright, it was only between me and him; only you gave me that ten-shilling note I started winning with, so I thought you were lucky. You won't let it go any further, will you?"

The boy gazed at his uncle from those big, hot, blue eyes, set rather close together. The uncle stirred and laughed uneasily.

"Right you are, son! I'll keep your tip private. Daffodil, eh? How much are you putting on him?"

"All except twenty pounds," said the boy. "I keep that in reserve."

The uncle thought it a good joke.

"You keep twenty pounds in reserve, do you, you young romancer? What are you betting, then?"

"I'm betting three hundred," said the boy gravely. "But it's between you and me, Uncle Oscar! Honour bright?"

The uncle burst into a roar of laughter.

"It's between you and me all right, you young Nat Gould," he said, laughing. "But where's your three hundred?"

"Bassett keeps it for me. We're partners."

"You are, are you! And what is Bassett putting on Daffodil?"

"He won't go quite as high as I do, I expect. Perhaps he'll go a hundred and fifty."

"What, pennies?" laughed the uncle.

"Pounds," said the child, with a surprised look at his uncle. "Bassett keeps a bigger reserve than I do."

Between wonder and amusement Uncle Oscar was silent. He pursued the matter no further, but he determined to take his nephew with him to the Lincoln races.

"Now, son," he said, "I'm putting twenty on Mirza, and I'll put five for you on any horse you fancy. What's your pick?"

"Daffodil, uncle."

"No, not the fiver on Daffodil!"

"I should if it was my own fiver," said the child.

"Good! Good! Right you are! A fiver for me and a fiver for you on Daffodil."

The child had never been to a race meeting before, and his eyes were blue fire. He pursed his mouth tight, and watched. A Frenchman just in front had put his money on Lancelot. Wild with excitement, he flayed his arms up and down, yelling "Lancelot! Lancelot!" in his French accent.

Daffodil came in first, Lancelot second, Mirza third. The child, flushed and with eyes blazing, was curiously serene. His uncle brought him four five-pound notes, four to one.

"What am I to do with these?" he cried, waving them before the boy's eyes.

"I suppose we'll talk to Bassett," said the boy. "I expect I have fifteen hundred now; and twenty in reserve; and this twenty."

His uncle studied him for some moments.

"Look here, son!" he said. "You're not serious about Bassett and that fifteen hundred, are you?"

"Yes, I am. But it's between you and me, uncle. Honour bright!"

"Honour bright all right, son! But I must talk to Bassett."

"If you'd like to be a partner, uncle, with Bassett and me, we could all be partners. Only, you'd have to promise, honour bright, uncle, not to let it go beyond us three. Bassett and I are lucky, and you must be lucky, because it was your ten shillings I started winning with. . . ."

Uncle Oscar took both Bassett and Paul into Richmond Park for an afternoon, and there they talked.

"It's like this, you see, sir," Bassett said. "Master Paul would get me talking about racing events, spinning yarns, you know, sir. And he was always keen on knowing if I'd made or if I'd lost. It's about a year since, now, that I put five shillings on Blush of Dawn for him—and we lost. Then the luck turned, with that ten shillings he had from you, that we put on Singhalese. And since that time, it's been pretty steady, all things considering. What do you say, Master Paul?"

"We're all right when we're sure," said Paul. "It's when we're not quite sure that we go down."

"Oh, but we're careful then," said Bassett.

"But when are you sure?" smiled Uncle Oscar.

"It's Master Paul, sir," said Bassett, in a secret, religious voice. "It's as if he had it from heaven. Like Daffodil, now, for the Lincoln. That was as sure as eggs."

"Did you put anything on Daffodil?" asked Oscar Cresswell.

"Yes, sir, I made my bit."

"And my nephew?"

Bassett was obstinately silent, looking at Paul.

"I made twelve hundred, didn't I, Bassett? I told uncle I was putting three hundred on Daffodil."

"That's right," said Bassett, nodding.

"But where's the money?" asked the uncle.

"I keep it safe locked up, sir. Master Paul he can have it any minute he likes to ask for it."

"What, fifteen hundred pounds?"

"And twenty! and forty, that is, with the twenty he made on the course."

"It's amazing!" said the uncle.

"If Master Paul offers you to be partners, sir, I would, if I were you; if you'll excuse me," said Bassett.

Oscar Cresswell thought about it.

"I'll see the money," he said.

They drove home again, and sure enough, Bassett came round to the garden-house with fifteen hundred pounds in notes. The twenty pounds reserve was left with Joe Glee, in the Turf Commission deposit.

"You see, it's all right, uncle, when I'm sure! Then we go strong, for all we're worth. Don't we, Bassett?"

"We do that, Master Paul."

"And when are you sure?" said the uncle, laughing.

"Oh, well, sometimes I'm absolutely sure, like about Daffodil," said the boy; "and sometimes I have an idea; and sometimes I haven't even an idea, have I, Bassett? Then we're careful, because we mostly go down."

"You do, do you! And when you're sure, like about Daffodil, what makes you sure, sonny?"

"Oh, well, I don't know," said the boy uneasily. "I'm sure, you know, uncle; that's all."

"It's as if he had it from heaven, sir," Bassett reiterated.

"I should say so!" said the uncle.

But he became a partner. And when the Leger was coming on, Paul was "sure" about Lively Spark, which was a quite inconsiderable horse. The boy insisted on putting a thousand on the horse, Bassett went for five hundred, and Oscar Cresswell two hundred. Lively Spark came in first, and the betting had been ten to one against him. Paul had made ten thousand.

"You see," he said, "I was absolutely sure of him."

Even Oscar Cresswell had cleared two thousand.

"Look here, son," he said, "this sort of thing makes me nervous."

"It needn't, uncle! Perhaps I shan't be sure again for a long time."

"But what are you going to do with your money?" asked the uncle.

"Of course," said the boy, "I started it for mother. She said she had no luck, because father is unlucky, so I thought if I was lucky, it might stop whispering."

"What might stop whispering?"

"Our house. I hate our house for whispering."

"What does it whisper?"

"Why—why"—the boy fidgeted—"why, I don't know. But it's always short of money, you know, uncle."

"I know it, son, I know it."

"You know people send mother writs, don't you, uncle?"

"I'm afraid I do," said the uncle.

"And then the house whispers, like people laughing at you behind your back. It's awful, that is! I thought if I was lucky . . ."

"You might stop it," added the uncle.

The boy watched him with big blue eyes that had an uncanny cold fire in them, and he said never a word.

"Well, then!" said the uncle. "What are we doing?"

"I shouldn't like mother to know I was lucky," said the boy.

"Why not, son?"

"She'd stop me."

"I don't think she would."

"Oh!"—and the boy writhed in an odd way—"I don't want her to know, uncle."

"All right, son! We'll manage it without her knowing."

They managed it very easily. Paul, at the other's suggestion, handed over five thousand pounds to his uncle, who deposited it with the family lawyer, who was then to inform Paul's mother that a relative had put five thousand pounds into his hands, which sum was to be paid out a thousand pounds at a time, on the mother's birthday, for the next five years.

"So she'll have a birthday present of a thousand pounds for five successive years," said Uncle Oscar. "I hope it won't make it all the harder for her later."

Paul's mother had her birthday in November. The house had been "whispering" worse than ever lately, and, even in spite of his luck, Paul could not bear up against it. He was very anxious to see the effect of the birthday letter, telling his mother about the thousand pounds.

When there were no visitors, Paul now took his meals with his parents, as he was beyond the nursery control. His mother went into town nearly every day. She had discovered that she had an odd knack of sketching furs and dress materials, so she worked secretly in the studio of a friend who was the chief "artist" for the leading drapers. She drew the figures of ladies in furs and ladies in silk and sequins for the newspaper advertisements. This young woman artist earned several thousand pounds a year, but Paul's mother only made several hundreds, and she was again dissatisfied. She so wanted to be first in something, and she did not succeed, even in making sketches for drapery advertisements.

She was down to breakfast on the morning of her birthday. Paul watched her face as she read her letters. He knew the lawyer's letter. As his mother read it, her face hardened and became more expressionless. Then a cold, determined look came on her mouth. She hid the letter under the pile of others, and said not a word about it.

"Didn't you have anything nice in the post for your birthday, mother?" said Paul.

"Quite moderately nice," she said, her voice cold and absent.

She went away to town without saying more.

But in the afternoon Uncle Oscar appeared. He said Paul's mother had had a long interview with the lawyer, asking if the whole five thousand could be advanced at once, as she was in debt.

"What do you think, uncle?" said the boy.

"I leave it to you, son."

"Oh, let her have it, then! We can get some more with the other," said the boy.

"A bird in the hand is worth two in the bush, laddie!" said Uncle Oscar.

"But I'm sure to know for the Grand National; or the Lincolnshire;

or else the Derby. I'm sure to know for one of them," said Paul.

So Uncle Oscar signed the agreement, and Paul's mother touched the whole five thousand. Then something very curious happened. The voices in the house suddenly went mad, like a chorus of frogs on a spring evening. There were certain new furnishings, and Paul had a tutor. He was really going to Eton, his father's school, in the following autumn. There were flowers in the winter, and a blossoming of the luxury Paul's mother had been used to. And yet the voices in the house, behind the sprays of mimosa and almond blossom, and from under the piles of iridescent cushions, simply trilled and screamed in a sort of ecstasy: "There must be more money! Oh-h-h, there must be more money. Oh, now, now-w! Now-w-w—there must be more money!—more than ever! More than ever!"

It frightened Paul terribly. He studied away at his Latin and Greek with his tutors. But his intense hours were spent with Bassett. The Grand National had gone by: he had not "known," and had lost a hundred pounds. Summer was at hand. He was in agony for the Lincoln. But even for the Lincoln he didn't "know" and he lost fifty pounds. He became wild-eyed and strange, as if something were going to explode in him.

"Let it alone, son! Don't you bother about it!" urged Uncle Oscar. But it was as if the boy couldn't really hear what his uncle was saying.

"I've got to know for the Derby! I've got to know for the Derby!" the child reiterated, his big blue eyes blazing with a sort of madness.

His mother noticed how overwrought he was.

"You'd better go to the seaside. Wouldn't you like to go now to the seaside, instead of waiting? I think you'd better," she said, looking down at him anxiously, her heart curiously heavy because of him.

But the child lifted his uncanny blue eyes.

"I couldn't possibly go before the Derby, mother!" he said. "I couldn't possibly!"

"Why not?" she said, her voice becoming heavy when she was opposed. "Why not? You can still go from the seaside to see the Derby with your Uncle Oscar, if that's what you wish. No need for you to wait here. Besides, I think you care too much about these races. It's a bad sign. My family has been a gambling family, and you won't know till you grow up how much damage it has done. But it has done damage. I shall have to send Bassett away, and ask Uncle Oscar not to talk racing to you, unless you promise to be reasonable about it; go away to the seaside and forget it. You're all nerves!"

"I'll do what you like, mother, so long as you don't send me away till after the Derby," the boy said.

"Send you away from where? Just from this house?"

"Yes," he said, gazing at her.

"Why, you curious child, what makes you care about this house so much, suddenly? I never knew you loved it."

He gazed at her without speaking. He had a secret within a secret, something he had not divulged, even to Bassett or to his Uncle Oscar.

But his mother, after standing undecided and a little bit sullen for some moments, said:

"Very well, then! Don't go to the seaside till after the Derby, if you don't wish it. But promise me you won't let your nerves go to pieces. Promise you won't think so much about horse racing and events, as you call them!"

"Oh, no," said the boy casually. "I won't think much about them, mother. You needn't worry. I wouldn't worry, mother, if I were you."

"If you were me and I were you," said his mother, "I wonder what we should do!"

"But you know you needn't worry, mother, don't you?" the boy repeated.

"I should be awfully glad to know it," she said wearily.

"Oh, well, you can, you know. I mean, you ought to know you needn't worry," he insisted.

"Ought I? Then I'll see about it," she said.

Paul's secret of secrets was his wooden horse, that which had no name. Since he was emancipated from a nurse and a nursery-governess, he had had his rocking horse removed to his own bedroom at the top of the house.

"Surely, you're too big for a rocking horse!" his mother had remonstrated.

"Well, you see, mother, till I can have a real horse, I like to have some sort of animal about," had been his quaint answer.

"Do you feel he keeps you company?" she laughed.

"Oh, yes! He's very good, he always keeps me company, when I'm there," said Paul.

So the horse, rather shabby, stood in an arrested prance in the boy's bedroom.

The Derby was drawing near, and the boy grew more and more tense. He hardly heard what was spoken to him, he was very frail, and his eyes were really uncanny. His mother had sudden seizures of uneasiness about him. Sometimes, for half-an-hour, she would feel a sudden anxiety about him that was almost anguish. She wanted to rush to him at once, and know he was safe.

Two nights before the Derby, she was at a big party in town, when one of her rushes of anxiety about her boy, her first-born, gripped her heart till she could hardly speak. She fought with the feeling, might and main, for she believed in common sense. But it was too strong. She had to leave the dance and go downstairs to telephone to the country. The children's nursery-governess was terribly surprised and startled at being rung up in the night.

"Are the children all right, Miss Wilmot?"

"Oh, yes, they are quite all right."

"Master Paul? Is he all right?"

"He went to bed as right as a trivet. Shall I run up and look at him?"

"No," said Paul's mother reluctantly. "No! Don't trouble. It's all right. Don't sit up. We shall be home fairly soon." She did not want her son's privacy intruded upon.

"Very good," said the governess.

It was about one o'clock when Paul's mother and father drove up to their house. All was still. Paul's mother went to her room and slipped off her white fur coat. She had told her maid not to wait up for her. She heard her husband downstairs, mixing a whisky-and-soda.

And then, because of the strange anxiety at her heart, she stole upstairs to her son's room. Noiselessly she went along the upper corridor. Was there a faint noise? What was it?

She stood, with arrested muscles, outside his door, listening. There was a strange, heavy, and yet not loud noise. Her heart stood still. It was a soundless noise, yet rushing and powerful. Something huge, in violent, hushed motion. What was it? What in God's name was it? She ought to know. She felt that she knew the noise. She knew what it was.

Yet she could not place it. She couldn't say what it was. And on and on it went, like a madness.

Softly, frozen with anxiety and fear, she turned the door handle.

The room was dark. Yet in the space near the window, she heard and saw something plunging to and fro. She gazed in fear and amazement.

Then suddenly she switched on the light, and saw her son, in his green pyjamas, madly surging on the rocking horse. The blaze of light suddenly lit him up, as he urged the wooden horse, and lit her up, as she stood, blonde, in her dress of pale green and crystal, in the doorway.

"Paul!" she cried. "Whatever are you doing?"

"It's Malabar!" he screamed, in a powerful, strange voice. "It's Malabar."

His eyes blazed at her for one strange and senseless second, as he ceased urging his wooden horse. Then he fell with a crash to the ground, and she, all her tormented motherhood flooding upon her, rushed to gather him up.

But he was unconscious, and unconscious he remained, with some brain-fever. He talked and tossed, and his mother sat stonily by his side.

"Malabar! It's Malabar! Bassett, Bassett, I know! It's Malabar!"

So the child cried, trying to get up and urge the rocking horse that gave him his inspiration.

"What does he mean by Malabar?" asked the heart-frozen mother.

"I don't know," said the father stonily.

"What does he mean by Malabar?" she asked her brother Oscar.

"It's one of the horses running for the Derby," was the answer.

And, in spite of himself, Oscar Cresswell spoke to Bassett, and himself put a thousand on Malabar: at fourteen to one.

The third day of the illness was critical: they were waiting for a change. The boy, with his rather long, curly hair, was tossing ceaselessly on the pillow. He neither slept nor regained consciousness, and his eyes were like blue stones. His mother sat, feeling her heart had gone, turned actually into a stone.

In the evening, Oscar Cresswell did not come, but Bassett sent a message, saying could he come up for one moment, just one moment? Paul's mother was very angry at the intrusion, but on second thought she agreed. The boy was the same. Perhaps Bassett might bring him to consciousness.

The gardener, a shortish fellow with a little brown moustache, and sharp little brown eyes, tiptoed into the room, touched his imaginary cap to Paul's mother, and stole to the bedside, staring with glittering, smallish eyes, at the tossing, dying child.

"Master Paul!" he whispered. "Master Paul! Malabar come in first all right, a clean win. I did as you told me. You've made over seventy thousand pounds, you have; you've got over eighty thousand. Malabar came in all right, Master Paul."

"Malabar! Malabar! Did I say Malabar, mother? Did I say Malabar? Do you think I'm lucky, mother? I knew Malabar, didn't I? Over eighty thousand pounds! I call that lucky, don't you, mother? Over eighty thousand pounds! I knew, didn't I know I knew? Malabar came in all right. If I ride my horse till I'm sure, then I tell you, Bassett, you can go as high as you like. Did you go for all you were worth, Bassett?"

"I went a thousand on it, Master Paul."

"I never told you, mother, that if I can ride my horse, and get there, then I'm asbolutely sure—oh, absolutely! Mother, did I ever tell you? I am lucky."

"No, you never did," said the mother.

But the boy died in the night.

And even as he lay dead, his mother heard her brother's voice saying to her: "My God, Hester, you're eighty-odd thousand to the good and a poor devil of a son to the bad. But, poor devil, poor devil, he's best gone out of a life where he rides his rocking horse to find a winner."

For Discussion

1. What is your impression of the family relationships?
2. Was the boy motivated to bet on the horses by his love for his mother or by his own selfishness? Explain.
3. Should the mother have made the boy so aware of the family's financial needs?
4. In using the boy the way he did, was the uncle fulfilling his responsibility toward his nephew? Toward his sister? Why?
5. Who ultimately was responsible for the boy's death?

For Comparison

1. What evidences of "The Broken Home" exist in this story? Is it possible to have a broken home even though the parents are living together?
2. In "Autobiography" Rod McKuen writes specifically about missing the presence of his father in his life. To what extent is Paul also experiencing this void? Why isn't his uncle an appropriate replacement?

For Composition

1. Children should (should not) share financial responsibilities.
2. Danger of keeping up with the Joneses.
3. Real versus pretended love in the home.

ROD McKUEN

AUTOBIOGRAPHY

For my mother

1.

I remember hearing children
in the street outside
above the noise
of pots and pans and bickering.
They had their world
I had my room.
I envied them only
for the day long sunshine
of their lives
and their fathers.
Mine I never knew.

2.

I grew
not necessarily erect.
I bent sometimes
but never to the lowest branch
and learned to love the smell
of people's bodies making love to me
as much as I loved lilacs.

3.

I try to play as many games
as games there are.
To lie a little's not so bad
if it get you through the night.
Bach and The Supremes help too
and I've a cat
who's learned to like my music.

4.

I read sometimes obituaries
in towns that I pass through
hoping I might find a man

who spells his name the same as me.
If he's dead then I'll know where he lived
and if he lived.

5.

In the end
the songs I sing
are of my own invention.
They mirror what has happened to me
since I was abandoned by my father
and by love.

6.

I stay alone
confined to me
imposing my philosophy on no one else
(The words that make this book
were written for myself
except a few that were a letter
written to a love now gone
who lived on *Stanyan Street.*)
but I have saved them up
and give them here
to those I hope might understand.

                                           May 16, 1966

For Discussion

1. McKuen addresses this poem to his mother, but he never mentions
   her in the body of the work. What is he trying to suggest? Who is the
   "he" in stanza four?
2. Why does the poet equate his father with love in stanza five? Might
   this reference throw some light on question one above?
3. What does McKuen want the reader to understand in stanza six?
4. Who is responsible for the type of person the poet now is? Himself?
   His mother? His father?

For Comparison

1. Perhaps McKuen has idealized the idea of his father too much. Using
   ideas from Rollin's "motherhood myth" as a springboard, discuss the
   "fatherhood myth" suggested in this poem.

2. McKuen says that he has been abandoned by his father and by love. Could one of the children in Van Doren's "Nobody Say a Word" write a poem on this theme when grown older? How might the ideas in such a poem be similar? How different?

For Composition

1. My parents' influence on me.
2. My parents never care.
3. Lonely among friends.

THEODORE ROETHKE

MY PAPA'S WALTZ

The whisky on your breath
Could make a small boy dizzy;
But I hung on like death;
Such waltzing was not easy.

We romped until the pans
Slid from the kitchen shelf;
My mother's countenance
Could not unfrown itself.

The hand that held my wrist
Was battered on one knuckle;
At every step you missed
My right ear scraped a buckle.

You beat time on my head
With a palm caked hard by dirt,
Then waltzed me off to bed
Still clinging to your shirt.

"My Papa's Waltz" by Theodore Roethke. Copyright 1942 by Hearst Magazines Inc. From *The Collected Poems of Theodore Roethke*. Reprinted by permission of Doubleday & Company, Inc.

For Discussion

1. What impression of family life does Roethke want to get across to you?
2. What sort of person is the mother? Does the son respect her, or does he fear her?
3. Do you get a positive or a negative feeling toward this family's situation? What effect could this type of family life possibly have on the young boy?

For Comparison

1. Compare the father in this poem with the father described by Patmore in "The Toys." Which do you feel is the more responsible?
2. Compare the parent-child relationship in this poem with that described in "A Domestic Dilemma." Will Martin ever be able to relate to his children the way Roethke's father related to him? Is Martin's intensity a negative influence? Which of the two men would you rather have as father?

For Composition

1. My strange parents.
2. A fun evening at my home.
3. Mother (or Father) is too stern.

COVENTRY PATMORE

THE TOYS

My little Son, who looked from thoughtful eyes
And moved and spoke in quiet grown-up wise,
Having my law the seventh time disobeyed,
I struck him, and dismissed
With hard words and unkissed,
His Mother, who was patient, being dead.

Then, fearing lest his grief should hinder sleep,
I visited his bed,
But found him slumbering deep,
With darkened eyelids, and their lashes yet
From his late sobbing wet.
And I, with moan,
Kissing away his tears, left others of my own;
For, on a table drawn beside his head,
He had put, within his reach,
A box of counters and a red-veined stone,
A piece of glass abraded by the beach,
And six or seven shells,
A bottle with bluebells,
And two French copper coins, ranged there with careful art,
To comfort his sad heart.
So when that night I prayed
To God, I wept, and said:
Ah, when at last we lie with tranced breath,
Not vexing Thee in death,
And thou rememberest of what toys
We made our joys,
How weakly understood
Thy great commanded good,
Then, fatherly not less
Than I whom Thou hast moulded from the clay,
Thou'lt leave Thy wrath, and say,
"I will be sorry for their childishness."

For Discussion

1. Why does the father feel guilty for punishing his son? Is his guilt intensified because the boy's mother is dead?
2. How is the father much like his son? What are some of the father's toys and some of his childish ways?
3. The father evidences both punishment and love. Is it necessary that a responsible parent use both? Or do you agree with the modern theory which suggests that love alone is sufficient?

For Comparison

1. The poet suggests that adults also have their "toys." What are some of the toys mentioned in Rod McKuen's "Autobiography"?

2. Read the last eleven lines of this poem carefully and then discuss them
   in terms of the grandmother's attitude in "A Visit to Grandmother"
   by Kelley.

For Composition

1. Parents should (should not) punish children.
2. Parents are sometimes children.

JAMES MERRILL

THE BROKEN HOME

Crossing the street,
I saw the parents and the child
At their window, gleaming like fruit
With evening's mild gold leaf.

In a room on the floor below,
Sunless, cooler—a brimming
Saucer of wax, marbly and dim—
I have lit what's left of my life.

I have thrown out yesterday's milk
And opened a book of maxims.
The flame quickens. The word stirs.

Tell me, tongue of fire,
That you and I are as real
At least as the people upstairs.

My father, who had flown in World War I,
Might have continued to invest his life
In cloud banks well above Wall Street and wife.
But the race was run below, and the point was to win.

Too late now, I make out in his blue gaze
(Through the smoked glass of being thirty-six)
The soul eclipsed by twin black pupils, sex
And business; time was money in those days.

From the book *Nights and Days* by James Merrill. Copyright © 1965, 1966 by James Merrill. Reprinted by permission of Atheneum Publishers. This poem appeared originally in *The New Yorker*.

Each thirteenth year he married. When he died
There were already several chilled wives
In sable orbit — rings, cars, permanent waves.
We'd felt him warming up for a green bride.

He could afford it. He was "in his prime"
A three score ten. But money was not time.

When my parents were younger this was a popular act:
A veiled woman would leap from an electric, wine-dark car
To the steps of no matter what — the Senate or the Ritz Bar —
And bodily, at newsreel speed, attack
No matter whom — Al Smith or José Maria Sert
Or Clemenceau — veins standing out on her throat
As she yelled *War mongerer! Pig! Give us the vote!*,
And would have to be hauled away in her hobble skirt.

What had the man done? Oh, made history.
Her business (he had implied) was giving birth,
Tending the house, mending the socks.

Always that same old story —
Father Time and Mother Earth,
A marriage on the rocks.

One afternoon, red, satyr-thighed
Michael, the Irish setter, head
Passionately lowered, led
The child I was to a shut door. Inside,

Blinds beat sun from the bed.
The green-gold room throbbed like a bruise.
Under a sheet, clad in taboos
Lay whom we sought, her hair undone, outspread,

And of a blackness found, it ever now, in old
Engravings where the acid bit.
I must have needed to touch it
Or the whiteness — was she dead?
Her eyes flew open, startled strange and cold.
The dog slumped to the floor. She reached for me. I fled.

Tonight they have stepped out onto the gravel.
The party is over. It's the fall
Of 1931. They love each other still.

She: Charlie, I can't stand the pace.
He: Come on, honey—why, you'll bury us all!

A lead soldier guards my windowsill:
Khaki rifle, uniform, and face.
Something in me grows heavy, silvery, pliable.

How intensely people used to feel!
Like metal poured at the close of a proletarian novel,
Refined and glowing from the crucible,
I see those two hearts, I'm afraid,
Still. Cool here in the graveyard of good and evil,
They are even so to be honored and obeyed.

. . . Obeyed, at least, inversely. Thus
I rarely buy a newspaper, or vote.
To do so, I have learned, is to invite
The tread of a stone guest within my house.

Shooting this rusted bolt, though, against him,
I trust I am no less time's child than some
Who on the heath impersonate Poor Tom
Or on the barricades risk life and limb.

Nor do I try to keep a garden, only
An avocado in a glass of water—
Roots pallid, gemmed with air. And later,

When the small gilt leaves have grown
Fleshy and green, I let them die, yes, yes,
And start another, I am earth's no less.

A child, a red dog roam the corridors,
Still, of the broken home. No sound. The brilliant
Rag runners halt before wide-open doors.
My old room! Its wallpaper—cream, medallioned
With pink and brown—brings back the first nightmares,
Long summer colds, and Emma, sepia-faced,
Perspiring over broth carried upstairs
Aswim with golden fats I could not taste.

The real house became a boarding-school.
Under the ballroom ceiling's allegory
Someone at last may actually be allowed
To learn something; or, from my window, cool
With the unstiflement of the entire story,
Watch a red setter stretch and sink in cloud.

For Discussion

1. The author says, "How intensely people used to feel!" Has the rapid pace of modern life cut down man's ability to share personal feelings? How might the inability to share feelings be partially responsible for broken homes?
2. The poem suggests that men make history and that women do less important things. Why do you agree or disagree? What is your opinion of working mothers? Do you feel the new professional independence of American women has weakened the structure of the home?
3. On the basis of his own family background, do you think the narrator will ever marry? Why? Why not? What kind of husband and father might he be?
4. He blames his retreat from life on his parents. Is this a reasonable, responsible attitude?

For Comparison

1. In what specific ways do Merrill and McKuen ("Autobiography") blame their retreats from life on their home backgrounds? Do you think the blame is rightly placed? Is their position responsible, or should they try to outgrow their past?
2. If Adler ("The Family Constellation") created another category to list the child from a broken home, what personality traits might he assign him? How is this child going to be different from the child in a similar constellation position who has two parents?

For Composition

1. People don't care about people anymore.
2. How my home life has affected me.
3. Mothers should (should not) hold jobs.

GREGORY CORSO

MARRIAGE

Should I get married? Should I be good?
Astound the girl next door with my velvet suit and faustus hood?
Don't take her to movies but to cemeteries
tell all about werewolf bathtubs and forked clarinets
then desire her and kiss her and all the preliminaries
and she going just so far and I understanding why
not getting angry saying You must feel! It's beautiful to feel!
Instead take her in my arms lean against an old crooked tombstone
and woo her the entire night the constellations in the sky—

When she introduces me to her parents
back straightened, hair finally combed, strangled by a tie,
should I sit knees together on their 3rd degree sofa
and not ask Where's the bathroom?
How else to feel other than I am,
often thinking Flash Gordon soap—
O how terrible it must be for a young man
seated before a family and the family thinking
We never saw him before! He wants our Mary Lou!
After tea and homemade cookies they ask What do you do for a living?

Should I tell them? Would they like me then?
Say All right get married, we're losing a daughter
but we're gaining a son—
And should I then ask Where's the bathroom?

O God, and the wedding! All her family and her friends
and only a handful of mine all scroungy and bearded
just waiting to get at the drinks and food—
And the priest! he looking at me as if I masturbated
asking me Do you take this woman for your lawful wedded wife?
And I trembling what to say say Pie Glue!
I kiss the bride all those corny men slapping me on the back
She's all yours, boy! Ha-ha-ha!
And in their eyes you could see some obscene honeymoon going on—
Then all that absurd rice and clanky cans and shoes
Niagra Falls! Hordes of us! Husbands! Wives! Flowers! Chocolates!
All streaming into cozy hotels

All going to do the same thing tonight
The indifferent clerk he knowing what was going to happen
The lobby zombies they knowing what
The whistling elevator man he knowing
The winking bellboy knowing
Everybody knowing! I'd be almost inclined not to do anything!
Stay up all night! Stare that hotel clerk in the eye!
Screaming: I deny honeymoon! I deny honeymoon!
running rampant into those almost climactic suites
yelling Radio belly! Cat shovel!
O I'd live in Niagra forever! in a dark cave beneath the Falls
I'd sit there the Mad Honeymooner
devising ways to break marriages, a scourge of bigamy
a saint of divorce—

But I should get married I should be good
How nice it'd be to come home to her
and sit by the fireplace and she in the kitchen
aproned young and lovely wanting my baby
and so happy about me she burns the roast beef
and comes crying to me and I get up from my big papa chair
saying Christmas teeth! Radiant brains! Apple deaf!
God what a husband I'd make! Yes, I should get married!
So much to do! like sneaking into Mr. Jones' house late at night
and cover his golf clubs with 1920 Norwegian books
Like hanging a picture of Rimbaud on the lawnmower
like pasting Tannu Tuva postage stamps all over the picket fence
like when Mrs. Kindhead comes to collect for the Community Chest
grab her and tell her There are unfavorable omens in the sky.
And when the mayor comes to get my vote tell him
When are you going to stop people killing whales!
And when the milkman comes leave him a note in the bottle
Penguin dust, bring me penguin dust, I want penguin dust—

Yet if I should get married and it's Connecticut and snow
and she gives birth to a child and I am sleepless, worn,
up for nights, head bowed against a quiet window, the past behind me,
finding myself in the most common of situations a trembling man
knowledged with responsibility not twig-smear nor Roman coin soup—
O what would that be like!
Surely I'd give it for a nipple a rubber Tacitus
For a rattle a bag of broken Bach records
Tack Della Francesca all over its crib
Sew the Greek alphabet on its bib
And build for its playpen a roofless Parthenon

No, I doubt I'd be that kind of father
not rural not snow no quiet window
but hot smelly tight New York City
seven flights up, roaches and rats in the walls
a fat Reichian wife screeching over potatoes Get a job!
And five nose running brats in love with Batman
And the neighbors all toothless and dry haired
like those hag masses of the 18th century
all wanting to come in and watch TV
The landlord wants his rent
Grocery store Blue Cross Gas & Electric Knights of Columbus
Impossible to lie back and dream Telephone snow, ghost parking—
No! I should not get married I should never get married!
But—imagine If I were married to a beautiful sophisticated woman
tall and pale wearing an elegant black dress and long black gloves
holding a cigarette holder in one hand and a highball in the other
and we lived high up in a penthouse with a huge window
from which we could see all of New York and ever farther on clearer days
No, can't imagine myself married to that pleasant prison dream—

O but what about love? I forget love
not that I am incapable of love
it's just that I see love as odd as wearing shoes—
I never wanted to marry a girl who was like my mother
And Ingrid Bergman was always impossible
And there's maybe a girl now but she's already married
And I don't like men and—
but there's got to be somebody!
Because what if I'm 60 years old and not married,
all alone in a furnished room with pee stains on my underwear
and everybody else is married! All the universe married but me!

Ah, yet well I know that were a woman possible as I am possible
then marriage would be possible—
Like SHE in her lonely alien gaud waiting her Egyptian lover
so I wait—bereft of 2,000 years and the bath of life.

For Discussion

1. What stereotyped images of marriage and homelife are presented in
   this poem?

2. Corso's style permits you to laugh, but you have probably felt many of these feelings and thought many of these thoughts yourself. Which ones? Have you rejected or seriously changed your attitudes toward marriage as a result of these thoughts and feelings?
3. Is Corso arguing that marriage be abolished, or is he suggesting that many of the rituals of marriage are meaningless?
4. The poet describes two types of wives and rejects one as a "pleasant prison dream." Why does he reject this type? Is it possible that he is rejecting both types in this one line?
5. Why is "SHE" capitalized in the second line from the end of the poem? Does this suggest to you an excessively idealized concept of women? Is there other evidence in the poem to this effect?
6. The poet suggests he might get married to escape growing old alone. Could such a marriage—or any instance of doing the right thing for the wrong reasons—be successful?

For Comparison

1. Based on what you know about his background, do you think Chig ("A Visit to Grandmother") might grow up with some of the attitudes expressed in this poem?
2. Is Corso fundamentally in agreement with Cadwallader's essay "Marriage as a Wretched Institution," or is he merely criticizing aspects of the marriage ritual? How might he and Cadwallader discuss marriage should they meet?

For Composition

1. We need (do not need) rituals.
2. The marriage myth.
3. The need to love and be loved.

photo by Suzanne Arms/Jeroboam, Inc.

Part Three

INDIVIDUAL-PEERS

In contemporary society it is impossible for an individual to live forever protected by the boundaries of family forces, however secure those forces might be. One of the most important and basic of all human desires is to be socially accepted, and this, the third level of involvement we will examine, adds an additional dimension to an individual's personal responsibilities.

Whether a person's friendships grow out of social or business reasons, they involve definite responsibilities. Often very complex problems evolve from these relationships because the knowledge friends have of each other and the obligations they feel toward each other are much more limited than within the family. Everyone makes friends for purely social reasons, and each individual friendship involves different but important attitudes toward responsibility. Friendships are constantly threatened because there is no natural force to make them permanent; but when they are faced by both parties with an attitude of good peer responsibility, they can develop into lasting, mutually rewarding experiences. Those relationships developed solely for business reasons also demand responsible attitudes. No business, however large, can exist for long without maintaining mutual trust and good will.

When you add peer responsibility to family and self-responsibility, you create a very complicated picture indeed; but it is a picture of the world in which you must learn to live. Some questions that you must answer are these: Should a person attempt to change the personality of another? Can one become too involved with other people? What is the significance of peer responsibility in light of the race issue? How may a person relate properly to peers without losing the sense of personal identity and responsibility?

145

NORMAN COUSINS

A COMMUNITY OF HOPE AND RESPONSIBILITY

The other day a friend of mine, like countless thousands of others throughout the country, received a telephone call from his broker. The stock market was in a deep dive. The broker advised my friend to sell, while there was still something left to sell. And, like many others, my friend sold—not because he thought there was anything wrong or unsound about the companies in which he had invested, but because he had been hit by a chain reaction of fear. It didn't occur to him that he might be helping to produce the very crash he dreaded, or that he might be contributing to a state of panic that might crack the economy and do grave damage to the country.

When I spoke to my friend about this, asking whether he didn't feel any sense of responsibility beyond his own Profit & Loss position, he stared at me coldly and said: "Let someone else be responsible. I'm looking out for Number One."

I thought back to a conversation I had with a Soviet economics professor in Moscow two years earlier. The Soviet professor said that Marxist scholars believed that capitalism would collapse ultimately—not solely because of inherent flaws in the structure of capitalism itself but because it wasn't really an ideology. He said that it inspired no sense of basic allegiance or willingness to sacrifice—the prime test of a strong ideology.

"Even your capitalists don't really believe in it," he said. "Whenever there is a real test of confidence, they turn and run. And the result is that the structure of capitalism will topple—because it won't have enough support from the people themselves."

He went on to say that the difference between communism and capitalism as economic doctrines was that the first was built to cope with adversity while the second was prone to it.

I told the Soviet economist that I believed he was mistaken about the notion that all Americans reacted the same way and would crumple in any genuine showdown. And his greatest error was the assumption that America lacked an ideology.

As I say, this discussion with a Soviet economist came to mind when my friend told me the other day that he felt no special responsibility beyond his own financial condition. There was no connection in his own mind between what he did and the gloating that took place in *Pravda* and in Communist circles throughout the world over the gyrations on Wall Street. In fact, my friend prides himself on being militantly anti-

Norman Cousins, "A Community of Hope and Responsibility," *Saturday Review*, June 16, 1962. Copyright 1962 Saturday Review, Inc.

Communist. He would yield second place in the decibel count to no one in his proclamations against communism. But his proclamations are meaningless alongside his actions. He doesn't comprehend that the best way of defending his society against totalitarianism is by doing all the things, small or large, that are required to make freedom work.

I think my friend would probably reply to this by saying that I am exaggerating his importance. After all, he might say, he is only one man. Why should I suppose that his one finger in the dyke could hold back the flood when everyone else was rushing for the dry highlands? More specifically, even if he hadn't told his broker to sell that Blue Monday, would it have made one whit of difference? Or would he have been left holding the bag—and an empty one at that?

In a sense, my friend represents the eternal and ultimate problem of a free society. It is the problem of the individual who thinks that one man cannot possibly make a difference in the destiny of that society.

It is the problem of the individual who doesn't really understand the nature of a free society or what is required to make it work.

It is the problem of the individual who has no comprehension of the multiplying power of single but sovereign units.

It is the problem of the individual who regards the act of pulling a single lever in a voting booth in numerical terms rather than historical terms.

It is the problem of the individual who has no real awareness of the millions of bricks that had to be put into place, one by one, over many centuries in order for him to dwell in the penthouse of freedom. Nor does he see any special obligation to those who built the structure or those who will have to live in it after him, for better or worse.

It is the problem of the individual who recognizes no direct relationship between himself and the decisions made by government in his name. Therefore, he feels no special obligation to dig hard for the information necessary to an understanding of the issues leading to those decisions.

In short, freedom's main problem is the problem of the individual who takes himself lightly historically—however well-rounded and indeed bloated he may take himself personally.

Having said this, I must admit that there are at least a few contributing factors. The individual is always responsible for the shape or direction a free society may take, but at the same time he is affected or conditioned by the general environment and by the general values he himself has helped to create.

My office is located in the largest city in the world. I look out from my window and see huge slabs of steel, concrete, and glass invading the sky. Many of these are new. A few of them have distinction, grace, spirit, even elegance. They make for expansion of the mind. Most of the others, however, look alike. Their claim on the esthetic imagination is quickly exhausted. Their sides contain row upon row of honeycombed slots, repeating themselves endlessly. It makes for a powerful spectacle, but it places at least some strain on the idea that an individual is a sovereign cause. An environment of compression, repetition, and massive routine does not quite furnish the ideal conditions for advancing a belief in the creative splendor and dignity of the individual.

When, suddenly, at the lunch hour or at five o'clock these monolithic hives disgorge their occupants, the notion of human individuality requires something approaching an act of faith. It would be a mistake to suppose that this has no effect on the human subconscious, pressing down upon it the constant evidence of individual inconsequentiality. Jefferson might have made at least a slight alteration here and there in his definition of human uniqueness if he had had to ride sixty floors in a crowded elevator four times a day. John Keats might have found it somewhat difficult to meditate on beauty or even to contemplate a Grecian urn after driving a car through mid-town traffic or spending an hour in search of a parking place.

There is no point in extolling the concept of human individuality without recognizing the increasing difficulties such individuality is expected to sustain. The idea that a glass box can light up from the inside and make it possible for the individual to witness events far away is surely one of the most magnificent ideas to come out of the inventive intelligence. Television still has this potential and some day, Mr. Minow willing, it may achieve it. At present, and for the most part, however, it has depressed individuality rather than expanded it. I make note of all the good things it has done, but its total effect has been to cheapen respect for life. The insistence of television on making people clobber one another constantly with fists or clubs, on making them fire bullets at each other —all this is having a debilitating effect on the preciousness and fragility of life, without which there can be no true respect for human individuality.

A casual attitude toward human hurt and pain is the beginning of the end of a free society. Long before a child learns how to read he learns how to turn on a television set. He is quickly introduced to a world of howling drunks, pampered idiots, wild-swinging and trigger-happy bullies, and gyp artists. He learns that sex is just another toy, and that there are always flashier ones for the taking. He learns that the way to express your disagreement with a man or your distaste for him is to clout him in the kisser or pour hot lead into his belly.

Education is not just what takes place in a building marked "school." Education is the sum total of all the experiences and impressions to which a young and plastic mind is exposed. The parent who insists on sending his child to the finest schools, but who sees no problem in allowing that child to spend at least an equal amount of time looking at TV gangster serials or Mickey Spillane, should not be surprised if the mind of his off-spring gives back the meanness and the sordidness put into it.

A free society—at least, this free society—has certain propositions that have gone into its making. These propositions aren't all political. One of the main propositions that had a certain vitality at the time this particular society was founded was that the individual man has a natural goodness inside him, that he is capable of responding to truth, that he is endowed with the capacity to recognize beauty and be enlarged by it.

These propositions, I submit, are now under attack—and not just by television. Whether with respect to motion pictures, or writing, or art today, I think we can find disturbing evidence that man is being cheapened—and cut down to a size much smaller than by natural rights he ought to be. The epic theme seems to be in retreat on a wide front. There seems to be a fascination with aberrations, a preoccupation with neuroticism, an obsession with aimlessness. The trend is to the harsh, the brassy, the abrasive. Nobility, sacrifice, idealism, beauty—these are too often dismissed as tall corn.

Not long ago, a friend suggested that I see the film "La Dolce Vita." It was, he said, quite remarkable and beautiful. I saw it. It was remarkable, all right; but I didn't see any beauty in it. The photography was striking, and I am even willing that the word beauty be used to describe some of the camera work. But I saw nothing beautiful about the people, or the lives they led, or their emotions, or their values, or what they did. The film was lacking in both sequence and consequence. The only point it had to make was that life was pointless. But what troubled me most of all was not the film itself but that our critical standards have themselves become so desensitized that the film could be called beautiful.

To offset this, fortunately, the other day I saw the Japanese film "The Island." It had no frenzy. It had no bashings or thrashings or wailings. It didn't make heroes of degenerates. It was not afraid of honest emotion. All it did was to show real people trying to cope with real problems. It was concerned with fundamentals of human relationships and response. It dealt with the fact of human devotion, even sacrifice. And because of all this there was an essential beauty in it. According to some definitions, perhaps, the film will be regarded as corny or sentimental. If it is corn, then it is high time we relished the kernel.

Incidentally, I was interested in the reaction of a friend who also saw the Japanese film. When I asked him his opinion, he said: "I know you will probably think it stupid of me, but I rather liked it." He almost found it necessary to apologize for responding to the simple but beautiful appeal of the film. He was almost afraid to trust his natural responses. He had become so intimidated by the dry-eyed, hard-boiled approach to life that he felt sheepish about acknowledging the existence inside him of that which distinguished him most of all from the ape.

One more instance. Recently, outside an art gallery on Fifty-Seventh Street in New York, I overheard two women discussing an abstract painting in the window. The painting, to my eyes, lacked creative thrust. It seemed to follow along meekly behind the works of better-known abstract artists. One of the women said to the other: "It looks like an inferior work to me; but I hate to say it out loud. You know, one feels like an idiot these days if he doesn't lavish the greatest praise on anything that seems incomprehensible."

I see no reason why anyone should allow himself to be intimidated into a feeling of total nullity or grim acquiescence if he sees something he happens not to like. He has the best credentials in the world for reacting; he has his individual taste buds. They may not coincide with those of others; they may run counter to those of experts, but at least they are his own, and the more he uses them the keener they become. No critic of stature—whether in literature or art or music—expects people to blot out their senses whenever he speaks. The critic applies his special training and knowledge to the work before him. He defines his standards. He sees himself as part of the total process by which a culture advances towards excellence. He certainly doesn't resent disagreement. And he doesn't discourage or disparage individual reactions—not if he is worth listening to, that is.

What I have been trying to suggest is that a free society cannot long remain free if man is in full retreat from man. For such a society pays a high price if the individual loses faith in his own centrality or in his ability to respond to creative beauty or in the stark fact of his ultimate responsibility.

This is a great deal of weight for a free man to carry; but if it is political and cultural weightlessness we are seeking, we don't have to get into outer space to find it. We can find it right here on earth and it goes by the name of totalitarianism.

There is no greater political or philosophical fallacy than the notion that freedom is not really an ideology. The ideology of freedom has the deepest foundation of all. It is fused with the nature of man. It exists in the molecular structure of man's own natural rights.

What is this ideology?

It is based on the proposition that government exists for the purpose of enhancing and protecting the natural and fundamental rights of individual human beings.

These rights do not have to be created or contrived. They exist. They are natural, essential, irrevocable. They come with the gift of life. The good society may recognize these rights but it cannot invent them. It cannot alter them; it cannot expunge them. Its obligation is to create the conditions under which they can grow and be secure.

Highest among these natural rights is the right of man to own himself. He cannot be owned by a nation, a group, or another man.

He owns the right to grow and to meet his potential.

He owns the right to appraise his abilities and to develop them and apply them, consistent with the rights of others.

He owns his thoughts and the right to nourish them and speak them, again consistent with the rights of others.

He owns the right to make mistakes, whether of thought or deed, without unreasonable punishment.

He owns the right to his hopes.

He owns the right to justice, whether his claim is against a person, an aggregation, or his own government.

He owns the right to contemplate human destiny and the mysteries of universal purpose, or the right to detach himself altogether from these pursuits.

He owns the right to hold grievances against his society and to make them known to other men in order to magnify his own voice.

He owns the right to make a better life for his young.

It is in these respects that a free society is not just a nation. It is an idea. It is a national sovereignty committed to the cause of human sovereignty. It seeks to create a proper environment for man's most enduring hopes. It is an instrument through which man may work for a fuller life —whether in terms of his physical needs or his creative and spiritual reach.

Our own free society has not yet fulfilled all these purposes. No one knows how near to or far from such fulfillment the American people may be. But the direction is clear. And the effort, however vast, will continue to be made. The great ideals and ordeals of human history go together.

The unfinished nature of our struggle should not separate or insulate us from an awareness of the needs and the rights of other peoples, nor does it sever this nation from the community of hope and responsibility in the world. The American people see a reflection of their own early history in those peoples who do not yet own their own nations. They see the cause of freedom from outside rule as a cause that connects all men. They accept that connection and are inspired by it.

The lands and cultures of man today are various, but they are all compressed into a single geographic abode. The question to be determined in our time is whether this abode can be preserved for man or whether it will become the arena of his last great combat. The means are now sufficient to punish nature itself, to put a torch to all of man's works, and to deprive him of the decencies that have given him distinction and pride.

In looking back at their own past, and in assessing their own purposes and ideals, the American people also look to the duty that unites them to all mankind—to create an enduring peace under law for this generation and the generations to come; to make the world safe for its diversity; to advance the cause of independence wherever peoples are not free and to create a pattern of interdependence for the whole; to use the resources of nature and the intelligence of man in the common good; to serve man's capacity to be free, and to justify the fact of life.

This is the ideology. It is real and it is ours.

For Discussion

1. What does Cousins mean when he writes, "a free society cannot long remain free if man is in full retreat from man"? How does he suggest that individuals retreat from one another?
2. What, according to Cousins, is the eternal and ultimate problem facing a free society? Do you agree? Why?
3. Do individuals have as much influence in society as Cousins suggests? Would his friend have been partially responsible if the stock market had crashed after he sold his stock?
4. Is there a danger that America might ultimately collapse because individuals are selfishly guarding their own interests rather than the broader interests of the country?
5. What are some of the especially important problems faced by someone who wants to be loyal to himself and to his society at the same time?

For Comparison

1. What might the husband in "The Bitter Bread" say about the rights detailed by Cousins near the end of this essay? Does he have any of those rights? Are his opportunities for having them better now than they were, say, a decade ago?
2. Cousins says "A casual attitude toward human hurt and pain is the beginning of the end of a free society." Relate this idea to Cather's "The Sculptor's Funeral."

For Composition

1. The individual in society.
2. The importance of one vote.
3. My responsibility to (club, church, social group, etc.).

JAMES BALDWIN

MY DUNGEON SHOOK: LETTER TO MY NEPHEW ON THE ONE HUNDREDTH ANNIVERSARY OF THE EMANCIPATION

Dear James:

I have begun this letter five times and torn it up five times. I keep seeing your face, which is also the face of your father and my brother. Like him, you are tough, dark, vulnerable, moody—with a very definite tendency to sound truculent because you want no one to think you are soft. You may be like your grandfather in this, I don't know, but certainly both you and your father resemble him very much physically. Well, he is dead, he never saw you, and he had a terrible life; he was defeated long before he died because, at the bottom of his heart, he really believed what white people said about him. This is one of the reasons that he became so holy. I am sure that your father has told you something about all that. Neither you nor your father exhibit any tendency towards holiness: you really *are* of another era, part of what happened when the Negro left the land and came into what the late E. Franklin Frazier called "the cities of destruction." You can only be destroyed by believing that you really are what the white world calls a *nigger*. I tell you this because I love you, and please don't you ever forget it.

I have known both of you all your lives, have carried your Daddy in my arms and on my shoulders, kissed and spanked him and watched him learn to walk. I don't know if you've known anybody from that far back; if you've loved anybody that long, first as an infant, then as a child, then as a man, you gain a strange perspective on time and human pain and effort. Other people cannot see what I see whenever I look into your father's face, for behind your father's face as it is today are all those other faces which were his. Let him laugh and I see a cellar your father does not remember and a house he does not remember and I hear in his present laughter his laughter as a child. Let him curse and I remember him falling down the cellar steps, and howling, and I remember, with pain, his tears, which my hand or your grandmother's so easily wiped away. But no one's hand can wipe away those tears he sheds invisibly today, which one hears in his laughter and in his speech and in his songs. I know what the world has done to my brother and how narrowly he has survived it. And I know, which is much worse, and this is the crime of which I accuse my country and my countrymen, and for which neither I nor time nor history will ever forgive them, that they have destroyed and are destroying hundreds of thousands of lives and do not know it and do not want to know it. One can be, indeed one must strive to become, tough and philosophical concerning destruction and death, for this is what most of mankind has been best at since we have heard of man. (But remember: *most* of mankind is not *all* of mankind.) But it is not permissible that the authors of devastation should also be innocent. It is the innocence which constitutes the crime.

Now, my dear namesake, these innocent and well-meaning people, your countrymen, have caused you to be born under conditions not very far removed from those described for us by Charles Dickens in the London of more than a hundred years ago. (I hear the chorus of the innocents screaming, "No! This is not true! How *bitter* you are!"—but I am writing this letter to *you*, to try to tell you something about how to handle *them*, for most of them do not yet really know that you exist. I *know* the conditions under which you were born, for I was there. Your countrymen were *not* there, and haven't made it yet. Your grandmother was also there, and no one has ever accused her of being bitter. I suggest that the innocents check with her. She isn't hard to find. Your countrymen don't know that *she* exists, either, though she has been working for them all their lives.)

Well, you were born, here you came, something like fifteen years ago; and though your father and mother and grandmother, looking about the streets through which they were carrying you, staring at the walls into which they brought you, had every reason to be heavyhearted, yet they were not. For here you were, Big James, named for me—you were a big baby, I was not—here you were: to be loved. To be loved, baby, hard, at once, and forever, to strengthen you against the loveless world. Remember that: I know how black it looks today, for you. It looked bad that day, too, yes, we were trembling. We have not stopped trembling yet, but if we had not loved each other none of us would have survived. And now you must survive because we love you, and for the sake of your children and your children's children.

This innocent country set you down in a ghetto in which, in fact, it intended that you should perish. Let me spell out precisely what I mean by that, for the heart of the matter is here, and the root of my dispute with my country. You were born where you were born and faced the future that you faced because you were black and *for no other reason.* The limits of your ambition were, thus, expected to be set forever. You were born into a society which spelled out with brutal clarity, and in as many ways as possible, that you were a worthless human being. You were not expected to aspire to excellence: you were expected to make peace with mediocrity. Wherever you have turned, James, in your short time on this earth, you have been told where you could go and what you could do (and *how* you could do it) and where you could live and whom you could marry. I know your countrymen do not agree with me about this, and I hear them saying, "You exaggerate." They do not know Harlem, and I do. So do you. Take no one's word for anything, including mine— but trust your experience. Know whence you came. If you know whence you came, there is really no limit to where you can go. The details and symbols of your life have been deliberately constructed to make you believe what white people say about you. Please try to remember that what they believe, as well as what they do and cause you to endure, does not testify to your inferiority but to their inhumanity and fear. Please try to be clear, dear James, through the storm which rages about your youthful head today, about the reality which lies behind the words *acceptance* and *integration*. There is no reason for you to try to become like white people and there is no basis whatever for their impertinent assumption that *they* must accept *you*. The really terrible thing, old buddy, is that *you* must accept *them*. And I mean that very seriously. You must accept them and accept them with love. For these innocent people have no other hope. They are, in effect, still trapped in a history which they do not understand; and until they understand it, they cannot be released from it. They have had to believe for many years, and for innumerable reasons, that black men are inferior to white men. Many of them, indeed, know better, but, as you will discover, people find it very difficult to act on what they know. To act is to be committed, and to be committed is to be in danger. In this case, the danger, in the minds of most white Americans, is the loss of their identity. Try to imagine how you would feel if you woke up one morning to find the sun shining and all the stars aflame. You would be frightened because it is out of the order of nature. Any upheaval in the universe is terrifying because it so profoundly attacks one's sense of one's own reality. Well, the black man has functioned in the white man's world as a fixed star, as an immovable pillar: and as he moves out of his place, heaven and earth are shaken to their foundations. You, don't be afraid. I said that it was intended that you should perish in the ghetto, perish by never being allowed to go behind the white man's definitions, by never being allowed to spell your proper name. You have, and many of us have, defeated this intention; and, by a terrible law, a terrible paradox, those innocents who believed that your imprisonment made them safe are losing their grasp of reality. But these men are your brothers—your lost, younger brothers. And if the word *integration* means anything, this is what it means: that we, with love, shall force our brothers to see themselves as they are, to cease fleeing from reality and begin to change it. For this is your home, my friend, do not be driven from it; great men have done great things here, and will again, and we can make America what America must become. It will be hard, James, but you come from sturdy, peasant stock, men who picked cotton and dammed rivers and built railroads, and, in the teeth of the most terrifying odds, achieved an unassailable and monumental dignity. You come from a long line of great poets, some of the greatest poets since Homer. One of them said, *The very time I thought I was lost, My dungeon shook and my chains fell off.*

You know, and I know, that the country is celebrating one hundred years of freedom one hundred years too soon. We cannot be free until they are free. God bless you, James, and Godspeed.

> Your uncle,
> James

For Discussion

1. What does Baldwin mean when he writes, "We cannot be free until they are free"?
2. What difference does Baldwin see between the two words "acceptance" and "integration"? How does an interpretation of these two words affect a person's attitude toward racial issues?
3. Baldwin places all of the blame for racial tension upon white society. For how much of the tension is the white community responsible? Why is it also important for the Black person to realize that a portion of the responsibility is his?

For Comparison

1. What kind of letter would Baldwin write to Ornita ("Black Is My Favorite Color")? What kind of letter would he write to Nat Lime?
2. Baldwin's ideas represent those of a Black author. What are some similar feelings expressed in "Lost Together with Our Children" regarding alienation from a Mexican-American point of view?

For Composition

1. Acceptance versus integration.
2. White society answers Baldwin.
3. Individual responsibility and minority groups.

MICHAEL GOLD

THE SOUL OF A LANDLORD

I

On the East Side people buy their groceries a pinch at a time; three cents' worth of sugar, five cents' worth of butter, everything in penny fractions. The good Jewish black bread that smells of harvest-time is sliced into a dozen parts and sold for pennies. But that winter even pennies were scarce.

There was a panic on Wall Street. Multitudes were without work; there were strikes, suicides, and food riots. The prostitutes roamed our street like wolves; never was there so much competition among them.

Life froze. The sun vanished from the deathly gray sky. The streets reeked with snow and slush. There were hundreds of evictions. I walked down a street between dripping tenement walls. The rotten slush ate through my shoes. The wind beat on my face. I saw a stack of furniture before a tenement: tables, chairs, a washtub packed with crockery and bed-clothes, a broom, a dresser, a lamp.

The snow covered them. The snow fell, too, on a little Jew and his wife and three children. They huddled in a mournful group by their possessions. They had placed a saucer on one of the tables. An old woman with a market bag mumbled a prayer in passing. She dropped a penny in the saucer. Other people did the same. Each time the evicted family lowered its eyes in shame. They were not beggars, but "respectable" people. But if enough pennies fell in the saucer, they might have rent for a new home. This was the one hope left them.

Winter. Building a snow fort one morning, we boys dug out a litter of frozen kittens and their mother. The little ones were still blind. They had been born into it, but had never seen our world.

Other dogs and cats were frozen. Men and women, too, were found dead in hallways and on docks. Mary Sugar Bum met her end in an alley. She was found half-naked, clutching a whisky bottle in her blue claw. This was her last "love" affair.

Horses slipped on the icy pavement, and quivered there for hours with broken legs, until a policeman arrived to shoot them.

The boys built a snow man. His eyes were two coals; his nose a potato. He wore a derby hat and smoked a corncob pipe. His arms were flung

From *Jews Without Money* by Michael Gold (New York: Liveright, 1930). By permission of the Evelyn Singer Agency, Inc.

wide; in one of them he held a broom, in the other a newspaper. This Golem with his amazed eyes and idiotic grin amused us all for an afternoon.

The next morning we found him strangely altered. His eyes and nose had been torn out; his grin smashed, like a war victim's. Who had played this joke? The winter wind.

II

Mrs. Rosenbaum owned a grocery store on our street. She was a widow with four children, and lived in two rooms back of the store. She slaved from dawn until midnight; a big, clumsy woman with a chapped face and masses of untidy hair; always grumbling, groaning, gossiping about her ailments. Sometimes she was nervous and screamed at her children, and beat them. But she was a kind-hearted woman, and that winter suffered a great deal. Everyone was very poor, and she was too good not to give them groceries on credit.

"I'm crazy to do it!" she grumbled in her icy store. "I'm a fool! But when a child comes for a loaf of bread, and I have the bread, and I know her family is starving, how can I refuse her? Yet I have my own children to think of! I am being ruined! The store is being emptied! I can't meet my bills!"

She was kind. Kindness is a form of suicide in a world based on the law of competition.

One day we watched the rewards of kindness. The sheriff's men arrived to seize Mrs. Rosenbaum's grocery. They tore down the shelves and fixtures, they carted off tubs of butter, drums of kerosene, sacks of rice, flour, and potatoes.

Mrs. Rosenbaum stood by, watching her own funeral. Her fat, kind face was swollen with crying as with toothache. Her eyes blinked in bewilderment. Her children clung to her skirts and cried. Snow fell from the sky, a crowd muttered in sympathy, a policeman twirled his club.

What happened to her after that, I don't know. Maybe the Organized Charities helped her; or maybe she died. O golden dyspeptic God of America, you were in a bad mood that winter. We were poor, and you punished us harshly for this worst of sins.

III

My father lay in bed. His shattered feet ached in each bone. His painter's sickness came back on him; he suffered with lung and kidney pains.

He was always depressed. His only distraction was to read the Yiddish newspapers, and to make gloomy conversation at night over the suicides, the hungry families, the robberies, murders, and catastrophes that newspapers record.

"It will come to an end!" said my father. "People are turning into wolves! They will soon eat each other! They will tear down the cities, and destroy the world in flames and blood!"

"Drink your tea," said my mother cheerfully, "God is still in the world. You will get better and work and laugh again. Let us not lose courage."

My father was fretful and nervous with an invalid's fears.

"But what if we are evicted, Katie?"

"We won't be evicted, not while I have my two hands and can work," said my mother.

"But I don't want you to work!" my father cried. "It breaks up our home!"

"It doesn't!" said my mother. "I have time and strength for everything."

IV

At first my mother had feared going out to work in a cafeteria among Christians. But after a few days she settled easily into the life of the polyglot kitchen, and learned to fight, scold, and mother the Poles, Germans, Italians, Irish, and Negroes who worked there. They liked her, and soon called her "Momma," which made her vain.

"You should hear how the big black dishwasher named Joe, how he comes to me today, and says, 'Momma, I'm going to quit. Everyone is against me here because I am black,' he says. 'The whole world is against us black people.'

"So I said to him, 'Joe, I am not against you. Don't be foolish, don't go out to be a bum again. The trouble with you here is you are lazy. If you would work harder the others would like you, too.' So he said, 'Momma, all right, I'll stay.' So that's how it is in the restaurant. They call me Momma, even the black ones."

It was a large, high-priced cafeteria for businessmen on lower Broadway. My mother was a chef's helper, and peeled and scoured tons of vegetables for cooking. Her wages were seven dollars a week.

She woke at five, cooked our breakfast at home, then had to walk a mile to her job. She came home at five-thirty, and made supper, cleaned the house, was busy on her feet until bedtime. It hurt my father's masculine pride to see his wife working for wages. But my mother liked it all; she was proud of earning money, and she liked her fights in the restaurant.

My dear, tireless, little dark-faced mother! Why did she always have to fight? Why did she have to give my father a new variety of headache with accounts of her battles for "justice" in the cafeteria? The manager there was a fat, blonde Swede with a *Kaiserliche* mustache, and the manners of Mussolini. All the workers feared this bull-necked tyrant, except my mother. She told him "what was what." When the meat was rotten, when the drains were clogged and smelly, or the dishwashers overworked, she told him so. She scolded him as if he were her child, and he listened meekly. The other workers fell into the habit of telling their complaints to my mother, and she would relay them to the Swedish manager.

"It's because he needs me," said my mother proudly. "That's why he lets me scold him. I am one of his best workers; he can depend on me in the rush. And he knows I am not like the other kitchen help; they work a day or two; then quit, but I stay on. So he's afraid to fire me, and I tell him what is what."

It was one of those super-cafeterias, with flowers on the tables, a string orchestra during the lunch hour, and other trimmings. But my mother had no respect for it. She would never eat the lunch served there to the employees, but took along two cheese sandwiches from home.

"Your food is *Dreck*, it is fit only for pigs," she told the manager bluntly. And once she begged me to promise never to eat hamburger steak in a restaurant when I grew up.

"Swear it to me, Mikey!" she said. "Never, never eat hamburger!"

"I swear it, momma."

"Poison!" she went on passionately. "They don't care if they poison the people, so long as there's money in it. I've seen with my own eyes. If I could write English, I'd write a letter to all the newspapers."

"Mind your own business!" my father growled. "Such things are for Americans. It is their country and their hamburger steak."

For Discussion

1. How is the snow man symbolic of the real people in this essay? To what extent is the fate of the people dependent upon nature? To what extent is it dependent upon other people?
2. What does Gold mean by the statement, "Kindness is a form of suicide in a world based on the law of competition"? Do you agree or disagree?
3. What specific attitudes expressed by the mother distinguish her from the father in the latter parts of this story? Which one do you feel is more responsible?
4. Why is the title of this essay important?

For Comparison

1. How would Nat Lime ("Black Is My Favorite Color") feel about the mother in this story? If you feel his attitude would differ sharply from the way it is depicted in his own story, explain exactly why.
2. In his own way, was the owner of the cafeteria providing "a clean, well-lighted place" for the mother? Was he helping her or using her?

For Composition

1. Poverty and pride.
2. Women should (should not) have to work.
3. Working for "The Man."

SHIRLEY JACKSON

AFTER YOU, MY DEAR ALPHONSE

Mrs. Wilson was just taking the gingerbread out of the oven when she heard Johnny outside talking to someone.

"Johnny," she called, "you're late. Come in and get your lunch."

"Just a minute, Mother," Johnny said. "After you, my dear Alphonse."

"After *you*, my dear Alphonse," another voice said.

"No, after *you*, my dear Alphonse," Johnny said.

Mrs. Wilson opened the door. "Johnny," she said, "you come in this minute and get your lunch. You can play after you've eaten."

Johnny came in after her, slowly. "Mother," he said, "I brought Boyd home for lunch with me."

"Boyd?" Mrs. Wilson thought for a moment. "I don't believe I've met Boyd. Bring him in, dear, since you've invited him. Lunch is ready."

"Boyd!" Johnny yelled. "Hey, Boyd, come on in!"

"I'm coming. Just got to unload this stuff."

"Well, hurry, or my mother'll be sore."

"Johnny, that's not very polite to either your friend or your mother," Mrs. Wilson said. "Come sit down, Boyd."

As she turned to show Boyd where to sit, she saw he was a Negro boy, smaller than Johnny but about the same age. His arms were loaded with split kindling wood. "Where'll I put this stuff, Johnny?" he asked.

Mrs. Wilson turned to Johnny, "Johnny," she said, "What is that wood?"

"Dead Japanese," Johnny said mildly. "We stand them in the ground and run over them with tanks."

"How do you do, Mrs. Wilson?" Boyd said.

"How do you do, Boyd? You shouldn't let Johnny make you carry all that wood. Sit down now and eat lunch, both of you."

"Why shouldn't he carry the wood, Mother? It's his wood. We got it at his place."

"Johnny," Mrs. Wilson said, "go on and eat your lunch."

"Sure," Johnny said. He held out the dish of scrambled eggs to Boyd. "After you, my dear Alphonse."

"After *you*, my dear Alphonse," Boyd said.

"After *you*, my dear Alphonse," Johnny said. They began to giggle.

"Are you hungry, Boyd?" Mrs. Wilson asked.

"Yes, Mrs. Wilson."

"Well, don't you let Johnny stop you. He always fusses about eating, so you just see that you get a good lunch. There's plenty of food here for you to have all you want."

"Thank you, Mrs. Wilson."

"Come on, Alphonse," Johnny said. He pushed half the scrambled eggs on to Boyd's plate. Boyd watched while Mrs. Wilson put a dish of stewed tomatoes beside his plate.

"Boyd don't eat tomatoes, do you, Boyd?" Johnny said.

"*Doesn't* eat tomatoes, Johnny. And just because you don't like them, don't say that about Boyd. Boyd will eat *anything*."

"Bet he won't," Johnny said, attacking his scrambled eggs.

"Boyd wants to grow up and be a big strong man so he can work hard," Mrs. Wilson said. "I'll bet Boyd's father eats stewed tomatoes."

"My father eats anything he wants to," Boyd said.

"So does mine," Johnny said. "Sometimes he doesn't eat hardly anything. He's a little guy, though. Wouldn't hurt a flea."

"Mine's a little guy, too," Boyd said.

"I'll bet he's strong, though," Mrs. Wilson said. She hesitated. "Does he . . . work?"

"Sure," Johnny said "Boyd's father works in a factory."

"There, you see?" Mrs. Wilson said. "And he certainly has to be strong to do that—all that lifting and carrying at a factory."

"Boyd's father doesn't have to," Johnny said. "He's a foreman."

Mrs. Wilson felt defeated. "What does your mother do, Boyd?"

"My mother?" Boyd was surprised. "She takes care of us kids."

"Oh. She doesn't work, then?"

"Why should she?" Johnny said through a mouthful of eggs. "You don't work."

"You really don't want any stewed tomatoes, Boyd?"

"No, thank you, Mrs. Wilson," Boyd said.

"No, thank you, Mrs. Wilson, no, thank you, Mrs. Wilson, no, thank you, Mrs. Wilson," Johnny said. "Boyd's sister's going to work, though. She's going to be a teacher."

"That's a very fine attitude for her to have, Boyd." Mrs. Wilson restrained an impulse to pat Boyd on the head. "I imagine you're all very proud of her?"

"I guess so," Boyd said.

"What about all your other brothers and sisters? I guess all of you want to make just as much of yourselves as you can."

"There's only me and Jean," Boyd said. "I don't know yet what I want to be when I grow up."

"We're going to be tank drivers, Boyd and me," Johnny said. "Zoom." Mrs. Wilson caught Boyd's glass of milk as Johnny's napkin ring, suddenly transformed into a tank plowed heavily across the table.

"Look, Johnny," Boyd said. "Here's a foxhole. I'm shooting at you."

Mrs. Wilson, with the speed born of long experience, took the gingerbread off the shelf and placed it carefully between the tank and the foxhole.

"Now eat as much as you want to, Boyd," she said. "I want to see you get filled up."

"Boyd eats a lot, but not as much as I do," Johnny said. "I'm bigger than he is."

"You're not much bigger," Boyd said. "I can beat you running."

Mrs. Wilson took a deep breath. "Boyd," she said. Both boys turned to her. "Boyd, Johnny has some suits that are a little too small for him, and a winter coat. It's not new, of course, but there's lots of wear in it still. And I have a few dresses that your mother or sister could probably use. Your mother can make them over into lots of things for all of you, and I'd be very happy to give them to you. Suppose before you leave I make up a big bundle and then you and Johnny can take it over to your mother right away . . ." Her voice trailed off as she saw Boyd's puzzled expression.

"But I have plenty of clothes, thank you," he said. "And I don't think my mother knows how to sew very well, and anyway I guess we buy about everything we need. Thank you very much though."

"We don't have time to carry that old stuff around, Mother," Johnny said. "We got to play tanks with the kids today."

Mrs. Wilson lifted the plate of gingerbread off the table as Boyd was about to take another piece. "There are many little boys like you, Boyd, who would be grateful for the clothes someone was kind enough to give them."

"Boyd will take them if you want him to, Mother," Johnny said.

"I didn't mean to make you mad, Mrs. Wilson," Boyd said.

"Don't think I'm angry, Boyd. I'm just disappointed in you, that's all. Now let's not say anything more about it."

She began clearing the plates off the table, and Johnny took Boyd's hand and pulled him to the door. " 'Bye, Mother," Johnny said. Boyd stood for a minute, staring at Mrs. Wilson's back.

"After you, my dear Alphonse," Johnny said, holding the door open.

"Is your mother still mad?" Mrs. Wilson heard Boyd ask in a low voice.

"I don't know," Johnny said. "She's screwy sometimes."

"So's mine," Boyd said. He hesitated. "After *you*, my dear Alphonse."

For Discussion

1. What is the significance of the title of this story?
2. In what specific ways does Mrs. Wilson show that she feels Boyd inferior? How typical of white, middle-class society are her attitudes?
3. What are the two boys' feelings toward one another? Why do their racial differences not matter to them? Is their indifference to race something they have learned or is it natural? Is Mrs. Wilson's racial discrimination something learned or is it natural?
4. When he is older, will Johnny's attitude be similar to his mother's? Do you feel that racial issues will be more easily solved by the members of the present younger generation than by their parents? Why?

For Comparison

1. What would be Boyd's response if he received a letter similar to Baldwin's "Letter to My Nephew"? With what parts of the letter would he agree? With what parts would he disagree?
2. Do you think Johnny will develop similar attitudes toward Negroes as those held by Nat Lime in "Black Is My Favorite Color"? How is Johnny's relationship with Boyd similar or different to that early relationship between Nat and his first Black playmate?

For Composition

1. Racial tolerance is (is not) natural.
2. Racial discrimination is (is not) natural.
3. If I brought home a (member of any racial minority group).

ERNEST HEMINGWAY

A CLEAN, WELL-LIGHTED PLACE

It was late and everyone had left the café except an old man who sat in the shadow the leaves of the tree made against the electric light. In the day time the street was dusty, but at night the dew settled the dust and the old man liked to sit late because he was deaf and now at night it was quiet and he felt the difference. The two waiters inside the café knew that the old man was a little drunk, and while he was a good client they knew that if he became too drunk he would leave without paying, so they kept watch on him.

"Last week he tried to commit suicide," one waiter said.

"Why?"

"He was in despair."

"What about?"

"Nothing."

"How do you know it was nothing?"

"He has plenty of money."

They sat together at a table that was close against the wall near the door of the café and looked at the terrace where the tables were all empty except where the old man sat in the shadow of the leaves of the tree that moved slightly in the wind. A girl and a soldier went by in the street. The street light shone on the brass number on his collar. The girl wore no head covering and hurried beside him.

"The guard will pick him up," one waiter said.

"What does it matter if he gets what he's after?"

"He had better get off the street now. The guard will get him. They went by five minutes ago."

The old man sitting in the shadow rapped on his saucer with his glass. The younger waiter went over to him.

"What do you want?"

The old man looked at him. "Another brandy," he said.

"You'll be drunk," the waiter said. The old man looked at him. The waiter went away.

"He'll stay all night," he said to his colleague. "I'm sleepy now. I never get into bed before three o'clock. He should have killed himself last week."

The waiter took the brandy bottle and another saucer from the counter inside the café and marched out to the old man's table. He put down the saucer and poured the glass full of brandy.

"You should have killed yourself last week," he said to the deaf man. The old man motioned with his finger. "A little more," he said. The waiter poured on into the glass so that the brandy slopped over and ran down the stem into the top saucer of the pile. "Thank you," the old man said. The waiter took the bottle back inside the café. He sat down at the table with his colleague again.

"He's drunk now," he said.

"He's drunk every night."

"What did he want to kill himself for?"

"How should I know."

"How did he do it?"

"He hung himself with a rope."

"Who cut him down?"

"His niece."

"Why did they do it?"

"Fear for his soul."

"How much money has he got?"

"He's got plenty."

"He must be eighty years old."

"Anyway I should say he was eighty."

"I wish he would go home. I never get to bed before three o'clock. What kind of hour is that to go to bed?"

"He stays up because he likes it."

"He's lonely. I'm not lonely. I have a wife waiting in bed for me."

"He had a wife once too."

"A wife would be no good to him now."

"You can't tell. He might be better with a wife."

"His niece looks after him. You said she cut him down."

"I know."

"I wouldn't want to be that old. An old man is a nasty thing."

"Not always. This old man is clean. He drinks without spilling. Even now, drunk. Look at him."

"I don't want to look at him. I wish he would go home. He has no regard for those who must work."

The old man looked from his glass across the square, then over at the waiters.

"Another brandy," he said, pointing to his glass. The waiter who was in a hurry came over.

"Finished," he said, speaking with that omission of syntax stupid people employ when talking to drunken people or foreigners. "No more tonight. Close now."

"Another," said the old man.

"No. Finished." The waiter wiped the edge of the table with a towel and shook his head.

The old man stood up, slowly counted the saucers, took a leather coin purse from his pocket and paid for the drinks, leaving half a peseta tip.

The waiter watched him go down the street, a very old man walking unsteadily but with dignity.

"Why didn't you let him stay and drink?" the unhurried waiter asked. They were putting up the shutters. "It is not half-past two."

"I want to go home to bed."

"What is an hour?"

"More to me than to him."

"An hour is the same."

"You talk like an old man yourself. He can buy a bottle and drink at home."

"It's not the same."

"No, it is not," agreed the waiter with a wife. He did not wish to be unjust. He was only in a hurry.

"And you? You have no fear of going home before your usual hour?"

"Are you trying to insult me?"

"No, hombre, only to make a joke."

"No," the waiter who was in a hurry said, rising from pulling down the metal shutters. "I have confidence. I am all confidence."

"You have youth, confidence, and a job," the older waiter said. "You have everything."

"And what do you lack?"

"Everything but work."

"You have everything I have."

"No. I have never had confidence and I am not young."

"Come on. Stop talking nonsense and lock up."

"I am of those who like to stay late at the café," the older waiter said. "With all those who do not want to go to bed. With all those who need a light for the night."

"I want to go home and into bed."

"We are of two different kinds," the older waiter said. He was now dressed to go home. "It is not only a question of youth and confidence although those things are very beautiful. Each night I am reluctant to close up because there may be some one who needs the café."

"Hombre, there are bodegas open all night long."

"You do not understand. This is a clean and pleasant café. It is well lighted. The light is very good and also, now there are shadows of the leaves."

"Good night," said the younger waiter.

"Good night," the other said. Turning off the electric light he continued the conversation with himself. It is the light of course but it is necessary that the place be clean and pleasant. You do not want music. Certainly you do not want music. Nor can you stand before a bar with dignity although that is all that is provided for these hours. What did he fear? It was not fear or dread. It was a nothing that he knew too well. It was all a nothing and a man was nothing too. It was only that and light was all it needed and a certain cleanness and order. Some lived in it and never felt it but he knew it all was nada y pues nada y nada y pues nada. Our nada who art in nada, nada be thy name thy kingdom nada thy will be nada in nada as it is in nada. Give us this nada our daily nada and nada us our nada as we nada our nadas and nada us not into nada but deliver us from nada; pues nada. Hail nothing full of nothing, nothing is with thee. He smiled and stood before a bar with a shining steam pressure coffee machine.

"What's yours?" asked the barman.

"Nada."

"Otro loco mas," said the barman and turned away.

"A little cup," said the waiter.

The barman poured it for him.

"The light is very bright and pleasant but the bar is unpolished," the waiter said.

The barman looked at him but did not answer. It was too late at night for conversation.

"You want another copita?" the barman asked.

"No, thank you," said the waiter and went out. He disliked bars and bodegas. A clean, well-lighted café was a very different thing. Now, without thinking further, he would go home to his room. He would lie in the bed and finally, with daylight, he would go to sleep. After all, he said to himself, it is probably only insomnia. Many must have it.

For Discussion

1. How do the two waiters reveal their very different attitudes? What are their individual attitudes? How much do you think their attitudes reflect thinking typical of their respective ages?
2. Did the old man's niece have a responsibility to save him from his suicide attempt? Does a person have the right to take his own life?

3. How true is the older waiter's comment that life "was all a nothing and a man was nothing too"?
4. Do we have a responsibility to provide clean, well-lighted places for other persons? What are some such places which you feel society has already provided? What are some others which you suggest be created?

For Comparison

1. Who has provided a "clean, well-lighted place" for Harvey in "The Sculptor's Funeral"? What speakers in Cather's story suggest the selfishness of Hemingway's younger waiter?
2. Hemingway's story seems to suggest that every man is an island unto himself. Is his story really a rejection of Donne's philosophy ("No Man Is an Island"), or is there a deeper meaning in Hemingway's story which supports Donne's ideas? Explain.

For Composition

1. The hell of being lonely.
2. Our brother's keeper.
3. The older waiter is right.

JESSE HILL FORD

THE BITTER BREAD

It was after Christmas, towards the end of December. There had come a sudden thaw. The roads got soft—the Devil was baking his bread, as the saying is, getting ready to pass out the hard luck for the New Year.

"Yes, yes," said the midwife, coming behind Robert in the narrow lane, toting her black suitcase. "It happen this way every year."

Maybe, thought Robert, maybe not. The damp cold tugged at his hands. Tonight the roads would freeze again. He looked back, "Can't you walk no faster?" he said.

"The first chile alway slow," she replied.

"She alone by herself though," Robert said. "Lemme tote that bag—"

"Don't nobody tote this bag but me."

From *Fishes, Birds and Sons of Men* by Jesse Hill Ford, by permission of Little, Brown and Co. in association with The Atlantic Monthly Press. Copyright © 1966 by Jesse Hill Ford; and Sarah Davis Ford and Katherine Kieffer Musgrove, Trustees.

He waited up until she came alongside him and then, reluctantly, he matched his pace with her own. A hawk went hunting rabbits above the dun-colored fields to the left, patiently tracing back and forth, hovering along the shaggy fence rows. Woods already dark with the cold shadows of winter lay to the right of the lane.

He smelled woodsmoke. His dog, a little brown fice, yapped three times, nervously, like a fox, and ran under the house.

"He won't bite," Robert said leading the way across the porch and entering the little room ahead of the midwife. On the bed beside the fireplace, Jeannie had not raised up.

"It's just me," said the midwife. Jeannie stirred. "How old is she?"

"She sixteen," Robert said. He squatted down and set two hickory logs into the fire. The logs hissed. Flame flickered from the red and yellow embers. It fluttered above the logs in the smoke. "How you feeling, Jeannie?" He asked without looking at the bed.

"No, no, no," said the midwife. Robert stood up. He looked around. The midwife had opened her suitcase. "We must take her to the hospital. Wrap her up warm. See how drowsy she is? Feel her?"

"Yes'm."

"Fever," said the midwife. "You ain't got a truck?"

"No."

"Wagon?"

"No."

"Then we have to tote her. Down to the main road we can flag somebody." The midwife leaned over the bed. "We got to get you to town, understand me? Can you hear? You too drowsy—hear?"

"Yes," Jeannie said. She did not open her eyes.

"How you feel?" Robert said.

"I hurt some," Jeannie said in a sleepy voice.

Robert got her shoes from the hearth.

"Don't bother with that. We'll wrap her up like a baby, see here? Now, lift her," said the midwife. "That's the time."

"She feel hot," Robert said.

The midwife was ahead of him, out the door and across the bare yard. "Makase," she said, going ahead of him almost at a trot now. Carrying Jeannie held close against her knees and her shoulders, Robert followed the midwife down the lane. The mud was already beginning to freeze crisp. Sunset made a dark red glow in the sky beyond soft fields of dead grass. Ahead and above him he saw the stars of evening.

Dark had come swiftly down by the time they reached the embankment to the highway. The midwife took off her scarf and waved the first approaching headlights. A pickup truck stopped. The midwife opened the door. "This girl need to go to the hospital . . . ."

"Get in," said the white man.

Robert climbed into the warm cab, holding Jeannie on his lap like a child. The midwife closed the door and waved good-bye. The truck moved down the highway.

"She having a baby."

"Oh." The white man turned the heater up and stepped harder on the gas pedal. Robert's feet began to tingle and get warm. The lights of Somerton appeared. At the Negro entrance to the hospital, down a narrow drive at the rear of the flat stopped the truck. He climbed out and came around to Robert's side. He opened the door.

"How much do I owe you?" Robert said, climbing down with Jeannie in his arms.

"Nothing," the man said. "I was coming in town anyhow." He walked ahead and opened the door to the hospital.

"I'm much obliged to," Robert said.

"You're welcome," said the man. "Good luck." And he was gone.

In one corner of the waiting room there was a statue of Lord Jesus, standing on a pedestal. Beside the Coca-Cola machine in the hall stood another statue, Mary, dressed in blue robes. "Yes, can I help you?" The white nurse came from behind the counter.

"We need the white doctor," Robert said.

"What's her troubles?"

"Baby," said Robert.

The nurse turned and walked up the corridor. She came back rolling a narrow hospital cart.

Now it's going to be all right, Robert thought. He put Jeannie on the cart.

"Straight down the hall to the front office. You'll see a window. The sign says 'Hospital Admissions.' "

"What about the doctor, please ma'am?"

"After she's admitted to the hospital we'll call the doctor. Meanwhile she can lie here in the hall."

"Yes'm," Robert said.

He went down the strange corridor. The woman behind the admissions window was a Sister in black robes. Robert answered her questions one after another while she filled in a white form.

"Fifty dollars," the Sister said.

"Yes'm. Put it on the book, I'll pay it."

"Cash, now," she said.

He reached into the pocket of his denim jacket and brought out the bills and the change, six dollars and forty-seven cents. He laid it out for her. "I can put this here down."

"Didn't you hear me just explain to you a while ago? We have rules.

Your wife can't be admitted until you've paid fifty dollars cash in advance."

"Fifty dollars," Robert said.

"Fifty dollars," the Sister said. "I didn't make the rule."

"She need the white doctor," Robert said.

"I'm sure she does, and we'll call the doctor as soon as we can get her into a hospital bed. The doctor can't deliver babies out in the hall. I'll hold these papers while you go for the money."

"Yes'm, I don't have it."

"Then you'll have to borrow it, won't you?"

"Yes'm."

She turned away in the bright, silent room beyond the glass, bent about other business. Robert went out the front and walked quickly down the road. For the first time he knew he had been sweating in the warm corridor because the cold came through his clothes. The sweat combined with it to chill him. He pushed his hands into the pockets of his coat and set off walking. Fear caught at him then. He began suddenly to run down the side of the road. He turned and waved at the lights of a car. It passed him slowly by, its exhaust making a steamy white plume in the air that was freezing him. He began running again. He ran down towards the intersection, past a row of neat white houses. Dogs rushed down the lawns and leaped the ditch, barking. He walked then. The dogs backed nervously away, whining at the strange smell of him.

At the corner he stopped. There was a filling station on his right, well lit, and painted blue and red. Inside the station two white men warmed themselves beside a kerosene heater. He crossed the street. A sidewalk took up on the other side and he began running again. He had a glimpse of white faces peering at him from the passing cars. He ran doggedly on, sweating again, breathing through his mouth, and tasting the bite of the cold air. By now, he thought, the land would be frozen—nearly hard as this sidewalk, by now.

He passed the last houses in the white section of town. He saw the cotton gin and the railroad crossing. He stopped running and walked along enough for his heart to stop pounding so, long enough for the ache inside to ease a bit. Beyond the rail crossing and up a side street he saw Joe-Thell's barbecue stand and the beer hall.

Robert had passed some time in the place on Saturday evenings at strawberry harvest and during cotton season. He ran up the street and pushed through the flimsy door. Joe-Thell looked up, frightened. "What's wrong?" he said. "Say, Robert?" There were no customers in the place.

"I need to borrow fifty dollars," Robert said.

"That quick," said Joe-Thell. He was an old man, wise in the ways of the world and never at a loss for words. He listened as Robert explained, nodding to let Robert know he had heard the same story six dozen times before. Joe-Thell nodded, sadly amused. He struck a kitchen match and lit his cigarette. He wiped his hands on his apron.

"This time of year though," said Joe-Thell, "people ain't got any work. People ain't got no money, and you got nothing to hock."

"If it was another time of year I wouldn't need to borrow," Robert said. "I can pay back."

"If I had it you could have it," said Joe-Thell. "But I don't have it. Here it is already after dark."

"Then who does have it?" Robert said. "Jeannie up there laying in the hall."

"You got to have a lender, Robert. Mama Lavorn about the only one I know that might go that high with you this time of year."

"Mama Lavorn?"

"Sure," Joe-Thell said. "Over to the Cafe and Tourist. Don't you know the Cafe and Tourist?" Joe-Thell was smiling a weary smile. "Look here, Robert. Go back to the crossing then follow the dirt street by the tracks, that's south on a dirt street that angles and slants off. Mama Lavorn got a red light that winks on and off above her front entrance. It's up that road on the right-hand side."

"Mama Lavorn," Robert said.

"Tell her I sent you. Say to her Joe-Thell said she might go that high."

Robert was already backing away to the door. He turned suddenly out into the cold again, running back the way he had come, crossing the railroad and running; crashing through thin ice into a puddle of freezing water. He leaped up, the front of him wet through. He was stung by the cold water. Almost without knowing it he was running again, but carefully now, watching for the pale gleam of the frozen puddles. His thin clothes began to stiffen in front where the puddle had wet them. His hands burned.

He crossed the porch beneath the blinking red light bulb and opened the front door. He saw Mama Lavorn smiling at him. She sat in a high chair behind the cash register. She was a fat, dark woman in a purple dress. She wore earbobs that glittered like ice when she moved her head.

"Lord, look here!" said Mama Lavorn. "I mean somebody's in a hurry!"

Her smile disappeared as he began talking. "So you need fifty dollars," she said. "You know anyplace else you can get it?" She didn't wait for him to say no, but went on: "Because if you do I'm going to give you good advice. Go there and get it. I'm a lender. If you get it here it's going to cost you money—if you get it."

"Please . . ." he said.

"The interest on a dollar for one week is two bits—twenty-five cents," she said. "In a week this fifty dollars gonna come to sixty-two fifty. Put it another way, you can bring me twelve and a half dollars every Saturday to take care of the interest and keep the fifty dollars until strawberry season if you have to."

Robert nodded. "Sign here, on this line." She pushed him a check on the Farmers and Merchants Bank. She handed him her fountain pen. He signed the check. "If you come up and don't pay, or if you miss a payment, all I have to do is take this check to court and they'll come after you. It means jail then, don't you know?"

"Yes'm."

She counted the money out of the cash drawer and into his big hand. "How come you so wet?"

"I fell," he said. Clutching the money, he made himself walk out the door. Then he ran.

Now, he was thinking, it will be all right. Running was easier now. The way back seemed shorter. The sidewalk started again. Almost before he knew it he saw the blue-and-red filling station, then the two white men, standing inside as before, beside the heater. They drew back as though astonished and let him pass. Lightly he bounded over the dead short grass on the hospital lawn and took his time then, opening the front door approaching the admissions window. He laid the five bills on the black marble shelf.

Silently the sister took the money, counted it, and pushed him a receipt. "Take this to the nurse."

"The doctor?"

"The doctor will be called."

He went down to the Negro waiting room. The nurse took the receipt. "Do you have a regular doctor?"

"No," he said, "no, Ma'am."

The nurse picked up the phone. Robert walked around the corner and into the hall to the cart. The hallway was dim. It didn't seem proper to touch his wife, not here.

"What took me so long," he said softly, "I had to go after the money."

Jeannie made no answer. Resting, he thought.

He walked back to the waiting room. It was deserted. Only Christ and Mary looked at him from pale, hard eyes. The red eye in the cold-drink machine said "Nickels Only." The doctor came briskly up the hall, nodded in Robert's direction, and muttered something to the nurse. The two of them went into the dim hallway. Presently they came back. "Should have called me at once!" the doctor said. "How long ago did you bring her in?"

"I think . . . ."

"You think?" The doctor came slowly from behind the counter. "Robert?" The doctor's white face had a smooth powdered look. His eyes were soft and blue.

"Sir?"

"Your wife's dead. She's been dead maybe half an hour. Sister will refund your fifty dollars. There'll be no fee for my services. There's the body to be taken care of—I usually call the L. B. Jones Funeral Parlor for Colored."

"And they bury her?"

"Well, they fix her and arrange a burial for her, yes. You have a burial policy?"

"I don't have one," Robert said.

"Doctor?" It was the nurse. The doctor went to the counter. The doctor took out his fountain pen. In a moment he returned, holding a slip of paper. He handed the paper to Robert.

"That's the death certificate. However you decide about handling the burial will be all right. Whoever does it will need this."

"Thank you, sir," Robert said. He sat down on the yellow patterned sofa. The doctor went away.

Presently a priest appeared. "I'm sorry about your wife, my son. She's in the arms of God now. She's with God. Are you a Catholic?"

"No, sir."

"We always ask. Not many Negroes are Catholics. We've few converts among the Negro personnel who work here at the hospital."

"Yes, sir."

"Can I help you in any way? With arrangements?"

The nurse handed something to the priest, who then handed it to Robert—the fifty dollars. Robert put the bills in the damp, cold pocket of his cloth jacket. He carefully folded the death certificate then. The embarrassment of grief had begun to blind him a little—to make him dizzy. He stood up and pushed the slip of white paper into the watch pocket of his overalls.

A big man, taller than the white people, he felt better standing up.

"We can't keep the body here," the nurse was saying.

Robert walked down the hall to the cart. He pulled the white sheet away. Then he wrapped Jeannie carefully in her quilt. He lifted her in his arms.

"If I can help in any way," the priest was saying. "If there's anyone I can call . . . ."

"Just open the door, please sir," Robert said.

The priest looked at the nurse. "Oh, this happens, it happens," the nurse said. "Wait till you've been here long as I have."

The priest opened the door. "God love you," he said.

Robert stepped into the cold. He walked slowly at first, until he reached the road, then he shifted his burden to his shoulder. It rested lightly. He walked at a quick steady pace and was soon out of town, beyond the last yellow street lamp. He chose the longer way, by the old road, a hard, narrow winding road that soon played out to gravel wending between the frozen fields.

At last he crossed the highway, climbed down the embankment, and entered the lane. His shoulder was numb. His side had begun to ache. As he had known it would be, the earth in the lane was frozen hard. The ground everywhere would be hard this night. Like a taste of sudden sickness, grief welled up inside him again, bone-hard and hard as the frozen ground, yet after the first few strokes of the pick the crust finally would give way. He knew the spade would bite and bite again, deeper and deeper still.

For Discussion

1. What elements of description and dialogue give this story a regional tone?
2. Examine the description of the hawk hunting rabbits. What symbolism might be found in this scene that will help interpret later events in the story?
3. Explain the role of the white man who drove Jeannie and Robert to the hospital. Was he being responsible, or was he trapped into the situation?
4. What dimension is added to the story when you discover that the hospital is run by a religious order?
5. What is your opinion of Joe-Thell? What role does he play in the story? What about Mama Lavorn?
6. Do you feel the priest, who is obviously new to situations like this, will be able to change them in any way, or will he finally fall into the pattern of acceptance?

For Comparison

1. This story and Gold's essay "The Soul of a Landlord" both deal with minority groups living in poverty. Discuss elements of poverty in each selection. In which does poverty seem the most oppressive?

2. McKuen ("Channing Way, I") says "It's always the strangers that do the most damage." Is this statement true in Robert's experience? Who were the strangers? Would you include Joe-Thell and Mama Lavorn among the strangers?

For Composition

1. Robert would (would not) find help easily today.
2. How I feel about the hospital in the story.
3. A time when I had no money and was desperate.

AMBROSE BIERCE

THE COUP DE GRÂCE

The fighting had been hard and continuous; that was attested by all the senses. The very taste of battle was in the air. All was now over; it remained only to succor the wounded and bury the dead—to "tidy up a bit," as the humorist of a burial squad put it. A good deal of "tidying up" was required. As far as one could see through the forests, among the splintered trees, lay wrecks of men and horses. Among them moved the stretcher-bearers, gathering and carrying away the few who showed signs of life. Most of the wounded had died of neglect while the right to minister to their wants was in dispute. It is an army regulation that the wounded must wait; the best way to care for them is to win the battle. It must be confessed that victory is a distinct advantage to a man requiring attention, but many do not live to avail themselves of it.

The dead were collected in groups of a dozen or a score and laid side by side in rows while the trenches were dug to receive them. Some, found at too great a distance from these rallying points, were buried where they lay. There was little attempt at identification, though in most cases, the burial parties being detailed to glean the same ground which they had assisted to reap, the names of the victorious dead were known and listed. The enemy's fallen had to be content with counting. But of that they got enough: many of them were counted several times, and the total, as given afterward in the official report of the victorious commander, denoted rather a hope than a result.

From Ambrose Bierce, *The Collected Writings of Ambrose Bierce*, copyright 1946, Citadel Press, Inc., 222 Park Avenue South, New York 10003.

At some little distance from the spot where one of the burial parties had established its "bivouac of the dead," a man in the uniform of a Federal officer stood leaning against a tree. From his feet upward to his neck his attitude was that of weariness reposing; but he turned his head uneasily from side to side; his mind was apparently not at rest. He was perhaps uncertain in which direction to go; he was not likely to remain long where he was, for already the level rays of the setting sun straggled redly through the open spaces of the wood and the weary soldiers were quitting their task for the day. He would hardly make a night of it alone there among the dead. Nine men in ten whom you meet after a battle inquire the way to some fraction of the army—as if any one could know. Doubtless this officer was lost. After resting himself a moment he would presumably follow one of the retiring burial squads.

When all were gone he walked straight away into the forest toward the red west, its light staining his face like blood. The air of confidence with which he now strode along showed that he was on familiar ground; he had recovered his bearings. The dead on his right and on his left were unregarded as he passed. An occasional low moan from some sorely-stricken wretch whom the relief-parties had not reached, and who would have to pass a comfortless night beneath the stars with his thirst to keep him company, was equally unheeded. What, indeed, could the officer have done, being no surgeon and having no water?

At the head of a shallow ravine, a mere depression of the ground, lay a small group of bodies. He saw, and swerving suddenly from his course walked rapidly toward them. Scanning each one sharply as he passed, he stopped at last above one which lay at a slight remove from the others, near a clump of small trees. He looked at it narrowly. It seemed to stir. He stooped and laid his hand upon its face. It screamed.

The officer was Captain Downing Madwell, of a Massachusetts regiment of infantry, a daring and intelligent soldier, an honorable man.

In the regiment were two brothers named Halcrow—Caffal and Creede Halcrow. Caffal Halcrow was a sergeant in Captain Madwell's company, and these two men, the sergeant and the captain, were devoted friends. In so far as disparity of rank, difference in duties and considerations of military discipline would permit they were commonly together. They had, indeed, grown up together from childhood. A habit of the heart is not easily broken off. Caffal Halcrow had nothing military in his taste nor disposition, but the thought of separation from his friend was disagreeable; he enlisted in the company in which Madwell was second-lieutenant. Each had taken two steps upward in rank, but between the highest non-commissioned and the lowest commissioned officer the gulf is deep and wide and the old relation was maintained with difficulty and a difference.

Creede Halcrow, the brother of Caffal, was the major of the regiment—a cynical, saturnine man, between whom and Captain Madwell there was a natural antipathy which circumstances had nourished and strengthened to an active animosity. But for the restraining influence of their mutual relation to Caffal these two patriots would doubtless have endeavored to deprive their country of each other's services.

At the opening of the battle that morning the regiment was performing outpost duty a mile away from the main army. It was attacked and nearly surounded in the forest, but stubbornly held its ground. During a lull in the fighting, Major Halcrow came to Captain Madwell. The two exchanged formal salutes, and the major said: "Captain, the colonel directs that you push your company to the head of this ravine and hold your place there until recalled. I need hardly apprise you of the dangerous character of the movement, but if you wish, you can, I suppose, turn over the command to your first-lieutenant. I was not, however, directed to authorize the substitution; it is merely a suggestion of my own, unofficially made."

To this deadly insult Captain Madwell coolly replied:

"Sir, I invite you to accompany the movement. A mounted officer would be a conspicuous mark, and I have long held the opinion that it would be better if you were dead."

The art of repartee was cultivated in military circles as early as 1862.

A half-hour later Captain Madwell's company was driven from its position at the head of the ravine, with a loss of one-third its number. Among the fallen was Sergeant Halcrow. The regiment was soon afterward forced back to the main line, and at the close of the battle was miles away. The captain was now standing at the side of his subordinate and friend.

Sergeant Halcrow was mortally hurt. His clothing was deranged; it seemed to have been violently torn apart, exposing the abdomen. Some of the buttons of his jacket had been pulled off and lay on the ground beside him and fragments of his other garments were strewn about. His leather belt was parted and had apparently been dragged from beneath him as he lay. There had been no great effusion of blood. The only visible wound was a wide, ragged opening in the abdomen. It was defiled with earth and dead leaves. Protruding from it was a loop of small intestine. In all his experience Captain Madwell had not seen a wound like this. He could neither conjecture how it was made nor explain the attendant circumstances—the strangely torn clothing, the parted belt, the besmirching of the white skin. He knelt and made a closer examination. When he rose to his feet, he turned his eyes in different directions as if looking for an enemy. Fifty yards away, on the crest of a low, thinly wooded hill, he saw several dark objects moving about among the fallen men—a herd of swine. One stood with its back to him, its shoulders sharply elevated. Its forefeet were upon a human body, its head was depressed and invisible. The bristly ridge of its chine showed black against the red west. Captain Madwell drew away his eyes and fixed them again upon the thing which had been his friend.

The man who had suffered these monstrous mutilations was alive. At intervals he moved his limbs; he moaned at every breath. He stared blankly into the face of his friend and if touched screamed. In his giant agony he had torn up the ground on which he lay; his clenched hands were full of leaves and twigs and earth. Articulate speech was beyond his power; it was impossible to know if he were sensible to anything but pain. The expression of his face was an appeal; his eyes were full of prayer. For what?

There was no misreading that look; the captain had too frequently seen it in eyes of those whose lips had still the power to formulate it by an entreaty for death. Consciously or unconsciously, this writhing fragment of humanity, this type and example of acute sensation, this handiwork of man and beast, this humble, unheroic Prometheus, was imploring everything, all, the whole non-ego, for the boon of oblivion. To the earth and the sky alike, to the trees, to the man, to whatever took form in sense or consciousness, this incarnate suffering addressed that silent plea.

For what, indeed? For that which we accord to even the meanest creature without sense to demand it, denying it only to the wretched of our own race: for the blessed release, the rite of uttermost compassion, the *coup de grâce.*

Captain Madwell spoke the name of his friend. He repeated it over and over without effect until emotion choked his utterance. His tears plashed upon the livid face beneath his own and blinded himself. He saw nothing but a blurred and moving object, but the moans were more distinct than ever, interrupted at briefer intervals by sharper shrieks. He turned away, struck his hand upon his forehead, and strode from the spot. The swine, catching sight of him, threw up their crimson muzzles regarding him suspiciously a second, and then with a gruff, concerted grunt, raced away out of sight. A horse, its foreleg splintered by a cannon-shot, lifted its head sidewise from the ground and neighed piteously. Madwell stepped forward, drew his revolver and shot the poor beast between the eyes, narrowly observing its death-struggle, which, contrary to his expectation, was violent and long; but at last it lay still. The tense muscles of its lips, which had uncovered the teeth in a horrible grin, relaxed; the sharp, clean-cut profile took on a look of profound peace and rest.

Along the distant, thinly wooded crest to westward the fringe of sunset fire had now nearly burned itself out. The light upon the trunks of the trees had faded to a tender gray; shadows were in their tops, like great dark birds aperch. Night was coming and there were miles of haunted forest between Captain Madwell and camp. Yet he stood there at the side of the dead animal, apparently lost to all sense of his surroundings. His eyes were bent upon the earth at his feet; his left hand hung loosely at his side, his right still held the pistol. Presently he lifted his face, turned it toward his dying friend and walked rapidly back to his side. He knelt upon one knee, cocked the weapon, placed the muzzle against the man's forehead, and turning away his eyes pulled the trigger. There was no report. He had used his last cartridge for the horse.

The sufferer moaned and his lips moved convulsively. The froth that ran from them had a tinge of blood.

Captain Madwell rose to his feet and drew his sword from the scabbard. He passed the fingers of his left hand along the edge from hilt to point. He held it out straight before him, as if to test his nerves. There was no visible tremor of the blade; the ray of bleak skylight that it reflected was steady and true. He stooped and with his left hand tore away the dying man's shirt, rose and placed the point of the sword just over the heart. This time he did not withdraw his eyes. Grasping the hilt with both hands, he thrust downward with all his strength and weight. The blade sank into the man's body—through his body into the earth; Captain Madwell came near falling forward upon his work. The dying man drew up his knees and at the same time threw his right arm across his breast and grasped the steel so tightly that the knuckles of the hand visibly whitened. By a violent but vain effort to withdraw the blade the wound was enlarged; a rill of blood escaped, running sinuously down into the deranged clothing. At that moment three men stepped silently forward from behind the clump of young trees which had concealed their approach. Two were hospital attendants and carried a stretcher.

The third was Major Creede Halcrow.

For Discussion

1. Why is it necessary that this story occur in some very remote place?
2. Why is the personal relationship among the three men important to an understanding of the story? What would Captain Madwell have done if he had come upon an unknown soldier? Would his personal reactions have been the same?

3. A major scene is that in which Madwell kills the horse. How is this scene important? What similarities and differences exist between the horse and the dying Caffal?
4. Was Madwell justified in killing Caffal? Would a present-day military court condemn his act? What would you have done?

For Comparison

1. Just how much is the narrator motivated by the idea summarized by Donne in "No Man Is an Island"?
2. The narrator is obviously directly responsible for killing Caffal. Is anyone directly responsible for what happens to Eben Flood ("Mr. Flood's Party")? How can you "kill" someone without overtly taking his or her life?

For Composition

1. Captain Madwell did what was necessary.
2. Captain Madwell is a murderer.
3. Why I think (do not think) human life is sacred.

BERNARD MALAMUD

BLACK IS MY FAVORITE COLOR

Charity Sweetness sits in the toilet eating her two hardboiled eggs while I'm having my ham sandwich and coffee in the kitchen. That's how it goes only don't get the idea of ghettoes. If there's a ghetto I'm the one that's in it. She's my cleaning woman from Father Divine and comes in once a week to my small three-room apartment on my day off from the liquor store. "Peace," she says to me, "Father reached on down and took me right up in Heaven." She's a small person with a flat body, frizzy hair, and a quiet face that the light shines out of, and Mama had such eyes before she died. The first time Charity Sweetness came in to clean, a little more than a year and a half, I made the mistake to ask her to sit down at the kitchen table with me and eat her lunch. I was still feeling not so hot after Ornita left but I'm the kind of a man—Nat Lime, forty-four, a bachelor with a daily growing bald spot on the back of my head, and

I could lose frankly fifteen pounds—who enjoys company so long as he has it. So she cooked up her two hardboiled eggs and sat down and took a small bite out of one of them. But after a minute she stopped chewing and she got up and carried the eggs in a cup in the bathroom, and since then she eats there. I said to her more than once, "Okay, Charity Sweetness, so have it your way, eat the eggs in the kitchen by yourself and I'll eat when you're done," but she smiles absentminded, and eats in the toilet. It's my fate with colored people.

Although black is still my favorite color you wouldn't know it from my luck except in short quantities even though I do all right in the liquor store business in Harlem, on Eighth Avenue between 110th and 111th. I speak with respect. A large part of my life I've had dealings with Negro people, most on a business basis but sometimes for friendly reasons with genuine feeling on both sides. I'm drawn to them. At this time of my life I should have one or two good colored friends but the fault isn't necessarily mine. If they knew what was in my heart towards them, but how can you tell that to anybody nowadays? I've tried more than once but the language of the heart either is a dead language or else nobody understands it the way you speak it. Very few. What I'm saying is, personally for me there's only one human color and that's the color of blood. I like a black person if not because he's black, then because I'm white. It comes to the same thing. If I wasn't white my first choice would be black. I'm satisfied to be white because I have no other choice. Anyway, I got an eye for color. I appreciate. Who wants everybody to be the same? Maybe it's like some kind of a talent. Nat Lime might be a liquor dealer in Harlem, but once in the jungle in New Guinea in the Second War, I got the idea when I shot at a running Jap and missed him, that I had some kind of a talent, though maybe it's the kind where you have a marvelous idea now and then but in the end what do they come to? After all, it's a strange world.

Where Charity Sweetness eats her eggs makes me think about Buster Wilson when we were both boys in the Williamsburg section of Brooklyn. There was this long block of run-down dirty frame houses in the middle of a not-so-hot white neighborhood full of pushcarts. The Negro houses looked to me like they had been born and died there, dead not long after the beginning of the world. I lived on the next street. My father was a cutter with arthritis in both hands, big red knuckles and swollen fingers so he didn't cut, and my mother was the one who went to work. She sold paper bags from a second-hand pushcart in Ellery Street. We didn't starve but nobody ate chicken unless we were sick or the chicken was. This was my first acquaintance with a lot of black people and I used to poke around on their poor block. I think I thought, brother, if there can be like this, what can't there be? I mean I caught an early idea what life

was about. Anyway I met Buster Wilson there. He used to play marbles
by himself. I sat on the curb across the street, watching him shoot one
marble lefty and the other one righty. The hand that won picked up the
marbles. It wasn't so much of a game but he didn't ask me to come over.
My idea was to be friendly, only he never encouraged, he discouraged.
Why did I pick him out for a friend? Maybe because I had no others then,
we were new in the neighborhood, from Manhattan, Also I liked his type.
Buster did everything alone. He was a skinny kid and his brothers'
clothes hung on him like worn-out potato sacks. He was a beanpole boy,
about twelve, and I was then ten. His arms and legs were burnt out
matchsticks. He always wore a brown wool sweater, one arm half unrav-
eled, the other went down to the wrist. His long and narrow head had a
white part cut straight in the short wooly hair, maybe with a ruler there,
by his father, a barber but too drunk to stay a barber. In those days
though I had little myself. I was old enough to know who was better off,
and the whole block of colored houses made me feel bad in the daylight.
But I went there as much as I could because the street was full of life.
In the night it looked different, it's hard to tell a cripple in the dark.
Sometimes I was afraid to walk by the houses when they were dark and
quiet. I was afraid there were people looking at me that I couldn't see.
I liked it better when they had parties at night and everybody had a good
time. The musicians played their banjos and saxophones and the houses
shook with the music and laughing. The young girls, with their pretty
dresses and ribbons in their hair, caught me in my throat when I saw
them through the windows.

But with the parties came drinking and fights. Sundays were bad days
after the Saturday night parties. I remember once that Buster's father,
also long and loose, always wearing a dirty gray Homburg hat, chased
another black man in the street with a half-inch chisel. The other one,
maybe five feet high, lost his shoe and when they wrestled on the ground
he was already bleeding through his suit, a thick red blood smearing the
sidewalk. I was frightened by the blood and wanted to pour it back in
the man who was bleeding from the chisel. On another time Buster's
father was playing in a crap game with two big bouncy red dice, in the
back of an alley between two middle houses. Then about six men started
fist-fighting there, and they ran out of the alley and hit each other in the
street. The neighbors, including children, came out and watched, everybody afraid but nobody moving to do anything. I saw the same thing
near my store in Harlem, years later, a big crowd watching two men in
the streets, their breaths hanging in the air on a winter night, murdering
each other with switch knives, but nobody moved to call a cop. I didn't
either. Anyway, I was just a young kid but I still remember how the cops
drove up in a police paddy wagon and broke up the fight by hitting every-

body they could hit with big nightsticks. This was in the days before LaGuardia. Most of the fighters were knocked out cold, only one or two got away. Buster's father started to run back in his house but a cop ran after him and cracked him on his Homburg hat with a club, right on the front porch. Then the Negro men were lifted up by the cops, one at the arms and the other at the feet, and they heaved them in the paddy wagon. Buster's father hit the back of the wagon and fell, with his nose spouting very red blood, on top of three other men. I personally couldn't stand it, I was scared of the human race so I ran home, but I remember Buster watching without any expression in his eyes. I stole an extra fifteen cents from my mother's pocketbook and I ran back and asked Buster if he wanted to go to the movies. I would pay. He said yes. This was the first time he talked to me.

So we went more than once to the movies. But we never got to be friends. Maybe because it was a one-way proposition—from me to him. Which includes my invitations to go with me, my (poor mother's) movie money, Hershey chocolate bars, watermelon slices, even my best Nick Carter and Merriwell books that I spent hours picking up in the junk shops, and that he never gave me back. Once he let me go in his house to get a match so we could smoke some butts we found, but it smelled so heavy, so impossible, I died till I got out of there. What I saw in the way of furniture I won't mention—the best was falling apart in pieces. Maybe we went to the movies all together five or six matinees that spring and in the summertime, but when the shows were over he usually walked home by himself.

"Why don't you wait for me, Buster?" I said. "We're both going in the same direction."

But he was walking ahead and didn't hear me. Anyway he didn't answer.

One day when I wasn't expecting it he hit me in the teeth. I felt like crying but not because of the pain. I spit blood and said, "What did you hit me for? What did I do to you?"

"Because you a Jew bastard. Take your Jew movies and your Jew candy and shove them up your Jew ass."

And he ran away.

I thought to myself how was I to know he didn't like the movies. When I was a man I thought, you can't force it.

Years later, in the prime of my life, I met Mrs. Ornita Harris. She was standing by herself under an open umbrella at the bus stop, crosstown 110th, and I picked up her green glove that she had dropped on the wet sidewalk. It was in the end of November. Before I could ask her was it hers, she grabbed the glove out of my hand, closed her umbrella, and stepped in the bus. I got on right after her.

I was annoyed so I said, "If you'll pardon me, Miss, there's no law that you have to say thanks, but at least don't make a criminal out of me."

"Well, I'm sorry," she said, "but I don't like white men trying to do me favors."

I tipped my hat and that was that. In ten minutes I got off the bus but she was already gone.

Who expected to see her again but I did. She came into my store about a week later for a bottle of scotch.

"I would offer you a discount," I told her, "but I know you don't like a certain kind of a favor and I'm not looking for a slap in the face."

Then she recognized me and got a little embarrassed.

"I'm sorry I misunderstood you that day."

"So mistakes happen."

The result was she took the discount. I gave her a dollar off.

She used to come in about every two weeks for a fifth of Haig and Haig. Sometimes I waited on her, sometimes my helpers, Jimmy or Mason, also colored, but I said to give the discount. They both looked at me but I had nothing to be ashamed. In the spring when she came in we used to talk once in a while. She was a slim woman, dark but not the most dark, about thirty years I would say, also well built, with a combination nice legs and a good-size bosom that I like. Her face was pretty, with big eyes and high cheek bones, but lips a little thick and nose a little broad. Sometimes she didn't feel like talking, she paid for the bottle, less discount, and walked out. Her eyes were tired and she didn't look to me like a happy woman.

I found out her husband was once a window cleaner on the big buildings, but one day his safety belt broke and he fell fifteen stories. After the funeral she got a job as a manicurist in a Times Square barber shop. I told her I was a bachelor and lived with my mother in a small three-room apartment on West Eighty-third near Broadway. My mother had cancer, and Ornita said she was very sorry.

One night in July we went out together. How that happened I'm still not so sure. I guess I asked her and she didn't say no. Where do you go out with a Negro woman? We went to the Village. We had a good dinner and walked in Washington Square Park. It was a hot night. Nobody was surprised when they saw us, nobody looked at us like we were against the law. If they looked maybe they saw my new lightweight suit that I bought yesterday and my shiny bald spot when we walked under a lamp, also how pretty she was for a man of my type. We went in a movie on West Eighth Street. I didn't want to go in but she said she had heard about the picture. We went in like strangers and we came out like strangers. I wondered what was in her mind and I thought to myself, whatever is in there it's not a certain white man that I know. All night long we went together like we were chained. After the movie she wouldn't let me take her back to Harlem. When I put her in a taxi she asked me, "Why did we bother?"

For the steak, I wanted to say. Instead I said, "You're worth the bother."

"Thanks anyway."

Kiddo, I thought to myself after the taxi left, you just found out what's what, now the best thing is forget her.

It's easy to say. In August we went out the second time. That was the night she wore a purple dress and I thought to myself, my God, what colors. Who paints that picture paints a masterpiece. Everybody looked at us but I had pleasure. That night when she took off her dress it was in a furnished room I had the sense to rent a few days before. With my sick mother, I couldn't ask her to come to my apartment, and she didn't want me to go home with her where she lived with her brother's family on West 115th near Lenox Avenue. Under her purple dress she wore a black slip, and when she took that off she had white underwear. When she took off the white underwear she was black again. But I know where the next white was, if you want to call it white. And that was the night I think I fell in love with her, the first time in my life though I have liked one or two nice girls I used to go with when I was a boy. It was a serious proposition. I'm the kind of a man when I think of love I'm thinking of marriage. I guess that's why I am a bachelor.

That same week I had a holdup in my place, two big men—both black —with revolvers. One got excited when I rang open the cash register so he could take the money and he hit me over the ear with his gun. I stayed in the hospital a couple of weeks. Otherwise I was insured. Ornita came to see me. She sat on a chair without talking much. Finally I saw she was uncomfortable so I suggested she ought to go home.

"I'm sorry it happened," she said.

"Don't talk like it's your fault."

When I got out of the hospital my mother was dead. She was a wonderful person. My father died when I was thirteen and all by herself she kept the family alive and together. I sat shive for a week and remembered how she sold paper bags on her pushcart. I remembered her life and what she tried to teach me. Nathan, she said, if you ever forget you are a Jew a goy will remind you. Mama, I said, rest in peace on this subject. But if I do something you don't like, remember, on earth it's harder than where you are. Then when my week of mourning was finished, one night I said, "Ornita, let's get married. We're both honest people and if you love me like I love you it won't be such a bad time. If you don't like New York

I'll sell out here and we'll move someplace else. Maybe to San Francisco where nobody knows us. I was there for a week in the Second War and I saw white and colored living together."

"Nat," she answered me, "I like you but I'd be afraid. My husband woulda killed me."

"Your husband is dead."

"Not in my memory."

"In that case I'll wait."

"Do you know what it'd be like—I mean the life we could expect?"

"Ornita," I said, "I'm the kind of a man, if he picks his own way of life he's satisfied."

"What about children? Were you looking forward to half-Jewish polka dots?"

"I was looking forward to children."

"I can't," she said.

Can't is can't. I saw she was afraid and the best thing was not to push. Sometimes when we met she was so nervous that whatever we did she couldn't enjoy it. At the same time I still thought I had a chance. We were together more and more. I got rid of my furnished room and she came to my apartment—I gave away Mama's bed and bought a new one. She stayed with me all day on Sundays. When she wasn't so nervous she was affectionate, and if I know what love is, I had it. We went out a couple of times a week, the same way—usually I met her in Times Square and sent her home in a taxi, but I talked more about marriage and she talked less against it. One night she told me she was still trying to convince herself but she was almost convinced. I took an inventory of my liquor stock so I could put the store up for sale.

Ornita knew what I was doing. One day she quit her job, the next day she took it back. She also went away a week to visit her sister in Philadelphia for a little rest. She came back tired but said maybe. Maybe is maybe so I'll wait. The way she said it it was closer to yes. That was the winter two years ago. When she was in Philadelphia I called up a friend of mine from the Army, now CPA, and told him I would appreciate an invitation for an evening. He knew why. His wife said yes right away. When Ornita came back we went there. The wife made a fine dinner. It wasn't a bad time and they told us to come again. Ornita had a few drinks. She looked relaxed, wonderful. Later, because of a twenty-four hour taxi strike I had to take her home on the subway. When we got to the 116th Street station she told me to stay on the train, and she would walk the couple of blocks to her house. I didn't like a woman walking alone on the streets at that time of the night. She said she never had any trouble but I insisted nothing doing. I said I would walk to her stoop with her and when she went upstairs I would go back to the subway.

On the way there, on 115th in the middle of the block before Lenox, we were stopped by three men—maybe they were boys. One had a black hat with a half-inch brim, one a green cloth hat, and the third wore a black leather cap. The green hat was wearing a short coat and the other two had long ones. It was under a street light but the leather cap snapped a six-inch switchblade open in the light.

"What you doin' with this white son of a bitch?" he said to Ornita.

"I'm minding my own business," she answered him, "and I wish you would too."

"Boys," I said, "we're all brothers. I'm a reliable merchant in the neighborhood. This young lady is my dear friend. We don't want any trouble. Please let us pass."

"You talk like a Jew landlord," said the green hat. "Fifty a week for a single room."

"No charge fo' the rats," said the half-inch brim.

"Believe me, I'm no landlord. My store is 'Nathan's Liquors' between Hundred Tenth and Eleventh. I also have two colored clerks, Mason and Jimmy, and they will tell you I pay good wages as well as I give discounts to certain customers."

"Shut your mouth, Jewboy," said the leather cap, and he moved the knife back and forth in front of my coat button. "No more black pussy for you."

"Speak with respect about this lady, please."

I got slapped on my mouth.

"That ain't no lady," said the long face in the half-inch brim, "that's black pussy. She deserve to have evvy bit of her hair shave off. How you like to have evvy bit of your hair shave off, black pussy?"

"Please leave me and this gentleman alone or I'm gonna scream long and loud. That's my house three doors down."

They slapped her. I never heard such a scream. Like her husband was falling fifteen stories.

I hit the one that slapped her and the next I knew I was lying in the gutter with a pain in my head. I thought, goodbye, Nat, they'll stab me for sure, but all they did was take my wallet and run in three different directions.

Ornita walked back with me to the subway and she wouldn't let me go home with her again.

"Just get home safely."

She looked terrible. Her face was gray and I still remembered her scream. It was a terrible winter night, very cold February, and it took me an hour and ten minutes to get home. I felt bad for leaving her but what could I do?

We had a date downtown the next night but she didn't show up, the first time.

In the morning I called her in her place of business.

"For God's sake, Ornita, if we got married and moved away we wouldn't have that kind of trouble that we had. We wouldn't come in that neighborhood any more."

"Yes, we would. I have family there and don't want to move anyplace else. The truth of it is I can't marry you, Nat. I got troubles enough of my own."

"I coulda sworn you love me."

"Maybe I do but I can't marry you."

"For God's sake, why?"

"I got enough trouble of my own."

I went that night in a cab to her brother's house to see her. He was a quiet man with a thin mustache. "She gone," he said, "left for a long visit to some close relatives in the South. She said to tell you she appreciate your intentions but didn't think it will work out."

"Thank you kindly," I said.

Don't ask me how I got home.

Once on Eighth Avenue, a couple of blocks from my store, I saw a blind man with a white cane tapping on the sidewalk. I figured we were going in the same direction so I took his arm.

"I can tell you're white," he said.

A heavy colored woman with a full shopping bag rushed after us.

"Never mind," she said, "I know where he live."

She pushed me with her shoulder and I hurt my leg on the fire hydrant.

That's how it is. I give my heart and they kick me in my teeth.

"Charity Sweetness—you hear me?—come out of that goddamn toilet!"

For Discussion

1. What importance do you attach to the fact that both of the principal characters represent frequently persecuted minority groups?
2. What is Charity Sweetness' attitude toward racial issues? How does she reveal this attitude in her relationship with Nat Lime?
3. Is Nat Lime going out of his way to be kind to Blacks? Do you feel that all of his actions are sincere? Is he really falling in love with Ornita, or is he merely using her to satisfy his own feelings of guilt or loneliness? Explain.
4. Ornita is afraid to marry Nat. Does society have a responsibility to create an environment in which such persons as Nat and Ornita can live safely? How can such an environment be created?

For Comparison

1. To what extent would Nat Lime agree with the waiter in "A Clean, Well-Lighted Place" that all is nothing and that all effort is ultimately wasted?
2. Exactly how might Nat react if he were riding the train ("Incident") and someone called Ornita "Nigger"? What if someone called him "Jew"?

For Composition

1. I do (do not) trust Nat.
2. Racial persecution.
3. My attitude on interracial marriages.

Willa Cather

THE SCULPTOR'S FUNERAL

A group of the townspeople stood on the station siding of a little Kansas town, awaiting the coming of the night train, which was already twenty minutes overdue. The snow had fallen thick over everything; in the pale starlight the line of bluffs across the wide, white meadows south of the town made soft, smoke-coloured curves against the clear sky. The men on the siding stood first on one foot and then on the other, their hands thrust deep into their trousers pockets, their overcoats open, their shoulders screwed up with the cold; and they glanced from time to time toward the southeast, where the railroad track wound along the river shore. They conversed in low tones and moved about restlessly, seeming uncertain as to what was expected of them. There was but one of the company who looked as though he knew exactly why he was there; and he kept conspicuously apart; walking to the far end of the platform, returning to the station door, then pacing up the track again, his chin sunk in the high collar of his overcoat, his burly shoulders drooping forward, his gait heavy and dogged. Presently he was approached by a tall, spare, grizzled man clad in a faded Grand Army suit, who shuffled out from the group and advanced with a certain deference, craning his neck forward until his back made the angle of a jack-knife three-quarters open.

Reprinted from *Youth and the Bright Medusa*, by Willa Cather, courtesy of Alfred A. Knopf, Inc.

"I reckon she's a-goin' to be pretty late again to-night, Jim," he remarked in a squeaky falsetto. "S'pose it's the snow?"

"I don't know," responded the other man with a shade of annoyance, speaking from out an astonishing cataract of red beard that grew fiercely and thickly in all directions.

The spare man shifted the quill toothpick he was chewing to the other side of his mouth. "It ain't likely that anybody from the East will come with the corpse, I s'pose," he went on reflectively.

"I don't know," responded the other, more curtly than before.

"It's too bad he didn't belong to some lodge or other. I like an order funeral myself. They seem more appropriate for people of some repytation," the spare man continued, with an ingratiating concession in his shrill voice, as he carefully placed his toothpick in his vest pocket. He always carried the flag at the G.A.R. funerals in the town.

The heavy man turned on his heel, without replying, and walked up the siding. The spare man shuffled back to the uneasy group. "Jim's ez full ez a tick, ez ushel," he commented commiseratingly.

Just then a distant whistle sounded, and there was a shuffling of feet on the platform. A number of lanky boys of all ages appeared as suddenly and slimily as eels wakened by the crack of thunder; some came from the waiting-room, where they had been warming themselves by the red stove, or half asleep on the slat benches; others uncoiled themselves from baggage trucks or slid out of express wagons. Two clambered down from the driver's seat of a hearse that stood backed up against the siding. They straightened their stooping shoulders and lifted their heads, and a flash of momentary animation kindled their dull eyes at that cold, vibrant scream, the world-wide call for men. It stirred them like the note of a trumpet; just as it had often stirred the man who was coming home to-night, in his boyhood.

The night express shot, red as a rocket, from out the eastward marsh lands and wound along the river shore under the long lines of shivering poplars that sentinelled the meadows, the escaping steam hanging in grey masses against the pale sky and blotting out the Milky Way. In a moment the red glare from the headlight streamed up the snow-covered track before the siding and glittered on the wet, black rails. The burly man with the dishevelled red beard walked swiftly up the platform toward the approaching train, uncovering his head as he went. The group of men behind him hesitated, glanced questioningly at one another, and awkwardly followed his example. The train stopped, and the crowd shuffled up to the express car just as the door was thrown open, the spare man in the G. A. R. suit thrusting his head forward with curiosity. The express messenger appeared in the doorway, accompanied by a young man in a long ulster and travelling cap.

"Are Mr. Merrick's friends here?" inquired the young man.

The group on the platform swayed and shuffled uneasily. Philip Phelps, the banker, responded with dignity: "We have come to take charge of the body. Mr. Merrick's father is very feeble and can't be about."

"Send the agent out here," growled the express messenger, "and tell the operator to lend a hand."

The coffin was got out of its rough box and down on the snowy platform. The townspeople drew back enough to make room for it and then formed a close semicircle about it, looking curiously at the palm leaf which lay across the black cover. No one said anything. The baggage man stood by his truck, waiting to get at the trunks. The engine panted heavily, and the fireman dodged in and out among the wheels with his yellow torch and long oil-can, snapping the spindle boxes. The young Bostonian, one of the dead sculptor's pupils who had come with the body, looked about him helplessly. He turned to the banker, the only one of that black, uneasy, stoop-shouldered group who seemed enough of an individual to be addressed.

"None of Mr. Merrick's brothers are here?" he asked uncertainly.

The man with the red beard for the first time stepped up and joined the group. "No, they have not come yet; the family is scattered. The body will be taken directly to the house." He stooped and took hold of one of the handles of the coffin.

"Take the long hill road up, Thompson, it will be easier on the horses," called the liveryman as the undertaker snapped the door of the hearse and prepared to mount to the driver's seat.

Laird, the red-bearded lawyer, turned again to the stranger: "We didn't know whether there would be any one with him or not," he explained. "It's a long walk, so you'd better go up in the hack." He pointed to a single battered conveyance, but the young man replied stiffly: "Thank you, but I think I will go up with the hearse. If you don't object," turning to the undertaker, "I'll ride with you."

They clambered up over the wheels and drove off in the starlight up the long, white hill toward the town. The lamps in the still village were shining from under the low, snow-burdened roofs; and beyond, on every side, the plains reached out into emptiness, peaceful and wide as the soft sky itself, and wrapped in a tangible, white silence.

When the hearse backed up to a wooden sidewalk before a naked, weather-beaten frame house, the same composite, ill-defined group that had stood upon the station siding was huddled about the gate. The front yard was an icy swamp, and a couple of warped planks, extending from the sidewalk to the door, made a sort of rickety footbridge. The gate hung on one hinge, and was opened wide with difficulty. Steavens, the young stranger, noticed that something black was tied to the knob of the front door.

The grating sound made by the casket, as it was drawn from the hearse, was answered by a scream from the house; the front door was wrenched open, and a tall, corpulent woman rushed out bareheaded into the snow and flung herself upon the coffin, shrieking: "My boy, my boy! And this is how you've come home to me!"

As Steavens turned away and closed his eyes with a shudder of unutterable repulsion, another woman, also tall, but flat and angular, dressed entirely in black, darted out of the house and caught Mrs. Merrick by the shoulders, crying sharply: "Come, come, mother; you musn't go on like this!" Her tone changed to one of obsequious solemnity as she turned to the banker: "The parlour is ready, Mr. Phelps."

The bearers carried the coffin along the narrow boards, while the undertaker ran ahead with the coffin-rests. They bore it into a large, unheated room that smelled of dampness and disuse and furniture polish, and set it down under a hanging lamp ornamented with jingling glass prisms and before a "Rogers group" of John Alden and Priscilla, wreathed with smilax. Henry Steavens stared about him with the sickening conviction that there had been some horrible mistake, and that he had somehow arrived at the wrong destination. He looked painfully about over the clover-green Brussels, the fat plush upholstery; among the hand-painted china placques and panels, and vases, for some mark of identification, for something that might once conceivably have belonged to Harvey Merrick. It was not until he recognized his friend in the crayon portrait of a little boy in kilts and curls hanging above the piano, that he felt willing to let any of these people approach the coffin.

"Take the lid off, Mr. Thompson; let me see my boy's face," wailed the elder woman between her sobs. This time Steavens looked fearfully, almost beseechingly into her face, red and swollen under its masses of strong, black, shiny hair. He flushed, dropped his eyes, and then, almost incredulously, looked again. There was a kind of power about her face— a kind of brutal handsomeness, even, but it was scarred and furrowed by violence, and so coloured and coarsened by fiercer passions that grief seemed never to have laid a gentle finger there. The long nose was distended and knobbed at the end, and there were deep lines on either side of it; her heavy, black brows almost met across her forehead, her teeth were large and square, and set far apart—teeth that could tear. She filled the room; the men were obliterated, seemed tossed about like twigs in an angry water, and even Steavens felt himself being drawn into the whirlpool.

The daughter—the tall, raw-boned woman in crêpe, with a mourning comb in her hair which curiously lengthened her long face—sat stiffly upon the sofa, her hands, conspicuous for their large knuckles, folded in her lap, her mouth and eyes drawn down, solemnly awaiting the opening of the coffin. Near the door stood a mulatto woman, evidently a servant in the house, with a timid bearing and an emaciated face pitifully sad and gentle. She was weeping silently, the corner of her calico apron lifted to her eyes, occasionally suppressing a long, quivering sob. Steavens walked over and stood beside her.

Feeble steps were heard on the stairs, and an old man, tall and frail, odorous of pipe smoke, with shaggy, upkept grey hair and a dingy beard, tobacco stained about the mouth, entered uncertainly. He went slowly up to the coffin and stood rolling a blue cotton handkerchief between his hands, seeming so pained and embarrassed by his wife's orgy of grief that he had no consciousness of anything else.

"There, there, Annie, dear, don't take on so," he quavered timidly, putting out a shaking hand and awkwardly patting her elbow. She turned with a cry, and sank upon his shoulder with such violence that he tottered a little. He did not even glance toward the coffin, but continued to look at her with a dull, frightened, appealing expression, as a spaniel looks at the whip. His sunken cheeks slowly reddened and burned with miserable shame. When his wife rushed from the room, her daughter strode after her with set lips. The servant stole up to the coffin, bent over it for a moment, and then slipped away to the kitchen, leaving Steavens, the lawyer and the father to themselves. The old man stood trembling and looking down at his dead son's face. The sculptor's splendid head seemed even more noble in its rigid stillness than in life. The dark hair had crept down upon the wide forehead; the face seemed strangely long, but in it there was not that beautiful and chaste repose which we expect to find in the faces of the dead. The brows were so drawn that there were two deep lines above the beaked nose, and the chin was thrust forward defiantly. It was as though the strain of life had been so sharp and bitter that death could not at once wholly relax the tension and smooth the countenance into perfect peace—as though he were still guarding something precious and holy, which might even yet be wrested from him.

The old man's lips were working under his stained beard. He turned to the lawyer with timid deference: "Phelps and the rest are comin' back to set up with Harve, ain't they?" he asked. "Thank 'ee, Jim, thank 'ee." He brushed the hair back gently from his son's forehead. "He was a good boy, Jim; always a good boy. He was ez gentle ez a child and the kindest of 'em all—only we didn't none of us ever onderstand him." The tears trickled slowly down his beard and dropped upon the sculptor's coat.

"Martin, Martin. Oh, Martin! come here," his wife wailed from the top of the stairs. The old man started timorously: "Yes, Annie, I'm coming." He turned away, hesitated, stood for a moment in miserable indecision; then reached back and patted the dead man's hair softly, and stumbled from the room.

"Poor old man, I didn't think he had any tears left. Seems as if his eyes would have gone dry long ago. At his age nothing cuts very deep," remarked the lawyer.

Something in his tone made Steavens glance up. While the mother had been in the room, the young man had scarcely seen any one else; but now, from the moment he first glanced into Jim Laird's florid face and blood-shot eyes, he knew that he had found what he had been heartsick at not finding before—the feeling, the understanding, that must exist in some-one, even here.

The man was red as his beard, with features swollen and blurred by dissipation, and a hot, blazing blue eye. His face was strained—that of a man who is controlling himself with difficulty—and he kept plucking at his beard with a sort of fierce resentment. Steavens, sitting by the win-dow, watched him turn down the glaring lamp, still its jangling pendants with an angry gesture, and then stand with his hands locked behind him, staring down into the master's face. He could not help wondering what link there could have been between the porcelain vessel and so sooty a lump of potter's clay.

From the kitchen an uproar was sounding; when the dining-room door opened, the import of it was clear. The mother was abusing the maid for having forgotten to make the dressing for the chicken salad which had been prepared for the watchers. Steavens had never heard anything in the least like it; it was injured, emotional, dramatic abuse, unique and masterly in its excruciating cruelty, as violent and unrestrained as had been her grief of twenty minutes before. With a shudder of disgust the lawyer went into the dining-room and closed the door into the kitchen.

"Poor Roxy's getting it now," he remarked when he came back. "The Merricks took her out of the poor-house years ago; and if her loyalty would let her, I guess the poor old thing could tell tales that would curdle your blood. She's the mulatto woman who was standing in here a while ago, with her apron to her eyes. The old woman is a fury; there never was anybody like her for demonstrative piety and ingenious cruelty. She made Harvey's life a hell for him when he lived at home; he was so sick ashamed of it. I never could see how he kept himself so sweet."

"He was wonderful," said Steavens slowly, "wonderful; but until to-night I have never known how wonderful."

"That is the true and eternal wonder of it, anyway; that it can come even from such a dung heap as this," the lawyer cried, with a sweeping gesture which seemed to indicate much more than the four walls within which they stood.

"I think I'll see whether I can get a little air. The room is so close I am beginning to feel rather faint," murmured Steavens, struggling with one of the windows. The sash was stuck, however, and would not yield, so he sat down dejectedly and began pulling at his collar. The lawyer came over, loosened the sash with one blow of his red fist and sent the window up a few inches. Steavens thanked him, but the nausea which had been gradually climbing into his throat for the last half hour left him with but one desire—a desperate feeling that he must get away from this place with what was left of Harvey Merrick. Oh, he comprehended well enough now the quiet bitterness of the smile that he had seen so often on his master's lips!

He remembered that once, when Merrick returned from a visit home, he brought with him a singularly feeling and suggestive bas-relief of a thin, faded old woman, sitting and sewing something pinned to her knee; while a full-lipped, full-blooded little urchin, his trousers held up by a single gallows, stood beside her, impatiently twitching her gown to call her attention to a butterfly he had caught. Steavens, impressed by the tender and delicate modelling of the thin, tired face, had asked him if it were his mother. He remembered the dull flush that had burned up in the sculptor's face.

The lawyer was sitting in a rocking-chair beside the coffin, his head thrown back and his eyes closed. Steavens looked at him earnestly, puzzled at the line of the chin, and wondering why a man should conceal a feature of such distinction under that disfiguring shock of beard. Suddenly, as though he felt the young sculptor's keen glance, he opened his eyes.

"Was he always a good deal of an oyster?" he asked abruptly. "He was terribly shy as a boy."

"Yes, he was an oyster, since you put it so," rejoined Steavens. "Although he could be very fond of people, he always gave one the impression of being detached. He disliked violent emotion; he was reflective, and rather distrustful of himself—except, of course, as regarded his work. He was sure-footed enough there. He distrusted men pretty thoroughly and women even more, yet somehow without believing ill of them. He was determined, indeed, to believe the best, but he seemed afraid to investigate."

"A burnt dog dreads the fire," said the lawyer grimly, and closed his eyes.

Steavens went on and on, reconstructing that whole miserable boyhood. All this raw, biting ugliness had been the portion of the man whose tastes were refined beyond the limits of the reasonable—whose mind was an exhaustless gallery of beautiful impressions, and so sensitive that the mere shadow of a poplar leaf flickering against a sunny wall would be etched and held there forever. Surely, if ever a man had the magic word in his finger tips, it was Merrick. Whatever he touched, he revealed its holiest secret; liberated it from enchantment and restored it to its pristine loveliness, like the Arabian prince who fought the enchantress spell for spell. Upon whatever he had come in contact with, he had left a beautiful record of the experience—a sort of ethereal signature; a scent, a sound, a colour that was his own.

Steavens understood now the real tragedy of his master's life; neither love nor wine, as many had conjectured; but a blow which had fallen earlier and cut deeper than these could have done—a shame not his, and yet so unescapably his, to hide in his heart from his very boyhood. And without—the frontier warfare; the yearning of a boy, cast ashore upon a desert of newness and ugliness and sordidness, for all that is chastened and old, and noble with traditions.

At eleven o'clock the tall, flat woman in black crêpe entered and announced that the watchers were arriving, and asked them "to step into the dining-room." As Steavens rose, the lawyer said dryly: "You go on —it'll be a good experience for you, doubtless; as for me, I'm not equal to that crowd to-night; I've had twenty years of them."

As Steavens closed the door after him he glanced back at the lawyer, sitting by the coffin in the dim light, with his chin resting on his hand.

The same misty group that had stood before the door of the express car shuffled into the dining-room. In the light of the kerosene lamp they separated and became individuals. The minister, a pale, feeble-looking man with white hair and blond chin-whiskers, took his seat beside a small side table and placed his Bible upon it. The Grand Army man sat down behind the stove and tilted his chair back comfortably against the wall, fishing his quill toothpick from his waistcoat pocket. The two bankers, Phelps and Elder, sat off in a corner behind the dinner-table, where they could finish their discussion of the new usury law and its effect on chattel security loans. The real estate agent, an old man with a smiling, hypocritical face, soon joined them. The coal and lumber dealer and the cattle shipper sat on opposite sides of the hard coal-burner, their feet on the nickel-work. Steavens took a book from his pocket and began to read. The talk around him ranged through various topics of local interest while the house was quieting down. When it was clear that the members of the family were in bed, the Grand Army man hitched his shoulders and, untangling his long legs, caught his heels on the rounds of his chair.

"S'pose there'll be a will, Phelps?" he queried in his weak falsetto.

The banker laughed disagreeably, and began trimming his nails with a pearl-handled pocket-knife.

"There'll scarcely be any need for one, will there?" he queried in his turn.

The restless Grand Army man shifted his position again, getting his knees still nearer his chin. "Why, the ole man says Harve's done right well lately," he chirped.

The other banker spoke up. "I reckon he means by that Harve ain't asked him to mortgage any more farms lately, so as he could go on with his education."

"Seems like my mind don't reach back to a time when Harve wasn't bein' edycated," tittered the Grand Army man.

There was a general chuckle. The minister took out his handkerchief and blew his nose sonorously. Banker Phelps closed his knife with a snap. "It's too bad the old man's sons didn't turn out better," he remarked with reflective authority. "They never hung together. He spent money enough on Harve to stock a dozen cattle-farms and he might as well have poured it into Sand Creek. If Harve had stayed at home and helped nurse what little they had, and gone into stock on the old man's bottom farm, they might all have been well fixed. But the old man had to trust everything to tenants and was cheated right and left."

"Harve never could have handled stock none," interposed the cattle-man. "He hadn't it in him to be sharp. Do you remember when he bought Sander's mules for eight-year olds, when everybody in town knew that Sander's father-in-law give 'em to his wife for a wedding present eighteen years before, an' they was full-grown mules then."

Every one chuckled, and the Grand Army man rubbed his knees with a spasm of childish delight.

"Harve never was much account for anything practical, and he shore was never fond of work," began the coal and lumber dealer. "I mind the last time he was home; the day he left, when the old man was out to the barn helpin' his hand hitch up to take Harve to the train, and Cal Moots was patchin' up the fence, Harve, he come out on the step and sings out, in his lady-like voice: "Cal Moots, Cal Moots! please come cord my trunk.""

"That's Harve for you," approved the Grand Army man gleefully. "I kin hear him howlin' yet when he was a big feller in long pants and his mother used to whale him with a rawhide in the barn for lettin' the cows git foundered in the cornfield when he was drivin' 'em home from pasture. He killed a cow of mine that-a-way onct—a pure Jersey and the best milker I had, an' the ole man had to put up for her. Harve, he was watchin' the sun set acrost the marshes when the anamile got away; he argued that sunset was oncommon fine."

"Where the old man made his mistake was in sending the boy East to school," said Phelps, stroking his goatee and speaking in a deliberate, judicial tone. "There was where he got his head full of trapseing to Paris and all such folly. What Harve needed, of all people, was a course in some first-class Kansas City business college."

The letters were swimming before Steavens's eyes. Was it possible that these men did not understand, that the palm on the coffin meant nothing to them? The very name of their town would have remained forever buried in the postal guide had it not been now and again mentioned in the world in connection with Harvey Merrick's. He remembered what his master had said to him on the day of his death, after the congestion of both lungs had shut off any probability of recovery, and the sculptor had asked his pupil to send his body home. "It's not a pleasant place to be lying while the world is moving and doing and bettering," he had said with a feeble smile, "but it rather seems as though we ought to go back to the place we came from in the end. The townspeople will come in for a look at me; and after they have had their say I shan't have much to fear from the judgment of God. The wings of the Victory, in there"— with a weak gesture toward his studio—"will not shelter me."

The cattleman took up the comment. "Forty's young for a Merrick to cash in; they usually hang on pretty well. Probably he helped it along with whisky."

"His mother's people were not long lived, and Harvey never had a robust constitution," said the minister mildly. He would have liked to say more. He had been the boy's Sunday-school teacher, and had been fond of him; but he felt that he was not in a position to speak. His own sons had turned out badly, and it was not a year since one of them had made his last trip home in the express car, shot in a gambling-house in the Black Hills.

"Nevertheless, there is no disputin' that Harve frequently looked upon the wine when it was red, also variegated, and it shore made an oncommon fool of him," moralized the cattleman.

Just then the door leading into the parlour rattled loudly and every one started involuntarily, looking relieved when only Jim Laird came out. His red face was convulsed with anger, and the Grand Army man ducked his head when he saw the spark in his blue, blood-shot eye. They were all afraid of Jim; he was a drunkard, but he could twist the law to suit his client's needs as no other man in all western Kansas could do; and there were many who tried. The lawyer closed the door gently behind him, leaned back against it and folded his arms, cocking his head a little to one side. When he assumed this attitude in the court-room, ears were always pricked up, as it usually foretold a flood of withering sarcasm.

"I've been with you gentlemen before," he began in a dry, even tone, "when you've sat by the coffins of boys born and raised in this town; and, if I remember rightly, you were never any too well satisfied when you checked them up. What's the matter, anyhow? Why is it that reputable young men are as scarce as millionaires in Sand City? It might almost seem to a stranger that there was some way something the matter with your progressive town. Why did Ruben Sayer, the brightest young lawyer you ever turned out, after he had come home from the university as straight as a die, take to drinking and forge a check and shoot himself? Why did Bill Merrit's son die of the shakes in a saloon in Omaha? Why was Mr. Thomas's son, here, shot in a gambling-house? Why did young Adams burn his mill to beat the insurance companies and go to the pen?"

The lawyer paused and unfolded his arms, laying one clenched fist quietly on the table. "I'll tell you why. Because you drummed nothing but money and knavery into their ears from the time they wore knicker-bockers; because you carped away at them as you've been carping here to-night, holding our friends Phelps and Elder up to them for their mod-els, as our grandfathers held up George Washington and John Adams. But the boys, worse luck, were young, and raw at the business you put them to; and how could they match coppers with such artists as Phelps and Elder? You wanted them to be successful rascals; they were only un-successful ones—that's all the difference. There was only one boy ever raised in this borderland between ruffianism and civilization, who didn't come to grief, and you hated Harvey Merrick more for winning out than you hated all the other boys who got under the wheels. Lord, Lord, how you did hate him! Phelps, here, is fond of saying that he could buy and sell us all out any time he's a mind to; but he knew Harve wouldn't have given a tinker's damn for his bank and all his cattle-farms put together; and a lack of appreciation, that way, goes hard with Phelps.

"Old Nimrod, here, thinks Harve drank too much; and this from such as Nimrod and me!

"Brother Elder says Harve was too free with the old man's money— fell short in filial consideration, maybe. Well, we can all remember the very tone in which brother Elder swore his own father was a liar, in the county court; and we all know that the old man came out of that partner-ship with his son as bare as a sheared lamb. But maybe I'm getting per-sonal, and I'd better be driving ahead at what I want to say."

The lawyer paused a moment, squared his heavy shoulders, and went on: "Harvey Merrick and I went to school together, back East. We were dead in earnest, and we wanted you all to be proud of us some day. We meant to be great men. Even I, and I haven't lost my sense of humour, gentlemen, I meant to be a great man. I came back here to practise, and I found you didn't in the least want me to be a great man. You wanted me to be a shrewd lawyer—oh, yes! Our veteran here wanted me to get him an increase of pension, because he had dyspepsia; Phelps wanted a new county survey that would put the widow Wilson's little bottom farm inside his south line; Elder wanted to lend money at 5 per cent a month, and get it collected; old Stark here wanted to wheedle old women up in Vermont into investing their annuities in real-estate mortgages that are not worth the paper they are written on. Oh, you needed me hard enough, and you'll go on needing me; and that's why I'm not afraid to plug the truth home to you this once.

"Well, I came back here and became the damned shyster you wanted me to be. You pretend to have some sort of respect for me; and yet you'll stand up and throw mud at Harvey Merrick, whose soul you couldn't dirty and whose hands you couldn't tie. Oh, you're a discriminating lot of Christians! There have been times when the sight of Harvey's name in some Eastern paper has made me hang my head like a whipped dog; and, again, times when I liked to think of him off there in the world, away from all this hog-wallow, doing his great work and climbing the big, clean up-grade he'd set for himself.

"And we? Now that we've fought and lied and sweated and stolen, and hated as only the disappointed strugglers in a bitter, dead little Western town know how to do, what have we got to show for it? Harvey Merrick wouldn't have given one sunset over your marshes for all you've got put together, and you know it. It's not for me to say why, in the inscrutable wisdom of God, a genius should ever have been called from his place of hatred and bitter waters; but I want this Boston man to know that the drivel he's been hearing here to-night is the only tribute any truly great man could ever have from such a lot of sick, side-tracked, burnt-dog, land-poor sharks as the here-present financiers of Sand City—upon which town may God have mercy!"

The lawyer thrust out his hand to Steavens as he passed him, caught up his overcoat in the hall, and had left the house before the Grand Army man had had time to lift his ducked head and crane his long neck about at his fellows.

Next day Jim Laird was drunk and unable to attend the funeral services. Steavens called twice at his office, but was compelled to start East without seeing him. He had a presentiment that he would hear from him again, and left his address on the lawyer's table; but if Laird found it, he never acknowledged it. The thing in him that Harvey Merrick had loved must have gone under ground with Harvey Merrick's coffin; for it never spoke again, and Jim got the cold he died of driving across the Colorado mountains to defend one of Phelps's sons who had got into trouble out there by cutting government timber.

For Discussion

1. Why did the townspeople dislike Harvey Merrick? How was he different from all of them?

2. Does anyone other than Steavens really grieve for Harvey? What about his mother?
3. How typical is the conversation about Harvey to that about anyone whose death is especially tragic? What would have been the attitude of the townspeople if Harvey had returned home alive and unusually successful?
4. Why did Steavens accompany the body back home? Was this act a product of the responsibility of friendship? Do you think that he regretted the trip?
5. The last paragraph suggests that any involvement risks possible dangers. Are the possible rewards of involvement sufficient to justify the possible dangers?

For Comparison

1. Apply Frost's definition of home ("The Death of the Hired Man") as "the place where, when you have to go there, / They have to take you in" to Harvey's return home. Why did he not request to be buried somewhere else?
2. Harvey was not accepted by his townspeople because he was a sensitive, creative person. Applying the principles of individuality from "A Community of Hope and Responsibility," discuss the unusual problems faced in an organized society by the creative individual.

For Composition

1. The responsibility of friendship.
2. Society rejects the creative person.
3. Dangers and opportunities of involvement.

JOHN DONNE

NO MAN IS AN ISLAND

No man is an island entire of itself; every man is a piece of the continent, a part of the main. If a clod be washed away by the sea, Europe is the less, as well as if a promontory were, as well as if a manor of thy friends or of thine own were. Any man's death diminishes me, because I am involved in mankind, and therefore never send to know for whom the bell tolls; it tolls for thee.

For Discussion

1. Why does Donne say that no man is an island? Does this mean that it is impossible to be individuals? Do you agree with Donne?
2. In a mechanized society such as ours, is such an attitude as Donne's feasible? Is it ever possible to feel totally involved with all of mankind?
3. When has someone's death created a permanent unfilled place in your life? How different is your attitude when reading about the death of a total stranger?
4. How can you relate Donne's poem to the fact that you sometimes feel the most lonely at twelve noon on a crowded downtown street?

For Comparison

1. Are the townspeople in "The Sculptor's Funeral" at all "diminished" by Harvey's death? Is Steavens?
2. Is the poem in direct conflict with Tennessee Williams' poem "Life Story," or is Williams' poem a realistic modern-day expression of Donne's idea?

For Composition

1. We're all one family.
2. Hurt me, hurt my brother.
3. I suffered with (name of friend).

COUNTEE CULLEN

INCIDENT

Once riding in old Baltimore,
    Heart-filled, head-filled with glee,
I saw a Baltimorean
    Keep looking straight at me.

Now I was eight and very small,
    And he was no whit bigger,
And so I smiled, but he poked out
    His tongue, and called me, "Nigger."

I saw the whole of Baltimore
From May until December;
Of all the things that happened there
That's all that I remember.

For Discussion

1. Why does the narrator remember only the one incident from Baltimore? Wouldn't this episode seem relatively minor to an eight-year-old boy?
2. Is this the first time the boy had such an encounter? If so, how did he know the meaning of "Nigger"?
3. Who is responsible for the incident?

For Comparison

1. How does Cullen's poem reflect ideas from McKuen's "Channing Way, I"?
2. How do you account for the different racial attitudes expressed in this poem and in "After You, My Dear Alphonse"?

For Composition

1. An incident that affected me.
2. The harm strangers do.
3. My most ugly memory.

LEONARD ADAMÉ

LOST TOGETHER WITH OUR CHILDREN

In the barber shop
    I see your ebony face
    against fluorescent lights
    black pebble eyes
looking down
    your clubfoot

boot wax on your hands
they read old newspapers
                    afraid of
                    your touching
                    even their shoes.

We look into our eyes
not speaking
                    we smile
                    a little
                    we know
                    of each other
                    and

of our accents
                    lost together
                    with our children
                    crying in
                    the playground
not wanting to
                    come home.

For Discussion

1. Why are eyes and seeing symbolically important to the meaning of this poem?
2. Who is the "we" in the poem? Who is the "they"?
3. Does the narrator lament the "lost accents"?
4. What is meant by the children "not wanting to come home"? Is such an attitude, in its symbolic interpretation, typical of the younger generation of minority groups today?
5. What is meant by being lost?

For Comparison

1. Does the narrator in "The Soul of a Landlord" belong to the younger generation of children who are in the process of change? Explain your answer.
2. Apply the rather famous definition of "home" given by Frost in "The Death of the Hired Man" to the concept of home in this poem. How does home viewed from this vantage point take on a different meaning?

For Composition

1. Lost heritage.
2. The new generation changes.
3. Sometimes I don't want to go home.

EDWIN ARLINGTON ROBINSON

MR. FLOOD'S PARTY

Old Eben Flood, climbing alone one night
Over the hill between the town below
And the forsaken upland hermitage
That held as much as he should ever know
On earth again of home, paused warily.
The road was his with not a native near;
And Eben, having leisure, said aloud,
For no man else in Tilbury Town to hear:

"Well, Mr. Flood, we have the harvest moon
Again, and we may not have many more;
The bird is on the wing, the poet says,
And you and I have said it here before.
Drink to the bird." He raised up to the light
The jug that he had gone so far to fill,
And answered huskily: "Well, Mr. Flood,
Since you propose it, I believe I will."

Alone, as if enduring to the end
A valiant armor of scarred hopes outworn,
He stood there in the middle of the road
Like Roland's ghost winding a silent horn.
Below him, in the town among the trees,
Where friends of other days had honored him,
A phantom salutation of the dead
Rang thinly till old Eben's eyes were dim.

Reprinted with permission of The Macmillan Company from *Collected Poems* by Edwin Arlington Robinson. Copyright 1921 by Edwin Arlington Robinson renewed 1949 by Ruth Nivison.

Then, as a mother lays her sleeping child
Down tenderly, fearing it may awake,
He set the jug down slowly at his feet
With trembling care, knowing that most things break;
And only when assured that on firm earth
It stood, as the uncertain lives of men
Assuredly did not, he paced away,
And with his hand extended paused again:

"Well, Mr. Flood, we have not met like this
In a long time; and many a change has come
To both of us, I fear, since last it was
We had a drop together. Welcome home!"
Convivially returning with himself,
Again he raised the jug up to the light;
And with an acquiescent quaver said:
"Well, Mr. Flood, if you insist, I might.

"Only a very little, Mr. Flood —
For auld lang syne. No more, sir; that will do."
So, for the time, apparently it did,
And Eben evidently thought so too;
For soon amid the silver loneliness
Of night he lifted up his voice and sang,
Secure, with only two moons listening,
Until the whole harmonious landscape rang —

"For auld lang syne." The weary throat gave out,
The last word wavered; and the song being done,
He raised again the jug regretfully
And shook his head, and was again alone.
There was not much that was ahead of him,
And there was nothing in the town below —
Where strangers would have shut the many doors
That many friends had opened long ago.

For Discussion

1. What happened to Flood's friends? Were they really friends if they deserted him in his time of need?
2. Did Flood turn to drink because his friends deserted him, or did his friends desert him because he drank? Is either action responsible?
3. What significance do you see in the name Eben Flood?
4. What is your feeling toward Flood? Do you feel sorry for him or do you feel resentment toward him?

5. What responsibility do we have to friends who have fallen upon hard times?

For Comparison

1. Would Eben Flood agree with the concepts presented in Williams' "Life Story"? What symbols of loneliness are found in both poems?
2. Answers to some of the problems raised in "The Death of the Hired Man" are simplified by the fact that Silas is "a good guy." What would be the attitude of Mary and Warren if Eben Flood had worked for them and if it were he who had returned to their place to die?

For Composition

1. Fair-weather friends.
2. How society could help its Eben Floods.
3. A fallen friend I once helped.

Rod McKuen

CHANNING WAY, I

It's always the strangers that do the most damage.
The ones you never get to know.
Seen in passing cars
mirrored in windows
and remembered.

And the others—
the ones who promise everything, then go away.

Sometimes I think people were meant to be strangers.
Not to get to know one another,
not to get close enough to damage the heart
made older by each new encounter.

But then,
someone comes along
and changes all that.
For a while anyway.

Still, as the years go by
it's easier to remember
the streets where it happened
                than the names
and who was the one on Channing Way.

For Discussion

1. What do you think would be McKuen's definitions of friendship and love?
2. Are the poet's attitudes toward friendship and love pessimistic or realistic?
3. How do strangers do the most damage to us?
4. Do we have a right to expect any more from friendship than the temporary change that McKuen suggests?

For Comparison

1. How can you apply McKuen's concept of the stranger to Cullen's poem "Incident"?
2. What specific ideas in this poem can be related to Hemingway's "A Clean, Well-Lighted Place"?

For Composition

1. My ideas about friendship.
2. The risk of being hurt.
3. Strangers in the night.

TENNESSEE WILLIAMS

LIFE STORY

After you've been to bed together for the first time,
without the advantage or disadvantage of any prior acquaintance,
the other party very often says to you,
Tell me about yourself, I want to know all about you,
what's your story? And you think maybe they really and truly do

sincerely want to know your life story, and so you light up
a cigarette and begin to tell it to them, the two of you
lying together in completely relaxed positions
like a pair of rag dolls a bored child dropped on a bed.

You tell them your story, or as much of your story
as time or a fair degree of prudence allows, and they say,
Oh, oh, oh, oh, oh,
each time a little more faintly, until the oh
is just an audible breath, and then of course

there's some interruption. Slow room service comes up
with a bowl of melting ice cubes, or one of you rises to pee
and gaze at himself with mild astonishment in the bathroom mirror.
And then, the first thing you know, before you've had time
to pick up where you left off with your enthralling life story,
they're telling you *their* life story, exactly as they'd intended to all along,

and you're saying, Oh, oh, oh, oh, oh,
each time a little more faintly, the vowel at last becoming
no more than an audible sigh,
as the elevator, halfway down the corridor and a turn to the left,
draws one last, long, deep breath of exhaustion
and stops breathing forever. Then?

Well, one of you falls asleep
and the other one does likewise with a lighted cigarette in his mouth,
and that's how people burn to death in hotel rooms.

For Discussion

1. Why is it important to this poem that the effort at communication occurs in bed?
2. Is either party really interested in knowing each other, or is this merely post-sex conversation?
3. To what extent are variations of this "life story" true for almost everyone?
4. The final line of the poem has a symbolic meaning. What is it?

For Comparison

1. Does McKuen's poem ("Channing Way, I") suggest the same feelings of despair and loneliness as those you find in this poem? Is one more optimistic than the other in any degree?

2. How might the old waiter in "A Clean, Well-Lighted Place" relate to this poem? Compare the absence of really significant communication in these two works.

For Composition

1. No one really cares.
2. My "Life Story."
3. Elevators—and other interruptions.

ROBERT FROST

THE DEATH OF THE HIRED MAN

Mary sat musing on the lamp-flame at the table
Waiting for Warren. When she heard his step,
She ran on tip-toe down the darkened passage
To meet him in the doorway with the news
And put him on his guard. "Silas is back."
She pushed him outward with her through the door
And shut it after her. "Be kind," she said.
She took the market things from Warren's arms
And set them on the porch, then drew him down
To sit beside her on the wooden steps.

"When was I ever anything but kind to him?
But I'll not have the fellow back," he said.
"I told him so last haying, didn't I?
'If he left then,' I said, 'that ended it.'
What good is he? Who else will harbor him
At his age for the little he can do?
What help he is there's no depending on.
Off he goes always when I need him most.
'He thinks he ought to earn a little pay,
Enough at least to buy tobacco with,
So he won't have to beg and be beholden.'
'All right,' I say, 'I can't afford to pay
Any fixed wages, though I wish I could.'

'Someone else can.' 'Then someone else will have to.'
I shouldn't mind his bettering himself
If that was what it was. You can be certain,
When he begins like that, there's someone at him
Trying to coax him off with pocket-money, —
In haying time, when any help is scarce.
In winter he comes back to us. I'm done."

"Sh! not so loud: he'll hear you," Mary said.

"I want him to: he'll have to soon or late."

"He's worn out. He's asleep beside the stove.
When I came up from Rowe's I found him here,
Huddled against the barn-door fast asleep,
A miserable sight, and frightening, too —
You needn't smile — I didn't recognize him —
I wasn't looking for him — and he's changed.
Wait till you see."

       "Where did you say he'd been?"

"He didn't say. I dragged him to the house,
And gave him tea and tried to make him smoke.
I tried to make him talk about his travels.
Nothing would do: he just kept nodding off."

"What did he say? Did he say anything?"

"But little."

       "Anything? Mary, confess
He said he'd come to ditch the meadow for me."

"Warren!"

       "But did he? I just want to know."

"Of course he did. What would you have him say?
Surely you wouldn't grudge the poor old man
Some humble way to save his self-respect.
He added, if you really care to know,
He meant to clear the upper pasture, too.
That sounds like something you have heard before?
Warren, I wish you could have heard the way
He jumbled everything. I stopped to look
Two or three times — he made me feel so queer —
To see if he was talking in his sleep.
He ran on Harold Wilson — you remember —

The boy you had in haying four years since.
He's finished school, and teaching in his college.
Silas declares you'll have to get him back.
He says they two will make a team for work.
Between them they will lay this farm as smooth!
The way he mixed that in with other things.
He thinks young Wilson a likely lad, though daft
On education—you know how they fought
All through July under the blazing sun,
Silas up on the cart to build the load,
Harold along beside to pitch it on."

"Yes, I took care to keep well out of earshot."

"Well, those days trouble Silas like a dream.
You wouldn't think they would. How some things linger!
Harold's young college boy's assurance piqued him.
After so many years he still keeps finding
Good arguments he sees he might have used.
I sympathize. I know just how it feels
To think of the right thing to say too late.
Harold's associated in his mind with Latin.
He asked me what I thought of Harold's saying
He studied Latin like the violin
Because he liked it—that an argument!
He said he couldn't make the boy believe
He could find water with a hazel prong—
Which showed how much good school had ever done him.
He wanted to go over that. But most of all
He thinks if he could have another chance
To teach him how to build a load of hay—"

"I know, that's Silas' one accomplishment.
He bundles every forkful in its place,
And tags and numbers it for future reference,
So he can find and easily dislodge it
In the unloading. Silas does that well.
He takes it out in bunches like big birds' nests.
You never see him standing on the hay
He's trying to lift, straining to lift himself."

"He thinks if he could teach him that, he'd be
Some good perhaps to someone in the world.
He hates to see a boy the fool of books.
Poor Silas, so concerned for other folk,
And nothing to look backward to with pride,
And nothing to look forward to with hope,
So now and never any different."

Part of a moon was falling down the west,
Dragging the whole sky with it to the hills.
Its light poured softly in her lap. She saw
And spread her apron to it. She put out her hand
Among the harp-like morning-glory strings,
Taut with the dew from garden bed to eaves,
As if she played unheard the tenderness
That wrought on him beside her in the night.
"Warren," she said, "he has come home to die:
You needn't be afraid he'll leave you this time."

"Home," he mocked gently.

        "Yes, what else but home?
It all depends on what you mean by home.
Of course he's nothing to us, anymore
Than was the hound that came a stranger to us
Out of the woods, worn out upon the trail."

"Home is the place where, when you have to go there,
They have to take you in."

        "I should have called it
Something you somehow haven't to deserve."
Warren leaned out and took a step or two,
Picked up a little stick, and brought it back
And broke it in his hand and tossed it by.
"Silas has better claims on us, you think,
Than on his brother? Thirteen little miles
As the road winds would bring him to his door.
Silas has walked that far no doubt today.
Why didn't he go there? His brother's rich,
A somebody—director in the bank."

"He never told us that."

        "We know it though."

"I think his brother ought to help, of course.
I'll see to that if there is need. He ought of right
To take him in, and might be willing to—
He may be better than appearances.
But have some pity on Silas. Do you think
If he'd had any pride in claiming kin
Or anything he looked for from his brother,
He'd keep so still about him all this time?"

"I wonder what's between them."

                                "I can tell you.
Silas is what he is—we wouldn't mind him—
But just the kind that kinsfolk can't abide.
He never did a thing so very bad.
He don't know why he isn't quite as good
As anyone. He won't be made ashamed
To please his brother, worthless though he is."

"I can't think Si ever hurt anyone."

"No, but he hurt my heart the way he lay
And rolled his old head on that sharp-edged chairback.
He wouldn't let me put him on the lounge.
You must go in and see what you can do.
I made the bed up for him there tonight.
You'll be surprised at him—how much he's broken.
His working days are done; I'm sure of it."

"I'd not be in a hurry to say that."

"I haven't been. Go, look, see for yourself.
But, Warren, please remember how it is:
He's come to help you ditch the meadow.
He has a plan. You mustn't laugh at him.
He may not speak of it, and then he may.
I'll sit and see if that small sailing cloud
Will hit or miss the moon."

                               It hit the moon.
Then there was three there, making a dim row,
The moon, the little silver cloud, and she.

Warren returned—too soon, it seemed to her,
Slipped to her side, caught up her hand and waited.

"Warren," she questioned.

                            "Dead," was all he answered.

For Discussion

1. Compare Mary's and Warren's attitudes toward Silas. How are they
   typical of attitudes representing their two sexes?

2. Compare the relative value of Silas' type of education with that of Harold's. Which seems most important in today's society?
3. Do you agree with Frost's definition of home as "the place where, when you have to go there, / They have to take you in"? Why does Silas feel that Warren's place is more home than his brother's? Is home always necessarily related to immediate family?
4. How responsible were Mary and Warren for Silas? If he had lived, would Warren have been responsible to take him in?
5. How responsible was Silas to Mary and Warren? Did his relationship with them justify his coming back there to die? Was this too much a demand on their friendship?

For Comparison

1. How are the attitudes of a formal versus an informal education in this poem similar to those expressed in "The Sculptor's Funeral"?
2. Compare Mary's attitudes with those of the narrator in "The Coup de Grâce." Was she, in her own way, trying to provide Silas a "coup de grâce"?

For Composition

1. Formal versus informal education.
2. Mary and Warren are (are not) responsible.
3. The right to self-respect.

photo by Lou de la Torre/BBM Associates

Part Four

INDIVIDUAL–SCHOOL

School is one of the first formally structured forces an individual encounters. People's attitudes are strongly shaped by the type of education they receive, by the personality of their school and teachers, and by the suitability of the education to their career objectives. A person's response to the immediate educational environment is molded by personal opinions and attitudes of family and peers.

Responsibility in education is reciprocal: the educational system is responsible to the individual, and the individual is responsible to the educational system. Many contemporary forces argue loudly that education today is not immediately relevant to our current needs. If this is true, then the entire structure of the educational system must be reorganized. If the proposition is false, then it is the responsibility of the educational system to justify itself. No educational program can do a valid job, however, unless the individual student is committed to working within the objectives of the system. However formal or informal a person's education may be, each student must know exactly what to expect from it and what responsibilities it demands.

Any person in a position of responsibility within a formally structured group must continually examine his or her responsibility to self, family, and peers. All of these concepts are involved in answering questions such as: What is a proper education? What are the qualities of a good teacher? Is a formal education better than an informal one? Do students have a right to dissent? Is the social environment of a college campus artificial? What is the difference between education and indoctrination?

219

BERTRAND RUSSELL

THE FUNCTION OF A TEACHER

Teaching, more even than most other professions, has been transformed during the last hundred years from a small, highly skilled profession concerned with a minority of the population, to a large and important branch of the public service. The profession has a great and honorable tradition, extending from the dawn of history until recent times, but any teacher in the modern world who allows himself to be inspired by the ideals of his predecessors is likely to be made sharply aware that it is not his function to teach what he thinks, but to instill such beliefs and prejudices as are thought useful by his employers. In former days a teacher was expected to be a man of exceptional knowledge or wisdom, to whose words men would do well to attend. In antiquity, teachers were not an organized profession, and no control was exercised over what they taught. It is true that they were often punished afterwards for their subversive doctrines. Socrates was put to death and Plato is said to have been thrown into prison, but such incidents did not interfere with the spread of their doctrines. Any man who has the genuine impulse of the teacher will be more anxious to survive in his books than in the flesh. A feeling of intellectual independence is essential to the proper fulfillment of the teacher's functions, since it is his business to instill what he can of knowledge and reasonableness into the process of forming public opinion. In antiquity he performed this function unhampered except by occasional spasmodic and ineffective interventions of tyrants or mobs. In the middle ages teaching became the exclusive prerogative of the church, with the result that there was little progress either intellectual or social. With the Renaissance, the general respect for learning brought back a very considerable measure of freedom to the teacher. It is true that the Inquisition compelled Galileo to recant, and burned Giordano Bruno at the stake, but each of these men had done his work before being punished. Institutions such as universities largely remained in the grip of the dogmatists, with the result that most of the best intellectual work was done by independent men of learning. In England, especially, until near the end of the nineteenth century, hardly any men of first-rate eminence except Newton were connected with universities. But the social system was such that this interfered little with their activities or their usefulness.

In our more highly organized world we face a new problem. Something called education is given to everybody, usually by the state, but sometimes by the churches. The teacher has thus become, in the vast majority of cases, a civil servant obliged to carry out the behests of men who have not his learning, who have no experience of dealing with the young, and whose only attitude towards education is that of the propagandist. It is not very easy to see how, in these circumstances, teachers can perform the functions for which they are specially fitted.

State education is obviously necessary, but as obviously involves certain dangers against which there ought to be safeguards. The evils to be feared were seen in their full magnitude in Nazi Germany and are still seen in Russia. Where these evils prevail no man can teach unless he subscribes to a dogmatic creed which few people of free intelligence are likely to accept sincerely. Not only must he subscribe to a creed, but he must condone abominations and carefully abstain from speaking his mind on current events. So long as he is teaching only the alphabet and the multiplication table, as to which no controversies arise, official dogmas do not necessarily warp his instruction; but even while he is teaching these elements he is expected, in totalitarian countries, not to employ the methods which he thinks most likely to achieve the scholastic result, but to instill fear, subservience, and blind obedience by demanding unquestioned submission to his authority. And as soon as he passes beyond the bare elements, he is obliged to take the official view on all controversial questions. The result is that the young in Nazi Germany became, and in Russia become, fanatical bigots, ignorant of the world outside their own country, totally unaccustomed to free discussion, and not aware that their opinions can be questioned without wickedness. This state of affairs, bad as it is, would be less disastrous than it is if the dogmas instilled were, as in medieval Catholicism, universal and international; but the whole conception of an international culture is denied by the modern dogmatists, who preached one creed in Germany, another in Italy, another in Russia, and yet another in Japan. In each of these countries fanatical nationalism was what was most emphasized in the teaching of the young, with the result that the men of one country have no common ground with the men of another, and that no conception of a common civilization stands in the way of warlike ferocity.

The decay of cultural internationalism has proceeded at a continually increasing pace ever since the First World War. When I was in Leningrad in 1920, I met the Professor of Pure Mathematics, who was familiar with London, Paris, and other capitals, having been a member of various international congresses. Nowadays the learned men of Russia are very seldom permitted such excursions, for fear of their drawing comparisons unfavorable to their own country. In other countries nationalism in learning is less extreme, but everywhere it is far more powerful than it was. There is a tendency in England (and, I believe in the United States) to dispense with Frenchmen and Germans in the teaching of French and German. The practice of considering a man's nationality rather than his competence in appointing him to a post is damaging to education and an offense against the ideal of international culture, which was a heritage from the Roman Empire and the Catholic Church, but is now being submerged under a new barbarian invasion, proceeding from below rather than from without.

In democratic countries these evils have not yet reached anything like the same proportions, but it must be admitted that there is grave danger of similar developments in education, and that this danger can only be averted if those who believe in liberty of thought are on the alert to protect teachers from intellectual bondage. Perhaps the first requisite is a clear conception of the services which teachers can be expected to perform for the community. I agree with the governments of the world that the imparting of definite uncontroversial information is one of the least of the teacher's functions. It is, of course, the basis upon which the others are built, and in a technical civilization such as ours it has undoubtedly a considerable utility. There must exist in a modern community a sufficient number of men who possess the technical skill required to preserve the mechanical apparatus upon which our physical comforts depend. It is, moreover, inconvenient if any large percentage of the population is unable to read and write. For these reasons we are all in favor of universal compulsory education. But governments have perceived that it is easy, in the course of giving instruction, to instill beliefs on controversial matters and to produce habits of mind which may be convenient or inconvenient to those in authority. The defense of the state in all civilized countries is quite as much in the hands of teachers as in those of the armed forces. Except in totalitarian countries, the defense of the state is desirable, and the mere fact that education is used for this purpose is not in itself a ground of criticism. Criticism will only arise if the state is defended by obscurantism and appeals to irrational passion. Such methods are quite unnecessary in the case of any state worth defending. Nevertheless, there is a natural tendency towards their adoption by those who have no firsthand knowledge of education. There is widespread belief that nations are made strong by uniformity of opinion and by the suppression of liberty. One hears it said over and over again that democracy weakens a country in war, in spite of the fact that in every important war since the year 1700 the victory has gone to the more democratic side. Nations have been brought to ruin much more often by insistence upon a narrow-minded doctrinal uniformity than by free discussion and the toleration of divergent opinions. Dogmatists the world over believe that although the truth is known to them, others will be led into false beliefs provided they are allowed to hear the arguments on both sides. This is a view which leads to one or another of two misfortunes: either one set of dogmatists con-

quers the world and prohibits all new ideas, or, what is worse, rival dogmatists conquer different regions and preach the gospel of hate against
each other, the former of these evils existing in the middle ages, the latter
during the wars of religion, and again in the present day. The first makes
civilization static, the second tends to destroy it completely. Against both,
the teacher should be the main safeguard.

It is obvious that organized party spirit is one of the greatest dangers
of our time. In the form of nationalism it leads to wars between nations,
and in other forms it leads to civil war. It should be the business of teachers to stand outside the strife of parties and endeavor to instill into the
young the habit of impartial inquiry, leading them to judge issues on
their merits and to be on their guard against accepting *ex parte* statements at their face value. The teacher should not be expected to flatter
the prejudices either of the mob or of officials. His professional virtue
should consist in a readiness to do justice to all sides, and in an endeavor
to rise above controversy into a region of dispassionate scientific investigation. If there are people to whom the results of his investigation are inconvenient, he should be protected against their resentment, unless it
can be shown that he has lent himself to dishonest propaganda by the
dissemination of demonstrable untruths.

The function of the teacher, however, is not merely to mitigate the
heat of current controversies. He has more positive tasks to perform,
and he cannot be a great teacher unless he is inspired by a wish to perform these tasks. Teachers are more than any other class the guardians
of civilization. They should be intimately aware of what civilization is,
and desirous of imparting a civilized attitude to their pupils. We are thus
brought to the question: what constitutes a civilized community?

This question would very commonly be answered by pointing to merely
material tests. A country is civilized if it has much machinery, many
motor cars, many bathrooms, and a great deal of rapid locomotion. To
these things, in my opinion, most modern men attach much too much
importance. Civilization, in the more important sense, is a thing of the
mind, not of material adjuncts to the physical side of living. It is a matter
partly of knowledge, partly of emotion. So far as knowledge is concerned,
a man should be aware of the minuteness of himself and his immediate
environment in relation to the world in time and space. He should see
his own country not *only* as home, but as one among the countries of the
world, all with an equal right to live and think and feel. He should see
his own age in relation to the past and the future, and be aware that its
own controversies will seem as strange to future ages as those of the past
seem to us now. Taking an even wider view, he should be conscious of the
vastness of geological epochs and astronomical abysses; but he should be
aware of all this, not as a weight to crush the individual human spirit,

but as a vast panorama which enlarges the mind that contemplates it. On the side of the emotions, a very similar enlargement from the purely personal is needed if a man is to be truly civilized. Men pass from birth to death, sometimes happy, sometimes unhappy; sometimes generous, sometimes grasping and petty; sometimes heroic, sometimes cowardly and servile. To the man who views the procession as a whole, certain things stand out as worthy of admiration. Some men have been inspired by love of mankind; some by supreme intellect have helped us to understand the world in which we live; and some by exceptional sensitiveness have created beauty. These men have produced something of positive good to outweigh the long record of cruelty, oppression and superstition. These men have done what lay in their power to make human life a better thing than the brief turbulence of savages. The civilized man, where he cannot admire, will aim rather at understanding than at reprobating. He will seek rather to discover and remove the impersonal causes of evil than to hate the men who are in its grip. All this should be in the mind and heart of the teacher, and if it is in his mind and heart he will convey it in his teaching to the young who are in his care.

No man can be a good teacher unless he has feelings of warm affection towards his pupils and a genuine desire to impart to them what he himself believes to be of value. This is not the attitude of the propagandist. To the propagandist his pupils are potential soldiers in an army. They are to serve purposes that lie outside their own lives, not in the sense in which every generous purpose transcends self, but in the sense of ministering to unjust privilege or to despotic power. The propagandist does not desire that his pupils should survey the world and freely choose a purpose which to them appears of value. He desires, like a topiarian artist, that their growth shall be trained and twisted to suit the gardener's purpose. And in thwarting their natural growth he is apt to destroy in them all generous vigor, replacing it by envy, destructiveness, and cruelty. There is no need for men to be cruel; on the contrary, I am persuaded that most cruelty results from thwarting in early years, above all from thwarting what is good.

Repressive and persecuting passions are very common, as the present state of the world only too amply proves. But they are not an inevitable part of human nature. On the contrary, they are, I believe, always the outcome of some kind of unhappiness. It should be one of the functions of the teacher to open vistas before his pupils showing them the possibility of activities that will be as delightful as they are useful, thereby letting loose their kind impulses and preventing the growth of a desire to rob others of joys that they will have missed. Many people decry happiness as an end, both for themselves and for others, but one may suspect them of sour grapes. It is one thing to forgo personal happiness for a public end, but it is quite another to treat the general happiness as a thing of no account. Yet this is often done in the name of some supposed heroism. In those who take this attitude there is generally some vein of cruelty based probably upon an unconscious envy, and the source of the envy will usually be found in childhood or youth. It should be the aim of the educator to train adults free from these physical misfortunes, and not anxious to rob others of happiness because they themselves have not been robbed of it.

As matters stand today, many teachers are unable to do the best of which they are capable. For this there are a number of reasons, some more or less accidental, others very deep-seated. To begin with the former, most teachers are overworked and are compelled to prepare their pupils for examinations rather than to give them a liberalizing mental training. The people who are not accustomed to teaching—and this includes practically all educational authorities—have no idea of the expense of spirit that it involves. Clergymen are not expected to preach sermons for several hours every day, but the analogous effort is demanded of teachers. The result is that many of them become harassed and nervous, out of touch with recent work in the subjects that they teach, and unable to inspire their students with a sense of the intellectual delights to be obtained from new understanding and new knowledge.

This, however, is by no means the gravest matter. In most countries certain opinions are recognized as correct, and others as dangerous. Teachers whose opinions are not correct are expected to keep silent about them. If they mention their opinions it is propaganda, while the mentioning of correct opinions is considered to be merely sound instruction. The result is that the inquiring young too often have to go outside the classroom to discover what is being thought by the most vigorous minds of their own time. There is in America a subject called civics, in which, perhaps more than in any other, the teaching is expected to be misleading. The young are taught a sort of copybook account of how public affairs are supposed to be conducted, and are carefully shielded from all knowledge as to how in fact they are conducted. When they grow up and discover the truth, the result is too often a complete cynicism in which all public ideals are lost; whereas if they had been taught the truth carefully and with proper comment at an earlier age they might have become men able to combat evils in which, as it is, they acquiesce with a shrug.

The idea that falsehood is edifying is one of the besetting sins of those who draw up educational schemes. I should not myself consider that a man could be a good teacher unless he had made a firm resolve never in the course of his teaching to conceal truth because it is what is called "unedifying." The kind of virtue that can be produced by guarded ignorance is frail and fails at the first touch of reality. There are, in this world, many men who deserve admiration, and it is good that the young should be taught to see the ways in which these men are admirable. But it is not good to teach them to admire rogues by concealing their roguery. It is thought that the knowledge of things as they are will lead to cynicism, and so it may do if the knowledge comes suddenly with a shock of surprise and horror. But if it comes gradually, duly intermixed with a knowledge of what is good, and in the course of a scientific study inspired by the wish to get at the truth, it will have no such effect. In any case, to tell lies to the young, who have no means of checking what they are told, is morally indefensible.

The thing, above all, that a teacher should endeavor to produce in his pupils, if democracy is to survive, is the kind of tolerance that springs from an endeavor to understand those who are different from ourselves. It is perhaps a natural human impulse to view with horror and disgust all manners and customs different from those to which we are used. Ants and savages put strangers to death. And those who have never traveled either physically or mentally find it difficult to tolerate the queer ways and outlandish beliefs of other nations and other times, other sects and other political parties. This kind of ignorant intolerance is the antithesis of a civilized outlook, and is one of the gravest dangers to which our overcrowded world is exposed. The educational system ought to be designed to correct it, but much too little is done in this direction at present. In every country nationalistic feeling is encouraged, and school children are taught, what they are only too ready to believe, that the inhabitants of other countries are morally and intellectually inferior to those of the country in which the school children happen to reside. Collective hysteria, the most mad and cruel of all human emotions, is encouraged instead of being discouraged, and the young are encouraged to believe what they hear frequently said rather than what there is some rational ground for believing. In all this the teachers are not to blame. They are not free to teach as they would wish. It is they who know most intimately the needs of the young. It is they who through daily contact have come to care for them. But it is not they who decide what shall be taught or what the methods of instruction are to be. There ought to be a great deal more freedom than there is for the scholastic profession. It ought to have more opportunities of self-determination, more independence from the interference of bureaucrats and bigots. No one would consent in our day to subject the medical men to the control of non-medical authorities as to how they should treat their patients, except of course where they depart criminally from the purpose of medicine, which is to cure the patient. The teacher is a kind of medical man whose purpose is to cure the patient of childishness, but he is not allowed to decide for himself on the basis of experience what methods are most suitable to this end. A few great historic universities, by the weight of their prestige, have secured vital self-determination, but the immense majority of educational institutions are hampered and controlled by men who do not understand the work with which they are interfering. The only way to prevent totalitarianism in our highly organized world is to secure a certain degree of independence for bodies performing useful public work, and among such bodies teachers deserve a foremost place.

The teacher, like the artist, the philosopher, and the man of letters, can only perform his work adequately if he feels himself to be an individual directed by an inner creative impulse, not dominated and fettered by an outside authority. It is very difficult in this modern world to find a place for the individual. He can subsist at the top as a dictator in a totalitarian state or a plutocratic magnate in a country of large industrial enterprises, but in the realm of the mind it is becoming more and more difficult to preserve independence of the great organized forces that control the livelihoods of men and women. If the world is not to lose the benefit to be derived from its best minds, it will have to find some method of allowing them scope and liberty in spite of organization. This involves a deliberate restraint on the part of those who have power, and a conscious realization that there are men to whom free scope must be afforded. Renaissance Popes could feel in this way towards Renaissance artists, but the powerful men of our day seem to have more difficulty in feeling respect for exceptional genius. The turbulence of our times is inimical to the fine flower of culture. The man in the street is full of fear, and therefore unwilling to tolerate freedoms for which he sees no need. Perhaps we must wait for quieter times before the claims of civilization can again override the claims of party spirit. Meanwhile, it is important that some at least should continue to realize the limitations of what can be done by organization. Every system should allow loopholes and exceptions, for if it does not it will in the end crush all that is best in man.

For Discussion

1. What particular problems are created for the teacher by state-and church-supported education?
2. Do you agree with Russell that "the imparting of definite uncontroversial information is one of the least of the teacher's functions"? Is Russell suggesting that a good teacher must be controversial?

3. What is the difference between teaching students to explore for truth and indoctrinating them? In what way is much modern education more a form of indoctrination?
4. What difference does Russell see between preparing students for examinations and giving them a liberalizing mental training?
5. How can a responsible teacher best instruct his students in the learning of tolerance? Do you agree that tolerance is the thing to learn?

For Comparison

1. Think about the final stanza of "An Elementary School Class Room in a Slum" in relation to this essay. What would be Russell's attitude toward the concept of education suggested in Spender's poem? Discuss his attitude in terms of what he says about the exploration for truth versus mere indoctrination.
2. What would be Russell's attitude toward the type of teaching done by Herndon in "The Way It Spozed to Be"? What would be Russell's attitude toward the school principal?

For Composition

1. Teaching versus indoctrination.
2. Censorship in the classroom.
3. The best teacher I have had.

MARGARET MEAD AND RHODA METRAUX

EDUCATION FOR DIVERSITY

May, 1967

How can parents give their children a solid education today and at the same time prepare them for life in a racially diverse world?

Traveling around the country, I meet a great number of parents who are deeply troubled about what action to take to achieve both these ends. Should they try to stick it out in a changing neighborhood? Should they struggle with all the difficulties of a newly integrated school? Should they move to a different kind of community for the sake of the children's education? Should they decide in favor of private schools?

Reprinted from *Redbook Magazine*, May 1967, Copyright © 1967, The Redbook Publishing Company.

Urgency is part of the problem, because the time for children's education is always *now*.

Parents want schooling for their children that will give them access to the knowledge and the skills that will open the doors of the world to them in later years. But farsighted parents also realize that their children must acquire a readiness to move into a highly diversified world in which they will live and work with men and women of markedly different backgrounds. No one can predict where these children, just taking their first tentative steps away from home, will be working twenty years from now, on what continent or at what tasks. And it is this double demand on education that poses the parents' dilemma.

In the past, schools did prepare American children to move freely in what was then a more circumscribed world. Two factors seem to have been important in achieving this. Most American families lived in small communities, where rich and poor jostled elbows and the children of new immigrants learning to speak the language and eat the food of the new country mingled with those who had come before them. And most children attended public schools, where our fundamental belief in the value of free education gave meaning to their meeting and learning together. However much they differed in their background and in the prospects for their future, their common experience in school taught them the easy give-and-take, the friendliness and trust that made them into people who were at home anywhere in the country.

There were, of course, regions of the country where this was not so. Schools in the southeast were segregated, and in our largest cities immigrants of one nationality often were crowded together in one grim reception slum. But for most Americans in small towns and in the mixed neighborhoods of larger cities, the public school was a good preparation for the kind of diversity they were likely to meet later in life. Children learned what we then understood to be democracy—how to get along comfortably with people of many different backgrounds.

But young children today will move into a world that is global in its dimensions. They will face a far more complex diversity. As adults they may have to learn to speak any one of forty or fifty languages, and they may find themselves working as supervisors or subordinates, colleagues or neighbors, with individuals of any of the world's races. Instead of learning what they must so that they can get along as well in Chicago as they can in Boston, whether with second-generation Italians, Germans, Irish or their parents' own ethnic group, today's children must learn how to live and work with people anywhere in the world.

And they are ill prepared to do so, for our schools long ago ceased to be small replicas of a larger world. Great numbers of Americans now live in neighborhoods and communities where their principal associations are with families very similar to their own, of the same class, color and religion, having the same kind of education and interests, and even, within a narrow range, the same kinds of occupations. Where those belonging to ethnically disadvantaged groups have become isolated, we speak of their crowded slum neighborhoods as ghettos, borrowing the term used to describe the old segregated Jewish settlements in Europe. Where the community is made up of more-privileged people, we call it a suburb or a "nice residential section." One result for the ghetto children has been an ever-increasing inequality of opportunity for good schooling. But from the point of view of human experience, segregation is equally damaging for the privileged, who are cut off from experiencing others—and themselves—as full human beings.

What we are facing now is the hard struggle to reverse this process. In most of what we are undertaking in rezoning neighborhoods, changing real-estate regulations, trying to integrate housing and schools, attempting to open up employment and to give everyone access to recreational facilities, the emphasis is on the rights and needs of those who have suffered from poverty and prejudice. However tardily, we have come to realize that it is devastatingly destructive for children to grow up trapped in ghettos. But we are much less clear that it is deeply damaging for children to grow up isolated in suburbs and in "select" sections of the city.

Instead, where privileged children are concerned our attention is focused on the more limited problem of how they will get a sound basic education. And in the midst of the uneasy process of transition and the pressures that are brought to bear on everyone, there is a real danger that the diversity we once valued for all children will come to be defined as a privilege for the deprived and as a penalty for the previously privileged.

Talking all these problems over with parents today, I have been struck both by the similarity and the contrast between their situation now and mine twenty years ago, when my own daughter was ready for school. I knew what I wanted for her. I wanted a school where she could learn all that we depend on schools to teach. But I also wanted her to grow up able to move freely, responsibly and with sophistication anywhere in the world. I wanted her to feel at home and welcome anywhere in the New World, where all the great races of man have mingled, and in the Old World, where so many groups have lived apart from one another. I wanted her to understand that skin color and eye color and hair form are signs of special ability and disability only where, temporarily, people have treated them as such.

Particularly I wanted her to overcome the peculiar American belief that African heritage, in whatever proportion, is determining as no other heritage, European or Asian, is. I wanted her to know members of other groups so that she would not classify individuals by such categories as skin color, language or religion, but would be able to respond to each of them as a person whom she liked or found uncongenial for individual reasons. I wanted her to experience living with others as full human beings.

But we lived in New York City, and there seemed no way of providing good schooling based on diversity within the then-deteriorating school system. I was faced, as parents now are faced, with the fact that children are young only once. If they are to have the right kind of education, they must have it now, not in some far future when we have reorganized the school system. And so, very reluctantly (for I grew up believing firmly in public schools), I joined with a group of parents in starting a new school where a few children, at least, could have the things we wanted for all children: a good formal education, a rich artistic experience and the daily give-and-take of growing up with children and with adults—teachers, trustees, maintenance staff—of diverse ethnic, religious and cultural backgrounds.

My conscience troubled me. A good school should be rooted in the community, and our children came from distant parts of the city. The long bus trips were hard on the children, and keeping the school going was hard on the parents. Most of them were young and had little money. They were scarcely able to afford tuition for their own children, much less contribute to the many scholarships that were needed.

The school often faced disaster. We paid the staff less than they could have earned in a different kind of school, and sometimes we couldn't pay them on time. The Negro families faced the greatest difficulties. Their children had the longest bus rides and the Negro parents made the greatest sacrifices in sharing the costs. No one now can count the hours everyone gave to make the school a living thing. Our children had a good education, but at great cost.

Today we have the legal framework for creating such diversity in all our public schools. But we are still a long way from having created the social climate in which each child can have both a good formal education and a happy experience of human diversity. Our attempts nationally to bring together children who differ from one another in color, religion, language and in ethnic, economic and social background are still clumsy and crude. Breaking old neighborhood patterns, bringing together children and teachers and parents who are strangers to one another, using old schools and new schools, finding methods of teaching the deprived and the privileged simultaneously—all this is hard on everyone, the children most of all.

Can we make it work? Can we give our children, all our children, the kind of education they will need? Some parents I know have given up and are sending their children to private schools; others are founding new private schools. Even the parents who care the most are discouraged. We are finding that what we want is expensive in time and money, and especially in effort. We are discovering that it is not enough to try to work toward our older, already existing standards. If a fully integrated school is to benefit all its students, it must have better teachers and better facilities than any ordinary school. And everyone will have to work much harder—the teachers, the school boards, the parents, the children themselves and the whole community. It will not be easy.

But I think we can succeed—on one condition: that is, that we continue to value diversity. Today that is not simply an ideal. It is the reality of our children's world.

For Discussion

1. What are all the implications of the word "diversity" as it is used in this essay?
2. Do you feel that parents who "are deeply troubled about what action to take" are always motivated by their concern for a solid education for their children? Could they be reacting to a conscious or unconscious racial bias?
3. Do you agree with the authors' suggestion that it is just as unfortunate to grow up in a select suburb as to grow up in a ghetto?
4. Was the parent in this essay responsible by sending her daughter to a private school? Would it have been more responsible to work to make the public school more adequate, or is that asking too much? Does it matter that this experimental school was integrated and not segregated?
5. This essay was written before various busing laws. In your opinion, has busing brought about any of the positive ideas suggested in this essay?

For Comparison

1. What would be the attitude of Mead and Metraux to the theme assignment given at the beginning of "Theme for English B"? What would be their attitude toward the theme itself?

2. With which concepts of teaching expressed by Russell ("The Function of a Teacher") would Mead and Metraux be in agreement? What new function might they add to the list?

For Composition

1. What education for the future demands.
2. My experiences in a ghetto (or select suburb) school.
3. Busing does (does not) aid in "education for diversity."

JULIAN BOND

THE BLACK MIND ON THE AMERICAN CAMPUS

The crisis in race that exists on the college campus is of course only a reflection of a larger, more serious crisis in the country and, indeed, throughout the world.

The roots of the crisis are as old as the world itself; they involve the continuing failure of the white minority of peoples of the world to share power and wealth with the nonwhite majority.

That struggle has been in the streets of every city in this country, both violently and non-violently. It is part of the struggle that inspired Fidel Castro to overthrow a dictator in Cuba, and it is the same struggle that is inspiring the patriots of Vietnam to continue, successfully, it seems, their 20-year-old struggle to resist foreign domination of their homeland.

That it should come to the college campus is not at all unusual; here, after all, are the people who have been told since the day they graduated from high school that the earth is theirs for taking, that they are the inheritors of tomorrow. Who is to blame if they believe it? That it is spreading downward into high schools, and even elementary schools is not surprising either.

It ought not to be surprising that young people who learned how to organize the poor and powerless in the Mississippi Delta would transfer their expertise to the powerless at Berkeley and Cornell.

From *The Black Politician*, published by Windsor University, Los Angeles, California; Dr. Chester M. Wright, President. Reprinted with permission.

And it ought not be surprising that race has played a large part in the continuing struggle of man against man.

To tie today's on-campus unrest only to yesterday's off-campus protests is unreal. However, there is a great deal more at stake than that.

A great deal has been made by some scholars and pollsters of the difference in the demands of black and white student activists. The whites want revolution, the experts say, while all the blacks want, despite their revolutionary rhetoric, is reform, a chance to bend the established system to their own ends, which are as safe and as ordinary as those shared by the rest of middle-class America.

Therein lies, I think, the conflict present in the black mind on the American campus. The black student is torn between the need for a regular, formal education, part of the socialization process that we are told everyone needs in order to seek an acceptable role in society, and his need to carve out a new education experience, one that is meaningful to him as a black person.

A young girl, a student at Tougaloo College in Mississippi, summed up this feeling when she wrote of her reaction to learning that Tougaloo and Brown University had entered into an education compact, with Brown acting as big brother.

"We argued," she wrote, "that Tougaloo could do better, that we did not have to pattern ourselves after Brown or any of the Ivy League schools, that we have a unique opportunity to make Tougaloo a revolutionary institute of learning. We questioned the notion that places like Brown offered a superior education; we felt in fact that they dealt in mis-education. We felt that if schools like Brown had been truly educating their students then the state of the country and the world would be a lot different."

Change the Tougaloos

The dilemma of whether to change the Tougaloos of the world or to get what can be gotten from the Browns is the continuing one among young blacks.

The demand for a black dorm or an Afro-American center is a part of this dilemma. The unscholarly attacks on black educational institutions by scholars who should know better are a part of that dilemma.

So the current and future course for those blacks interested in solving —or rather eliminating the crisis of race is unclear.

One has to realize that it is educated and civilized man who has put us where we are today. The rape of Vietnam was not begun by high school dropouts, but by liberally educated men. The pollution of the air and water is not carried out by fools and idiots, but by men educated at the best scientific and technical centers. The ability to shape a society that spends nearly $100 billion on conquering space and dominating the globe militarily comes from men of genius, not from men whose minds are limited.

Civilized man, or educated man, is supposed to solve his problems in a civilized manner.

But the problems of the 20th century are so vast that many have quite properly been urged to seek uncivilized solutions to them. These problems include the poisoning of the air and water; the rape of the land; the new colonization of peoples, both here and abroad; the new imperialism practiced by Western democracy, and the continuing struggle of those who have not against those who have.

Birth of the Colossus

With the birth, 200 years ago, of the colossus called the United States, rational and educated men began to believe that civilization stretched to its highest order had begun. Building on a heritage of revolution, expressing a belief in the equality of most, if not all men, this new democracy was to be the highest elevation of man's relations, one to the other, and a new beginning of decency between nations.

Civilization, as it was then defined, included imposing limitations on war between nations, encouraging the spread of industrialization, the civilizing of so-called heathen elements, the harnessing of nature for the benefit and pleasure of man. It was believed generally that man's better nature would triumph over his base desire to conquer and rule and make war, and that intellect, reason, and logic would share equally with morality in deciding man's fate.

Of course it has not been so. Man still makes war. He still insists that one group subordinate its wishes and desires to that of another. He still insists on gathering material wealth at the expense of his fellows and his environment.

Men and nations have grown arrogant, and the struggle of the twentieth century has continued.

And while the struggle has continued, the university has remained aloof, a center for the study of why man behaves as he does, but never a center for the study of how to make man behave in a civilized manner.

Robert M. Hutchins, former chancellor of the University of Chicago, describes the present-day university thus: It was hoped "it would lead the way to national power and prosperity . . . become the central factory of the knowledge industry, the foundation of our future. [But it became] . . . the national screening device through which individuals were to be put in the proper productive relationship to the national program of power and prosperity.

"[But] the world has moved too fast for the university. The leaders of the younger generations see that the problem is not to get wealth and power [nations] have enough of those already. The problem is justice, or what to do with wealth and power. An institution that evidently has little interest in this question cannot command the allegiance of the young."

That the allegiance of some of the young is not with the university but with the oppressed and downtrodden is evident. Every continent has seen its young rise up against the evils the university is supposed to teach them how to destroy, and many have risen up against the university itself.

Despite its goal of producing individuals who know their relationship to be managers of the new industrial and technological society, the university has thankfully, probably against its desires, produced a new crop of people, a group of activists whose current demands on the university will hopefully be expanded to include assaults on the foundations of a society which has perverted education to reinforce inequity.

Entire Fabric Attacked

So then it is the entire fabric of education that is being attacked, its purpose, its ends. All black students have done is allowed their demands to be colored by their race.

Why should we not demand amnesty, the young ask, when you have allowed amnesty for over 300 years? Why should we negotiate, they ask, when you have received it since you came to power? Why should we not use weapons, when you have used them time and time again against us? Why should we be accused of tearing down the university and having nothing to put in its place, when you have torn down Vietnam and left the ghetto standing?

Why should we not have a black house on campus, the blacks ask, when the Methodists, Episcopalians, Jews, and Catholics often have theirs?

Why shouldn't we take over a building and evict the deans? Isn't every big-city university, in connivance with urban renewal, doing the same thing to entire families on a permanent basis every day?

Why should we not learn about ourselves, the blacks ask? Haven't we been made to learn more than we ever wanted to know about you?

Why shouldn't any and every black high school graduate be admitted freely to this college, the blacks ask? Aren't they being taught by your graduates, and therefore shouldn't they have learned what it takes to fit in here?

Why should Dow Chemical or ROTC be on campus, the students ask?

We are not here to learn to make napalm or to learn how to be soldiers. This is not a vocational school for *any* employer. Or at least it should not be.

This ought to be, the students say, a center for the shaping of civilized man; a center for the study of not just why man behaves as he does, but also a center for the study of how to make him behave better.

To do this, the university must rid itself of several old notions. First of all, higher education can no longer be regarded as a privilege for a few, but must be seen as a right for the many. None of the rhetoric of the past several years about an education for everyone really approaches this aim; higher education is still an elitist and largely white preserve in America today.

In an age when education itself is being questioned, to permit or even to require that everyone receive a piece of parchment which will establish that he knows what millions of people already know with little profit to mankind will not suffice; it is simply not enough and simply will not do.

What is it then that is lacking? What is there beyond four years of compressing all the world's knowledge from lecture notes to the little blue book?

For the blacks, it must be more than Swahili lessons and Afro-American centers, although these have their place. For white universities, it must be more than raiding Southern black schools and taking their most talented faculty and students. For the black school it must be more than pride in blackness.

A writer in *The Center Magazine* described the school's failing action. He wrote: "Students are encouraged to relinquish their own wills, their freedom of volition: they are taught that value and culture reside outside oneself, and must be acquired from the institutions, and almost everything in their education is designed to discourage them from activity, from the wedding of idea and act. It is almost as if we hoped to discourage them from thought itself, by making ideas so lifeless, so hopeless, that their despair would be enough to make them manipulable and obedient."

While the university may have bred despair, it thankfully has not bred obedience. Violence occurs where there is no politics; while there is no politics of race, or rather while there is no anti-racist politics in the university, violence—physical and intellectual—will flourish.

The University in Doubt

Until the university develops a politics or, in better terms perhaps for this gathering, a curriculum and a discipline that stifles war and poverty and racism, until then, the university will be in doubt.

If education is a socializing process, in our society it has prepared white people to continue enjoying privileged traditions and positions, while black people, through it, have been programmed for social and economic oblivion.

Today's black and white students see this. They see the university nurturing war and directing counter-revolution; they see their professors employed in the Pentagon; they see their presidents serving on commission after commission investigating and recommending last year's solution to the last century's problems; they see the university recruit ghetto students with substandard backgrounds and then submit these students to standards of white, middle-class America.

They believe, as does the Tougaloo student I quoted from earlier that "the task for black students and black Americans is much greater than trying to change white institutions and their white counterparts in the South. The task is to create revolutionary institutes of learning. The act of trying to be a better person, of trying to imagine and create humane institutions is formidable, but we have no other alternative. We must have a prototype from which to build a good society.

"The point which I make is an old one: that revolution is not only the seizure of power, but is also the building of a society that is qualitatively better than the one we presently live in."

But perhaps what the university's response ought to be in sentiments like that is best expressed in the words of the late W. E. B. DuBois, words written almost 50 years ago.

Dr. DuBois said: " . . . We believe that the vocation of man in a modern civilized land includes not only the technique of his actual work but intelligent comprehension of his elementary duties as a father, citizen, maker of public opinion . . . a conserver of the public health, an intelligent follower of moral customs, and one who can appreciate if not partake something of the higher spiritual life of the world.

"We do not pretend that this can be taught to each individual in school, but it can be put into social environment, and the more that environment is restricted and curtailed the more emphatic is the demand that . . . [man] shall be trained and trained thoroughly in these matters of human development if he is to share the surrounding civilization." Or, indeed, if there is to be any civilization at all.

For Discussion

1. Have educators been wrong to tell students "that the earth is theirs for the taking"? Has this bred a false sense of security that ultimately leads to disappointment and hostility?
2. The heart of Bond's essay is phrased in his thesis sentence and occurs in the ninth paragraph. What are the possibilities and frustrations at both extremes of education? Which do you feel is the most significant one for today's world?
3. Evaluate the statement made by the girl from Tougaloo. Is her position valid, or is a compromise between Tougaloo and Brown a better solution?
4. Bond says universities study how people behave but do not study or teach ways of changing human behavior to a more "civilized manner." How might courses of instruction work to accomplish this goal? Have you personally experienced any such courses or known teachers who might design them. If so, explain their effectiveness.
5. Bond includes in his essay a series of paragraphs beginning with "Why" which ask pertinent questions about education in today's society. How valid is each of these questions? What questions might you add to this list?
6. Carefully evaluate the statement from W. E. B. DuBois that ends this essay. What is the range of its implications? Has American education made any progress toward this goal in the half-century since DuBois made this statement?

For Comparison

1. Compare ideas in this essay with those in "Education for Diversity." Would the authors of that essay agree with the girl from Tougaloo, or would they feel her position to be separatist? What would be their attitude toward the final statement by DuBois?
2. What aspects of "The Campus on the Hill" might qualify it to be what Bond calls "the university in doubt"?

For Composition

1. Tougaloo versus Brown.
2. Learning for change.
3. My experience with elitist education.

DONALD BARTHELME

ME AND MISS MANDIBLE

13 September

Miss Mandible wants to make love to me but she hesitates because I am officially a child; I am, according to the records, according to the gradebook on her desk, according to the card index in the principal's office, eleven years old. There is a misconception here, one that I haven't quite managed to get cleared up yet. I am in fact thirty-five, I've been in the Army, I am six feet one, I have hair in the appropriate places, my voice is a baritone, I know very well what to do with Miss Mandible if she ever makes up her mind.

In the meantime we are studying common fractions. I could, of course, answer all the questions, or at least most of them (there are things I don't remember). But I prefer to sit in this too-small seat with the desktop cramping my thighs and examine the life around me. There are thirty-two in the class, which is launched every morning with the pledge of allegiance to the flag. My own allegiance, at the moment, is divided between Miss Mandible and Sue Ann Brownly, who sits across the aisle from me all day long and is, like Miss Mandible, a fool for love. Of the two I prefer, today, Sue Ann; although between eleven and eleven and a half (she refuses to reveal her exact age) she is clearly a woman, with a woman's disguised aggression and a woman's peculiar contradictions. Strangely neither she nor any of the other children seem to see any incongruity in my presence here.

15 September

Happily our geography text, which contains maps of all the principal land-masses of the world, is large enough to conceal my clandestine journal-keeping, accomplished in an ordinary black composition book. Every day I must wait until Geography to put down such thoughts as I may have had during the morning about the situation and my fellows. I have tried writing at other times and it does not work. Either the teacher is walking up and down the aisles (during this period, luckily, she sticks close to the map rack in the front of the room) or Bobby Vanderbilt, who sits behind me, is punching me in the kidneys and wanting to know what I am doing. Vanderbilt, I have found out from certain desultory conversations on the playground, is hung up on sports cars, a veteran consumer of *Road & Track*. This explains the continual roaring sounds which seem to emanate from his desk; he is reproducing a record album called *Sounds of Sebring.*

19 September

Only I, at times (only at times), understand that somehow a mistake has been made, that I am in a place where I don't belong. It may be that Miss Mandible also knows this, at some level, but for reasons not fully understood by me she is going along with the game. When I was first assigned to this room I wanted to protest, the error seemed obvious, the stupidest principal could have seen it; but I have come to believe it was deliberate, that I have been betrayed again.

Now it seems to make little difference. This life-role is as interesting as my former life-role, which was that of a claims adjuster for the Great Northern Insurance Company, a position which compelled me to spend my time amid the debris of our civilization: rumpled fenders, roofless sheds, gutted warehouses, smashed arms and legs. After ten years of this one has a tendency to see the world as a vast junkyard, looking at a man and seeing only his (potentially) mangled parts, entering a house only to trace the path of the inevitable fire. Therefore when I was installed here, although I knew an error had been made, I countenanced it, I was shrewd; I was aware that there might well be some kind of advantage to be gained from what seemed a disaster. The role of The Adjuster teaches one much.

22 September

I am being solicited for the volleyball team. I decline, refusing to take unfair profit from my height.

23 September

Every morning the roll is called: Bestvina, Bokenfohr, Broan, Brownly, Cone, Coyle, Crecelius, Darin, Durbin, Geiger, Guiswite, Heckler, Jacobs, Kleinschmidt, Lay, Logan, Masei, Mitgang, Pfeilsticker. It is like the litany chanted in the dim miserable dawns of Texas by the cadre sergeant of our basic training company.

In the Army, too, I was ever so slightly awry. It took me a fantastically long time to realize what the others grasped almost at once: that much of what we were doing was absolutely pointless, to no purpose. I kept wondering why. Then something happened that proposed a new question. One day we were commanded to whitewash, from the ground to the top-most leaves, all of the trees in our training area. The corporal who relayed the order was nervous and apologetic. Later an off-duty captain sauntered by and watched us, white-splashed and totally weary, strung out among the freakish shapes we had created. He walked away swearing. I understood the principle (orders are orders), but I wondered: Who decides?

29 September

Sue Ann is a wonder. Yesterday she viciously kicked my ankle for not paying attention when she was attempting to pass me a note during History. It is swollen still. But Miss Mandible was watching me, there was nothing I could do. Oddly enough Sue Ann reminds me of the wife I had in my former role, while Miss Mandible seems to be a child. She watches me constantly, trying to keep sexual significance out of her look; I am afraid the other children have noticed. I have already heard, on that ghostly frequency that is the medium of classroom communication, the words *"Teacher's pet!"*

2 October

Sometimes I speculate on the exact nature of the conspiracy which brought me here. At times I believe it was instigated by my wife of former days, whose name was . . . I am only pretending to forget. I know her name very well, as well as I know the name of my former motor oil (Quaker State) or my old Army serial number (US 54109268). Her name was Brenda, and the conversation I recall best, the one which makes me suspicious now, took place on the day we parted. "You have the soul of a whore," I said on that occasion, stating nothing less than literal, unvarnished fact. "You," she replied, "are a pimp, a poop, and a child. I am leaving you forever and I trust that without me you will perish of your own inadequacies. Which are considerable."

I squirm in my seat at the memory of this conversation, and Sue Ann watches me with malign compassion. She has noticed the discrepancy between the size of my desk and my own size, but apparently sees it only as a token of my glamour, my dark man-of-the-world-ness.

7 October

Once I tiptoed up to Miss Mandible's desk (when there was no one else in the room) and examined its surface. Miss Mandible is a clean-desk teacher, I discovered. There was nothing except her gradebook (the one in which I exist as a sixth-grader) and a text, which was open at a page headed *Making the Processes Meaningful*. I read: "Many pupils enjoy working fractions when they understand what they are doing. They have confidence in their ability to take the right steps and to obtain correct answers. However, to give the subject full social significance, it is necessary that many realistic situations requiring the processes be found. Many interesting and lifelike problems involving the use of fractions should be solved . . ."

8 October

I am not irritated by the feeling of having been through all this before. Things are different now. The children, moreover, are in some ways different from those who accompanied me on my first voyage through the elementary schools: *"They have confidence in their ability to take the right steps and to obtain correct answers."* This is surely true. When Bobby Vanderbilt, who sits behind me and has the great tactical advantage of being able to maneuver in my disproportionate shadow, wishes to bust a classmate in the mouth he first asks Miss Mandible to lower the blind, saying that the sun hurts his eyes. When she does so, *bip!* My generation would never have been able to con authority so easily.

13 October

It may be that on my first trip through the schools I was too much under the impression that what the authorities (who decides?) had ordained for me was right and proper, that I confused authority with life itself. My path was not particularly of my own choosing. My career stretched out in front of me like a paper chase, and my role was to pick up the clues. When I got out of school, the first time, I felt that this estimate was substantially correct, and eagerly entered the hunt. I found clues abundant: diplomas, membership cards, campaign buttons, a marriage license, insurance forms, discharge papers, tax returns, Certificates of Merit. They seemed to prove, at the very least, that I was *in the running*. But that was before my tragic mistake on the Mrs. Anton Bichek claim.

I misread a clue. Do not misunderstand me: it was a tragedy only from the point of view of the authorities. I conceived that it was my duty to obtain satisfaction for the injured, for this elderly lady (not even one of our policyholders, but a claimant against Big Ben Transfer & Storage, Inc.) from the company. The settlement was $165,000; the claim, I still believe, was just. But without my encouragement Mrs. Bichek would never have had the self-love to prize her injury so highly. The company paid, but its faith in me, in my efficacy in the role, was broken. Henry Goodykind, the district manager, expressed this thought in a few not altogether unsympathetic words, and told me at the same time that I was to have a new role. The next thing I knew I was here, at Horace Greeley Elementary, under the lubricious eye of Miss Mandible.

17 October

Today we are to have a fire drill. I know this because I am a Fire Marshal, not only for our room but for the entire right wing of the second floor. This distinction, which was awarded shortly after my arrival, is interpreted by some as another mark of my somewhat dubious relations with our teacher. My armband, which is red and decorated with white felt letters reading FIRE, sits on the little shelf under my desk, next to the brown paper bag containing the lunch I carefully make for myself each morning. One of the advantages of packing my own lunch (I have no one to pack it for me) is that I am able to fill it with things I enjoy. The peanut butter sandwiches that my mother made in my former existence, many years ago, have been banished in favor of ham and cheese. I have found that my diet has mysteriously adjusted to my new situation; I no longer drink, for instance, and when I smoke, it is in the boy's john, like everybody else. When school is out I hardly smoke at all. It is only in the matter of sex that I feel my own true age; this is apparently something that, once learned, can never be forgotten. I live in fear that Miss Mandible will one day keep me after school, and when we are alone, create a compromising situation. To avoid this I have become a model pupil: another reason for the pronounced dislike I have encountered in certain quarters. But I cannot deny that I am singed by those long glances from the vicinity of the chalkboard; Miss Mandible is in many ways, notably about the bust, a very tasty piece.

24 October

There are isolated challenges to my largeness, to my dimly realized position in the class as Gulliver. Most of my classmates are polite about this matter, as they would be if I had only one eye, or wasted, metal-wrapped legs. I am viewed as a mutation of some sort but essentially a peer. However Harry Broan, whose father has made himself rich manufacturing the Broan Bathroom Vent (with which Harry is frequently reproached; he is always being asked how things are in Ventsville), today inquired if I wanted to fight. An interested group of his followers had gathered to observe this suicidal undertaking. I replied that I didn't feel quite up to it, for which he was obviously grateful. We are now friends forever. He has given me to understand privately that he can get me all the bathroom vents I will ever need, at a ridiculously modest figure.

25 October

"*Many interesting and lifelike problems involving the use of fractions should be solved . . .*" The theorists fail to realize that everything that is either interesting or lifelike in the classroom proceeds from what they would probably call interpersonal relations: Sue Ann Brownly kicking me in the ankle. How lifelike, how womanlike, is her tender solicitude after the deed! Her pride in my newly acquired limp is transparent; everyone knows that she has set her mark upon me, that it is a victory in her unequal struggle with Miss Mandible for my great, overgrown heart. Even

Miss Mandible knows, and counters in perhaps the only way she can, with sarcasm. "Are you wounded, Joseph?" Conflagrations smoulder behind her eyelids, yearning for the Fire Marshall clouds her eyes. I mumble that I have bumped my leg.

30 October

I return again and again to the problem of my future.

4 November

The underground circulating library has brought me a copy of *Movie-TV Secrets*, the multicolor cover blazoned with the headline, "Debbie's Date Insults Liz!" It is a gift from Frankie Randolph, a rather plain girl who until today has had not one word for me, passed on via Bobby Vanderbilt. I nod and smile over my shoulder in acknowledgment; Frankie hides her head under her desk. I have seen these magazines being passed around among the girls (sometimes one of the boys will condescend to inspect a particularly lurid cover). Miss Mandible confiscates them whenever she finds one. I leaf through *Movie-TV Secrets* and get an eyeful. "The exclusive picture on these pages isn't what it seems. We know how it looks and we know what the gossipers will do. So in the interests of a nice guy, we're publishing the facts first. Here's what really happened!" The picture shows a rising young movie idol in bed, pajama-ed and bleary-eyed, while an equally blowzy young woman looks startled beside him. I am happy to know that the picture is not really what it seems; it seems to be nothing less than divorce evidence.

What do these hipless eleven-year-olds think when they come across, in the same magazine, the full-page ad for Maurice de Paree, which features "Hip Helpers" or what appear to be padded rumps? ("A real undercover agent that adds appeal to those hips and derriere, both!") If they cannot decipher the language the illustrations leave nothing to the imagination. "Drive him frantic . . ." the copy continues. Perhaps this explains Bobby Vanderbilt's preoccupation with Lancias and Maseratis; it is a defense against being driven frantic.

Sue Ann has observed Frankie Randolph's overture, and catching my eye, she pulls from her satchel no less than seventeen of these magazines, thrusting them at me as if to prove that anything any one of her rivals has to offer, she can top. I shuffle through them quickly, noting the broad editorial perspective:

"Debbie's Kids Are Crying"
"Eddie Asks Debbie: Will You . . .?"
"The Nightmares Liz Has About Eddie!"
"The Things Debbie Can Tell About Eddie"

"The Private Life of Eddie and Liz"
"Debbie Gets Her Man Back"
"A New Life for Liz"
"Love Is a Trick Affair"
"Eddie's Taylor-Made Love Nest"
"How Liz Made a Man of Eddie"
"Are They Planning to Live Together?"
"Isn't It Time to Stop Kicking Debbie Around?"
"Debbie's Dilemma"
"Eddie Becomes a Father Again"
"Is Debbie Planning to Re-wed?"
"Can Liz Fulfill Herself?"
"Why Debbie Is Sick of Hollywood"

Who are these people, Debbie, Eddie, Liz, and how did they get themselves in such a terrible predicament? Sue Ann knows, I am sure; it is obvious that she has been studying their history as a guide to what she may expect when she is suddenly freed from this drab, flat classroom.

I am angry and I shove the magazines back at her with not even a whisper of thanks.

5 November

The sixth grade at Horace Greeley Elementary is a furnace of love, love, love. Today it is raining, but inside the air is heavy and tense with passion. Sue Ann is absent; I suspect that yesterday's exchange has driven her to bed. Guilt hangs over me. She is not responsible, I know, for what she reads, for the models proposed to her by a venal publishing industry; I should not have been so harsh. Perhaps it is only the flu.

Nowhere have I encountered an atmosphere as charged with aborted sexuality as this. Miss Mandible is helpless; nothing goes right today. Amos Darin has been found drawing a dirty picture in the cloakroom. Sad and inaccurate, it was offered not as a sign of something else but as an act of love in itself. It has excited even those who have not seen it, even those who saw but understood only that it was dirty. The room buzzes with imperfectly comprehended titillation. Amos stands by the door, waiting to be taken to the principal's office. He wavers between fear and enjoyment of his temporary celebrity. From time to time Miss Mandible looks at me reproachfully, as if blaming me for the uproar. But I did not create this atmosphere, I am caught in it like all the others.

8 November

Everything is promised my classmates and I, most of all the future. We accept the outrageous assurances without blinking.

9 November

I have finally found the nerve to petition for a larger desk. At recess I can hardly walk, my legs do not wish to uncoil themselves. Miss Mandible says she will take it up with the custodian. She is worried about the excellence of my themes. Have I, she asks, been receiving help? For an instant I am on the brink of telling her my story. Something, however, warns me not to attempt it. Here I am safe, I have a place; I do not wish to entrust myself once more to the whimsy of authority. I resolve to make my themes less excellent in the future.

11 November

A ruined marriage, a ruined adjusting career, a grim interlude in the Army when I was almost not a person. This is the sum of my existence to date, a dismal total. Small wonder that re-education seemed my only hope. It is clear even to me that I need reworking in some fundamental way. How efficient is the society that provides thus for the salvage of its clinkers!

Plucked from my unexamined life among other pleasant, desperate, money-making young Americans, thrown backward in space and time, I am beginning to understand how I went wrong, how we all go wrong. (Although this was far from the intention of those who sent me here; they require only that I *get right*.)

14 November

The distinction between children and adults, while probably useful for some purposes, is at bottom a specious one, I feel. There are only individual egos, crazy for love.

15 November

The custodian has informed Miss Mandible that our desks are all the correct size for sixth-graders, as specified by the Board of Estimate and furnished the schools by the Nu-Art Educational Supply Corporation of Englewood, California. He has pointed out that if the desk size is correct, then the pupil size must be incorrect. Miss Mandible, who has already arrived at this conclusion, refuses to press the matter further. I think I know why. An appeal to the administration might result in my removal from the class, in a transfer to some sort of setup for "exceptional children." This would be a disaster of the first magnitude. To sit in a room with child geniuses (or, more likely, children who are "retarded") would shrivel me in a week. Let my experience here be that of the common run, I say; let me be, please God, typical.

20 November

We read signs as promises. Miss Mandible understands by my great height, by my resonant vowels, that I will one day carry her off to bed. Sue Ann interprets these same signs to mean that I am unique among her male acquaintances, therefore most desirable, therefore her special property as is everything that is Most Desirable. If neither of these propositions work out then life has broken faith with them.

I myself, in my former existence, read the company motto ("Here to Help in Time of Need") as a description of the duty of the adjuster, drastically mislocating the company's deepest concerns. I believed that because I had obtained a wife who was made up of wife-signs (beauty, charm, softness, perfume, cookery) I had found love. Brenda, reading the same signs that have now misled Miss Mandible and Sue Ann Brownly, felt she had been promised that she would never be bored again. All of us, Miss Mandible, Sue Ann, myself, Brenda, Mr. Goodykind, still believe that the American flag betokens a kind of general righteousness.

But I say, looking about me in this incubator of future citizens, that signs are signs, and that some of them are lies. This is the great discovery of my time here.

23 November

It may be that my experience as a child will save me after all. If only I can remain quietly in this classroom, making my notes while Napoleon plods through Russia in the droning voice of Harry Broan, reading aloud from our History text. All of the mysteries that perplexed me as an adult have their origins here, and one by one I am numbering them, exposing their roots.

2 December

Miss Mandible will refuse to permit me to remain ungrown. Her hands rest on my shoulders too warmly, and for too long.

7 December

It is the pledges that this place makes to me, pledges that cannot be redeemed, that confuse me later and make me feel I am not *getting anywhere*. Everything is presented as the result of some knowable process; if I wish to arrive at four I get there by way of two and two. If I wish to burn Moscow the route I must travel has already been marked out by another visitor. If, like Bobby Vanderbilt, I yearn for a wheel of the Lancia 2.4-liter coupé, I have only to go through the appropriate process, that is, get the money. And if it is money itself that I desire, I have only to make it. All of these goals are equally beautiful in the sight of the Board of

Estimate; the proof is all around us, in the no-nonsense ugliness of this steel and glass building, in the straightline matter-of-factness with which Miss Mandible handles some of our less reputable wars. Who points out that arrangements sometimes slip, that errors are made, that signs are misread? *"They have confidence in their ability to take the right steps and to obtain correct answers."* I take the right steps, obtain the correct answers, and my wife leaves me for another man.

8 December

My enlightenment is proceeding wonderfully.

9 December

Disaster once again. Tomorrow I am to be sent to a doctor, for observation. Sue Ann Brownly caught Miss Mandible and me in the cloakroom, during recess, and immediately threw a fit. For a moment I thought she was actually going to choke. She ran out of the room weeping, straight for the principal's office, certain now which of us was Debbie, which Eddie, which Liz. I am sorry to be the cause of her disillusionment, but I know that she will recover. Miss Mandible is ruined but fulfilled. Although she will be charged with contributing to the delinquency of a minor, she seems at peace; *her* promise has been kept. She knows now that everything she has been told about life, about America, is true.

I have tried to convince the school authorities that I am a minor only in a very special sense, that I am in fact mostly to blame—but it does no good. They are as dense as ever. My contemporaries are astounded that I present myself as anything other than an innocent victim. Like the Old Guard marching through the Russian drifts, the class marches to the conclusion that truth is punishment.

Bobby Vanderbilt has given me his copy of *Sounds of Sebring*, in farewell.

For Discussion

1. How important to the story is the fact that the narrator is older than the other students? What other variables might have been used by Barthelme to tell the same or a similar story?
2. Does the narrator overemphasize sex as a source of tension in the classroom? What are some reasons for the emphasis that he gives it?
3. Characterize Miss Mandible. Does her name help you get a visual concept of her? If so, what do you think she looks like?

4. What is the importance of the quotation taken from the math text and quoted in the 7 October entry? What does the quotation suggest about much of education?
5. What valid comparisons does the narrator draw between the classroom experience and his prior army life? Examine, particularly, concepts of authority.
6. Discuss the meaning of the narrator's statement "that everything that is either interesting or lifelike in the classroom proceeds from what they (the theorists) would probably call interpersonal relations."
7. What is the symbolic meaning of the episode involving the size of the desk? What other incidents might have been used to prove the same point?
8. Is education correct in teaching that taking the right steps will lead to the correct answers? How does this assumption lead to frustration in later life?

For Comparison

1. In his essay "The Black Mind on the American Campus" Bond criticizes educators for telling students "that the earth is theirs for the taking." To what extent and in what manner is Miss Mandible guilty of this same approach?
2. What meaning would the narrator of this story get from "The Campus on the Hill"? What does that poem suggest about authority?

For Composition

1. I think Miss Mandible taught me too.
2. Sexual tension in the classroom.
3. Misplaced authority in the classroom.

JOHN UPDIKE

A SENSE OF SHELTER

Snow fell against the high school all day, wet big-flaked snow that did not accumulate well. Sharpening two pencils, William looked down on a parking lot that was a blackboard in reverse; car tires had cut smooth arcs of black into its white, and where the school buses had backed around, there were handsome pairs of arabesque V's. The snow, though at moments it whirled opaquely, could not quite bleach these scars away. The temperature must be exactly 32°. The window was open a crack, and a canted pane of glass lifted outdoor air into his face, coating the cedarwood smell of pencil shavings with the transparent odor of the wet window sill. With each revolution of the handle his knuckles came within a fraction of an inch of the tilted glass, and the faint chill this proximity breathed on them sharpened his already acute sense of shelter.

The sky behind the shreds of snow was stone-colored. The murk inside the high classroom gave the air a solidity that limited the overhead radiance to its own vessels; six globes of dull incandescence floated on the top of a thin sea. The feeling the gloom gave him was not gloomy, it was joyous: he felt they were all sealed in, safe; the colors of cloth were dyed deeper, the sound of whispers was made more distinct, the smells of tablet paper and wet shoes and varnish and face powder pierced him with a vivid sense of possession. These were his classmates sealed in, his, the stupid as well as the clever, the plain as well as the lovely, his enemies as well as his friends, his. He felt like a king and seemed to move to his seat between the bowed heads of subjects that loved him less than he loved them. His seat was sanctioned by tradition; for twelve years he had sat at the rear of classrooms, William Young, flanked by Marsha Wyckoff and Andy Zimmerman. Once there had been two Zimmermans, but one went to work in his father's greenhouse, and in some classes—Latin and Trig—there were none, and William sat at the edge of the class as if on the lip of a cliff, and Marsha Wyckoff became Marvin Wolf or Sandra Wade, but it was always the same desk, whose surface altered from hour to hour but from whose blue-stained ink-hole his mind could extract, like a chain of magician's handkerchiefs, a continuity of years. As a senior he was kind of king and as a teacher's pet another kind, a puppet king, who had gathered in appointive posts and even, when the moron vote split between two football heroes, some elective ones. He was not popular, he had never had a girl, his intense friends of childhood had drifted off into teams and gangs, and in large groups—when the whole school, for instance, went in the fall to the beautiful, dung-and-cotton-candy-smelling county fair—he was always an odd man, without a seat on the bus home. But exclusion is itself a form of inclusion. He even had a nickname: Mip, because he stuttered. Taunts no longer much frightened him; he had come late into his inheritance of size, but this summer it had arrived, and he at last stood equal with his enormous, boisterous parents, and had to unbutton his shirt cuffs to get his wrists through them, and discovered he could pick up a basketball with one hand. So, his long legs blocking two aisles, he felt regal even in size and, almost trembling with happiness under the high globes of light beyond whose lunar glow invisible snow-flakes were drowning on the gravel roof of his castle, believed that the long delay of unpopularity had been merely a consolation, that he was at last strong enough to make his move. Today he must tell Mary Landis he loved her.

He had loved her since, a fat-faced toughie with freckles and green eyes, she deftly stole his rubber-lined schoolbag on the walk back from second grade along Jewett Street and outran him—simply had better legs. The superior speed a boy was supposed to have failed to come; his kidneys burned with panic. In front of the grocery store next to her home she stopped and turned. She was willing to have him catch up. This humiliation on top of the rest was too much to bear. Tears broke in his throat; he spun around and ran home and threw himself on the floor of the front parlor, where his grandfather, feet twiddling, perused the news-paper and soliloquized all morning. In time the letter slot rustled, and the doorbell rang, and his mother and Mary exchanged the schoolbag and polite apologies. Their gentle voices had been to him, lying there on the carpet with his head wrapped in his arms, indistinguishable. Mother had always liked Mary. From when she had been a tiny girl dancing along the hedge on the end of an older sister's arm, Mother had liked her. Out of all the children that flocked, similar as pigeons, around the neighbor-hood, Mother's heart had reached out with claws and fastened on Mary. He never took the schoolbag to school again, had refused to touch it. He supposed it was still in the attic, still faintly smelling of pink rubber.

The buzzer sounded the two-minute signal. In the middle of the class-room Mary Landis stood up, a Monitor badge pinned to her belt. She wore a lavender sweater with the sleeves pushed up to expose her fore-arms, a delicately cheap effect. Wild stories were told about her; perhaps it was merely his knowledge of these that put the hardness in her face. Her eyes in their shape seemed braced for squinting and their green was frosted. Her freckles had faded. William thought she laughed less this year; now that she was in the Secretarial Course and he in the College Preparatory, he saw her in only one class a day, this one, English. She stood a second, eclipsed at the thighs by Jack Stephens' shoulders, look-ing back at the room with a stiff glance, as if she had seen the same faces too many times before. Her habit of perfect posture emphasized the angularity she had grown into; there was a nervous edge, a boxiness in her bones, that must have been waiting all along under the childish fat. Her eye sockets were deeply indented and her chin had a prim square set that seemed defiant to him. Her brown skirt was snug and straight; she had less hips than bosom, and thin, athletic legs. Her pronged chest poised, she sauntered up the aisle and encountered a leg thrown in her path. She stared down until it withdrew; she was used to such attentions.

As she went out the door, somebody she saw in the hall made her smile, a wide smile full of warmth and short white teeth, and love scooped at his heart. He would tell her.

In another minute, the second bell rasped. Shuffling through the perfumed crowds to his next class, he crooned to himself, in the slow, over-enunciated manner of the Negro vocalist who had brought the song back this year,

> "Lah-vender blue, dilly dilly,
> Lavendih greeh-een;
> *Eef* I were king, dilly dilly,
> You would: be queen."

The song gave him an exultant sliding sensation that intertwined with the pleasures of his day. He knew all the answers, he had done all the work, the teachers called upon him only to rebuke the ignorance of the others. In Trig and Soc Sci both it was this way. In gym, the fourth hour of the morning, he, who was always picked near the last, startled his side by excelling at volleyball, leaping like a madman, shouting like a bully. The ball felt light as a feather against his big bones. His hair wet from the shower, he walked in the icy air to Luke's Luncheonette, where he ate three hamburgers in a booth with three juniors. There was Barry Kruppman, a tall, thyroid-eyed boy who came on the school bus from the country town of Bowsville and was an amateur hypnotist and occultist; he told them about a Portland, Oregon, businessman who under hypnosis had been taken back through sixteen reincarnations to the condition of an Egyptian concubine in the household of a high priest of Isis. There was his friend Lionel Griffin, a pudgy simp whose blond hair stood out above his ears in two slick waxed wings. He was supposed to be a fairy, and in fact did seem most excited by the transvestite aspect of the soul's transmigration. And there was Lionel's girl, Virginia, a drab little mystery who chain-smoked Herbert Tareytons and never said anything. She had sallow skin, and Lionel kept jabbing her and shrieking. William would rather have sat with members of his own class, who filled the other booths, but he would have had to force himself on them. These juniors admired him and welcomed his company. He asked, "Wuh-well, was he ever a c-c-c-cockroach, like Archy?"

Kruppman's face grew intense; his furry lids dropped down over the bulge of his eyes, and when they drew back, his pupils were as small and hard as BBs. "That's the really interesting thing. There was this gap, see, between his being a knight under Charlemagne and then a sailor on a ship putting out from Macedonia—that's where Yugoslavia is now—in the time of Nero; there was this gap when the only thing the guy would do was walk around the office snarling and growling, see, like this."

Kruppman worked his blotched ferret face up into a snarl and Griffin shrieked. "He tried to bite one of the assistants and they think that for six hundred years"—the uncanny, unhealthy seriousness of his whisper hushed Griffin momentarily—"for six hundred years he just was a series of wolves. Probably in the German forests. You see, when he was in Macedonia"—his whisper barely audible—"he murdered a woman."

Griffin squealed with pleasure and cried, "Oh, Kruppman! Kruppman, how you do go on!" and jabbed Virginia in the arm so hard a Herbert Tareyton jumped from her hand and bobbled across the Formica table.

The crowd at the soda bar had thinned and when the door to the outside opened he saw Mary come in and stand there for a second where the smoke inside and the snow outside swirled together. The mixture made a kind of—Kruppman's ridiculous story had put the phrase in his head—wolf-weather, and she was just a gray shadow against it. She bought a pack of cigarettes from Luke and went out again, a kerchief around her head, the pneumatic thing above the door hissing behind her. For a long time, always in fact, she had been at the center of whatever gang was the best one: in the second grade the one that walked home up Jewett Street together, and in the sixth grade the one that went bicycling as far away as the quarry and the Rentschler estate and played touch football Saturday afternoons, and in the ninth grade the one that went roller-skating at Candlebridge Park with the tenth-grade boys, and in the eleventh grade the one that held parties lasting past midnight and that on Sundays drove in caravans as far as Philadelphia and back. And all the while there had been a succession of boy friends, first Jack Stephens and Fritz March in their class and then boys a grade ahead and then Barrel Lord, who was a senior when they were sophomores and whose name was in the newspapers all football season, and then this last summer someone out of the school altogether, a man she met while working as a waitress in the city of Alton. So this year her weekends were taken up, and the party gang carried on as if she had never existed, and nobody saw her much except in school and when she stopped by in Luke's to buy a pack of cigarettes. Her silhouette against the big window had looked wan, her head hooded, her face nibbled by light, her fingers fiddling on the glassy counter with her coins. He yearned to reach out, to comfort her, but he was wedged deep in the shrill booths, between the jingling guts of the pinball machine and the hillbilly joy of the jukebox. The impulse left him with a disagreeable feeling. He had loved her too long to want to pity her; it endangered the investment of worship on which he had not yet realized any return.

The two hours of the school afternoon held Latin and a study hall. In study hall, while the five people at the table with him played ticktacktoe and sucked cough drops and yawned, he did all his homework for the next day. He prepared thirty lines of Vergil, Aeneas in the Underworld. The study hall was a huge low room in the basement of the building; its coziness crept into Tartarus. On the other side of the fudge-colored wall the circular saw in the woodworking shop whined and gasped and then whined again; it bit off pieces of wood with a rising, terrorized inflection—*bzzzzzup!* He solved ten problems in trigonometry. His mind cut neatly through their knots and separated them, neat stiff squares of correctness, one by one from the long but finite plank of problems that connected Plane with Solid Geometry. Lastly, as the snow on a ragged slant drifted down into the cement pits outside the steel-mullioned windows, he read a short story by Edgar Allan Poe. He closed the book softly on the pleasing sonority of its final note of horror, gazed at the red, wet, menthol-scented inner membrane of Judy Whipple's yawn, rimmed with flaking pink lipstick, and yielded his conscience to the smug sense of his work done, of the snow falling, of the warm minutes that walked through their shelter so slowly. The perforated acoustic tiling above his head seemed the lining of a long tube that would go all the way: high school merging into college, college into graduate school, graduate school into teaching at a college —section man, assistant, associate, *full* professor, possessor of a dozen languages and a thousand books, a man brilliant in his forties, wise in his fifties, renowned in his sixties, revered in his seventies, and then retired, sitting in a study lined with acoustical books until the time for the last transition from silence to silence, and he would die, like Tennyson, with a copy of "Cymbeline" beside him on the moon-drenched bed.

After school he had to go to Room 101 and cut a sports cartoon into a stencil for the school paper. He liked the building best when it was nearly empty. Then the janitors went down the halls sowing seeds of red wax and making an immaculate harvest with broad brooms, gathering all the fluff and hairpins and wrappers and powder that the animals had dropped that day. The basketball team thumped in the hollow gymnasium; the cheerleaders rehearsed behind drawn curtains on the stage. In Room 101 two giggly typists with stripes bleached into their hair banged away between mistakes. At her desk Mrs. Gregory, the faculty sponsor, wearily passed her pencil through misspelled news copy. William took the shadow box from the top of the filing cabinet and the styluses and shaders from their drawer and the typed stencils from the closet where they hung, like fragile blue scarves, on hooks. "B-BALLERS BOW, 57-42." was the headline. He drew a tall b-baller bowing to a stumpy pagan idol, labeled "W" for victorious Weiserton High, and traced it in the soft blue wax with a fine loop stylus. His careful breath grazed his fingers. His eyebrows frowned while his heart throbbed happily on the giddy prattle of the typists. The shadow box was simply a plastic frame holding a pane of glass and lifted at one end by two legs so the light bulb, fitted in a tin tray, could slide under; it was like a primitive lean-to sheltering a fire. As he worked, his eyes smarting, he mixed himself up with the light bulb, felt himself burning under a slanting roof upon which a huge hand scratched. The glass grew hot; the danger in the job was pulling the softened wax with your damp hand, distorting or tearing the typed letters. Sometimes the center of an o stuck to your skin like a bit of blue confetti. But he was expert and cautious. He returned the things to their places feeling airily tall, heightened by Mrs. Gregory's appreciation, which she expressed by keeping her back turned, in effect saying that other staff members were undependable but William did not need to be watched.

In the hall outside Room 101 only the shouts of a basketball scrimmage reverberated; the chant of the cheerleaders had been silenced. Though he had done everything, he felt reluctant to leave. Neither of his parents would be home yet. Since the death of his grandfather, both worked in Alton, and this building was as much his home. He knew all its nooks. On the second floor of the annex, beyond the art room, there was a strange, narrow boys' lavatory that no one ever seemed to use. It was here one time that Barry Kruppman tried to hypnotize him and thus cure his stuttering. Kruppman's voice purred and his irises turned tiny in the bulging whites, and for a moment William felt himself lean backward involuntarily, but he was distracted by the bits of bloodshot pink in the corners of these portentous eyes; the folly of giving up his will to an intellectual inferior occurred to him; he refused to let go and go under, and perhaps therefore his stuttering had continued.

The frosted window at the end of the long room cast a watery light on the green floor and made the porcelain urinals shine like slices of moon. The semiopacity of this window gave great denseness to the room's feeling of secrecy. William washed his hands with close attention, enjoying the lavish amount of powdered soap provided for him in this castle. He studied his face in the mirror, making infinitesimal adjustments to attain the absolutely most flattering angle, and then put his hands below his throat to get their strong, long-fingered beauty into the picture. As he walked toward the door he sang, closing his eyes and gasping as if he were a real Negro whose entire career depended upon this recording,

> "Who—told me so, dilly dilly,
> Who told me soho?
> *Aii* told myself, dilly dilly,
> I told: me so."

When he emerged into the hall it was not empty: one girl walked down its varnished perspective toward him, Mary Landis, in a heavy brown coat, with a scarf on her head and books in her arms. Her locker was up here, on the second floor of the annex. His own was in the annex basement. A ticking sensation that existed neither in the medium of sound nor of light crowded against his throat. She flipped the scarf back from her hair and in a conversational voice that carried well down the clean planes of the hall said, "Hi, Billy." The name came from way back, when they were both children, and made him feel small but brave.

"Hi. How are you?"

"Fine." Her smile broadened.

What was so funny? Was she really, as it seemed, pleased to see him? "Du-did you just get through cheer-cheer-cheerleading?"

"Yes. Thank God. *Oh* she's so awful. She makes us do the same stupid locomotives for every cheer; I told her, no wonder nobody cheers any more."

"This is M-M-Miss Potter?" He blushed, feeling that he made an ugly face in getting past the "M." When he got caught in the middle of a sentence the constriction was somehow worse. He admired the way words poured up her throat, distinct and petulant.

"Yes, Potbottom Potter," she said. "She's just aching for a man and takes it out on us. I wish she would get one. Honestly, Billy, I have half a mind to quit. I'll be so glad when June comes, I'll never set foot in this idiotic building again."

Her lips, pale with the lipstick worn off, crinkled bitterly. Her face, foreshortened from the height of his eyes, looked cross as a cat's. He was a little shocked that poor Miss Potter and this kind, warm school stirred her to what he had to take as actual anger; this grittiness in her was the first abrasive texture he had struck today. Couldn't she see around teachers, into their fatigue, their poverty, their fear? It had been so long since he had spoken to her, he didn't know how insensitive she had become. "Don't quit," he brought out of his mouth at last. "It'd be n-n-nuh—it'd be nothing without you."

He pushed open the door at the end of the hall for her and as she passed under his arm she looked up and said, "Why, aren't you sweet."

The stair well, all asphalt and iron, smelled of galoshes. It felt more private than the hall, more specially theirs; there was something magical in its shifting multiplicity of planes as they descended that lifted the spell on his tongue, so that words came as quickly as his feet pattered on the steps.

"No I mean it," he said, "you're really a beautiful cheerleader. But then you're beautiful period."

"I have skinny legs."

"Who told you that?"

"Somebody."

"Well, *he* wasn't very sweet."

"No."

"Why do you hate this poor old school?"

"Now, Billy. You know you don't care about this junky place any more than I do."

"I love it. It breaks my heart to hear you say you want to get out, because then I'll never see you again."

"You don't care, do you?"

"Why *sure* I care you *know*"—their feet stopped; they had reached bottom, the first-floor landing, two brass-barred doors and a grimy radiator—"I've always li-loved you."

"You don't mean that."

"I do too. It's ridiculous but there it is. I wanted to tell you today and now I have."

He expected her to go out of the door in derision but instead she showed a willingness to discuss this awkward matter. He should have realized before this that women enjoy being talked to. "It's a very silly thing to say," she asserted tentatively.

"I don't see why," he said, fairly bold now that he couldn't seem more ridiculous, and yet picking his words with a certain strategic care. "It's not *that* silly to love somebody, I mean what the hell. Probably what's silly is not to do anything about it for umpteen years but then I never had an opportunity, I thought."

He set his books down on the radiator and she set hers down beside his. "What kind of opportunity were you waiting for?"

"Well, see, that's it; I didn't know." He wished, in a way, she'd go out the door. But she had propped herself against the wall and plainly expected him to keep talking. "Yuh-you were such a queen and I was such a nothing and I just didn't really want to presume." It wasn't very interesting; he was puzzled that she seemed to be interested. Her face had grown quite stern, the mouth very small and thoughtful, and he made a gesture with his hands intended to release her from the bother of thinking about it; after all, it was just a disposition of his heart, nothing permanent or expensive; maybe it was just his mother's idea anyway. Half in impatience to close the account, he asked, "Will you marry me?"

"You don't want to marry me," she said. "You're going to go on and be a great man."

He blushed in pleasure; is this how she saw him, is this how they all saw him, as worthless now but in time a great man? "No, I'm not," he said, "but anyway, you're great now. You're so pretty, Mary."

"Oh, Billy," she said, "if you were me for just one day you'd hate it."

She said this rather blankly, watching his eyes; he wished her voice had shown more misery. In his world of closed surfaces a panel, carelessly pushed, had opened, and he hung in this openness paralyzed, unable to think what to say. Nothing he could think of quite fitted the abruptly immense context. The radiator cleared its throat; its heat made, in the intimate volume just on this side of the doors on whose windows the snow beat limply, a provocative snugness; he supposed he should try, and stepped forward, his hands lifting toward her shoulders. Mary sidestepped between him and the radiator and put the scarf back on, lifting the cloth like a broad plaid halo above her head and then wrapping it around her chin and knotting it so she looked, in her red galoshes and bulky coat, like a peasant woman in a European movie. With her thick hair swathed, her face seemed pale and chunky, and when she recradled the books in her arms her back bent humbly under the point of the kerchief. "It's too hot in here," she said. "I have to wait for somebody." The disconnectedness of the two statements seemed natural in the fragmented atmosphere his stops and starts had produced. She bucked the brass bar with her shoulder and the door slammed open; he followed her into the weather.

"For the person who thinks your legs are too skinny?"

"Uh-huh." As she looked up at him a snowflake caught on the lashes of one eye. She jerkily rubbed that cheek on the shoulder of her coat and stamped a foot, splashing slush. Cold water gathered on the back of his shirt. He put his hands in his pockets and pressed his arms against his sides to keep from shivering.

"Thuh-then you wo-wo-won't marry me?" His wise instinct told him the only way back was by going forward, through absurdity.

"We don't know each other," she said.

"My God," he said. "Why not? I've known you since I was two."

"What do you know about me?"

This awful seriousness of hers; he must dissolve it. "That you're not a virgin." But instead of making her laugh, this made her face go dead and turned it away. Like beginning to kiss her, it had been a mistake; in part, he felt grateful for his mistakes. They were like loyal friends, who are nevertheless embarrassing. "What do you know about *me?*" he asked, setting himself up for a finishing insult but dreading it. He hated the stiff feel of his smile between his cheeks; glimpsed, as if the snow were a mirror, how hateful he looked.

"That you're basically very nice."

Her returning good for evil blinded him to his physical discomfort, set him burning with regret. "Listen," he said, "I did love you. Let's at least get that straight."

"You never loved anybody," she said. "You don't know what it is."

"O.K.," he said. "Pardon me."

"You're excused."

"You better wait in the school," he said. "He's-eez-eez going to be a long time."

She didn't answer and walked a little distance, toeing out in the child-ish way common to the women of the county, along the slack cable that divided the parking lot from the softball field. One bicycle, rusted as if it had been there for years, leaned in the rack, its fenders supporting thin crescents of white.

The warmth inside the door felt heavy, like a steamed towel laid against his face. William picked up his books and ran his pencil along the black ribs of the radiator before going down the stairs to his locker in the annex basement. The shadows were thick at the foot of the steps; suddenly it felt late, he must hurry and get home. He had the irrational fear they were going to lock him in. The cloistered odors of paper, sweat, and, from the woodshop at the far end of the basement hall, sawdust were no longer delightful to him. The tall green double lockers appeared to study him through the three air slits near their tops. When he opened his locker, and put his books on his shelf, below Marvin Wolf's, and re-moved his coat from his hook, his self seemed to crawl into the long dark space thus made vacant, the ugly, humiliated, educable self. In answer to a flick of his great hand the steel door weightlessly slammed shut, and through the length of his body he felt so clean and free he smiled. Be-tween now and the happy future predicted for him he had nothing, almost literally nothing, to do.

For Discussion

1. Characterize William Young. What kind of student is he? How typical is he of other high-school seniors? Will he be successful in college? Why?
2. What aspects of his school life make Billy feel secure?
3. What does Updike mean when he makes reference to Billy's "ugly, humiliated, educable self"?
4. Billy plans to be a teacher. What kind of teacher do you think he would become? Would you enjoy having him as your teacher? How tolerant would he be?

For Comparison

1. At what stage of the education process described by Hall in "The Three Movements" is William Young? How far will he progress in search of the "it" discussed in Hall's poem?
2. What would be William Young's attitude toward the teacher and class in Herndon's "The Way It Spozed to Be"?

For Composition

1. Education and social security.
2. Billy is (is not) a responsible student.
3. Billy will (will not) become a good teacher.

JAMES HERNDON

THE WAY IT SPOZED TO BE

We had come out of the library from our first meeting with the principal, just the new teachers. I walked down the hall with a man named Skates whom I'd just met. It was mid-afternoon; the hall was dark. Suddenly, a trio of girls burst upon us as if they had been lying in ambush. One jumped ahead, pointing a finger at me.

You a new teacher?

Uh-huh. Yes.

What grade?

All of them, it looks like.

You teach the eighth?

Yes. Eighth too.

What you teach to the eighth grade?

English. Social studies. No, only English to the eighth grade.

The other two girls were hanging back, giggling. This girl crowded me, standing right next to me, looking straight up. I kept my head absurdly raised, feeling that if I bent down I'd graze the top of her head with my chin. I kept stepping back in order to get a look at her, and also to get away from her. She kept moving forward. She talked very loudly, smiling and grinning all the time but still almost shouting every word, having a fine time. It was okay with me.

What your name?

Herndon. Mr. Herndon.

Okay, Mr. Hern-don, saying Hern-dawn, accent last syllable as I was to hear it spoken from then on by all students. Okay, Mr. Hern-don, you all right. I'm gonna be in your class. You better believe it! I'm in your class!

Well, fine, I said. Good. The two girls giggled in the background. Skates stood around, waiting. The girl ignored all of them; her business was with me.

Reprinted from *Harper's Magazine*, September 1965, by permission of James Herndon.

It seemed to be over. I waved my hand at her and started to move off. She grabbed me by the arm.

I ain't done! Listen you Mr. Hern-don, my name Ruth. Ruth! You'll hear about me, don't worry about it! And what I say, Mr. Hern-don, you don't cause me no trouble and I don't cause you none! You hear?

That suits me, I said. Well, see you later, Ruth, girls. Skates and I started off.

You don't cause me none, and I don't cause you none! she yelled once more, and then the three of them took off, sprinting down the hall away from us, laughing like hell and yelling at the top of their lungs.

The first day, sure enough, there was Ruth in my eighth grade B class. She was absolutely the craziest-looking girl I've ever seen. Her hair was a mass of grease, matted down flat in some places, sticking straight out in several others. Her face was faintly Arabic, and she was rather handsome, and very black. Across her forehead a tremendous scar ran in a zigzag pattern from somewhere above the hairline on her left side across to her right eye, cutting into the eyebrow. The scar was dead white. Her entire figure seemed full of energy and power; she was, every time I saw her, completely alert and ready. She could have been any age from fifteen to twenty-five. I once tried to look up her age, but on every sheet, the space after *Age* was simply left blank. No one knew, and apparently no one knew why it was that no one knew.

True to her word, she didn't cause me any trouble that first day. She sat in the second desk in her row and all she did was grab all the pencils I handed out for that row and refuse to pass them back. The row burst into an uproar, demanding their pencils. The other rows, not having thought of this themselves, yelled derisively, That row ain't gittin' any!

Please pass the pencils back, Ruth, I said, reasonably but loudly, since I wanted to be heard. In the back of my mind I was still wondering how she got in my class, or at least how she knew she was going to be in my class.

Ruth jumped up immediately. Don't go to hollowing at me! she yelled. You got *plenty* of pencils! You *spozed* to give 'em all out! They ain't your pencils! You *spozed* to give 'em out! I *need* these pencils!

The class yelled out, Whooooo-eee Whooo-eee! They all made the same sound. Everyone stood up, laughing and yelling whoo-eee except for the kids in Ruth's row who all screamed, We ain't got no pyenculs!

I advanced on the row. Sit down! I shouted at everybody. I did have plenty of pencils, and I was going to give one to each kid in the row and forget about it. Let her keep the goddam pencils! But as I came toward the row, Ruth suddenly flung the handful of pencils out into the room, screeched No! and launched herself backwards into space. She actually flew through the air and landed on her back on the floor after crashing

—some part of her body or head, I couldn't tell—against a desk and a kid or two. Later—as other girls from other classes landed on their heads with a bang—I came to call this the Plop Reflex but all I could think of at the time was getting this damn girl off the floor. As I moved, she jumped up, full of life, and fled for the door.

I'm trying to tell about my year teaching—learning to teach—in a junior high school near San Francisco. It was a Negro school, about 98 per cent Negro they told me downtown in the district office, as if to say not entirely Negro. Its principal, Mr. Grisson, announced candidly that he was new at his job, that he expected to make some mistakes himself and certainly would not be surprised if we made some too. The vice principal, Miss Bentley, likened us to the Army. The Army, she submitted, was an organization of people given certain tasks to perform. So was a school. The school's overall mission was the education of children. "So that learning may take place," Miss Bentley explained, "there must first be order."

Skates had another comparison to suggest. He called our students "The Tribe." Watch out today, he'd yell to me, coming down the hall for lunch, The Tribe's getting edgy! Or, Come into my room; The Tribe's holding a talent show, tap-dancing, strippers, the whole bit. It's a little gift from me, in appreciation of the fact that they didn't eat me up last week.

Still, that was later. On this first day all I knew about my students was that they were divided up into four different groups—a seventh-grade B class which I had twice, an eighth-grade B class, a ninth-grade D class, and a seventh-grade H class. Inquiring around the coffee tables in the teachers' rooms, I learned that the kids were all rated A (high) to H (low) and placed in classrooms together accordingly.

The first day, third period, I pretended to ignore 9D—making out cards and alphabetizing lists while trying to figure out what they might have in mind. They ignored me in turn, steadfastly and actually, roaming the room to try out new seats, applying cosmetics, and listening to transistors. So on the second day, I determined to pass out English books and spellers, to make everything official, and get down to work. The main work, I'd decided, was going to be composition, freely done and at length. The kids were bound to be interested in things they'd written themselves and we could later make some corrections, show up some common faults, use the books to find practical standards for usage and punctuation. The spellers I'd use for regularity; they weren't much good, being just lists of words and a number of rather silly things to do with those words.

Nine D scrambled around for the books and spellers, but then quickly withdrew as soon as it became clear there were enough to go around, which was only when every single person had one of each. Cosmetics came out, kids got up and began searching for new places to sit, a boy took out a transistor radio. I passed out paper; I began to talk about what we were going to do. Cosmetics and conversation continued—not loudly or aggressively, but just as if I weren't addressing them. I began to insist on everyone's attention. Finally a voice said, Teacher, why don't you let us alone?

That stopped it. Oooooh? they all went. The speaker was Verna, a tall, lanky girl, brown, lithe and strong-looking, plain-faced, kinky-haired, without make-up. The tone of the class implied apprehension and excitement; I was now going to throw Verna out. Actually I didn't give a damn. We had everyone's attention; they had momentarily lost. Verna had to say something. I expected an outburst, but instead she said, You should have made us get to work yesterday. All the other teachers made us get to work. If you want us to do work, why didn't you make us yesterday?

She stopped talking and immediately turned around, her back toward me. The class rallied to her support by taking up their conversations where they had left off. Now I was losing. I got ready to start insisting again, wondering what I was going to say if and when they started listening.

Then the door swung open, and a kid walked in, came over and handed me a slip, and found a seat near the back of the room. The class turned around and conversed in a different key. The subject was the newcomer, Maurice, particularly the fact that he had just gotten out of Juvenile Hall in time to make the second day of school. Teacher, Maurice just back from Juvi! shouted somebody, so I wouldn't have any trouble finding out. Maurice himself was subdued, having been warned, I suppose, to be nice or find himself right back in Juvi. But I was winning again; they were so curious about what I was going to say to Maurice that they had to recognize me. I passed a book and speller down the row to him. You spozed to report to the parole officer about Maurice, Teacher! How he do, if he do his work! Do he get in trouble or fighting! . . .

Well now, I said, actually this is not a class about Juvi, but about English. Whoooo-eee! That broke them up. But when they stopped laughing they were attentive enough. I began to talk about how English meant using the language; I was well into my speech about figuring out together what was relatively interesting to do and then figuring out how to do it—which was, naturally, crap since I already had the business of composition in mind—and they were just beginning to get bored (they knew it was crap too) seeing as how I wasn't going either to lecture Maurice about Crime Not Paying or to say anything humorous again, when Bang! Maurice and another boy, locked in each other's arms, fell over their desks and across the desks of the next row and lay there stretched out, struggling. Books, papers, and kids scattered. Whoooo-eee!

Hell! I got over there. Silence. Let go! I shouted, but nothing happened. Maurice was on top, the other kid across a desk, and as I got there Maurice loosed an arm and belted the other kid in the face. Cut it out! I grabbed Maurice. The kid on the bottom let go, but Maurice didn't. I tugged him rather gently. He belted the kid again. I got mad, grabbed Maurice under the arms, and heaved as hard as I could. He flew backwards over the row of desks and landed with a crash on the next row. He landed plenty hard; I imagine it hurt and, also, he must have thought it was all up with him, back to Juvi. He was frantic and mad. He jumped up and started for me. I stood there; he stopped and stood there. He glared. Everybody was frightened. No one in the class looked forward, suddenly, to what was going to happen, which was that Maurice was going to come for me and hit me or I him; the end would be the speedy return of Maurice to Juvenile Hall beaten up by me previously or not. It was inevitable.

We stood there quite a few seconds and then I nodded, turned, and walked swiftly back to my desk and sat down. I hoped I was implying a mutual cease-fire among equals. When I turned around toward the class, Maurice had likewise retreated and was sitting at his desk. We carefully didn't look right at each other, but still in the same general direction, so as not to be accused of avoiding anything either. Maurice had seen the issue—I'd say we saw it exactly alike. We both had something at stake, and we cooperated perfectly.

The class was dumbfounded. They waited, disappointed, but certainly somewhat relieved. The Tribe courted disaster; that doesn't mean they liked it. But they didn't believe the action was over, so they were all attention when I got ready to say something. All right, I said, I guess we can start classwork. The first English assignment is to write a story about what just happened. You can begin writing now, finish it tonight, and have it ready for tomorrow's class.

Whatever they'd expected, that wasn't it. It suddenly seemed like a lousy idea to me, and I decided to admit it and do something else, but before I could Verna said Sh—! loudly and turned around in her seat so her back was to me. The class woke up at that signal and began to yell demands and questions at me. What to write! How we spozed to write without no paper! That ain't no schoolwork, Teacher! You can't make us write about that! I ain't got no pencil! You trying to get us into trouble! No pen! No paper! What to write! What to do!

Shhh—loudly again. This time not from Verna, but from Leon LaTour in the back. None of The Tribe said Shit, only Sh! or, to express extreme disgust, Sheee . . . ! Sh! said Leon LaTour, nobody going to write that. He was addressing the class, not me. He just want to pin it on somebody.

He want to find out about it. He want to pull you in on it!

Protestations of innocence and as many accusations and counter-accusations followed that. Finally people's Mamas began to be mentioned, and I had to yell Quiet! again. Well, what if I do want to know? I yelled. Do you know? Something started it didn't it? Here's Maurice pounding on somebody, on Fletcher there, all of a sudden. Do you think he wanted to? So who did start it then?

Accusations, etc. Leon LaTour grinned in the back. Finally Verna jumped up and yelled, Hush up you-all! Sit down big-leg! came an unidentified voice. Forget you! said Verna coldly and everybody hushed. You don't have to get all shook up, said Verna. She was talking to me. Everybody know who start it. Earl he took hold of Maurice's notebook while Maurice writing on them cards you give him for the books, and slip it over onto Fletcher's desk and Maurice look up and find it gone and then he see it on Fletcher's desk and grab it, but Fletcher don't know it Maurice's because he didn't see that Earl put it there so he grab it back and there they go.

No one denied it. Earl was out of his seat and backed up in the corner of the room like John Dillinger facing the FBI. Sit down, Earl, I said. Oooooh? went the class softly. Sh! said Leon LaTour. Verna wasn't convinced. Ain't you sendin' Earl to the office, Teacher? she said flatly.

I was tired of the whole thing. Property. Your Mama. It seemed likely that at the moment Earl was slipping Maurice's notebook over, every other kid in the class was grabbing, poking, pushing, or pulling at some piece of someone else's stuff. I told them so, and looked at the clock; there were only about five minutes left. Okay, I said, now go on and write the assignment, now we all know all about it.

Actually no one wrote the assignment; no one, that is, except for Maurice, who perhaps figured he'd better. The next day all denied any knowledge of its being assigned. I read Maurice's Composition, as it was entitled. A boy took another boy ['s notebook] in the class and so the boy jump [ed] him to beat [him] the teacher broke it up But the teacher didn't send the boys to the office. (*Corrections mine.*)

Teachers are always willing to give advice to new (or old) teachers, and I talked to them all during those first six or seven weeks. The advice was of two kinds. The first kind, useful enough, was about methods and equipment—sets of flash cards, controlled readers, recorders, easy-corecting tests, good films—but after a short time I was already using most of these. My problem was not what to use but how to get the kids to respond in such a way that they learned something. That brought up the other kind of advice, which was also the most common and which was useless to me. It was about a conglomeration of dodges, tricks, gimmicks to get the kids to do what they were spozed to do, that is, whatever the teacher had in mind for them to do. The purpose of all these tricks was to get and keep an aspect of order, which was reasonable enough I suppose. But the purpose of this order was to enable "learning to take place" (so everyone said—not wanting to be guilty of the authoritarian predilection for order for its own sake) and we all knew that most of the kids weren't learning anything. Everyone agreed that our students were on the average a couple of years below grade level, everyone agreed that was because they were "deprived" kids, but no one agreed that simply because their methods weren't working they ought to try something else.

It's not my purpose or even desire to criticize these teachers—they were as good as or better than most and they had a difficult job—but frankly I could never come to terms with their attitude. They knew certain ways to get control of the class, although even these didn't work consistently because the kids were not easily threatened, having little to lose. The material which was so important, which had to be "covered" once order was established, was supposed to lead toward specific understanding and broader knowledge. But actually what was happening was that teachers were presenting the students, every day, with something for them either to do or not-do, while keeping them through "order" from any other alternative. If a kid couldn't or wouldn't copy a paragraph from the board, he had only the choice of not-doing it, of doing nothing. Almost every teacher admitted that this last was the choice of half the class on any given day. Since their teaching methods were right in other schools, they argued, it must be the fact of "deprivation" which was at fault here. If deprivation was the problem, then something should be done about that deprivation. After that, the school program, being essentially right, would work, since the only reason it didn't work now was that the students were of the wrong kind, *i.e.*, they were deprived.

But I began to think something else was the trouble. Long before we met, my wife had worked for Dr. Thomas French at the Institute for Psychoanalysis in Chicago, and during this time I was reading the first volume of his book *The Integration of Behavior*, which he had sent her. In it he noted that the disintegration of reactions in abnormal behavior seemed to show up goals and processes in a kind of relief, and motivational patterns which might be overlooked in normal behavior were clearly shown in the abnormal. It occurred to me that The Tribe's reactions to this teaching were not different, only more overt, violent, and easily seen than those of normal (or nondeprived) children. Where the middle-class kids were learning enough outside of the classroom or accepting conventional patterns of behavior more readily, so as to make it seem that they were actually learning in school, The Tribe was exposing the system as ineffective for everyone.

During Christmas vacation I came across something that did seem
effective: Paul Roberts' book *Patterns of English*, the first high-school
English text based on modern linguistics or structural grammar. What
impressed me about it was that the exercises seemed both practical and
extremely interesting. I immediately tried them out on 7B and they were
a great success.

Very briefly, the idea was to teach kids the various different kinds of
words (the "parts of speech") by the way in which they occurred in sentences, instead of according to the meaning of the word. That is, a word
wasn't to be called a noun because it was a person, place, or thing necessarily, but because it occurred in normal sentences in a certain way. If
you took a sentence, "The _____ is new," you could see that only certain words would fit that blank, and those words we could call nouns or
anything else; whatever we called them, they still were the only kinds of
words which would fit there.

This seemed simple and interesting, and 7B was enthusiastic. They
learned the various "patterns" easily, and by the time the year was over
had gone through about half the book, which was meant for upper-grade
high-school kids. I began now to try it out with 9D and 7H and the
results were, relatively, quite as good. We did these patterns once a week
and almost all the kids enjoyed making up huge lists of words which
would fit certain patterns, and became fairly sure of themselves when it
came to naming the patterns. The opposite exercise, that of taking a nonsense sentence like *"The groobs fleegled the grinty wilpentops"* and trying to figure out which words were nouns, adjectives, etc., was a great
favorite; it had all the virtues, being new, fun, and not difficult. At the
same time, Roberts assured the reader, they were learning the signaling
devices for the parts of speech in English. This was the only thing I was
able to point to to prove I was teaching something, in the ordinary classroom sense, and I was happy about it.

February and March are dull times in the morning sports page—nothing but the interminable scoring of pro-basketball teams and a vague
sense of something about minor-league hockey. The season made itself
felt at school. It was the beginning of the second semester and although
it was impossible to see just why, it was clear that we were pretty stable.
We had our schedule of events—reading, library, spellers—so that everyone would know just what they were not-doing, and the interminable and
intellectual discussions of the radicals, led by Verna, about what was
wrong with everything. Yet even the sports page began to tell us that
some baseball team was contemplating a trade, a new manager; and we
had a few changes too about this time.

In 9D Leon LaTour stopped coming to my class. In fact, he didn't come to any classes for the rest of the year. He didn't stop coming to school. He came on time, and spent the day roaming the halls or the yard, joining his class at passing periods to talk, going with them, stopping short at the door of whatever classroom they went into, and going on. Kids began to speak of students beaten up by him, of teachers threatened in the halls, of his talk about setting the fires in the big cans in the halls, which now became almost daily events. In the teachers' room it was branded a scandal—something had better be done, was the consensus. Skates told me that a number of his ninth-graders were coming in after lunch half-drunk and the kids all said they were buying wine from Leon LaTour at a nickel a drink. Skates was in favor of the whole thing, both on account of its being a revolutionary act and also because the student-drunks were too sleepy in class to cause any trouble or make any noise.

I began to stop regularly at the Plantation Club after school for a beer or two myself. The Plantation had South Seas decor, a good jukebox, and was dark and warm. There were always several businessmen from the Negro hotel next door, a traveling man's hotel as the bartender said. He often treated me in an extravagant Uncle Tom manner; he would hurry to serve me, wipe the bar over and over, ask me if the beer was cold enough, if I was comfortable, if the music was too loud or not loud enough. At other times he ignored me completely when I came in, until I began to think about getting up to leave, at which instant he would hurry over and become Uncle Tom again. I couldn't see any resemblance between the salesmen here and The Tribe, and indeed whenever I tried to imagine The Tribe grown up I found I couldn't do it. I could only imagine them now. I counted on something happening in my classes and soon, hoping I could hold out long enough for it. I counted on it. It did occur to me now that perhaps it wouldn't; there were too many things against it, the school structure, other teachers, America itself.

But something did. I still have an ordinary yellow-covered notebook which used to belong to Cerise. Open the cover, and there is a page decorated in ink with curlicues and flourishes which enclose a paragraph: "This is the Slambook belonging to Cerise, who says that nobody can read it without her permission and also anyone who steals it is guilty of a crime." It was all spelled correctly and signed with an elegant and unreadable script.

On the next page there is a list, numbered, of the students of 9D, and this is the key to what follows. For on each page afterwards, there is the name of a kid, and on that page other kids have been invited to comment on his or her character, appearance, courage, brains, or wealth, signing themselves only with a number corresponding to the key in the front. The beauty of this system is that the owner of the Slambook may then show the comments to the kid whose name is at the top of the page and have the pleasure of listening to him beg and plead with her to see the first page so that he may identify the commentators, the girl who said he was good-looking or the boy who said he was chicken. The authors of the remarks can also plead for her not to show it, and the owner thus becomes the center of frantic social activity.

I picked this Slambook up from the floor after the class left one period; when I gave it back to Cerise the next day, saying I didn't want to be guilty of a crime, she said it was already out of date and she had another, so I could have it.

Slambooks suddenly took precedence over everything. Charlene, Connie, and Cerise—the Three Cs, we called them—had them one day; everyone else was making them the next. The Three Cs were the prettiest and whitest girls in the class and their lead was bound to be followed. Since making up slambooks involved doing more work than many kids had done the entire year, I was delighted. Everyone was avidly writing in them, not perhaps in "complete sentences" or the rest of the paraphernalia expected for classwork, but the books were carefully made, the names spelled right, the style of the opening paragraph elegant and complicated and formal. From the appearance and behavior of the class, they might have been involved in some kind of engrossing class project or group work (as of course they were) discussing their progress with each other and writing entries into notebooks to be reported later with the results of their research, discussion, and inquiry.

The whole talk now in the teachers' room was about Slambook season and voices rose in excited competition about how many had been confiscated or destroyed. Methods for ridding the school of Slambooks forever were discussed and, I guess, tried out. All I could see, though, was that The Tribe had finally come across something which *needed to be written down* to be successful or interesting to them, which couldn't even exist without writing, and they were as enthusiastic about it as possible.

The next change in 9D began around the same time. It was, I think, the day I started reading Cerise's book that Geneva came into the room and, instead of going over to sit down, went to the board and began to write a list of the Top Forty songs on it. Geneva was a tall, big girl, middle in the hierarchy of skin-color, hair, features, etc., and middle in other ways too. This morning, as far as I could tell, she simply felt like writing tune titles on the board and did it.

The Top Forty, of course, were those forty rock 'n' roll songs played over and over, all day long, by the disc-jockeys of the local rock 'n' roll station. Geneva planned to write down only the first twenty—at least that's all she did write down and later on twenty became established as the proper number although we all still called it the Top Forty. As kids noticed Geneva chalking up titles, they began to question spellings, order, simple correctness; she made a couple of changes. Top Forty soon became a program, like the pledge of allegiance (or a paragraph on the board for everyone to copy). Something everyone could expect to start the class with from now on, except that almost everyone thought it was something important in itself, which made the difference.

During library periods I kept looking in the back storeroom for anything I could use with my classes and eventually I came across a series of playbooks. I kept them stacked in a corner of the room, since the librarian said that no one else ever used them. Occasionally kids from 9D or 7H would take a look at them.

One day, near the beginning of the period in 9D, with the kids hard at work or not-work, the Slambooks going through their courses, the Top Forty being laboriously written on the board under the watchful eye of Verna and a few critics, I was astonished to see the Three Cs approaching my desk in a body. They were clutching playbooks and they asked me why couldn't we read these plays out loud in class, everyone taking the parts? Why not? I'd already tried to get 9D interested in play-reading some time before. So I said it was a fine idea, but who was going to do the reading? It was an idiotic question. With the Three Cs planning to do something, everyone in the class was suddenly eager to take part. The Cs' own big table was quickly moved up to the front of the room—ten boys shoving each other for the honor of grabbing hold of it—desks shoved out of the way, folding chairs set around it. Trouble began as twenty kids dived for space around the table. I yelled. Everyone finally fell back and, taking the easy way out, I announced that the Three Cs, having introduced the idea, could pick out the players. There followed plenty of threats and counterthreats, some refusals-in-advance-of-expected-rejection, an incipient Plop Reflex or two; the Cs finally extorted enough promises and, with perhaps fifteen minutes left in the period, they began to read the play. That was the first time I realized that the play the Cs were so excited about was *Cinderella*.

It was a terrible reading. Unprepared, the kids stumbled and read too fast, giggled among themselves or argued, forgot their turn in haste to correct someone else, and the audience, prepared at first to listen, soon lost interest and drifted back to their spellers, Slambooks, and cosmetics.

The source of the trouble was the Three Cs. In their haste they had picked *Cinderella* because they saw there was a Prince and a fancy-dress ball and two sisters and a mother who were going to that ball; they saw themselves in starring roles, dancing, dining, diamonds shining and all. They weren't prepared to find Cinderella the heroine and had given that part to a girl named Grace, not concealing the fact that Grace looked, in their opinion, like someone who stayed home and cleaned up all the time. As the play went on and Grace steadily read all the most interesting parts with the fairy godmother and the Prince, the Cs became more and more upset and began to interpose remarks. How could the Prince dance with that ugly old thing? they wanted to know.

By the end of the play they had really become the three jealous women, so much so that they were almost speechless as the Prince began to go around with the glass slipper. When he got to their house and tried the slipper on the first of the mean sisters, he was supposed to read the line, "Oh no! Your foot is much too big for this slipper. You cannot be the lady I seek!" But by the time he got as far as "big," Charlene jumped up in a fury and yelled, Don't you say my feets too big you black monkey! and slammed her book down.

That broke up the play. Everyone began to laugh and yell Whoooo-eee! The other two Cs, having looked ahead now and seen the same fate reserved for them, quit the play too. We ain't playing no part where they get to say our feet too big, Mr. Hern-don! The bell rang about then, and the class rushed out still yelling Whooo-eee! They left *Cinderella* scattered about the room, the chairs knocked over, the table still up in front.

I left the table there. The next day the Cs tried to recruit someone to move it back for them, but the class objected. A number of them had playbooks out and were planning to read another play. But first, they called out to me, we got to finish that one about Cinderella. They wanted to know how it came out.

Springtime was the rioting season. The Tribe had given up and was becoming violent. By April the story of the year was over—some details, some dramatics left to tell, but the score was already in. All the promises had lost their appeal and The Tribe was busting out. Fights. Fires. Windows. Food thrown all over. Neighborhood complaints about vandalism. And we lost Ruth. She'd remained in the elite 8B all year, getting along well enough, but in the spring she became determined to carry out minor disturbances to the bitter end, insisting on her rights, why she didn't have to give back the other kid's pen or book, what I was spozed to do. One afternoon after school she imprisoned the school nurse, a secretary, and a woman teacher in a room for forty-five minutes, threatening them with an upraised chair if they moved, thereby giving us an idea of what she meant by trouble. Teachers who had kept things in check all year began to have their problems. Oddly enough, the faculty took it in stride. It happens every year, they seemed to say. We try. We hold 'em for as long as we can. . . .

I viewed the daily slaughter with detachment and no little vanity. If they were beginning to lose, I was just starting to win. If their programs were falling apart, we were just starting to move. 9D not only read almost every day, but they were discussing—all right, they were arguing, squabbling, making a lot of noise, using a lot of bad language—certain questions about play-reading. They were discussing who read well and why, they were telling each other what the play was about, they argued about where certain characters should sit at the table. The most important question to them was what relationship the reader should have to the character he was reading. Two solid factions arose, the first arguing that if the character was a giant, a big kid had to read the part. The second disagreed; they thought that, if the character was a beautiful girl, any girl who *read* beautifully, who *sounded* beautiful, should read it. The kids were making it. Rolling. I was enthusiastic, pleased, proud of them.

In this mood I met with Mr. Grisson in April for his official evaluation of my year's work. He opened the interview by stating that it was always painful to him to have to make judgments, but that it was best to be frank. In short, he found my work unsatisfactory on every count, he could not recommend me for rehire in the district. Furthermore he must say that he considered me unfit for the position of junior-high-school teacher in any school, anywhere, now or in the future, and would so state on my evaluation paper.

On the last day of school, Ramona and Hazel told me I was the nicest and best teacher they ever had. I told them I bet they said that to all their teachers; the class agreed loudly that they did.

Grisson had scheduled an assembly for the afternoon. I sat with Skates in the balcony of the auditorium, surrounded by excited students. On the stage Grisson was giving out awards for the year—for good citizenship, class officers and athletes, and finally for the district-wide spelling contest. He called off the names, waited for the kids to climb up onto the stage, shook their hands, led applause, and frowned into the audience as The Tribe expressed occasional disbelief in the spelling ability of such-and-such a watermelon-head. After it seemed that all the awards had been distributed, Grisson paused significantly. Everyone waited. Then he said, there is one more spelling award which may come as a little surprise. It is my great pleasure now to call up the last winner in the spelling contest—Leon LaTour!

The Tribe went wild, roaring out in what seemed to me equal parts of disbelief, astonishment, glee, and disgust, keeping it up long after Leon LaTour shook Grisson's hand and left the stage. Around us I could see other teachers nodding and smiling; it was another victory—the rebel brought back into the fold, a threat to the system conquered by the carrot. Grisson was leading the way, and everything was okay.

Unfortunately, I was aware that Leon LaTour hadn't ever taken the spelling tests. They were given only in English classes, and Leon LaTour only had one English class—mine; he hadn't been there when I gave it. He hadn't been in any classes then: I suppose Grisson could have called him in and given him the test privately, but it didn't seem likely, nor did it seem likely that Leon LaTour would have come in and taken that test.

In any case Leon LaTour couldn't spell.

So why the award? What the hell? Either Leon LaTour threatened some good-spelling kid to sign his—Leon's—name to his own spelling paper, or else the whole thing was rigged. Like many another event that year there wasn't an answer available, but it was the last day and I didn't have to worry about it. Forget you! I said, talking to myself out loud. Two kids in front of me started to giggle. You hear Mr. Hern-don? one of them said to the other. He say, Forget you!

The movie came on then, something about a Bullfighter and a Kid. The Tribe was restless during it, standing up, talking, scuffling. I was brooding about the position I found myself in. I couldn't remember when I'd worked so hard or concentrated what intelligence and energy I possessed so seriously on a single effort. It seemed unlikely that any kind of work besides teaching was going to satisfy me now, but it seemed even more unlikely that I was going to get another teaching job very soon. It was a kind of bind I wasn't used to.

Around Skates and me the kids stopped scuffling and began to cheer and yell. I looked at the screen. In the movie, the bull had just gored a matador. Two men came out to distract it, and the bull began to chase them around the ring, crashing into the wooden barriers as the men dodged behind them. Time and time again, the bull chased and crashed. The kids yelled and laughed and stood up and fell down again helpless with laughter. Hey Jim! Skates yelled to me, look, The Tribe likes it! They like it! He was laughing now too, raising his fist and waving it in the air.

Suddenly the lights went on in the auditorium, the film stopped, and Grisson appeared on the stage. He warned them that any further demonstrations of that sort wouldn't be tolerated; if it happened again the film would be stopped and they could return to their classrooms. Sh! said The Tribe.

Let 'em alone! Skates called out loudly from the balcony. Hell, he said to me, it's the first time all year they like something. So let 'em alone . . . .

Well, the lights went back out, the bull chased everyone around the ring, the kids yelled. In time the movie was over, the lights came on, the kids dismissed, the season over too, and we all went home.

———

For Discussion

1. In your own estimation, do you consider the narrator a good teacher? Why?
2. As a result of what happened to him during his first year, how do you suppose he will conduct his classes in the future? Will he then be filling the function of a good teacher?
3. What difference do you see between him and Skates? Which would you rather have for your teacher?
4. Do you feel that laws requiring compulsory attendance are wrong? Would those students in the 9D class have been better off outside the formal school structure? What type of education, if any, would you recommend for them?

For Comparison

1. Why is the school seen as a place for revolt by some students and as a place of shelter ("A Sense of Shelter") by others? What factors account for the different attitudes?
2. To what extent has the narrator structured his teaching technique to provide the education for diversity that Mead and Metraux advocate in their essay?

For Composition

1. Compulsory education is (is not) good.
2. The narrator is (is not) a good teacher.
3. How I would have taught the 9D class.

KARL SHAPIRO

UNIVERSITY

To hurt the Negro and avoid the Jew
Is the curriculum. In mid-September
The entering boys, identified by hats,
Wander in a maze of mannered brick
  Where boxwood and magnolia brood
  And columns with imperious stance
  Like rows of ante-bellum girls
    Eye them, outlanders.

In whited cells, on lawns equipped for peace,
Under the arch, and lofty banister,
Equals shake hands, unequals blankly pass;
The exemplary weather whispers, "Quiet, quiet,"
  And visitors on tiptoe leave
  For the raw North, the unfinished West
  As the young, detecting an advantage,
    Practice a face.

Where, on their separate hill, the colleges,
Like manor houses of an older law,
Gaze down embankments on a land in fee,
The Deans, dry spinsters over family plate,
  Ring out the English name like coin,
  Humor the snob and lure the lout.
  Within the precincts of this world
    Poise is a club.

But on the neighboring range, misty and high,
The past is absolute; some luckless race
Dull with inbreeding and conformity
Wears out its heart, and comes barefoot and bad
  For charity or jail. The scholar
  Sanctions their obsolete disease;
  The gentleman revolts with shame
    At his ancestor.

And the true nobleman, once a democrat,
Sleeps on his private mountain. He was one
Whose thought was shapely and whose dream was broad;
This school he held his art and epitaph.

But now it takes from him his name,
Falls open like a dishonest look,
And shows us, rotted and endowed,
    Its senile pleasure.

For Discussion

1. To what extent do you agree with Shapiro's criticism that modern education is basically a product of the conservative tradition?
2. Is the philosophy of American education "dull with inbreeding and conformity"? If so, what suggestions can you make to change this philosophy?
3. Shapiro suggests that much college life is artificial. Do you feel this criticism applies to the life on your own college campus? Among which groups?
4. If Shapiro's poem is true, then college education exists as a device to make man feel superior. Is this alone a valid foundation for education? Could this attitude be what is behind a lot of the current unrest on campuses around the country?

For Comparison

1. Shapiro and William Young ("A Sense of Shelter") hold some similar attitudes toward education. What are they? How would Young fit into the university scene described here?
2. In "The Function of a Teacher" Russell speaks of the limitations placed on education by church and state support. How has such support been responsible for the image of a university which Shapiro depicts?

For Composition

1. Snob appeal in education.
2. Colleges are too conservative.
3. The real purpose of a college.

LANGSTON HUGHES

THEME FOR ENGLISH B

The instructor said,

> *Go home and write*
> *a page tonight.*
> *And let that page come out of you—*
> *Then, it will be true.*

I wonder if it's that simple?

I am twenty-two, colored, born in Winston-Salem.
I went to school there, then Durham, then here
to this college on the hill above Harlem.
I am the only colored student in my class.
The steps from the hill lead down into Harlem,
through a park, then I cross St. Nicholas,
Eighth Avenue, Seventh, and I come to the Y,
the Harlem Branch Y, where I take the elevator
up to my room, sit down, and write this page:

It's not easy to know what is true for you or me
at twenty-two, my age. But I guess I'm what
I feel and see and hear, Harlem, I hear you:
hear you, hear me—we two—you, me, talk on this page.
(I hear New York, too.) Me—who?
Well, I like to eat, sleep, drink, and be in love.
I like to work, read, learn, and understand life.
I like a pipe for a Christmas present,
or records—Bessie, bop, or Bach.
I guess being colored doesn't make me *not* like
the same things other folks like who are other races.
So will my page be colored that I write?
Being me, it will not be white.
But it will be
a part of you, instructor.
You are white—
yet a part of me, as I am a part of you.
That's American.
Sometimes perhaps you don't want to be a part of me.
Nor do I often want to be a part of you.
But we are, that's true!

As I learn from you,
I guess you learn from me—
although you're older—and white—
and somewhat more free.

This is my page for English B.

For Discussion

1. Is the instructor's theme assignment a good one? Just how difficult is it to "let that page come out of you"?
2. How well does the subsequent "theme" meet the demands of the assignment? If you were teaching the course, what grade would you give this theme?
3. What does the narrator mean when he says his page "will be / a part of you, instructor"? What responsibilities does this idea imply for instructors?
4. What does the narrator do to describe himself as typical?
5. How important to the meaning of the poem is the fact that the teacher is white? Can you suggest how the poem would be different had the teacher been Black?

For Comparison

1. Both Hughes and Bond ("The Black Mind on the American Campus") are Black. What similarities do you find between their selections presented here? What differences? How do you account for these differences?
2. How would William Young ("A Sense of Shelter") react if he had given the assignment and received this theme?

For Composition

1. An honest theme.
2. Black and white in the classroom.
3. My theme for English B.

STEPHEN SPENDER

AN ELEMENTARY SCHOOL CLASS ROOM IN A SLUM

Far far from gusty waves, these children's faces.
Like rootless weeds the torn hair round their paleness.
The tall girl with her weighed-down head. The paper-seeming boy
    with rat's eyes. The stunted unlucky heir
Of twisted bones, reciting a father's gnarled disease,
His lesson from his desk. At back of the dim class,
One unnoted, sweet and young: his eyes live in a dream
Of squirrels' game, in tree room, other than this.

On sour cream walls, donations. Shakespeare's head
Cloudless at dawn, civilized dome riding all cities.
Belled, flowery, Tyrolese valley. Open-handed map
Awarding the world its world. And yet, for these
Children, these windows, not this world, are world,
Where all their future's painted with a fog,
A narrow street sealed in with a lead sky,
Far far from rivers, capes, and stars of words.

Surely Shakespeare is wicked, the map a bad example
With ships and sun and love tempting them to steal—
For lives that slyly turn in their cramped holes
From fog to endless night? On their slag heap, these children
Wear skins peeped through by bones and spectacles of steel
With mended glass, like bottle bits on stones.
All of their time and space are foggy slum
So blot their maps with slums as big as doom.

Unless, governor, teacher, inspector, visitor,
This map becomes their window and these windows
That open on their lives like crouching tombs
Break, O break open, till they break the town
And show the children to the fields and all their world
Azure on their sands, to let their tongues
Run naked into books, the white and green leaves open
The history theirs whose language is the sun.

For Discussion

1. This poem is filled with symbols: rootless weeds, fog, lead sky, slag heap, etc. Discuss what these various symbols mean to you and how they support the meaning of the entire poem.
2. What is the real world for these children?
3. Is the meaning of this poem limited because it is about education in a slum classroom? Which of the concepts are universally true?
4. How would you teach this class if you were the teacher?

For Comparison

1. There are similarities between the attitudes expressed in this poem and Shapiro's "University". What are they? What symbols in Shapiro's poem compare with symbols in Spender's poem?
2. Examine carefully the thesis of Bond's essay (his ninth paragraph in "The Black Mind on the American Campus") and apply it to the problem presented in this poem.

For Composition

1. These windows are world.
2. They don't have a chance.
3. How education might save them.

PHILIP LARKIN

A STUDY OF READING HABITS

When getting my nose in a book
Cured most things short of school,
It was worth ruining my eyes
To know I could still keep cool,
And deal out the old right hook
To dirty dogs twice my size.

From *The Whitsun Weddings*, by Philip Larkin. Copyright © 1964 by Philip Larkin. Reprinted by permission of Random House, Inc., and Faber and Faber, Ltd.

Later, with inch-thick specs,
Evil was just my lark:
Me and my cloak and fangs
Had ripping times in the dark.
The women I clubbed with sex!
I broke them up like meringues.

Don't read much now: the dude
Who lets the girl down before
The hero arrives, the chap
Who's yellow and keeps the store,
Seems far too familiar. Get stewed:
Books are a load of crap.

For Discussion

1. What kind of person do you think the narrator of this poem is? What was probably his favorite subject in school? Which one did he dislike the most?
2. What kinds of reading experiences are objected to in the last stanza of the poem? Can you suggest some book or story titles which fit the descriptions given? Judging from the kind of material he read, can you suggest why the narrator did not enjoy reading?
3. To what extent do you agree with the narrator that the real work-a-day world is more important than the world depicted in books? What aspect of the reading that you have done in school do you feel has been impractical?
4. What are the differences between a formal and an informal education?

For Comparison

1. How would Billy ("A Sense of Shelter") respond to the narrator of this poem?
2. What would this poem mean to the narrator in "Me and Miss Mandible"?

For Composition

1. Reading is (is not) a waste of time.
2. Formal versus informal education.
3. Reading that has helped me.

W. D. SNODGRASS

THE CAMPUS ON THE HILL

Up the reputable walks of old established trees
They stalk, children of the *nouveaux riches;* chimes
Of the tall Clock Tower drench their heads in blessing:
"I don't wanna play at your house;
I don't like you any more."
My house stands opposite, on the other hill,
Among meadows, with the orchard fences down and falling;
Deer come almost to the door.
You cannot see it, even in this clearest morning.
White birds hang in the air between
Over the garbage landfill and those homes thereto adjacent,
Hovering slowly, turning, settling down
Like the flakes sifting imperceptibly onto the little town
In a waterball of glass.
And yet, this morning, beyond this quiet scene,
The floating birds, the backyards of the poor,
Beyond the shopping plaza, the dead canal, the hillside lying tilted in the air,
Tomorrow has broken out today:
Riot in Algeria, in Cyprus, in Alabama;
Aged in wrong, the empires are declining,
And China gathers, soundlessly, like evidence.
What shall I say to the young on such a morning?—
Mind is the one salvation?—also grammar?—
No; my little ones lean not toward revolt. They
Are the Whites, the vaguely furiously driven, who resist
Their souls with such passivity
As would make Quakers swear. All day, dear Lord, all day
They wear their godhead lightly.
They look out from their hill and say,
To themselves, "We have nowhere to go but down;
The great destination is to stay."
Surely the nations will be reasonable;
They look at the world—don't they?—the world's way?
The clock just now has nothing more to say.

For Discussion

1. Why does Snodgrass stress the difference between the setting of the
   college and the setting of his home? How does the attitude toward
   these two settings contribute to the meaning of the poem?

2. Do you think that the children of the *nouveaux riches* (newly rich) are as concerned about the real world problems as their professor would like to imagine them to be? If they are not concerned, might the college be partially to blame?
3. Is the professor saying that grammar and other such fundamentals are not important in a world in which everything has suddenly turned wrong?
4. If the professor is objecting to the complacent attitude of his students, what would he do if they really cared and revolted?
5. How would you make modern education more relative to problems of life?

For Comparison

1. What similar criticisms of modern education are made in this poem and in Karl Shapiro's "University"?
2. How would this teacher of the *nouveaux riches* relate to students described by Spender in "An Elementary Class Room in a Slum"? How, particularly, would he relate to the final stanza of that poem?

For Composition

1. Education in an ideal vacuum.
2. Student apathy.
3. Changes I would make in current education.

DONALD HALL

THE THREE MOVEMENTS

It is not in the books
that he is looking, nor for
a new book, nor
documents of any kind, nor
does he expect it to be like the wind,
that, when you touch it, tears
without a sound of tearing, nor
like the rain

"The Three Movements" from *The Alligator Bride* by Donald Hall. Copyright © 1957 by Donald Hall. Reprinted by permission of Harper & Row, Publishers.

water
that becomes
grass in the sun. He
expects that when he finds it,
it will be
like a man, visible, alive
to what has happened and what
will happen, with
firmness in its face, seeing
exactly what is, without
measure of change, and not
like documents,
or rain in the grass.

But what, he says,
if it is not
for the finding, not
what you most expect, nor even
what you dread, nothing
but the books, the endless
documents, the banked
volumes that repeat
mile after mile
their names,
their information?
Perhaps there is nothing
except the rain
water
becoming the grass, the
sustenance. What
a man should do is
accumulate
information
until he has gathered, like a
farmer, as much
as his resources can contain.

Yet perhaps, he thinks,
I speak
with knowledge, but perhaps
forgetting the movement
that intrigues
all thinking. It is
the movement which works through,
which discovers itself
in alleys, in

sleep, not
expected and not
in the books of words and phrases
nor the various paints and edges
of scenery.

It is, he says,
familiar when come upon,
glimpsed
as in a mirror
unpredicted,
and it appears
to understand. It is
like himself, only visible.

For Discussion

1. What is the "it" for which Hall is searching?
2. What is the importance of the title? What are the three movements as Hall defines them?
3. Should all knowledge be made practical? Should a man attempt, as Hall suggests, to accumulate as much information "as his resources can contain"?
4. Applying Hall's principle, how long a time do you think it would take for a person to become educated? How responsible is an individual man to educate himself to the best of his potential?

For Comparison

1. How does the attitude expressed by Hall differ from that expressed by the narrator in "A Study of Reading Habits"? Do the two poems express different levels of responsibility?
2. To what extent has the "it" described by Hall been found already by the narrator in "Me and Miss Mandible"?

For Composition

1. All knowledge can (cannot) be practical.
2. Education is a constant process.
3. Man's responsibility to educate himself.

photo by L. S. Asbury

Part Five

INDIVIDUAL–RELIGION

People's religious beliefs, whatever they might be, become a part of their world and force upon them certain responsibilities. Whether individuals ultimately become members of a church or avowed atheists, the ideas about God and an afterlife they hold do much to shape the world in which they live. These beliefs inevitably cast the believer into certain social groups to which some loyalty is owed, groups which are probably in direct opposition to certain other social groups.

A person's first religious ideas are usually inherited, but a step toward personal maturity is the establishment of one's own religious convictions even though they ultimately may be the same as those suggested by parents. Once the decision is made, church membership sometimes places obligations and limitations upon a member. Church members often must decide between matters of personal integrity and group loyalty, determining the extent of control they are willing to permit the church to have in their personal lives. If a person rejects organized religious opinions, that rejection becomes itself a type of belief, demanding distinct responsibilities.

As is apparent in the following selections, the basic issue important to religious responsibility is the determination of the rights of the individual both inside and outside the formal religious structure. Typical questions include: Is organized religion valid in today's world? How much religious fervor is based on fear? Does an individual have the right or perhaps even the responsibility to try to convince someone else to accept his religious beliefs? What are some problems of religious importance raised by modern scientific knowledge? Can a person be religious for the wrong reasons?

HOWARD SINGER

DON'T TRY TO SELL ME YOUR RELIGION

All over the country solemn-faced people are getting together to eat tunafish sandwiches, drink lukewarm coffee, and carry out an activity called Interfaith Dialogue.

In Valyermo, Calif., a group of rabbis and the Benedictine monks of St. Andrews Priory recited Psalms together, the monks in Latin, the rabbis in Hebrew. In Latrobe, Pa., Catholic and Jewish scholars spent four days exploring religious problems. The Harvard Divinity School recently brought 100 Christian and Jewish scholars together to discuss Christian-Jewish relations. And the same thing is going on at lower levels. Apparently the shepherd of every little church or synagogue now wants to hold hands with the pastor of every other synagogue or church. And it isn't just churchmen; the number of laymen involved in interreligious dialogue boggles the mind.

The epidemic started only a few years ago. Shortly before the Ecumenical Council met at Rome one began to hear a good deal of talk about "new winds" blowing through the churches, and a wave of "progressive thinking" erupted among theologians. At first only Protestants and Catholics started talking to one another. Then Jews were brought in, at first only for social projects. But interfaith dialogues were soon blooming in every village and town.

Interreligious dialogue takes many forms. There is the formal Interfaith Conference, usually sponsored by a seminary, lasting two or three days. There may be panel discussions, or Christian and Jewish scholars may read learned papers to one another on, say, their differing concepts of revelation. There are many less ambitious formats—for instance, the local enterprise sponsored by a synagogue and church as part of their adult-education programs, and informal meetings of interested laymen gathered in somebody's living room.

The theory behind it all was first stated by Martin Buber, the Jewish philosopher, who spoke of "I-Thou" and "I-It" relationships. In an "I-Thou" relationship you don't try to score points or defeat your opponent; you try to understand him, to respect his uniqueness, to establish a warm relationship with him. People learn from the growth in personal relationships. So the theory goes.

Now all this sounds eminently reasonable, or at least harmless. All the same I think that interreligious dialogue between Christians and Jews is a farce, and, in addition, subtly demeaning.

Reprinted with permission from *The Saturday Evening Post.* © 1967 The Curtis Publishing Company.

But I want to be careful, and I want to be clear.

I am a rabbi, and I speak only of Christian-Jewish dialogue, not Protestant-Catholic.

What's more, I speak of theological dialogue only.

I have no objection to ministers, priests and rabbis getting together to discuss the poverty program or juvenile delinquency, or, for that matter, the prevalence of noisy motorcycles. We share society's problems, and we certainly ought to cooperate in finding solutions. And it is quite possible that such meetings can lessen the misunderstandings between Christians and Jews. But when Christians and Jews get together to discuss religious differences, I sigh and shake my head. The sad fact is that when laymen engage in theological dialogue they cheerfully exchange superficialities and misinformation. And when clergymen or scholars do it, they walk gingerly around certain topics, like infantrymen poking their way through a minefield.

Purely "theological" dialogue must start with the assumption that, for all their differences, the participants have some religious beliefs in common. Now that assumption is true as between Protestants and Catholics, who might well look forward to the reunion of the "separated brethren." But similar dialogues between Jews and Christians make no sense because there is neither common ground nor the possibility of important, unifying consequences.

But what about all that talk about the "Judeo-Christian heritage"? What about that reference in the Ecumenical Council's Declaration to "the great spiritual patrimony common to Christians and Jews"?

I think it's high time somebody broke down and admitted that the phrase "Judeo-Christian tradition" is one of the most successful public-relations triumphs of the century. Our ancestors, both Christian and Jewish, would hardly have understood it. It's true that both faiths have certain values in common, but we also share them with Moslems and Buddhists; they are the values of any civilized society. As Professor Walter Kaufmann of Princeton has pointed out, there is no more reason to talk about a Judeo-Christian tradition than there is to talk about a Judeo-Islamic or a Greco-Christian tradition. Christianity borrowed at least as much from the Greeks and Romans as it did from the Jews.

Then why is the phrase so popular?

One reason is that Jews are sharply conscious of their minority status, and their organizations understand the techniques of good public relations. The ancient Greeks and Romans, poor fellows, were not similarly oriented. Another reason is that Christians like the idea of a "Judeo-Christian" tradition because it fits their religious outlook. They like to think that since Jews came first, and they came later, Judaism was the seed and the root, Christianity the flower and the fruit. But as a Jew and a rabbi, obviously I don't accept that view. I don't see Christianity as the exquisite culmination of a long and painful Jewish evolution; I see Christianity, to use Santayana's phrase, as a "paganization" of monotheism, something with which I can have no real sense of kinship.

Not only is there no common ground in these dialogues; there is no sense of equality. In theory every Christian is a missionary, and a missionary can't respect the outsider's uniqueness; he must overcome it. Of course he believes it's for your own good, but it somehow never occurs to him that what is altruism to him is subversion to you. And make no mistake, the Christian duty to convert the non-Christian is not a quaint or minor obligation. It is central to Christianity. The last two verses of the Gospel according to Matthew urge the faithful to go forth and teach all the nations, and baptize them. This is still regarded by the major Christian churches as a basic tenet. It was forcefully restated in the first draft of the Ecumenical Council's Declaration on the Non-Christian Religions. And in the final version of the Declaration, according to no less an authority than Cardinal Bea of the Vatican, the church "explicitly and openly declares that it is both her duty and her desire to preach Christ." This is not merely a theoretical position; there are at this moment more than a thousand Christian missionaries of all denominations hard at work in, of all places, Israel. Alas, they're not doing too well. For some reason, a nation populated by so many Jewish survivors of extermination camps built by European Christians is deaf to missionary talk of the Christian God of Love.

Recently I read the remarks of Professor Arthur Piepkorn, head of the Department of Systematic Theology at Concordia Seminary and an editorial associate of *The American Lutheran*. He spoke at one of those dialogue sessions, sponsored jointly by the seminary and the Anti-Defamation League of B'nai B'rith. He remarked that "the concern of every Christian" will be to convert non-Christians, but conceded: "We know that in the past Christians sometimes tried to convert Jews in ways that created an understandable atmosphere of persisting suspicion and skepticism among the Jews." Then some terrifying examples follow—"and similar phenomena are deplorable facts of history" . . . . And yet: ". . . to the extent that the Lutheran fails to include the Jews in his evangelistic outreach, to that extent, the Lutheran is on his own terms culpably anti-Semitic."

This good Christian concedes that in the past his co-religionists were a little crude about it, which is regrettable. But the duty remains, though he'll abjure force for the future.

I can't quite decide what disturbs me more: the good professor's remarks, or the fact that the rabbi who shared that platform didn't walk off after hearing them. The nature of an aggressive intention is not changed by labeling it a Christian duty. There's only one fitting response to that sort of thing: "Please understand that my faith is as precious to me as yours is to you. If your imagination or your principles can't carry you that far, just go your own way, and leave me alone in my peaceful outer darkness."

Dialogues between clergymen are always fascinating exhibitions of double talk. In the first place, the vocabulary of theology is itself an endless swamp over a bottomless pit. In the second place, a Christian clergyman can't openly reveal his assumption of his faith's superiority without alienating the non-servile Jewish participants, if any; but he can't quite suppress it either. As a rule he muddles through, which is why listening to him in mid-dialogue is like watching some unusually spry youngsters doing the monkey. I can't help suspecting that clergymen know full well that dialogue is a colossal waste of time. But interfaith-conference-hopping is a great deal more glamorous than visiting old ladies in the hospital. And by now a kind of permanent interfaith clergymen's civil service has developed, with a strong vested interest in calling more meetings. It helps to remember that dialogue is a wondrous puffer-up of clerical reputations.

Laymen who go in for religious dialogue are likely to be decent, open-minded and warmhearted. Their discussions are less guarded, though often superficial, and they do sometimes strike a note of graceful spontaneity. There are good reasons for that too.

One pamphlet published by a Jewish group, intended for guidance on setting up interfaith dialogues, reminds us: "Experience has shown that . . . persons who have much in common are least likely to get sidetracked into controversies over extraneous matters. . . . It's a good idea to make sure that the two sides will be reasonably similar in education, social status and life style." Well, when Christians and Jews of that sort meet, a certain amount of ice-breaking is inevitable. But they would do just as well discussing whether bowling or tennis is more suitable for the middle-aged.

Better yet, let them do some good; let them discuss real problems of our society, not just vague subjective feelings about their faiths. There's something futile and fraudulent in even the most "successful" session of theological dialogue, something tasteless in the notion itself. When we are conscious of the guest or the stranger, we can't help dressing things up a little, and the faith is subtly falsified. There is something artificial in speechmaking about one's deepest religious principles; it's so easy to talk them to death. What goes on at a dialogue is what happens when those lovely tropical fish are brought to the surface; the fish die, and their brilliant colors quickly fade.

There's no reason why it should not be said: Dialogue is a new way to gain social status. But in that very fact lies a problem: When the dialogue is the main social contact between the two groups, the "dialogue" itself becomes a hostage and acquires a significance it doesn't deserve. Participants can even use the threat of withdrawal as a pressure tactic. During the Broadway run of *The Deputy*, the play about Pope Pius XII's attitude toward the Nazis' persecution of the Jews, a leading Catholic figure stated that unless the Jewish community repudiated the play, further dialogue would be impossible. To my sorrow several Jewish organizations and rabbis did signify their disapproval, even while some thoughtful Catholic writers (Hilda Graef in the *Catholic World* and George Shuster in *The New York Times*) agreed with the play's central thesis. Ironically, I believe the play probably was more effective in helping Christians confront the truth about their past than all the dialogues in history.

During the Korean War I participated in what was probably the longest continuous unstructured dialogue in history. It was held among Catholic, Protestant and Jewish chaplains in my barracks in Japan. We were at it almost every night. Our discussions were playful intellectual wrestling matches and usually they bubbled over with friendly, raucous laughter. But I learned something valuable from those evenings. I learned that dialogue doesn't lead to friendship; rather it's friendship, or at least the sharing of a predicament, that sometimes can lead to honest dialogue. It was great fun. And even so, it had a sour ending.

When I was about to return home, one of my fellow chaplains, accompanying me to the aircraft, pulled me aside and told me how wonderful it was that we were now friends. I was touched. I expressed similar sentiments with the utmost sincerity. Then he pressed something into my hand and said, "Howard, listen. Read this on the plane and try, prayerfully, to find your way to Jesus." I looked at what I was holding; it was the New Testament. I did a terrible thing then: I laughed.

I was sorry immediately, for he was stricken at my response, but for a moment I had honestly thought he was kidding. And then I understood.

For centuries good Christians just couldn't believe that Jews really accepted Judaism in good faith. It seemed so obvious to Christians that Christianity was superior. Those who resisted conversion had to be in league with the devil. Now my friend, to be sure, was a child of the 20th century. He didn't believe I was a devil's disciple. But he was also a good Christian. It didn't matter that every evening for a full year I had demonstrated a reasonable knowledge of the New Testament as well as my own scriptures. It didn't matter that I had made my wholehearted loyalty to Judaism clear in a hundred different ways. He was still going to save my soul. And because he insisted on trying, I hurt his feelings.

Ever since, when a Christian clergyman invites me to talk about religion, I make some careful comment about the weather.

For Discussion

1. How valid is Rabbi Singer's suggestion that every Christian feels a commitment to missionary activity? How can such a commitment on the part of one person violate the individual freedom of a second person?
2. Does anything of value come from the numerous efforts to bring together for discussion persons of different religious faiths? Is the value a spiritual or a social one?
3. Rabbi Singer says that it would be better for people to discuss "real problems of our society, not just vague subjective feelings about their faiths." Do you feel that the "real problems" are perhaps more important than the abstract, spiritual ones? What are some real problems that Rabbi Singer might have in mind?

For Comparison

1. Does this essay deal with the same problem as the poem "Debate with the Rabbi," or is there a difference? What definition of *religion* is intended in both works?
2. Martin Luther King, Jr.'s essay, "The Answer to a Perplexing Question," suggests that the individual has an obligation to become "an instrument of God" and work toward the removal of social evils. What would Singer's reaction be to this position? Would he see in this attitude the risk of doing the wrong things in the name of a religious goal? What are your opinions?

For Composition

1. Don't try to sell me your religion.
2. Interreligious dialogue is (is not) healthy.
3. My experience with religious zealots.

MARTIN LUTHER KING, JR.

THE ANSWER TO A PERPLEXING QUESTION

Human life through the centuries has been characterized by man's persistent efforts to remove evil from the earth. Seldom has man thoroughly adjusted himself to evil, for in spite of his rationalizations, compromises, and alibis, he knows the "is" is not the "ought" and the actual is not the possible. Though the evils of sensuality, selfishness, and cruelty often rise aggressively in his soul, something within him tells him that they are intruders and reminds him of his higher destiny and more noble allegiance. Man's hankering after the demonic is always disturbed by his longing for the divine. As he seeks to adjust to the demands of time, he knows that eternity is his ultimate habitat. When man comes to himself, he knows that evil is a foreign invader that must be driven from the native soils of his soul before he can achieve moral and spiritual dignity . . . .

How can evil be cast out? Men have usually pursued two paths to eliminate evil and thereby save the world. The first calls upon man to remove evil through his own power and ingenuity in the strange conviction that by thinking, inventing, he will at last conquer the nagging forces of evil. Give people a fair chance and a decent education, and they will save themselves. This idea, sweeping across the modern world like a plague, has ushered God out and escorted man in and has substituted human ingenuity for divine guidance. Some people suggest that this concept was introduced during the Renaissance when reason dethroned religion, or later when Darwin's *Origin of Species* replaced belief in creation by the theory of evolution, or when the industrial revolution turned the hearts of men to material comforts and physical conveniences. At any rate, the idea of adequacy of man to solve the evils of history captured the minds of people, giving rise to the easy optimism of the nineteenth century, the doctrine of inevitable progress, Rousseau's maxim of "the original goodness of human nature," and Condorcet's conviction that by reason alone the whole world would soon be cleansed of crime, poverty, and war.

Armed with this growing faith in the capability of reason and science modern man set out to change the world. He turned his attention from God and the human soul to the outer world and its possibilities. He observed, analyzed, and explored. The laboratory became man's sanctuary and scientists his priests and prophets. A modern humanist confidently affirmed:

The future is not with the churches but with the laboratories, not with prophets but with scientists, not with piety but with efficiency. Man is at last becoming aware that he alone is responsible for the realization of the world of his dreams, that he has within himself the power for its achievement.

Man has subpoenaed nature to appear before the judgment seat of scientific investigation. None doubt that man's work in the scientific laboratories has brought unbelievable advances in power and comfort, producing machines that think and gadgets that soar majestically through the skies, stand impressively on the land and move with stately dignity on the seas.

But in spite of these astounding new scientific developments, the old evils continue and the age of reason has been transformed into an age of terror. Selfishness and hatred have not vanished with an enlargement of our educational system and an extension of our legislative policies. A once optimistic generation now asks in utter bewilderment, "Why could not we cast it out?"

The answer is rather simple: Man by his own power can never cast evil from the world. The humanist's hope is an illusion, based on too great an optimism concerning the inherent goodness of human nature.

I would be the last to condemn the thousands of sincere and dedicated people outside the churches who have labored unselfishly through various humanitarian movements to cure the world of social evils, for I would rather a man be a committed humanist than an uncommitted Christian. But so many of these dedicated persons, seeking salvation within the human context, have become understandably pessimistic and disillusioned, because their efforts are based on a kind of self-delusion which ignores fundamental facts about our mortal nature.

Nor would I minimize the importance of science and the great contributions which have come in the wake of the Renaissance. These have lifted us from the stagnating valleys of superstition and half-truths to the sunlit mountains of creative analysis and objective appraisal. The unquestioned authority of the church in scientific matters needed to be freed from paralyzing obscurantism, antiquated notions, and shameful inquisitions. But the exalted Renaissance optimism, while attempting to free the mind of man, forgot about man's capacity for sin.

The second idea for removing evil from the world stipulates that if man waits submissively upon the Lord, in his own good time God alone will redeem the world. Rooted in a pessimistic doctrine of human nature, the idea, which eliminates completely the capability of sinful man to do anything, was prominent in the Reformation, that great spiritual movement which gave birth to the protestant concern for moral and spiritual freedom and served as a necessary corrective for a corrupt and stagnant medieval church. The doctrines of justification by faith and the priesthood of all believers are towering principles which we as Protestants must forever affirm, but the Reformation doctrine of human nature over-stressed the corruption of man. The Renaissance was too optimistic, and the Reformation too pessimistic. The former so concentrated on the good-ness of man that it overlooked his capacity for goodness. While rightly affirming the sinfulness of human nature and man's incapacity to save himself, the Reformation wrongly affirmed that the image of God has been completely erased from man.

This led to the Calvinistic concept of the total depravity of man and to a resurrection of the terrible idea of infant damnation. So depraved is human nature, said the doctrinaire Calvinist, that if a baby dies without baptism he will burn forever in hell. Certainly this carries the idea of man's sinfulness too far.

This lopsided Reformation theology has often emphasized a purely other-worldly religion, which stresses the utter hopelessness of this world and calls upon the individual to concentrate on preparing his soul for the world to come. By ignoring the need for social reform, religion is divorced from the mainstream of human life. A pulpit committee listed as the first essential qualification for a new minister: "He must preach the true gos-pel and not talk about social issues." This is a blueprint for a dangerously irrelevant church where people assemble to hear only pious platitudes.

By disregarding the fact that the gospel deals with man's body as well as with his soul, such a one-sided emphasis creates a tragic dichotomy between the sacred and the secular. To be worthy of its New Testament origin, the church must seek to transform both individual lives and the social situation that brings to many people anguish of spirit and cruel bondage.

The idea that man expects God to do everything leads inevitably to a callous misuse of prayer. For if God does everything, man then asks for anything, and God becomes little more than a "cosmic bellhop" who is summoned for every trivial need. Or God is considered so omnipotent and man so powerless that prayer is a substitute for work and intelligence. A man said to me, "I believe in integration, but I know it will not come until God wants it to come. You Negroes should stop protesting and start praying." I am certain we need to pray for God's help and guidance in this integration struggle, but we are gravely misled if we think the struggle will be won only with prayer. God, who gave us minds for think-ing and bodies for working, would defeat his own purpose if he permitted us to obtain through prayer what may come through work and intelli-gence. Prayer is a marvelous and necessary supplement of our feeble efforts, but it is a dangerous substitute. When Moses strove to lead the Israelites to the Promised Land God made it clear that he would not do for them what they could do for themselves. "And the Lord said unto

Moses, Wherefore criest thou unto me? speak unto the children of Israel, that they go forward."

We must pray earnestly for peace, but we must also work vigorously for disarmament and the suspension of weapon testing. We must use our minds as rigorously to plan for peace as we have used them to plan for war. We must pray with unceasing passion for racial justice, but we must also use our minds to develop a program, organize ourselves into mass nonviolent action, and employ every resource of our bodies and souls to bring into being those social changes that make for a better distribution of wealth within our nation and in the underdeveloped countries of the world.

Does not all of this reveal the fallacy of thinking that God will cast evil from the earth, even if man does nothing except sit complacently by the wayside? No prodigious thunderbolt from heaven will blast away evil. No mighty army of angels will descend to force men to do what their wills resist. The Bible portrays God, not as an omnipotent czar who makes all decisions for his subjects nor as a cosmic tyrant who with gestapolike methods invades the inner lives of men, but rather as a loving Father who gives to his children such abundant blessings as they may be willing to receive. Always man must do something. "Stand upon thy feet," says God to Ezekiel, "and I will speak unto you." Man is no helpless invalid left in a valley of total depravity until God pulls him out. Man is rather an upstanding human being whose vision has been impaired by the cataracts of sin and whose soul has been weakened by the virus of pride, but there is sufficient vision left for him to turn his weak and sin-battered life toward the Great Physician, the curer of the ravages of sin.

The real weakness of the idea that God will do everything is its false conception of both God and man. It makes God so absolutely sovereign that man is absolutely helpless. It makes man so absolutely depraved that he can do nothing but wait on God. It sees the world as so contaminated with sin that God totally transcends it and touches it only here and there through a mighty invasion. This view ends up with a God who is a despot and not a Father. It ends up with such a pessimism concerning human nature that it leaves man little more than a helpless worm crawling through the morass of an evil world. But man is neither totally depraved, nor is God an almighty dictator. We must surely affirm the majesty and sovereignty of God, but this should not lead us to believe that God is an Almighty Monarch who will impose his will upon us and deprive us of the freedom to choose what is good or what is not good. He will not thrust himself upon us nor force us to stay home when our minds are bent on journeying to some far country. But he follows us in love, and when we come to ourselves and turn our tired feet back to the Father's house, he stands waiting with outstretched arms of forgiveness.

Therefore we must never feel that God will, through some breathtaking miracle or a wave of the hand, cast evil out of the world. As long as we believe this we will pray unanswerable prayers and ask God to do things that he will never do. The belief that God will do everything for man is as untenable as the belief that man can do everything for himself. It, too, is based on a lack of faith. We must learn that to expect God to do everything while we do nothing is not faith, but superstition.

What, then is the answer to life's perplexing question: "How can evil be cast out of our individual and collective lives?" If the world is not to be purified by God alone nor by man alone, who will do it?

The answer is found in an idea which is distinctly different from the two we have discussed, for neither God nor man will individually bring the world's salvation. Rather, *both* man and God, made one in a marvelous unity of purpose through an overflowing love as the free gift of himself on the part of God and by perfect obedience and receptivity on the part of man, can transform the old into the new and drive out the deadly cancer of sin.

The principle which opens the door for God to work through man is faith. This is what the disciples lacked when they desperately tried to remove the nagging evil from the body of the sick child. Jesus reminded them that they had been attempting to do themselves what could be done only when their lives were open receptacles, as it were, into which God's strength could be freely poured.

Two types of faith in God are clearly set forth in the Scriptures. One may be called the mind's faith, wherein the intellect assents to a belief that God exists. The other may be referred to as the heart's faith, whereby the whole man is involved in a trusting act of self-surrender. To know God, a man must possess this latter type of faith, for the mind's faith is directed toward a theory, but the heart's faith is centered in a Person. Gabriel Marcel claims that faith is *believing in, not believing that.* It is "opening a credit; which puts me at the disposal of the one in whom I believe." When I believe, he says "I rally to with that sort of interior gathering of oneself which the act of rallying implies." Faith is the opening of all sides and at every level of one's life to the divine inflow.

This is what the Apostle Paul emphasized in his doctrine of salvation by faith. For him, faith is man's capacity to accept God's willingness through Christ to rescue us from the bondage of sin. In his magnanimous love, God freely offers to do for us what we cannot do for ourselves. Our humble and openhearted acceptance is faith. So by faith we are saved. Man filled with God and God operating through man bring unbelievable changes in our individual and social lives.

Social evils have trapped multitudes of men in a dark and murky corridor where there is no exit sign and plunged others into a dark abyss of psychological fatalism. These deadly, paralyzing evils can be removed by a humanity perfectly united through obedience with God. Moral victory will come as God fills man and man opens his life by faith to God, even as the gulf opens to the overflowing waters of the river. Racial justice, a genuine possibility in our nation and in the world, will come neither by our frail and often misguided efforts nor by God imposing his will on wayward men, but when enough people open their lives to God and allow him to pour his triumphant, divine energy into their souls. Our age-old and noble dream of a world of peace may yet become a reality, but it will come neither by man working alone nor by God destroying the wicked schemes of men, but when men so open their lives to God that he may fill them with love, mutual respect, understanding, and goodwill. Social salvation will come only through man's willing acceptance of God's mighty gift.

Let me apply what I have been saying to our personal lives. Many of you know what it means to struggle with sin. Year by year you were aware that a terrible sin—slavery to drink, perhaps, or untruthfulness, impurity, selfishness—was taking possession of your life. As the years unfolded and the vice widened its landmarks on your soul, you knew that it was an unnatural intruder. You may have thought, "One day I shall drive this evil out. I know it is destroying my character and embarrassing my family." At last you determined to purge yourself of the evil by making a New Year's resolution. Do you remember your surprise and disappointment when you discovered, three hundred and sixty-five days later, that your most sincere efforts had not banished the old habit from your life? In complete amazement you asked, "Why could not I cast it out?"

In despair you decided to take your problem to God, but instead of asking him to work through you, you said, "God, you must solve this problem for me. I can't do anything about it." But days and months later the evil was still with you. God would not cast it out, for he never removes sin without the cordial co-operation of the sinner. No problem is solved when we idly wait for God to undertake full responsibility.

One cannot remove an evil habit by mere resolution nor by simply calling on God to do the job, but only as he surrenders himself and becomes an instrument of God. We shall be delivered from the accumulated weight of evil only when we permit the energy of God to come into our souls.

For Discussion

1. How do you think the author would define the word *religion?* The word *evil?*

2. Do you believe that human beings are capable of ridding the world of evil? Do you agree with King's suggestion that evil will only be done away with if people work directly with God?
3. King talks about "a *callous misuse* of prayer." Give some examples of how individuals might be guilty of this offense.
4. What does King mean when he suggests "the mind's faith is directed toward a theory, but the heart's faith is centered in a Person"? Do you agree or disagree with this statement?
5. How might one be certain that what one identifies as a social evil really is one and not simply a product of one's own ego or selfishness?
6. In your opinion should the church concern itself with social evils, or is its role solely that of preparing people for life after death?

For Comparison

1. Would King agree with the concept of God projected by Crane in "Blustering God"? What about the concept of human beings in that same poem?
2. To what extent do the persons in "O Yes" have (or fail to have) the attitudes toward God and people that King recommends in his essay?

For Composition

1. King's concept of social evil.
2. God and human beings—Partners.
3. The Church in today's world.

Friedrich Nietzsche

THE GAY SCIENCE

The Madman. Have you not heard of that madman who lit a lantern in the bright morning hours, ran to the market place, and cried incessantly, "I seek God! I seek God!" As many of those who do not believe in God were standing around just then, he provoked much laughter. Why, did he get lost? said one. Did he lose his way like a child? said another. Or is he hiding? Is he afraid of us? Has he gone on a voyage? or emigrated?

Thus they yelled and laughed. The madman jumped into their midst and pierced them with his glances.

"Whither is God" he cried. "I shall tell you. *We have killed him*—you and I. All of us are his murderers. But how have we done this? How were we able to drink up the sea? Who gave us the sponge to wipe away the entire horizon? What did we do when we unchained this earth from its sun? Whither is it moving now? Wither are we moving now? Away from all suns? Are we not plunging continually? Backward, sideward, forward, in all directions? Is there any up or down left? Are we not straying as through an infinite nothing? Do we not feel the breath of empty space? Has it not become colder? Is not night and more night coming on all the while? Must not lanterns be lit in the morning? Do we not hear anything yet of the noise of the gravediggers who are burying God? Do we not smell anything yet of God's decomposition? Gods too decompose. God is dead. God remains dead. And we have killed him. How shall we, the murderers of all murderers, comfort ourselves? What was holiest and most powerful of all that the world has yet owned has bled to death under our knives. Who will wipe this blood off us? What water is there for us to clean ourselves? What festivals of atonement, what sacred games shall we have to invent? Is not the greatness of this deed too great for us? Must not we ourselves become gods simply to seem worthy of it? There has never been a greater deed; and whoever will be born after us—for the sake of this deed he will be part of a higher history than all history hitherto."

Here the madman fell silent and looked again at his listeners; and they too were silent and stared at him in astonishment. At last he threw his lantern on the ground, and it broke and went out. "I come too early," he said then; "my time has not come yet. This tremendous event is still on its way, still wandering—it has not yet reached the ears of man. Lightning and thunder require time, the light of the stars requires time, deeds require time even after they are done, before they can be seen and heard. This deed is still more distant from them than the most distant stars—*and yet they have done it themselves.*"

It has been related further that on that same day the madman entered divers churches and there sang his *requiem aeternam deo*. Led out and called to account, he is said to have replied each time, "What are these churches now if they are not the tombs and sepulchers of God?"

For Discussion

1. What is your definition of religion? Does it of necessity demand a supernatural basis? Does it demand formal organization?

2. What does Nietzsche mean when he says that God is dead? How has he been killed?
3. To what extent do you believe that modern churches are now the " 'tombs and sepulchers of God' "?
4. How possible is it to separate religious belief from religious affiliation with a church group?
5. With what does Nietzsche suggest we replace God?

For Comparison

1. Does cummings' poem "Jehovah buried,Satan dead" suggest the same concept of "God is dead" as that expressed by Nietzsche in this essay?
2. To what extent does Boyd's prayer "Here I am In Church Again, Jesus" support the final sentence in Nietzsche's essay?

For Composition

1. God is (is not) dead.
2. Religion is a crutch.
3. Religion and church can (cannot) be separated.

FRANK O'CONNOR

FIRST CONFESSION

It was a Saturday afternoon in early spring. A small boy whose face looked as though it had been but newly scrubbed was being led by the hand by his sister through a crowded street. The little boy showed a marked reluctance to proceed; he affected to be very interested in the shop-windows. Equally, his sister seemed to pay no attention to them. She tried to hurry him; he resisted. When she dragged him he began to bawl. The hatred with which she viewed him was almost diabolical, but when she spoke her words and tone were full of passionate sympathy.

"Ah, sha, God help us!" she intoned into his ear in a whine of commiseration.

"Leave me go!" he said, digging his heels into the pavement. "I don't want to go. I want to go home."

"But, sure, you can't go home, Jackie. You'll have to go. The parish priest will be up to the house with a stick."

"I don't care. I won't go."

"Oh, Sacred Heart, isn't it a terrible pity you weren't a good boy? Oh, Jackie, me heart bleeds for you! I don't know what they'll do to you at all, Jackie, me poor child. And all the trouble you caused your poor old nanny, and the way you wouldn't eat in the same room with her, and the time you kicked her on the shins, and the time you went for me with the bread knife under the table. I don't know will he ever listen to you at all, Jackie. I think meself he might sind you to the bishop. Oh, Jackie, how will you think of all your sins?"

Half stupefied with terror, Jackie allowed himself to be led through the sunny streets to the very gates of the church. It was an old one with two grim iron gates and a long, low, shapeless stone front. At the gates he stuck, but it was already too late. She dragged him behind her across the yard, and the commiserating whine with which she had tried to madden him gave place to a yelp of triumph.

"Now you're caught! Now, you're caught. And I hope he'll give you the pinitintial psalms! That'll cure you, you suppurating little caffler!"

Jackie gave himself up for lost. Within the old church there was no stained glass; it was cold and dark and desolate, and in the silence, the trees in the yard knocked hollowly at the tall windows. He allowed himself to be led through the vaulted silence, the intense and magical silence which seemed to have frozen within the ancient walls, buttressing them and shouldering the high wooden roof. In the street outside, yet seeming a million miles away, a ballad singer was drawling a ballad.

Nora sat in front of him beside the confession box. There were a few old women before her, and later a thin, sad-looking man with long hair came and sat beside Jackie. In the intense silence of the church that seemed to grow deeper from the plaintive moaning of the ballad singer, he could hear the buzz-buzz-buzz of a woman's voice in the box, and then the husky ba-ba-ba of the priest's. Lastly the soft thud of something that signalled the end of the confession, and out came the woman, head lowered, hands joined, looking neither to right nor left, and tiptoed up to the altar to say her penance.

It seemed only a matter of seconds till Nora rose and with a whispered injunction disappeared from his sight. He was all alone. Alone and next to be heard and the fear of damnation in his soul. He looked at the sad-faced man. He was gazing at the roof, his hands joined in prayer. A woman in a red blouse and black shawl had taken her place below him. She uncovered her head, fluffed her hair out roughly with her hand, brushed it sharply back, then, bowing, caught it in a knot and pinned it on her neck. Nora emerged. Jackie rose and looked at her with a hatred which was inappropriate to the occasion and the place. Her hands were joined on her stomach, her eyes modestly lowered, and her face had an expression of the most rapt and tender recollection. With death in his heart he crept into the compartment she left open and drew the door shut behind him.

He was in pitch darkness. He could see no priest nor anything else. And anything he had heard of confession got all muddled up in his mind. He knelt to the right-hand wall and said: "Bless me, father, for I have sinned. This is my first confession." Nothing happened. He repeated it louder. Still it gave no answer. He turned to the opposite wall, genu-flected first, then again went on his knees and repeated the charm. This time he was certain he would receive a reply, but none came. He repeated the process with the remaining wall without effect. He had the feeling of someone with an unfamiliar machine, of pressing buttons at random. And finally the thought struck him that God knew. God knew about the bad confession he intended to make and had made him deaf and blind so that he could neither hear nor see the priest.

Then as his eyes grew accustomed to the blackness, he perceived some-thing he had not noticed previously: a sort of shelf at about the height of his head. The purpose of this eluded him for a moment. Then he under-stood. It was for kneeling on.

He had always prided himself upon his powers of climbing, but this took it out of him. There was no foothold. He slipped twice before he succeeded in getting his knee on it, and the strain of drawing the rest of his body up was almost more than he was capable of. However, he did at last get his two knees on it, there was just room for those, but his legs hung down uncomfortably and the edge of the shelf bruised his shins. He joined his hands and pressed the last remaining button. "Bless me, father, for I have sinned. This is my first confession."

At the same moment the slide was pushed back and a dim light streamed into the little box. There was an uncomfortable silence, and then an alarmed voice asked, "Who's there?" Jackie found it almost im-possible to speak into the grille which was on a level with his knees, but he got a firm grip of the molding above it, bent his head down and side-ways, and as though he were hanging by his feet like a monkey found himself looking almost upside down at the priest. But the priest was looking sideways at him, and Jackie, whose knees were being tortured by this new position, felt it was a queer way to hear confessions.

"'Tis me, father," he piped, and then, running all his words together in excitement, he rattled off, "Bless me, father, for I have sinned. This is my first confession."

"What?" exclaimed a deep and angry voice, and the sombre soutaned figure stood bolt upright, disappearing almost entirely from Jackie's view. "What does this mean? What are you doing there? Who are you?"

And with the shock Jackie felt his hands lose their grip and his legs their balance. He discovered himself tumbling into space, and, falling, he knocked his head against the door, which shot open and permitted him to thump right into the center of the aisle. Straight on this came a small, dark-haired priest with a biretta well forward on his head. At the same time Nora came skeltering madly down the church.

"Lord God!" she cried. "The snivelling little caffler! I knew he'd do it! I knew he'd disgrace me!"

Jackie received a clout over the ear which reminded him that for some strange reason he had not yet begun to cry and that people might possibly think he wasn't hurt at all. Nora slapped him again.

"What's this? What's this?" cried the priest. "Don't attempt to beat the child, you little vixen!"

"I can't do me pinance with him," cried Nora shrilly, cocking a shocked eye on the priest. "He have me driven mad. Stop your crying, you dirty scut! Stop it now or I'll make you cry at the other side of your ugly puss!"

"Run away out of this, you little jade!" growled the priest. He suddenly began to laugh, took out a pocket handkerchief, and wiped Jackie's nose. "You're not hurt, sure you're not. Show us the ould head. . . . Ah, 'tis nothing. 'Twill be better before you're twice married. . . . So you were coming to confession?"

"I was, father."

"A big fellow like you should have terrible sins. Is it your first?"

"'Tis, father."

"Oh, my, worse and worse! Here, sit down there and wait till I get rid of these ould ones and we'll have a long chat. Never mind that sister of yours."

With a feeling of importance that glowed through his tears Jackie waited. Nora stuck her tongue out at him, but he didn't even bother to reply. A great feeling of relief was welling up in him. The sense of oppression that had been weighing him down for a week, the knowledge that he was about to make a bad confession, disappeared. Bad confession, indeed! He had made friends, made friends with the priest, and the priest expected, even demanded terrible sins. Oh, women! Women! It was all women and girls and their silly talk. They had no real knowledge of the world!

And when the time came for him to make his confession he did not beat about the bush. He may have clenched his hands and lowered his eyes, but wouldn't anyone?

"Father," he said huskily, "I made it up to kill me grandmother."

There was a moment's pause. Jackie did not dare to look up, but he could feel the priest's eyes on him. The priest's voice also seemed a trifle husky.

"Your grandmother?" he asked, but he didn't after all sound very angry.

"Yes, father."

"Does she live with you?"

"She do, father."

"And why did you want to kill her?"

"Oh, God, father, she's a horrible woman!"

"Is she now?"

"She is, father."

"What way is she horrible?"

Jackie paused to think. It was hard to explain.

"She takes snuff, father."

"Oh, my!"

"And she goes round in her bare feet, father."

"Tut-tut-tut!"

"She's a horrible woman, father," said Jackie with sudden earnestness. "She takes porter. And she ates the potatoes off the table with her hands. And me mother do be out working most days, and since that one came 'tis she gives us our dinner and I can't ate the dinner." He found himself sniffling. "And she gives pinnies to Nora and she doesn't give no pinnies to me because she knows I can't stand her. And me father sides with her, father, and he bates me, and me heart is broken and wan night in bed I made it up the way I'd kill her."

Jackie began to sob again, rubbing his nose with his sleeve, as he remembered his wrongs.

"And what way were you going to kill her?" asked the priest smoothly.

"With a hatchet, father."

"When she was in bed?"

"No, father."

"How, so?"

"When she ates the potatoes and drinks the porter she falls asleep, father."

"And you'd hit her then?"

"Yes, father."

"Wouldn't a knife be better?"

"'Twould, father, only I'd be afraid of the blood."

"Oh, of course. I never thought of the blood."

"I'd be afraid of that, father. I was near hitting Nora with the bread knife one time she came after me under the table, only I was afraid."

"You're a terrible child," said the priest with awe.

"I am, father," said Jackie noncommittally, sniffling back his tears.

"And what would you do with the body?"

"How, father?"

"Wouldn't someone see her and tell?"

"I was going to cut her up with a knife and take away the pieces and bury them. I could get an orange box for threepence and make a cart to take them away."

"My, my," said the priest. "You had it all well planned."

"Ah, I tried that," said Jackie with mounting confidence. "I borrowed a cart and practised it by meself one night after dark."

"And weren't you afraid?"

"Ah, no," said Jackie half-heartedly. "Only a bit."

"You have terrible courage," said the priest. "There's a lot of people I want to get rid of, but I'm not like you. I'd never have the courage. And hanging is an awful death."

"Is it?" asked Jackie, responding to the brightness of a new theme.

"Oh, an awful blooming death!"

"Did you ever see a fellow hanged?"

"Dozens of them, and they all died roaring."

"Jay!" said Jackie.

"They do be swinging out of them for hours and the poor fellows lepping and roaring, like bells in a belfry, and then they put lime on them to burn them up. Of course, they pretend they're dead but sure, they don't be dead at all."

"Jay!" said Jackie again.

"So if I were you I'd take my time and think about it. In my opinion 'tisn't worth it, not even to get rid of a grandmother. I asked dozens of fellows like you that killed their grandmothers about it, and they all said, no, 'twasn't worth it. . . ."

Nora was waiting in the yard. The sunlight struck down on her across the high wall and its brightness made his eyes dazzle. "Well?" she asked. "What did he give you?"

"Three Hail Marys."

"You mustn't have told him anything."

"I told him everything," said Jackie confidently.

"What did you tell him?"

"Things you don't know."

"Bah! He gave you three Hail Marys because you were a cry baby!"

Jackie didn't mind. He felt the world was very good. He began to whistle as well as the hindrance in his jaw permitted.

"What are you sucking?"

"Bull's eyes."

"Was it he gave them to you?"

"'Twas."

"Almighty God!" said Nora. "Some people have all the luck. I might as well be a sinner like you. There's no use in being good."

For Discussion

1. If the boy had confessed the first time he was in the confessional, how would his confession have differed from the one he finally made?
2. Much of the early detail in the story pits the boy and his youth against older society. Do you feel that churches are more directed toward meeting the needs of the older members of society? Why?
3. Nora assumes that as older sister she has responsibility for her brother and for his actions. Does she? If so, is such responsibility religious or merely social?
4. The priest finally offers some rather nonreligious counsel. Is it as effective as a traditional, religiously toned sermon might be? Is the priest assuming an attitude responsible to his position? What if his unusual approach had failed?

For Comparison

1. Compare this story with X. J. Kennedy's poem "First Confession." What similarities and what differences do you find in attitude?
2. Would Singer ("Don't Try To Sell Me Your Religion") agree with the counsel the priest gives, or would he see it as a kind of religious manipulation of the boy?

For Composition

1. My first personal encounter with a clergyman.
2. The generation gap in the church.
3. A casual approach to religion.

TILLIE OLSEN

O YES

1

They are the only white people there, sitting in the dimness of the Negro church that had once been a corner store, and all through the bubbling, swelling, seething of before the services, twelve-year-old Carol clenches tight her mother's hand, the other resting lightly on her friend, Parialee Phillips, for whose baptism she has come.

The white-gloved ushers hurry up and down the aisle, beckoning people to their seats. A jostle of people. To the chairs angled to the left for the youth choir, to the chairs angled to the right for the ladies' choir, even up to the platform, where behind the place for the dignitaries and the mixed choir, the new baptismal tank gleams—and as if pouring into it from the ceiling, the blue-painted River of Jordan, God standing in the waters, embracing a brown man in a leopard skin and pointing to the letters of gold:

REJOICE

GOD   IS   LOVE

I AM THE WAY   THE TRUTH   THE LIFE

At the clear window, the crucified Christ embroidered on the starched white curtain leaps in the wind of the sudden singing. And the choirs march in. Robes of wine, of blue, of red.

"We stands and sings too," says Parialee's mother, Alva, to Helen; though already Parialee has pulled Carol up. Singing, little Lucinda Phillips fluffs out her many petticoats; singing, little Bubbie bounces up and down on his heels.

> *Any day now I'll reach that land of freedom,*
> > *Yes, o yes*
> *Any day now, know that promised land*

The youth choir claps and taps to accent the swing of it. Beginning to tap, Carol stiffens. "Parry, look. Somebody from school."

"Once more once," says Parialee, in the new way she likes to talk now. "Eddie Garlin's up there. He's in my math."

"Couple cats from Franklin Jr. chirps in the choir. No harm or alarm."

Anxiously Carol scans the faces to see who else she might know, who else might know her, but looks quickly down to Lucinda's wide skirts, for it seems Eddie looks back at her, sullen or troubled, though it is hard to tell, faced as she is into the window of curtained sunblaze.

> *I know my robe will fit me well*
> *I tried it on at the gates of hell*

If it were a record she would play it over and over, Carol thought, to untwine the intertwined voices, to search how the many rhythms rock apart and yet are one glad rhythm.

> *When I get to heaven gonna sing and shout*
> *Nobody be able to turn me out*

"That's Mr. Chairback Evans going to invocate," Lucinda leans across Parry to explain. "He don't invoke good like Momma."

"Shhhh."

"Momma's the only lady in the church that invocates. She made the prayer last week. (Last month, Lucy.) I made the children's 'nouncement last time. (That was way back Thanksgiving.) And Bubbie's 'nounced too. Lots of times."

"Lucy-inda. SIT!"

Bible study announcements and mixed-choir practice announcements and Teen Age Hearts meeting announcements.

If Eddie said something to her about being there, worried Carol, if he talked to her right in front of somebody at school.

Messengers of Faith announcements and Mamboettes announcement and Committee for the Musical Tea.

Parry's arm so warm. Not realizing, starting up the old game from grade school, drumming a rhythm on the other's arm to see if the song could be guessed. "Parry, guess."

But Parry is pondering the platform.

The baptismal tank? "Parry, are you scared . . . the baptizing?"

"This cat? No." Shaking her head so slow and scornful, the barrette in her hair, sun fired, strikes a long rail of light. And still ponders the platform.

New Strangers Baptist Church invites you and Canaan Fair Singers announcements and Battle of Song and Cosmopolites meet. "O Lord, I couldn't find no ease," a solo. The ladies' choir:

> *O what you say seekers, o what you say seekers,*
> *Will you never turn back no more?*

The mixed choir sings:

> *Ezekiel saw that wheel of time*
> *Every spoke was of humankind . . .*

And the slim worn man in the pin-stripe suit starts his sermon On the Nature of God. How God is long-suffering. Oh, how long he has suffered. Calling the roll of the mighty nations that rose and fell and now are dust for grinding the face of man.

O voice of drowsiness and dream to which Carol does not need to listen. As long ago. Parry warm beside her too, as it used to be, there in the classroom at Mann Elementary, and the feel of drenched in sun and dimness and dream. Smell and sound of the chalk wearing itself away to nothing, rustle of books, drumming tattoo of fingers on her arm: *Guess.*

And as the preacher's voice spins happy and free, it is the used-to-be play-yard. Tag. Thump of the volley ball. Ectasy of the jump rope. Parry, do pepper. Carol, do pepper. Parry's bettern Carol, Carol's bettern Parry. . . .

Did someone scream?

It seemed someone screamed—but all were sitting as before, though the sun no longer blared through the windows. She tried to see up where Eddie was, but the ushers were standing at the head of the aisle now, the ladies in white dresses like nurses or waitresses wear, the men holding their white-gloved hands up so one could see their palms.

"And God is Powerful," the preacher was chanting. "Nothing for him to scoop out the oceans and pat up the mountains. Nothing for him to scoop up the miry clay and create man. Man, I said, create Man."

The lady in front of her moaned "*O yes*" and others were moaning "*O yes.*"

"And when the earth mourned the Lord said, Weep not, for all will be returned to you, every dust, every atom. And the tired dust settles back, goes back. Until that Judgment Day. That great day."

"*O yes.*"

The ushers were giving out fans. Carol reached for one and Parry said: "What *you* need one for?" but she took it anyway.

"You think Satchmo can blow; you think Muggsy can blow; you think Dizzy can blow?" He was straining to an imaginary trumpet now, his head far back and his voice coming out like a trumpet.

"Oh Parry, he's so good."

"Well. Jelly jelly."

"Nothing to Gabriel on that great getting-up morning. And the horn wakes up Adam, and Adam runs to wake up Eve, and Eve moans; Just one more minute, let me sleep, and Adam yells, Great Day, woman, don't you know it's the Great Day?"

"*Great Day, Great Day,*" the mixed choir behind the preacher rejoices:

> *When our cares are past*
> *when we're home at last . . .*

"And Eve runs to wake up Cain." Running round the platform, stooping and shaking imaginary sleepers, "and Cain runs to wake up Abel." Looping, scalloping his voice—"Grea-aaa-aat Daaaay." All the choirs thundering:

> *Great Day*
> *When the battle's fought*
> *And the victory's won*

Exultant spirals of sound. And Carol caught into it (Eddie forgotten, the game forgotten) chanting with Lucy and Bubbie: "*Great Day.*"

"Ohhhhhhhhh," his voice like a trumpet again, "the re-unioning. Ohhhhhhhhh, the rejoicing. After the ages immemorial of longing."

Someone *was* screaming. And an awful thrumming sound with it, like feet and hands thrashing around, like a giant jumping of a rope.

"*Great Day.*" And no one stirred or stared as the ushers brought a little woman out into the aisle, screaming and shaking, just a little shrunk-up woman, not much taller than Carol, the biggest thing about her her swollen hands and the cascades of tears wearing her face.

The shaking inside Carol too. Turning and trembling to ask: "What . . . that lady?" But Parry still ponders the platform; little Lucy loops the chain of her bracelet round and round; and Bubbie sits placidly, dreamily. Alva Phillips is up fanning a lady in front of her; two lady ushers are fanning other people Carol cannot see. And her mother, her mother looks in a sleep.

Yes. He raised up the dead from the grave. He made old death behave.

Yes. Yes. From all over, hushed.   *O Yes*
He was your mother's rock. Your father's mighty tower. And he gave us a little baby. A little baby to love.

                                                                      I am so glad
Yes, your friend, when you're friendless. Your father when you're fatherless. Way maker. Door opener.

                                                                              Yes
When it seems you can't go on any longer, he's there. You can, he says, you can.

                                                                              Yes
And that burden you been carrying—ohhhhh that burden—not for always will it be. No, not for always.

                                                                Stay with me, Lord
I will put my Word in you and it is power. I will put my Truth in you and it is power.

O Yes

Out of your suffering I will make you to stand as a stone. A tried stone. Hewn out of the mountains of ages eternal.

Yes

Ohhhhhhhhhhh. Out of the mire I will lift your feet. Your tired feet from so much wandering. From so much work and wear and hard times.

Yes

From so much journeying—and never the promised land. And I'll wash them in the well your tears made. And I'll shod them in the gospel of peace, and of feeling good. Ohhhhhhhhh.

O Yes

Behind Carol, a trembling wavering scream. Then the thrashing. Up above, the singing:

> *They taken my blessed Jesus and flogged him to the woods*
> *And they made him hew out his cross and they dragged him to Calvary*
> *Shout brother, Shout shout shout. He never cried a word.*

Powerful throbbing voices. Calling and answering to each other.

> *They taken my blessed Jesus and whipped him up the hill*
> *With a knotty whip and a raggedy thorn he never cried a word*
> *Shout, sister. Shout shout shout. He never cried a word.*

> *Go tell the people the Saviour has risen*
> *Has risen from the dead and will live forevermore*
> *And won't have to die no more.*

Halleloo.

> *Shout, brother, shout*
> *We won't have to die no more!*

A single exultant lunge of shriek. Then the thrashing. All around a clapping. Shouts with it. The piano whipping, whipping air to a froth. Singing now.

> *I once was lost who now am found*
> *Was blind who now can see*

On Carol's fan, a little Jesus walked on wondrously blue waters to where bearded disciples spread nets out of a fishing boat. If she studied the fan—became it—it might make a wall around her. If she could make what was happening (*what* was happening?) into a record small and round to listen to far and far as if into a seashell—the stamp and rills and spirals all tiny (but never any screaming).

> *wade wade in the water*

> *Jordan's water is chilly and wild*
> *I've got to get home to the other side*
> *God's going to trouble the waters*

Ladders of screamings. The music leaps and prowls. Drumming feet of ushers running. And still little Lucy fluffs her skirts, loops the chain on her bracelet; still Bubbie sits and rocks dreamily; and only eyes turn for an instant to the aisle—as if nothing were happening. "Mother, let's go home," Carol begs, but her mother holds her so tight. Alva Phillips, strong Alva, rocking too and chanting, *O Yes*. No, do not look.

> *Wade,*
> *Sea of trouble all mingled with fire*
> *Come on my brethren it's time to go higher*
> *Wade wade*

The voices in great humming waves, slow, slow (when did it become the humming?), everyone swaying with it too, moving like in slow waves and singing, and up where Eddie is, a new cry, wild and open, "O help me, Jesus," and when Carol opens her eyes she closes them again, quick, but still can see the new known face from school (not Eddie), the thrashing, writhing body, struggling against the ushers with the look of grave and loving support on their faces, and hear the torn, tearing cry: "Don't take me away, life everlasting, don't take me away."

And now the rhinestones in Parry's hair glitter wicked, the white hands of the ushers, fanning, foam in the air; the blue-painted waters of Jordan swell and thunder; Christ spirals on his cross in the window, and she is drowned under the sluice of the slow singing and the sway.

So high up and forgotten the waves and the world, so stirless the deep cool green and the wrecks of what had been. Here now Hostess Foods, where Alva Phillips works her nights—but different from that time Alva had taken them through before work, for it is all sunken under water, the creaking loading platform where they had left the night behind; the closet room where Alva's swaddles of sweaters, boots, and cap hung, the long hall lined with pickle barrels, the sharp freezer door swinging open.

Bubbles of breath that swell. A gulp of numbing air. She swims into the chill room where the huge wheels of cheese stand, and Alva swims too, deftly oiling each machine: slicers and wedgers and the convey, that at her touch start to roll and grind. The light of day blazes up and Alva is holding a cup, saying: Drink this, baby.

"DRINK IT." Her mother's voice and the numbing air demanding her to pay attention. Up through the waters and into the car.

"That's right, lambie, now lie back." Her mother's lap.

"Mother."

"Shhhhh. You almost fainted, lambie."

Alva's voice. "You gonna be all right, Carol . . . Lucy, I'm telling you for the last time, you and Buford get back into that church. Carol is *fine*."

"Lucyinda, if I had all your petticoats I could float." Crying. "Why didn't you let me wear my full skirt with the petticoats, Mother."

"Shhhhh, lamb." Smoothing her cheek. "Just breathe, take long deep breaths."

". . . How you doing now, you little ol' consolation prize?" It is Parry, but she does not come in the car or reach to Carol through the open window: "No need to cuss and fuss. You going to be sharp as a tack, Jack."

Answering automatically: "And cool as a fool."

Quick, they look at each other.

"Parry, we have to go home now, don't we, Mother. I almost fainted, didn't I, Mother? . . . Parry, I'm sorry I got sick and have to miss your baptism."

"Don't feel sorry. I'll feel better you not there to watch. It was our mommas wanted you to be there, not me."

"Parry!" Three voices.

"Maybe I'll come over to play kickball after. If you feeling better. Maybe. Or bring the pogo." Old shared joys in her voice: "Or any little thing."

In just a whisper: "Or any little thing. Parry. Good-bye, Parry."

And why does Alva have to talk now?

"You all right? You breathin' deep like your momma said? Was it too close 'n hot in there? Did something scare you, Carrie?"

Shaking her head to lie, "No."

"I blame myself for not paying attention. You not used to people letting go that way. Lucy and Bubbie, Parialee, they used to it. They been coming here since they lap babies.

"Alva, that's all right. Alva, Mrs. Phillips."

"You *was* scared. Carol, it's something to study about. You'll feel better if you understand."

Trying not to listen.

"You not used to hearing what people keeps inside, Carol. You know how music can make you feel things? Glad or sad or like you can't sit still? That was religion music, Carol."

"I have to breathe deep, Mother said."

"Not everybody feels religion the same way. Some it's in their mouth, but some it's like a hope in their blood, their bones. And they singing songs every word that's real to them, Carol, every word out of they own life. And the preaching finding lodgment in their hearts."

The screaming was tuning up in her ears again, high above Alva's patient voice and the waves lapping and fretting.

"Maybe somebody's had a hard week, Carol, and they locked up with it. Maybe a lot of hard weeks bearing down."

"Mother, my head hurts."

"And they're home, Carol, church is home. Maybe the only place they can feel how they feel and maybe let it come out. So they can go on. And it's all right."

"Please, Alva. Mother, tell Alva my head hurts."

"Get Happy, we call it, and most it's a good feeling, Carol, when you got all that locked up inside you."

"Tell her we have to go home. It's all right, Alva. Please, Mother. Say good-bye. Good-bye."

When I was carrying Parry and her father left me, and I fifteen years old, one thousand miles away from home, sin-sick and never really believing, as still I don't believe all, scorning, for what have it done to help, waiting there in the clinic and maybe sleeping, a voice called: Alva, Alva. So mournful and so sweet: Alva. Fear not, I have loved you from the foundation of the universe. And a little small child tugged on my dress. He was carrying a parade stick, on the end of it a star that outshined the sun. Follow me, he said. And the real sun went down and he hidden his stick. How dark it was, how dark. I could feel the darkness with my hands. And when I could see, I screamed. Dump trucks run, dumping bodies in hell, and a convey line run, never ceasing with souls, weary ones having to stamp and shove them along, and the air like fire. Oh I never want to hear such screaming. Then the little child jumped on a motorbike making a path no bigger than my little finger. But first he greased my feet with the hands of my momma when I was a knee baby. They shined like the sun was on them. Eyes he placed all around my head, and as I journeyed upward after him, it seemed I heard a mourning: "Mamma Mamma you must help carry the world." The rise and fall of nations I saw. And the voice called again Alva Alva, and I flew into a world of light, multitudes singing, Free, free, I am so glad.

2

Helen began to cry, telling her husband about it.

"You and Alva ought to have your heads examined, taking her there cold like that," Len said. "All right, wreck my best handkerchief. Anyway, now that she's had a bath, her Sunday dinner . . . ."

"And been fussed over," seventeen-year-old Jeannie put in.

"She seems good as new. Now *you* forget it, Helen."

"I can't. Something . . . deep happened. If only I or Alva had told her what it would be like. . . . But I didn't realize."

You don't realize a lot of things, Mother, Jeannie said, but not aloud.

"So Alva talked about it after instead of before. Maybe it meant more that way."

"Oh Len, she didn't listen."

"You don't know if she did or not. Or what there was in the experience for her. . . ."

Enough to pull that kid apart two ways even more, Jeannie said, but still not aloud.

"I was so glad she and Parry were going someplace together again. Now that'll be between them too. Len, they really need, miss each other. What happened in a few months? When I think of how close they were, the hours of makebelieve and dressup and playing ball and collecting. . . ."

"Grow up, Mother." Jeannie's voice was harsh. "Parialee's collecting something else now. Like her own crowd. Like jivetalk and rhythmand-blues. Like teachers who treat her like a dummy and white kids who treat her like dirt; boys who think she's really something and chicks who. . . ."

"Jeannie, I know. It hurts."

"Well, maybe it hurts Parry too. Maybe. At least she's got a crowd. Just don't let it hurt Carol though, 'cause there's nothing she can do about it. That's all through, her and Parialee Phillips, put away with their paper dolls."

"No, Jeannie, no."

"It's like Ginger and me. Remember Ginger, my best friend in Horace Mann. But you hardly noticed when it happened to us, did you . . . because she was white? Yes, Ginger, who's got two kids now, who quit school year before last. Parry's never going to finish either. What's she got to do with Carrie any more? They're going different places. Different places, different crowds. And they're sorting. . . ."

"Now wait, Jeannie. Parry's just as bright, just as capable."

"They're in junior high, Mother. Don't you know about junior high? How they sort? And it's all where you're going. Yes and Parry's colored and Carrie's white. And you have to watch everything, what you wear and how you wear it and who you eat lunch with and how much home-work you do and how you act to the teacher and what you laugh at. . . . And run with your crowd."

"It's that final?" asked Len. "Don't you think kids like Carol and Par-ry can show it doesn't *have* to be that way."

"They can't. They can't. They don't let you."

"No need to shout," he said mildly. "And who do you mean by 'they' and what do you mean by 'sorting'?"

How they sort. A foreboding of comprehension whirled within Helen. What was it Carol had told her of the Welcome Assembly the first day in junior high? The models showing How to Dress and How Not to Dress and half the girls in their loved new clothes watching their counterparts up on the stage—*their* straight skirt, their sweater, their earrings, lipstick, hairdo—"How Not to Dress," "a bad reputation for your school." It was nowhere in Carol's description, yet picturing it now, it seemed to Helen that a mute cry of violated dignity hung in the air. Later there had been a story of going to another Low 7 homeroom on an errand and seeing a teacher trying to wipe the forbidden lipstick off a girl who was fighting back and cursing. Helen could hear Carol's frightened, self-righteous tones: ". . . and I hope they expel her; she's the kind that gives Franklin Jr. a bad rep; she doesn't care about anything and always gets into fights." Yet there was nothing in these incidents to touch the heavy comprehension that waited. . . . Homework, the wonderings those times Jeannie and Carol needed help: "What if there's no one at home to give the help, and the teachers with their two hundred and forty kids a day can't or don't or the kids don't ask and they fall hopelessly behind, what then?"—but this too was unrelated. And what had it been that time about Parry? "Mother, Melanie and Sharon won't go if they know Parry's coming." Then of course you'll go with Parry, she's been your friend longer, she had answered, but where was it they were going and what had finally happened? Len, my head hurts, she felt like saying, in Carol's voice in the car, but Len's eyes were grave on Jeannie who was saying passionately:

"If you think it's so goddam important why do we have to live here where it's for real; why don't we move to Ivy like Betsy (yes, I know, money), where it's the deal to be buddies, in school anyway, three colored kids and their father's a doctor or judge or something big wheel and one always gets elected President or head song girl or something to prove o how we're democratic . . . What do you want of that poor kid anyway? Make up your mind. Stay friends with Parry—but be one of the kids. Sure. Be a brain—but not a square. Rise on up, college prep, but don't get separated. Yes, stay one of the kids, but. . . ."

"Jeannie. You're not talking about Carol at all, are you, Jeannie? Say it again. I wasn't listening. I was trying to think."

"She will not say it again," Len said firmly, "you look about ready to pull a Carol. One a day's our quota. And you, Jeannie, we'd better cool it. Too much to talk about for one session. . . . Here, come to the window and watch the Carol and Parry you're both so all worked up about."

In the wind and the shimmering sunset light, half the children of the block are playing down the street. Leaping, bouncing, hallooing, tugging the kites of spring. In the old synchronized understanding, Carol and Parry kick, catch, kick, catch. And now Parry jumps on her pogo stick (the last time), Carol shadowing her, and Bubbie, arching his body in a semicircle of joy, bounds after them, high, higher, higher.

And the months go by and supposedly it is forgotten, except for the now and then when, self-important, Carol will say: I really truly did nearly faint, didn't I, Mother, that time I went to church with Parry?

And now seldom Parry and Carol walk the hill together. Melanie's mother drives to pick up Carol and the several times Helen has suggested Parry, too, Carol is quick to explain: "She's already left" or "She isn't ready; she'll make us late."

And after school? Carol is off to club or skating or library or some-one's house, and Parry can stay for kickball only on the rare afternoons when she does not have to hurry home where Lucy, Bubbie, and the cous-ins wait to be cared for, now Alva works the four to twelve-thirty shift.

No more the bending together over the homework. All semester the teachers have been different, and rarely Parry brings her books home, for where is there space or time and what is the sense? And the phone never rings with: what you going to wear tomorrow, are you bringing your lunch, or come on over, let's design some clothes for the Katy Keane comic-book contest. And Parry never drops by with Alva for Saturday snack to or from grocery shopping.

And the months go by and the sorting goes on and seemingly it is over until that morning when Helen must stay home from work, so swollen and feverish is Carol with the mumps.

The afternoon before, Parry had come by, skimming up the stairs, spilling books and binders on the bed: Hey frail, lookahere and wail, your momma askin for homework, what she got against YOU? . . . look-ing quickly once then not looking again and talking fast. . . . Hey, you bloomed. You gonna be your own pumpkin, hallowe'en? Your momma know yet it's mu-umps? And lumps. Momma says: no distress, she'll be by tomorrow morning see do you need anything while your momma's to work. . .(Singing:*whole lotta shakin goin on.*) All your 'signments is inside; Miss Rockface says the teachers to write 'em cause I mightn't get it right all right.

But did not tell: Does your mother work for Carol's mother? Oh, you're neighbors! Very well, I'll send along a monitor to open Carol's locker but you're only to take these things I'm writing down, noth-ing else. Now say after me: Miss Campbell is   trusting me to be   a good responsible girl. And go   right to Carol's house. After school. Not stop anywhere   on the way. Not lose anything. And only take. What's written on the list.

You really gonna mess with that book stuff? Sign on *mine* says do-not-open-until-eX-mas. . . . That Mrs. Fernandez doll she didn't send nothin, she was the only, says feel better and read a book to report if you feel like and I'm the most for takin care for you; she's my most,

wish I could get her but she only teaches 'celerated. . . . Flicking the old
read books on the shelf but not opening to mock-declaim as once she
used to . . . Vicky, Eddie's g.f. in Rockface office, she's on suspended
for sure, yellin to Rockface: you bitchkitty don't you give me no more
bad shit. That Vicky she can sure slingating-ring it. Staring out the
window as if the tree not there in which they had hid out and rocked
so often. . . . For sure. (*Keep mo-o-vin.*) Got me a new pink top and
lilac skirt. Look sharp with this purple? Cinching in the wide belt as
if delighted with what newly swelled above and swelled below. Wear
it Saturday night to Sweet's, Sounds of Joy, Leroy and Ginny and me
goin if Momma'll stay home. IF. (*Shake my baby shake.*) How come
old folks still likes to party? Huh? Asking of Rembrandt's weary old
face looking from the wall. How come (softly) you long-gone you.
Touching her face to his quickly, lightly. NEXT mumps is your buddy-
bud Melanie's turn to tote your stuff. I'm getting the hoovus goovus.
Hey you so unneat, don't care what you bed with. Removing the books
and binders, ranging them on the dresser one by one, marking lipstick
faces—bemused or mocking or amazed—on each paper jacket. Better.
Fluffing out smoothing the quilt with exaggerated energy. Any little
thing I can get, cause I gotta blow. Tossing up and catching their year-
ago, arm-in-arm graduation picture, replacing it deftly, upside down,
into its mirror crevice. Joe. Bring you joy juice or fizz water or kicka-
poo? Adding a frown line to one bookface. Twanging the paper fish-
kite, the Japanese windbell overhead, setting the mobile they had
once made of painted eggshells and decorated straws to twirling and
rocking. And is gone.

She talked to the lipstick faces after, in her fever, tried to stand on her
head to match the picture, twirled and twanged with the violent overhead.
Sleeping at last after the disordered night. Having surrounded herself
with the furnishings of that world of childhood she no sooner learned to
live in comfortably, then had to leave.
The dollhouse stands there to arrange and rearrange; the shell and
picture card collections to re-sort and remember; the population of dolls
given away to little sister, borrowed back, propped all around to dress
and undress and caress.
She has thrown off her nightgown because of the fever, and her just
budding breast is exposed where she reaches to hold the floppy plush dog
that had been her childhood pillow.
Not for anything would her mother have disturbed her. Except that in
the unaccustomedness of a morning at home, in the bruised restlessness

after the sleepless night, Helen clicks on the radio—and the storm of singing whirls into the room:

> *... trouble all mingled with fire*
> *Come on my brethren we've got to go higher*
> *Wade, wade. . . .*

And Carol runs down the stairs, shrieking and shrieking. "Turn it off, Mother, turn it off." Hurling herself at the dial and wrenching it so it comes off in her hand.

"Ohhhhh," choked and convulsive, while Helen tries to hold her, to quiet.

"Mother, why did they sing and scream like that?"

"At Parry's church?"

"Yes." Rocking and strangling the cries. "I hear it all the time." Clinging and beseeching. ". . . What was it, Mother? Why?"

Emotion, Helen thought of explaining, *a characteristic of the religion of all oppressed peoples, yes your very own great-grandparents*—thought of saying. And discarded.

Aren't you now, haven't you had feelings in yourself so strong they had to come out some way? ("what howls restrained by decorum")—thought of saying. And discarded.

Repeat Alva: *hope . . . every word out of their own life. A place to let go. And church is home.* And discarded.

The special history of the Negro people—history?—just you try living what must be lived every day—thought of saying. And discarded.

And said nothing.

And said nothing.

And soothed and held.

"Mother, a lot of the teachers and kids don't like Parry when they don't even know what she's like. Just because. . ." Rocking again, convulsive and shamed. "And I'm not really her friend any more."

No news. Betrayal and shame. Who betrayed? Whose shame? Brought herself to say aloud: "But may be friends again. As Alva and I are."

The sobbing a whisper. "That girl Vicky who got that way when I fainted, she's in school. She's the one keeps wearing the lipstick and they wipe it off and she's always in trouble and now maybe she's expelled. Mother."

"Yes, lambie."

"She acts so awful outside but I remember how she was in church and whenever I see her now I have to wonder. And hear . . . like I'm her, Mother, like I'm her." Clinging and trembling. "Oh why do I have to feel it happens to me too?

"Mother, I want to forget about it all, and not care—like Melanie. Why can't I forget? *Oh why is it like it is and why do I have to care?*"

Caressing, quieting.

Thinking: *caring asks doing. It is a long baptism into the seas of humankind, my daughter. Better immersion than to live untouched.... Yet how will you sustain?*

Why is it like it is?

Sheltering her daughter close, mourning the illusion of the embrace.

And why do I have to care?

While in her, her own need leapt and plunged for the place of strength that was not—where one could scream or sorrow while all knew and accepted, and gloved and loving hands waited to support and understand.

For Margaret Heaton, who always taught.   *1956–7*

For Discussion

1. What dimension does the fact that Carol is white contribute to the story?
2. The songs sung reflect a strong belief in a heavenly life. Is such a belief an escape from the responsibilities of the present? How do these songs take on special meanings when sung by the black worshippers in this story?
3. Does Parry's attitude reflect sincerity and knowledge of the significance of her baptism, or is she doing it because it is expected of her?
4. What does Jeannie mean when she says, "You don't realize a lot of things, Mother"?
5. The story suggests that "church is home," "a place to let go." Does everyone need some such place, whether or not it is a church? Is letting go a responsible action?
6. Exactly what is meant by *"caring asks doing"*?

For Comparison

1. Compare Parry in this story with Jackie in "First Confession." How much is each a product of his or her environment? Discuss the sincerity of each character.
2. In "The Answer to a Perplexing Question" King says "the mind's faith is directed toward a theory, but the heart's faith is centered in a Person." Discuss this statement in terms of Olsen's story.

For Composition

1. Parry is (is not) ready for baptism.
2. What really is bothering Carol?
3. Religion and emotion.

E. M. FORSTER

THE OTHER SIDE OF THE HEDGE

My pedometer told me that I was twenty-five; and, though it is a shocking thing to stop walking, I was so tired that I sat down on a milestone to rest. People outstripped me, jeering as they did so, but I was too apathetic to feel resentful, and even when Miss Eliza Dimbleby, the great educationist, swept past, exhorting me to persevere, I only smiled and raised my hat.

At first I thought I was going to be like my brother, whom I had had to leave by the roadside a year or two round the corner. He had wasted his breath on singing, and his strength on helping others. But I had travelled more wisely, and now it was only the monotony of the highway that oppressed me—dust under foot and brown crackling hedges on either side, ever since I could remember.

And I had already dropped several things—indeed, the road behind was strewn with the things we all had dropped; and the white dust was settling down on them, so that already they looked no better than stones. My muscles were so weary that I could not even bear the weight of those things I still carried. I slid off the milestone into the road, and lay there prostrate, with my face to the great parched hedge, praying that I might give up.

A little puff of air revived me. It seemed to come from the hedge; and, when I opened my eyes, there was a glint of light through the tangle of boughs and dead leaves. The hedge could not be as thick as usual. In my weak, morbid state, I longed to force my way in, and see what was on the other side. No one was in sight, or I should not have dared to try. For we of the road do not admit in conversation that there is another side at all.

I yielded to the temptation, saying to myself that I would come back in a minute. The thorns scratched my face, and I had to use my arms as a shield, depending on my feet alone to push me forward. Halfway through I would have gone back, for in the passage all the things I was carrying

From *The Collected Tales of E. M. Forster*. Published 1947 by Alfred A. Knopf, Inc. Reprinted by permission of the publisher.

were scraped off me, and my clothes were torn. But I was so wedged that return was impossible, and I had to wriggle blindly forward, expecting every moment that my strength would fail me, and that I should perish in the undergrowth.

Suddenly cold water closed round my head, and I seemed sinking down for ever. I had fallen out of the hedge into a deep pool. I rose to the surface at last, crying for help, and I heard someone on the opposite bank laugh and say: "Another!" And then I was twitched out and laid panting on the dry ground.

Even when the water was out of my eyes, I was still dazed, for I had never been in so large a space, nor seen such grass and sunshine. The blue sky was no longer a strip, and beneath it the earth had risen gradually into hills—clean, bare buttresses, with beech trees in their folds, and meadows and clear pools at their feet. But the hills were not high, and there was in the landscape a sense of human occupation—so that one might have called it a park, or garden, if the words did not imply a certain triviality and constraint.

As soon as I got my breath, I turned to my rescuer and said:

"Where does this place lead to?"

"Nowhere, thank the Lord!" said he, and laughed. He was a man of fifty or sixty—just the kind of age we mistrust on the road—but there was no anxiety in his manner, and his voice was that of a boy of eighteen.

"But it must lead somewhere!" I cried, too much surprised at his answer to thank him for saving my life.

"He wants to know where it leads!" he shouted to some men on the hillside, and they laughed back, and waved their caps.

I noticed then that the pool into which I had fallen was really a moat which bent round to the left and to the right, and that the hedge followed it continually. The hedge was green on this side—its roots showed through the clear water, and fish swam about in them—and it was wreathed over with dog-roses and Traveller's Joy. But it was a barrier, and in a moment I lost all pleasure in the grass, the sky, the trees, the happy men and women, and realized that the place was but a prison, for all its beauty and extent.

We moved away from the boundary, and then followed a path almost parallel to it, across the meadows. I found it difficult walking, for I was always trying to out-distance my companion, and there was no advantage in doing this if the place led nowhere. I had never kept step with anyone since I left my brother.

I amused him by stopping suddenly and saying disconsolately, "This is perfectly terrible. One cannot advance: one cannot progress. Now we of the road——"

"Yes, I know."

"I was going to say, we advance continually."

"I know."

"We are always learning, expanding, developing. Why, even in my short life I have seen a great deal of advance—the Transvaal War, the Fiscal Question, Christian Science, Radium. Here for example—"

I took out my pedometer, but it still marked twenty-five, not a degree more.

"Oh, its stopped! I meant to show you. It should have registered all the time I was walking with you. But it makes me only twenty-five."

"Many things don't work in here," he said. "One day a man brought in a Lee-Metford, and that wouldn't work."

"The laws of science are universal in their application. It must be the water in the moat that has injured the machinery. In normal conditions everything works. Science and the spirit of emulation—those are the forces that have made us what we are."

I had to break off and acknowledge the pleasant greetings of people whom we passed. Some of them were singing, some talking, some engaged in gardening, hay-making, or other rudimentary industries. They all seemed happy; and I might have been happy too, if I could have forgotten that the place led nowhere.

I was startled by a young man who came sprinting across our path, took a little fence in the fine style, and went tearing over a ploughed field till he plunged into a lake, across which he began to swim. Here was true energy, and I exclaimed: "A cross-country race! Where are the others?"

"There are no others," my companion replied; and, later on, when we passed some long grass from which came the voice of a girl singing exquisitely to herself, he said again: "There are no others." I was bewildered at the waste in production, and murmured to myself, "What does it all mean?"

He said: "It means nothing but itself"—and he repeated the words slowly, as if I were a child.

"I understand," I said quietly, "but I do not agree. Every achievement is worthless unless it is a link in the chain of development. And I must not trespass on your kindness any longer. I must get back somehow to the road, and have my pedometer mended."

"First, you must see the gates," he replied, "for we have gates, though we never use them."

I yielded politely, and before long we reached the moat again, at a point where it was spanned by a bridge. Over the bridge was a big gate, as white as ivory, which was fitted into a gap in the boundary hedge. The gate opened outwards, and I exclaimed in amazement, for from it ran a road—just such a road as I had left—dusty under foot, with brown crackling hedges on either side as far as the eye could reach.

"That's my road!" I cried.

He shut the gate and said: "But not your part of the road. It is through this gate that humanity went out countless ages ago, when it was first seized with the desire to walk."

I denied this, observing that the part of the road I myself had left was not more than two miles off. But with the obstinacy of his years he repeated: "It is the same road. This is the beginning, and though it seems to run straight away from us, it doubles so often, that it is never far from our boundary and sometimes touches it." He stooped down by the moat, and traced on its moist margin an absurd figure like a maze. As we walked back through the meadows, I tried to convince him of his mistake.

"The road sometimes doubles, to be sure, but that is part of our discipline. Who can doubt that its general tendency is onward? To what goal we know not—it may be to some mountain where we shall touch the sky, it may be over precipices into the sea. But that it goes forward—who can doubt that? It is the thought of that that makes us strive to excel, each in his own way, and gives us an impetus which is lacking with you. Now that man who passed us—it's true that he ran well, and jumped well, and swam well; but we have men who can run better, and men who can jump better, and who can swim better. Specialization has produced results which would surprise you. Similarly, that girl——"

Here I interrupted myself to exclaim: "Good gracious me! I could have sworn it was Miss Eliza Dimbleby over there, with her feet in the fountain!"

He believed that it was.

"Impossible! I left her on the road, and she is due to lecture this evening at Tunbridge Wells. Why, her train leaves Cannon Street in—of course my watch has stopped like everything else. She is the last person to be here."

"People always are astonished at meeting each other. All kinds come through the hedge, and come at all times—when they are drawing ahead in the race, when they are lagging behind, when they are left for dead. I often stand near the boundary listening to the sounds of the road—you know what they are—and wonder if anyone will turn aside. It is my great happiness to help someone out of the moat, as I helped you. For our country fills up slowly, though it was meant for all mankind."

"Mankind have other aims," I said gently, for I thought him well-meaning; "and I must join them." I bade him good evening, for the sun was declining, and I wished to be on the road by nightfall. To my alarm, he caught hold of me, crying: "You are not to go yet!" I tried to shake him off, for we had no interests in common, and his civility was becoming irksome to me. But for all my struggles the tiresome old man would not let go; and, as wrestling is not my specialty, I was obliged to follow him.

It was true that I could have never found alone the place where I came in, and I hoped that, when I had seen the other sights about which he was worrying, he would take me back to it. But I was determined not to sleep in the country, for I mistrusted it, and the people too, for all their friendliness. Hungry though I was, I would not join them in their evening meals of milk and fruit, and, when they gave me flowers, I flung them away as soon as I could do so unobserved. Already they were lying down for the night like cattle—some out on the bare hillside, others in groups under the beeches. In the light of an orange sunset I hurried on with my unwelcome guide, dead tired, faint for want of food, but murmuring indomitably: "Give me life, with its struggles and victories, with its failures and hatreds, with its deep moral meaning and its unknown goal!"

At last we came to a place where the encircling moat was spanned by another bridge, and where another gate interrupted the line of the boundary hedge. It was different from the first gate; for it was half transparent like horn, and opened inwards. But through it, in the waning light, I saw again just such a road as I had left—monotonous, dusty, with brown crackling hedges on either side, as far as the eye could reach.

I was strangely disquieted at the sight, which seemed to deprive me of all self-control. A man was passing us, returning for the night to the hills, with a scythe over his shoulder and a can of some liquid in his hand. I forgot the destiny of our race. I forgot the road that lay before my eyes, and I sprang at him, wrenched the can out of his hand, and began to drink.

It was nothing stronger than beer, but in my exhausted state it overcame me in a moment. As in a dream, I saw the old man shut the gate, and heard him say: "This is where your road ends, and through this gate humanity—all that is left of it—will come in to us."

Though my senses were sinking into oblivion, they seemed to expand ere they reached it. They perceived the magic song of nightingales, and the odour of invisible hay, and stars piercing the fading sky. The man whose beer I had stolen lowered me down gently to sleep off its effects, and, as he did so, I saw that he was my brother.

For Discussion

1. Forster uses symbolism throughout the story to reinforce his theme. What do you think is symbolized by the road, the hedge, the other side?

2. What kind of life is on the other side? Does it seem ideal or somewhat dull? What is the author's judgment of it?

3. The narrator's brother "had wasted his breath on singing, and his

strength on helping others." Was his life really wasted? How is it
possible that these activities could be done for completely wrong reasons?
4. Where does happiness lie? Is it to be attained in this world? Is it
something we always strive for but never attain? What about progress?
5. Does man have a right to happiness in this life? How can happiness be
found in "life, with its struggles and victories, with its failures and
hatreds, with its deep moral meaning and its unknown goal"?
6. What is your concept of happiness if you do not believe in an after
life?

For Comparison

1. This story has some of the same characteristics of a parable as had
Nietzsche's "The Gay Science." What are the similarities and differences in the philosophy of the two pieces?
2. Does the narrator in Herbert's "The Collar" go through much the
same process of self-discovery that the narrator in Forster's story experiences? How do their final discoveries differ? Which seems to you
the most responsible?

For Composition

1. My definition of happiness.
2. An ideal life would (would not) be boring.
3. Religious symbolism in this story.

GERARD MANLEY HOPKINS

GOD'S GRANDEUR

The world is charged with the grandeur of God.
    It will flame out, like shining from shook foil;
    It gathers to a greatness, like the ooze of oil
Crushed. Why do men then now not reck his rod?
Generations have trod, have trod, have trod;
    And all is seared with trade; bleared, smeared with toil;
    And wears man's smudge and shares man's smell: the soil
Is bare now, nor can foot feel, being shod.

And for all this, nature is never spent;
There lives the dearest freshness deep down things;
And though the last lights off the black West went
Oh, morning at the brown brink eastward, springs—
Because the Holy Ghost over the bent
World broods with warm breast and with ah! bright wings.

For Discussion

1. What do you think Hopkins means by "the grandeur of God"? How is God's grandeur evidenced in the world?
2. Why does Hopkins feel that the grandeur of God will "flame out"?
3. Who is responsible for the loss of God's grandeur? Do you agree with the poet that man has crowded it out by his own greed?
4. Does man have a responsibility to restore a part of this grandeur to his world? How might he go about doing this?

For Comparison

1. With what specific ideas in Nietzsche's "The Gay Science" would Hopkins be in agreement?
2. Hopkins speaks of the generations that "have trod, have trod." Is he describing the endless walking toward a goal that Forster presents in "The Other Side of the Hedge"? Do both writers see life as a kind of maze in which man is trapped?

For Composition

1. Evidence of God's grandeur.
2. Greed versus grandeur.
3. Responsibility to restore goodness.

GEORGE HERBERT

THE COLLAR

I struck the board, and cried, "No more!
I will abroad!"
What? shall I ever sigh and pine?
My lines and life are free, free as the road,
Loose as the wind, as large as store.
Shall I be still in suit?

Have I no harvest but a thorn
To let me blood, and not restore
What I have lost with cordial fruit?
    Sure there was wine
Before my sighs did dry it.
    There was corn
Before my tears did drown it.
Is the year only lost to me?
Have I no bays to crown it?
No flowers, no garlands gay?
    All blasted?
    All wasted?
Not so, my heart!
    But there is fruit,
    And thou hast hands.
Recover all thy sigh-blown age
On double pleasures.
    Leave thy cold dispute
Of what is fit and not.
    Forsake thy cage,
    Thy rope of sands,
Which petty thoughts have made and made to thee
Good cable, to enforce and draw,
    And be thy law,
While thou didst wink and wouldst not see.
    Away! Take heed!
    I will abroad.
Call in thy death's head there! Tie up thy fears!
    He that forbears
    To suit and serve his need
    Deserves his load."
But as I raved, and grew more fierce and wild
    At every word,
Methoughts I heard one calling, "Child!"
And I replied, "My Lord!"

For Discussion

1. What is the significance of the title? How does the poet see God's relationship to man? Is man as free as Herbert suggests he is in the fourth line?
2. Is the poet responsible for the negative features of his life?
3. What could Herbert mean by man's "cold dispute," "cage," and "rope of sands"?

4. The poem suggests that man should be a law unto himself. How does such an idea increase the possibilities of responsibility to self, peers, and God?

For Comparison

1. Might the narrator of "Debate with the Rabbi" agree with much of the philosophy found in this poem? How does he see religion as a collar? Would he be in agreement with the final two lines of the poem?
2. How is this poem similar to "Jehovah buried,Satan dead"? What aspects of traditional religious philosophy are both writers questioning?

For Composition

1. Religion is (is not) a collar.
2. Freedom is a collar.
3. Responsible freedom.

X. J. KENNEDY

FIRST CONFESSION

Blood thudded in my ears. I scuffed,
    Steps stubborn, to the telltale booth
Beyond whose curtained portal coughed
    The robed repositor of truth.

The slat shot back. The universe
    Bowed down his cratered dome to hear
Enumerated my each curse,
    The sip snitched from my old man's beer,

My sloth pride envy lechery,
    The dime held back from Peter's Pence
With which I'd bribed my girl to pee
    That I might spy her instruments.

Hovering scale-pans when I'd done
    Settled their balance slow as silt

While in the restless dark I burned
  Bright as a brimstone in my guilt

Until as one feeds birds he doled
  Seven Our Fathers and a Hail
Which I to double-scrub my soul
  Intoned twice at the altar rail

Where Sunday in seraphic light
  I knelt, as full of grace as most,
And stuck my tongue out at the priest:
  A fresh roost for the Holy Ghost.

For Discussion

1. Is the narrator really sincere? Whether he is confessing to a priest or to God, how necessary is his sincerity?
2. How much do you feel the structure of religion operates to make man feel guilty and afraid? How can such a structure lead to insincerity?
3. How old do you think the boy is? How unusual are his "sins" for a person of his age?
4. Do you feel that the boy's actions violated a religious principle or merely a social code?
5. If the boy is sincere, must he now tell his father that he stole some of his beer? How necessary is it that a person confess to a fellow man whom he has wronged as well as to God or a priest?

For Comparison

1. Compare the sincerity of the narrator in this poem with that of Parry in "O Yes." What does religion mean to each person?
2. Does the young boy represent one of the fearers who worship "Much and Quick" as described in "Jehovah buried,Satan dead"? How much of the boy's attitude is motivated by fear?

For Composition

1. My definition of sin.
2. Sincerity in religious acts.
3. Confession is good for the soul.

QUANDRA PRETTYMAN

WHEN MAHALIA SINGS

We used to gather at the high window
of the holiness church and, on tip-toe,
look in and laugh at the dresses, too small
on the ladies, and how wretched they all
looked—an old garage for a church, for pews,
old wooden chairs. It seemed a lame excuse
for a church. Not solemn or grand,
with no real robed choir, but a loose jazz band,
or so it sounded to our mocking ears.
So we responded to their hymns with jeers.

Sometimes those holiness people would dance,
and this we knew sprang from deep ignorance
of how to rightly worship God, who after
all was pleased not by such foolish laughter
but by the stiffly still hands in our church
where we saw no one jump or shout or lurch
or weep. We laughed to hear those holiness
rhythms making a church a song fest:
we heard this music as the road to sin,
down which they traveled toward that end.

I, since then, have heard the gospel singing
of one who says I worship with clapping
hands and my whole body, God, whom we must
thank for all this richness raised from dust.
Seeing her high-thrown head reminded
me of those holiness high-spirited,
who like angels, like saints, worshiped as whole
men with rhythm, with dance, with singing soul.
Since then, I've learned of my familiar God—
He finds no worship alien or odd.

For Discussion

1. How typical is the youth-motivated response to religion as it is described in the first stanza? To what extent is this response a desire for
   peer acceptance? What fears might such a response cover?

2. Is the emotional service described in the poem necessarily any more or less sincere than the service at the narrator's own church "where we saw no one jump or shout or lurch / or weep"?
3. If you have heard Mahalia sing, what was your reaction? What reasons might you suggest for the narrator's change in attitude?

For Comparison

1. There are obvious comparisons between this poem and "O Yes." Focus your attention on the narrator of the poem and on Carol in the story. Will Carol ever come to the realization expressed in the last line of this poem? Why or why not?
2. Martin Luther King, Jr. discussed the social aspects of religion in "The Answer to a Perplexing Question." From his essay can you determine what his attitude would have been toward the church service described in this poem? What evidence in King's essay did you use?

For Composition

1. No worship alien or odd.
2. My favorite gospel singer.
3. Why we criticize emotion in religion.

---

e. e. cummings

Jehovah buried,Satan dead

Jehovah buried,Satan dead,
do fearers worship Much and Quick;
badness not being felt as bad,
itself thinks goodness what is meek;
obey says toc,submit says tic,
Eternity's a Five Year Plan:
if Joy with Pain shall hang in hock
who dares to call himself a man?

go dreamless knaves on Shadows fed,
your Harry's Tom,your Tom is Dick;

while Gadgets murder squawk and add,
the cult of Same is all the chic;
by instruments,both span and spic,
are justly measured Spic and Span:
to kiss the mike if Jew turn kike
who dares to call himself a man?

loudly for Truth have liars pled,
their heels for Freedom slaves will click;
where Boobs are holy,poets mad,
illustrious punks of Progress shriek;
when Souls are outlawed,Hearts are sick,
Hearts being sick,Minds nothing can:
if Hate's a game and Love's a φυκ
who dares to call himself a man?

King Christ,this world is all aleak;
and lifepreservers there are none:
and waves which only He may walk
who dares to call Himself a man.

For Discussion

1. What is cummings' definition of man? What personal qualities would he expect a real man to have?
2. What aspects of modern life is the poet really criticizing?
3. In what way may goodness be falsely equated with meekness? How necessary is it that modern religion be meek?
4. Cummings describes modern worshipers as being "fearers." How valid is a religious act that is based upon fear?
5. To what extent is an individual man responsible to work out his own religious ideas? Identify some of the conflicting problems that he must resolve.

For Comparison

1. Both this poem and Frank O'Connor's story "First Confession" have much to say about goodness and meekness. What distinctions are made? How does each work show the relation between aspects of the religious experience and fear?
2. How similar is the concept of God expressed in this poem with the concept expressed by Crane in "Blustering God"?

For Composition

1. Liars about truth.
2. Religion is (is not) necessarily meek.
3. My emerging religious philosophy.

STEPHEN CRANE

BLUSTERING GOD

I

Blustering god,
Stamping across the sky
With loud swagger,
I fear you not.
No, though from your highest heaven
You plunge your spear at my heart,
I fear you not.
No, not if the blow
Is as the lightning blasting a tree,
I fear you not, puffing braggart.

II

If thou can see into my heart
That I fear thee not,
Thou wilt see why I fear thee not,
And why it is right.
So threaten not, thou, with thy bloody spears,
Else thy sublime ears shall hear curses.

III

Withal, there is one whom I fear;
I fear to see grief upon that face.
Perchance, friend, he is not your god;
If so, spit upon him.
By it you will do no profanity.
But I—
Ah, sooner would I die
Than see tears in those eyes of my soul.

For Discussion

1. Do you feel that Crane is near blasphemy in the first two stanzas? Why?

2. If you agree with Crane's image of a "blustering god" or a "puffing braggart," offer some reasons for your opinion. If you disagree with Crane, explain why.
3. What sort of god does Crane not fear? What does he mean by "I fear to see grief upon that face"?
4. How does Crane's poem indicate that every man should have his own concept of the god he worships?

For Comparison

1. Both Crane and Nietzsche ("The Gay Science") reject the image of one type of God and accept the image of another type? Do they reject and accept essentially the same types?
2. How is the image of God rejected by Crane similar to the early concept of God held by the young boy in X. J. Kennedy's poem "First Confession"?

For Composition

1. My definition of blasphemy.
2. Crane's God.
3. Individual religious responsibility.

HOWARD NEMEROV

DEBATE WITH THE RABBI

You've lost your religion, the Rabbi said.
   It wasn't much to keep, said I.
You should affirm the spirit, said he,
And the communal solidarity.
   I don't feel so solid, I said.

We are the people of the Book, the Rabbi said.
   Not of the phone book, said I.
Ours is a great tradition, said he,
And a wonderful history.
   But history's over, I said.

> We Jews are creative people, the Rabbi said.
> Make something, then, said I.
> In science and in art, said he,
> Violinists and physicists have we.
> Fiddle and physic indeed, I said.
>
> Stubborn and stiff-necked man! the Rabbi cried.
> The pain you give me, said I.
> Instead of bowing down, said he.
> You go on in your obstinacy.
> We Jews are that way, I replied.

For Discussion

1. What concepts of religion are expressed in the first stanza? Do the narrator and the rabbi have the same idea of what religion is?
2. To what extent is all religion motivated by a sense of "communal solidarity"?
3. The rabbi builds his argument upon what has been done in the past, and the narrator seems more concerned with the present. Is one position more responsible than the other, or does the answer lie in the middle somewhere?

For Comparison

1. Compare the rabbi in this poem with the priest in O'Connor's "First Confession." Does one seem more willing than the other to deal with problems as they exist, or are they both motivated by their own sense of communal solidarity?
2. The dialogue in this poem has some similarities with conversation in Forster's "The Other Side of the Hedge." What, for instance, would the attitude of this narrator be to the statement of the Forster's narrator that "Every achievement is worthless unless it is a link in the chain of development"? What other significant comparisons can you make?

For Composition

1. Communal solidarity as religious experience.
2. Past versus present in religion.
3. My own debate with my minister (rabbi, priest).

MALCOLM BOYD

HERE I AM IN CHURCH AGAIN, JESUS

I love it here, but, as you know, for some of the wrong reasons. I sometimes lose myself completely in the church service and forget the people outside whom you love. I sometimes withdraw far, far inside myself when I am inside church, but people looking at me can see only my pious expression and imagine I am loving you instead of myself.

Help us, Lord, who claim to be your special people. Don't let us feel privileged and selfish because you have called us to you. Teach us our responsibilities to you, our brother, and to all the people out there. Save us from the sin of loving religion instead of you.

___

For Discussion

1. What are some of the wrong reasons for which a person may embrace religion?
2. The author makes a distinction between people inside the church and people outside. Is there a danger that organized religion may become something like a social club that rejects everyone who does "not belong"?
3. What danger is inherent in a belief that you are one of God's "special people"?
4. How may a person love religion instead of God? Is it possible for such a person to recognize the difference?

For Comparison

1. Explain how religious actions and attitudes can be taken for the wrong reasons in terms of this selection and X. J. Kennedy's "First Confession."
2. Would Boyd find the church service described by Prettyman ("When Mahalia Sings") a valid religious experience? Against what criteria would he measure it?

For Composition

1. The church and the world out there.
2. Religious for the wrong reasons.
3. Selfishness in modern religion.

___

Part Six

INDIVIDUAL–STATE

The individual's attitudes toward the government under which he or she lives are usually acquired from family and friends and are brought more sharply into focus by formal education. Responsible individuals must formalize for themselves a definite opinion about their relationship to government, whether local, state or national.

As with the educational system, the role of responsibility in state is a two-way street. The state has responsibilities to its citizens, and they have responsibilities to it. A mature individual must determine what he or she feels to be the proper role of government in contemporary society and then determine his or her own responsibilities to help the state meet its obligations without trespassing upon the rights of its citizens. Those persons who loudly criticize governmental forces must show another and better program. Those who support the same forces must shoulder the responsibility of defending them.

Questions to be answered as you read the following selections include: What is the proper function of government? Is government necessary? Who should help shape government policy? Is war justified? Is democracy practical today? Is a good citizen necessarily a quiet one? Is protest valid? What happens when private conscience conflicts with demands of state?

HENRY STEELE COMMAGER

THE DECLARATION IS FOR TODAY!

We celebrate on Wednesday the 175th birthday of the Declaration of Independence. But we must not assume that we are celebrating merely a historical event. It *was* a great historical event. "A greater," wrote John Adams, "never was nor will be decided among men." But it was not the kind of event that is over and done with. It has tremendous meaning for today.

It is not sufficiently appreciated that the Declaration did far more than declare independence. It did more even than display a "decent respect to the opinions of mankind" by setting forth the causes which impelled separation—though that itself was something new in history. What it did was to state the basic philosophy not of independence but of democracy and republicanism.

It is fashionable, now, in certain quarters to argue that the United States is not a democracy, that the Fathers established a Republic, not a democracy, and that the Fathers were in fact hostile to democracy and took care to guard against it in State and Federal Constitutions. To support this curious thesis, all the warnings that men uttered, all the institutions and mechanisms that men contrived to guard against unlimited government are conjured up and enlisted in the anti-democratic ranks. And from all this it is sought to draw the conclusion that democracy is somehow vaguely un-American.

Jefferson, who penned the Declaration; the committee of patriots—John Adams, Benjamin Franklin, Roger Sherman and R. R. Livingston—who passed on it, the Congress that approved it, Americans generally who rejoiced in it, did not so reason. They feared unlimited government; they feared the tyranny of factions or of majorities; but they never doubted the basic principle of democracy, that men make government.

This is the principle asserted in the Declaration, and it stamps the Declaration as the greatest of all statements of democracy in either the eighteenth or the twentieth century meaning of the word. Governments, says Jefferson—and only the felicity of the phrasing was new with him—governments derive their powers from the consent of the governed. The crucial word is *derive*. Government comes from below, not above; government comes from men, not from kings or lords or military masters; government looks to the source of all power in the consent of men. This is the very essence of democracy.

More, if government fails of its ends, if it fails to protect men in their rights to life, liberty and happiness, it is the right and duty of men to alter or abolish it. This is strong doctrine, so strong that now we pay it only lip service. Even the suggestion of altering government is looked upon as subversive, while the advocacy of the right of abolishing government is regarded in some quarters as treason.

But Jefferson himself was quite clear about the principle. Not only did he feel that men have a right to change their government whenever that government fails to serve the purposes for which it was established; he went even further and argued that ideally "every constitution and every law naturally expires" with each new generation. "If it be enforced longer," he wrote Madison, "it is an act of force and not of right." The earth, he said, belongs always to the living, not to the dead, and each new generation has the same right to make its own form of government that the original generation of constitution-makers had.

This sounds like revolutionary doctrine, and in a sense it is. But it is revolutionary in a new sense rather than in the old sense. At the time Jefferson wrote there was but one way of revolution—the appeal to arms. The right of revolution, even of violent revolution, was a moral right and must be invoked as long as there was no alternative.

But Jefferson's generation provided an alternative. For violent revolution they substituted legal revolution. For the appeal to arms they substituted the appeal to the will of the people. This is the historical meaning of that greatest of American political inventions, the constitutional convention. The constitutional convention derived its authority directly from people. It addressed itself exclusively to altering, abolishing or remaking a constitution. It referred its handiwork back to the source of all power—the people. It was revolution legalized. It was the constitutional alternative to revolution by force and violence. In the words of Jefferson's colleague, John Adams, it "realized the theories of the wisest writers."

These principles of what we must call democracy applied only indirectly to the specific purpose of the Declaration, that of justifying independence, but they applied directly to the larger purposes of the Declaration, that of providing a political philosophy adequate to the needs of this new people. And so, too, with what is unquestionably the most famous phrase in the great Declaration—the assertion that "all men are created equal." Certainly this assertion was not essential to the declaration of independence; it was not even essential to the other purposes that commanded the immediate attention of the Congress—the creation of an American union and the alliance with France.

It was superfluous, it was even gratuitous. But Jefferson felt—and rightly—that it was essential as a principle of political and social philosophy, essential for the kind of people who were now to assume a separate and equal station among the powers of the earth.

Who can doubt now that he was right? The phrase itself has given endless trouble and inspired endless controversy. What did it mean? How could Jefferson, himself a slave owner, assert that all men are created equal? How could Jefferson's generation, committed as it was to social, economic and even political inequalities, subscribe to such an assertion? How could Americans persist in it when it was so palpably contrary to reality?

From Fisher Ames to William Graham Summer, from John C. Calhoun to Henry L. Mencken, critics have attacked and derided this assertion of equality. Even those who rejoice in it have been apologetic about it. It meant, so they say, that all men are equal in the sight of God, equal before the last Judgment Seat. Or it meant that all have, equally, immortal souls. Or it meant that all whites (clearly the Negroes did not count) at the time it was written were equal before the law. Or it meant that in a state of nature, in some remote golden day of the past, men had been equal and that these men had come together and compacted for government.

It is doubtless true that Jefferson meant all these things, for they were commonplaces of political and social thought in the eighteenth century. But that he meant more is equally clear from his whole career. "Let us set up a standard to which the good and the wise can repair," Washington is supposed to have said of the Constitution, and the admonition applies equally to the assertion of equality in the Declaration.

The significance of this momentous phrase, as of most of the great phrases of history, lies not in its descriptive but in its prophetic, not in its actual but in its ideal, qualities. No one has expressed this better than Lincoln—Lincoln, who had to meet the charge that the phrase could not have been meant for Negro slaves and therefore did not mean what it said. In his Springfield speech of 1857 he spoke on what the signers did mean:

"They meant to set up a standard maxim for free society, which should be familiar to all, and revered by all; constantly looked to, constantly labored for, and even though never perfectly attained, constantly approximated, and thereby constantly spreading and deepening its influence and augmenting the happiness and value of life to all people of all colors everywhere . . . Its authors meant it to be . . . a stumbling block to all those who in after times might seek to turn a free people back into the hateful paths of despotism. They knew the proneness of prosperity to breed tyrants, and they meant when such should reappear in this fair land and commence their vocation, they should find left for them at least one hard nut to crack."

"A standard maxim for a free society." That is what the Declaration has ever been, and what it will long continue to be. Again and again in our history those who fought for the expansion of freedom, those who fought tyranny over the minds as over the bodies of men, have appealed to it, and rarely in vain. Each generation discovers it anew: with each generation it takes on new vitality and new meaning.

Each generation must not only familiarize itself with the philosophy of the great Declaration, it must justify and vindicate that philosophy anew. It must maintain the vitality of the democratic principle—that men make government. It must constantly enlarge the concept of majority rule, and see to it that all who are entitled to participate in the business of making and remaking government actually do participate. It must keep constantly before it the right of men to alter or abolish governments, and keep open and easy of access all those channels for alteration and recreation that the wisdom of the Fathers provided as alternatives to the use of force.

It must safeguard, therefore, as sacred the rights of speech and press and assembly and petition and association—those rights which enable men to achieve through reason and consent what in the past they tried to achieve through violence. It must take care that the doctrine of equality is substantial as well as rhetorical; that it means equality of opportunity as well as equality of right; that it means equality everywhere in the nation; that it means equality for Negro and for Jew and for alien as well as for those who claim descent from the Pilgrim Fathers —men who were heretics—or from the Revolutionary Fathers—men who were radicals.

It must not feebly look to the past, and only to the past, supposing that the Fathers exhausted political wisdom, but must take inspiration and courage from the boldness and the wisdom of the Fathers to apply to world problems those principles that were applied first to a people whom Jefferson called "the world's best hope."

For Discussion

1. What is the Declaration's meaning for today? How does man go about keeping the Declaration alive and meaningful today?
2. Do you agree with the Declaration's assertion that "all men are created equal"? Do you think the government's civil-rights program has helped to bring this phrase into reality? Why? Why not?

3. To what extent do you agree with Commager that the true power of government lies in the hands of the people?
4. Jefferson suggested that every new generation must pass its own constitution and establish its own laws. What are some changes in current laws that you would make if you had this opportunity?

For Comparison

1. Would Moore ("In Distrust of Merits") agree with Commager that the Declaration is meaningful today? What would be her reaction to Commager's suggestion that the real power of government lies in the hands of the people?
2. Reread the final two paragraphs in this essay; then relate their central idea to the one presented by Owens in "Mental Cases." To what extent is blind dependence upon the past responsible for the scene in Owens' poem?

For Composition

1. The Declaration does (does not) have meaning today.
2. The citizen's power in government.
3. Revolution is (is not) a necessity.

D. H. LAWRENCE

THE SPIRIT OF PLACE

Let us look at this American artist first. How did he ever get to America, to start with? Why isn't he a European still, like his father before him?

Now listen to me, don't listen to him. He'll tell you the lie you expect. Which is partly your fault for expecting it.

He didn't come in search of freedom of worship. England had more freedom of worship in the year 1700 than America had. Won by Englishmen who wanted freedom, and so stopped at home and fought for it. And got it. Freedom of worship? Read the history of New England during the first century of its existence.

Freedom anyhow? The land of the free! This the land of the free! Why, if I say anything that displeases them, the free mob will lynch me, and that's my freedom. Free? Why I have never been in any country where the individual has such an abject fear of his fellow countrymen. Because, as I say, they are free to lynch him the moment he shows he is not one of them.

No, no, if you're so fond of the truth about Queen Victoria, try a little about yourself.

Those Pilgrim Fathers and their successors never came here for freedom of worship. What did they set up when they got here? Freedom, would you call it?

They didn't come for freedom. Or if they did, they sadly went back on themselves.

All right then, what did they come for? For lots of reasons. Perhaps least of all in search of freedom of any sort: positive freedom, that is.

They came largely to get *away*—that most simple of motives. To get away. Away from what? In the long run, away from themselves. Away from everything. That's why most people have come to America, and still do come. To get away from everything they are and have been.

"Henceforth be masterless."

Which is all very well, but it isn't freedom. Rather the reverse. A hopeless sort of constraint. It is never freedom till you find something you really *positively want to be*. And people in America have always been shouting about the things they are *not*. Unless of course they are millionaires, made or in the making.

And after all there is a positive side to the movement. All that vast flood of human life that has flowed over the Atlantic in ships from Europe to America has not flowed over simply on a tide of revulsion from Europe and from the confinements of the European ways of life. This revulsion was, and still is, I believe, the prime motive in emigration. But there was some cause, even for the revulsion.

It seems as if at time man had a frenzy for getting away from any control of any sort. In Europe the old Christianity was the real master. The Church and the true aristocracy bore the responsibility for the working out of the Christian ideals: a little irregularly, maybe, but responsible nevertheless.

Mastery, kingship, fatherhood had their power destroyed at the time of the Renaissance.

And it was precisely at this moment that the great drift over the Atlantic started. What were men drifting away from? The old authority of Europe? Were they breaking the bonds of authority, and escaping to a new more absolute unrestrainedness? Maybe. But there was more to it.

Liberty is all very well, but men cannot live without masters. There is always a master. And men either live in glad obedience to the master they believe in, or they live in a frictional opposition to the master they wish to undermine. In America this frictional opposition has been the vital factor. It has given the Yankee his kick. Only the continual influx of more servile Europeans has provided America with an obedient labouring class. The true obedience never outlasting the first generation.

But there sits the old master, over in Europe. Like a parent. Somewhere deep in every American heart lies a rebellion against the old parenthood of Europe. Yet no American feels he has completely escaped its mastery. Hence the slow, smouldering patience of American opposition. The slow, smouldering, corrosive obedience to the old master Europe, the unwilling subject, the unremitting opposition.

Whatever else you are, be masterless.

> "Ca Ca Caliban
> Get a new master, be a new man."

Escaped slaves, we might say, people the republics of Liberia or Haiti. Liberia enough! Are we to look at America in the same way? A vast republic of escaped slaves. When you consider the hordes from eastern Europe, you might well say it: a vast republic of escaped slaves. But one dare not say this of the Pilgrim Fathers, and the great old body of idealist Americans, the modern Americans tortured with thought. A vast republic of escaped slaves. Look out, America! And a minority of earnest, self-tortured people.

The masterless.

> "Ca Ca Caliban
> Get a new master, be a new man."

What did the Pilgrim Fathers come for, then, when they came so gruesomely over the black sea? Oh, it was in a black spirit. A black revulsion from Europe, from the old authority of Europe, from kings and bishops and popes. And more. When you look into it, more. They were black, masterful men, they wanted something else. No kings, no bishops maybe. Even no God Almighty. But also, no more of this new "humanity" which followed the Renaissance. None of this new liberty which was to be so pretty in Europe. Something grimmer, by no means free-and-easy.

America has never been easy, and is not easy to-day. Americans have always been at a certain tension. Their liberty is a thing of sheer will, sheer tension: a liberty of THOU SHALT NOT. And it has been so from the first. The land of THOU SHALT NOT. Only the first commandment is: THOU SHALT NOT PRESUME TO BE A MASTER. Hence democracy.

"We are the masterless." That is what the American Eagle shrieks. It's a Hen-Eagle.

The Spaniards refused the post-Renaissance liberty of Europe. And the Spaniards filled most of America. The Yankees, too, refused, refused the post-Renaissance humanism of Europe. First and foremost, they hated masters. But under that, they hated the flowing ease of humour in Europe. At the bottom of the American soul was always a dark suspense, at the bottom of the Spanish-American soul the same. And this dark suspense hated and hates the old European spontaneity, watches it collapse with satisfaction.

Every continent has its own great spirit of place. Every people is polarized in some particular locality, which is home, the homeland. Different places on the face of the earth have different vital effluence, different vibration, different chemical exhalation, different polarity with different stars: call it what you like. But the spirit of place is a great reality. The Nile valley produced not only the corn, but the terrific religions of Egypt. China produces the Chinese, and will go on doing so. The Chinese in San Francisco will in time cease to be Chinese, for America is a great melting pot.

There was a tremendous polarity in Italy, in the city of Rome. And this seems to have died. For even places die. The Island of Great Britain had a wonderful terrestrial magnetism or polarity of its own, which made the British people. For the moment, this polarity seems to be breaking. Can England die? And what if England dies?

Men are less free than they imagine; ah, far less free. The freest are perhaps least free.

Men are free when they are in a living homeland, not when they are straying and breaking away. Men are free when they are obeying some deep, inward voice of religious belief. Obeying from within. Men are free when they belong to a living, organic, *believing* community, active in fulfilling some unfulfilled, perhaps unrealized purpose. Not when they are escaping to some wild west. The most unfree souls go west, and shout of freedom. Men are freest when they are most unconscious of freedom. The shout is a rattling of chains, always was.

Men are not free when they are doing just what they like. The moment you can do just what you like, there is nothing you care about doing. Men are only free when they are doing what the deepest self likes.

And there is getting down to the deepest self! It takes some diving.

Because the deepest self is way down, and the conscious self is an obstinate monkey. But of one thing we may be sure. If one wants to be free, one has to give up the illusion of doing what one likes, and seek what IT wishes done.

But before you can do what IT likes, you must first break the spell of the old mastery, the old IT.

Perhaps at the Renaissance, when kingship and fatherhood fell, Europe drifted into a very dangerous half-truth: of liberty and equality.

Perhaps the men who went to America felt this, and so repudiated the old world altogether. Went one better than Europe. Liberty in America has meant so far the breaking away from *all* dominion. The true liberty will only begin when Americans discover IT, and proceed possibly to fulfill IT. IT being the deepest *whole* self of man, the self in its wholeness, not idealistic halfness.

That's why the Pilgrim Fathers came to America, then; and that's why we come. Driven by IT. We cannot see that invisible winds carry us, as they carry swarms of locusts, that invisible magnetism brings us as it brings the migrating birds to their unforeknown goal. But it is so. We are not the marvellous choosers and deciders we think we are. IT chooses for us, and decides for us. Unless of course we are just escaped slaves, vulgarly cocksure of our ready-made destiny. But if we are living people, in touch with the source, IT drives us and decides us. We are free only so long as we obey. When we run counter, and think we will do as we like, we just flee around like Orestes pursued by the Eumenides.

And still, when the great day begins, when Americans have at last discovered America and their own wholeness, still there will be the vast number of escaped slaves to reckon with, those who have no cocksure, ready-made destinies.

Which will win in America, the escaped slaves, or the new whole men?

The real American day hasn't begun yet. Or at least, not yet sunrise. So far it has been the false dawn. That is, in the progressive American consciousness there has been the one dominant desire, to do away with the old thing. Do away with masters, exalt the will of the people. The will of the people being nothing but a figment, the exalting doesn't count for much. So, in the name of the will of the people, get rid of masters. When you have got rid of masters, you are left with this mere phrase of the will of the people. Then you pause and bethink yourself, and try to recover your own wholeness.

So much for the conscious American motive, and for democracy over here. Democracy in America is just the tool with which the old mastery of Europe, the European spirit, is undermined. Europe destroyed, potentially, American democracy will evaporate. America will begin.

American consciousness has so far been a false dawn. The negative ideal of democracy. But underneath, and contrary to this open ideal, the first hints and revelations of IT. IT, the American whole soul.

You have got to pull the democratic and idealistic clothes off American utterance, and see what you can of the dusky body of IT underneath.

"Henceforth be masterless."

Henceforth be mastered.

For Discussion

1. What does Lawrence mean by "The Spirit of Place"? What does he suggest has been contributed to America by its English ancestry?
2. Lawrence works out a specialized definition of *freedom* that ties it in very closely with responsibility. What is his concept of freedom?
3. The author suggests that freedom is not an escape from something but is to "find something you really *positively want to be.*" What possibilities for freedom are opened by this definition?
4. Do you agree with Lawrence that man is not successful unless he has a master? What force in American life is the master that motivates us all?

For Comparison

1. Is the idea of personal freedom and its relationship to responsibility similar in this essay and in the short story by Camus, "The Guest"?
2. Does Jeffers refute Lawrence's idea of responsible freedom when he suggests that it is better to live at a "distance from the thickening center" of corruption?

For Composition

1. The real freedom.
2. The freest are perhaps least free.
3. Responsibility and freedom.

WAYNE H. DAVIS

OVERPOPULATED AMERICA

I define as most seriously overpopulated that nation whose people by virtue of their numbers and activities are most rapidly decreasing the ability of the land to support human life. With our large population, our affluence and our technological monstrosities the United States wins first place by a substantial margin.

Let's compare the US to India, for example. We have 203 million people, whereas she has 540 million on much less land. But look at the impact of people on the land.

The average Indian eats his daily few cups of rice (or perhaps wheat, whose production on American farms contributed to our one percent per year drain in quality of our active farmland), draws his bucket of water from the communal well and sleeps in a mud hut. In his daily rounds to gather cow dung to burn to cook his rice and warm his feet, his footsteps, along with those millions of his countrymen, help bring about a slow deterioration of the ability of the land to support people. His contribution to the destruction of the land is minimal.

An American, on the other hand, can be expected to destroy a piece of land on which he builds a home, garage and driveway. He will contribute his share to the 142 million tons of smoke and fumes, seven million junked cars, 20 million tons of paper, 48 billion cans, and 26 billion bottles the overburdened environment must absorb each year. To run his air conditioner we will strip-mine a Kentucky hillside, push the dirt and slate down into the stream, and burn coal in a power generator, whose smokestack contributes to a plume of smoke massive enough to cause cloud seeding and premature precipitation from Gulf winds which should be irrigating the wheat farms of Minnesota.

In his lifetime he will personally pollute three million gallons of water, and industry and agriculture will use ten times this much water in his behalf. To provide these needs the US Army Corps of Engineers will build dams and flood farmland. He will also use 21,000 gallons of leaded gasoline containing boron, drink 28,000 pounds of milk and eat 10,000 pounds of meat. The latter is produced and squandered in a life pattern unknown to Asians. A steer on a Western range eats plants containing minerals necessary for plant life. Some of these are incorporated into the body of the steer which is later shipped for slaughter. After being eaten by man these nutrients are flushed down the toilet into the ocean or buried in the cemetery, the surface of which is cluttered with boulders called tombstones and has been removed from productivity. The result is a continual drain on the productivity of range land. Add to this the erosion of overgrazed lands, and the effects of the falling water table as we mine Pleistocene deposits of groundwater to irrigate to produce food for more people, and we can see why our land is dying far more rapidly than did the great civilization of the Middle East, which experienced the same cycle. The average Indian citizen, whose fecal material goes back to the land, has but a minute fraction of the destructive effect on the land that the affluent American does.

Thus I want to introduce a new term, which I suggest be used in future discussions of human population and ecology. We should speak of our numbers in "Indian equivalents". An Indian equivalent I define as the average number of Indian citizens required to have the same detrimental effect on the land's ability to support human life as would the average American. This value is difficult to determine, but let's take an extremely conservative working figure of 25. To see how conservative this is, imagine the addition of 1000 citizens to your town and 25,000 to an Indian village. Not only would the Americans destroy much more land for homes, highways and a shopping center, but they would contribute far more to environmental deterioration in hundreds of other ways as well. For example, their demand for steel for new autos might increase the daily pollution equivalent of 130,000 junk autos which *Life* tells us that US Steel Corp. dumps into Lake Michigan. Their demand for textiles would help the cotton industry destroy the life in the Black Warrior River in Alabama with endrin. And they would contribute to the massive industrial pollution of our oceans (we provide one third to one half the world's share) which has caused the precipitous downward trend in our commercial fisheries landings during the past seven years.

The per capita gross national product of the United States is 38 times that of India. Most of our goods and services contribute to the decline in the ability of the environment to support life. Thus it is clear that a figure of 25 for an Indian equivalent is conservative. It has been suggested to me that a more realistic figure would be 500.

In Indian equivalents, therefore, the population of the United States is at least four billion. And the rate of growth is even more alarming. We are growing at one percent per year, a rate which would double our numbers in 70 years. India is growing at 2.5 percent. Using the Indian equivalent of 25, our population growth becomes 10 times as serious as that of India. According to the Rienows in their recent book *Moment in the Sun*, just one year's crop of American babies can be expected to use up 25 billion pounds of beef, 200 million pounds of steel and 9.1 billion gallons of gasoline during their collective lifetime. And the demands on water and land for our growing population are expected to be far greater than the supply available in the year 2000. We are destroying our land at a rate of over a million acres a year. We now have only 2.6 agricultural acres per person. By 1975 this will be cut to 2.2, the critical point for the maintenance of what we consider a decent diet, and by the year 2000 we might expect to have 1.2.

You might object that I am playing with statistics in using the Indian equivalent on the rate of growth. I am making the assumption that today's child will live 35 years (the average Indian life span) at today's level of affluence. If he lives an American 70 years, our rate of population growth would be 20 times as serious as India's.

But the assumption of continued affluence at today's level is unfounded. If our numbers continue to rise, our standard of living will fall so sharply that by the year 2000 any surviving Americans might consider today's average Asian to be well off. Our children's destructive effects on their environment will decline as they sink ever lower into poverty.

The United States is in serious economic trouble now. Nothing could be more misleading than today's affluence, which rests precariously on a crumbling foundation. Our productivity, which had been increasing steadily at about 3.2 percent a year since World War II, has been falling during 1969. Our export over import balance has been shrinking steadily from $7.1 billion in 1964 to $0.15 billion in the first half of 1969. Our balance of payments deficit for the second quarter was $3.7 billion, the largest in history. We are now importing iron ore, steel, oil, beef, textiles, cameras, radios and hundreds of other things.

Our economy is based upon the Keynesian concept of a continued growth in population and productivity. It worked in an underpopulated nation with excess resources. It could continue to work only if the earth and its resources were expanding at an annual rate of 4 to 5 percent. Yet neither the number of cars, the economy, the human population, nor anything else can expand indefinitely at an exponential rate in a finite world. We must face this fact *now*. The crisis is here. When Walter Heller says that our economy will expand by 4 percent annually through the latter 1970s he is dreaming. He is in a theoretical world totally unaware of the realities of human ecology. If the economists do not wake up and devise a new system for us now somebody else will have to do it for them.

A civilization is comparable to a living organism. Its longevity is a function of its metabolism. The higher the metabolism (affluence), the shorter the life. Keynesian economics has allowed us an affluent but shortened life span. We have now run our course.

The tragedy facing the United States is even greater and more imminent than that descending upon the hungry nations. The Paddock brothers in their book, *Famine 1975!*, say that India "cannot be saved" no matter how much food we ship her. But India will be here after the United States is gone. Many millions will die in the most colossal famines India has ever known, but the land will survive and she will come back as she always has before. The United States, on the other hand, will be a desolate tangle of concrete and ticky-tacky, of strip-mined moonscape and silt-choked reservoirs. The land and water will be so contaminated with pesticides, herbicides, mercury fungicides, lead, boron, nickel, arsenic and hundreds of other toxic substances, which have been approaching critical levels of concentration in our environment as a result of our numbers and affluence, that it may be unable to sustain human life.

Thus as the curtain gets ready to fall on man's civilization let it come as no surprise that it shall first fall on the United States. And let no one make the mistake of thinking we can save ourselves by "cleaning up the environment." Banning DDT is the equivalent of the physician's treating syphilis by putting a bandaid over the first chancre to appear. In either case you can be sure that more serious and widespread trouble will soon appear unless the disease itself is treated. We cannot survive by planning to treat the symptoms such as air pollution, water pollution, soil erosion, etc.

What can we do to slow the rate of destruction of the United States as a land capable of supporting human life? There are two approaches. First, we must reverse the population growth. We have far more people now than we can continue to support at anything near today's level of affluence. American women average slightly over three children each. According to the *Population Bulletin* if we reduced this number to 2.5 there would still be 330 million people in the nation at the end of the century. And even if we reduced this to 1.5 we would have 57 million more people in the year 2000 than we have now. With our present longevity patterns it would take more than 30 years for the population to peak even when reproducing at this rate, which would eventually give us a net decrease in numbers.

Do not make the mistake of thinking that technology will solve our population problem by producing a better contraceptive. Our problem now is that people want too many children. Surveys show the average number of children wanted by the American family is 3.3. There is little difference between the poor and the wealthy, black and white, Catholic and Protestant. Production of children at this rate during the next 30 years would be so catastrophic in effect on our resources and the viability of the nation as to be beyond my ability to contemplate. To prevent this trend we must not only make contraceptives and abortion readily available to everyone, but we must establish a system to put severe economic pressure on those who produce children and reward those who do not. This can be done within our system of taxes and welfare.

The other thing we must do is to pare down our Indian equivalents. Individuals in American society vary tremendously in Indian equivalents. If we plot Indian equivalents versus their reciprocal, the percentage of land surviving a generation, we obtain a linear regression. We can then place individuals and occupation types on this graph. At one end would be the starving blacks of Mississippi; they would approach unity in Indian equivalents, and would have the least destructive effect on the land. At the other end of the graph would be the politicians slicing pork for the barrel, the highway contractors, strip-mine operators, real estate developers, and public enemy number one—the US Army Corps of Engineers.

We must halt land destruction. We must abandon the view of land and minerals as private property to be exploited in any way economically feasible for private financial gain. Land and minerals are resources upon which the very survival of the nation depends, and their use must be planned in the best interests of the people.

Rising expectations for the poor is a cruel joke foisted upon them by the Establishment. As our new economy of use-it-once-and-throw-it-away produces more and more products for the affluent, the share of our resources available for the poor declines. Blessed be the starving blacks of Mississippi with their outdoor privies, for they are ecologically sound, and they shall inherit a nation. Although I hope that we will help these unfortunate people attain a decent standard of living by divetring war efforts to fertility control and job training, our most urgent task to assure this nation's survival during the next decade is to stop the affluent destroyers.

For Discussion

1. Do you agree with Davis's definition of "overpopulation"? How valid is his comparison of America with India?
2. Is Davis really critical of America's overpopulation, or is he objecting more to the country's affluence? Can the two ultimately be separated?
3. What is your reaction to the statement by Davis that "India will be here after the United States is gone"?
4. One solution proposed by Davis is to reverse population growth. How much initiative should the government take in this approach? How can it become active without violating personal and religious privacy?
5. Davis's other suggestion is to reduce Indian equivalents. What ways can you suggest for doing this? Again, is there a danger that in doing this the government might become too powerful? For instance, discuss the energy crisis in terms of the second-to-last paragraph in the essay.

For Comparison

1. Examine this essay in relationship to Sandburg's "Four Preludes on Playthings of the Wind." Beginning with the first stanza of the poem, indicate the symbols of decay that give support to Davis' ideas.
2. Is this essay in direct opposition to Lawrence's "The Spirit of Place,"

or is population control a part of the "IT" that Lawrence speaks about as being necessary in America.

For Composition

1. Our overpopulation is (is not) serious.
2. The church and population control.
3. My concept of ideal family size.

WALTER VAN TILBURG CLARK

THE PORTABLE PHONOGRAPH

The red sunset, with narrow black cloud strips like threats across it, lay on the curved horizon of the prairie. The air was still and cold, and in it settled the mute darkness and greater cold of night. High in the air there was wind, for through the veil of the dusk the clouds could be seen gliding rapidly south and changing shapes. A queer sensation of torment, of two-sided, unpredictable nature, arose from the stillness of the earth air beneath the violence of the upper air. Out of the sunset, through the dead, matted grass and isolated weed stalks of the prairie, crept the narrow and deeply rutted remains of a road. In the road, in places, there were crusts of shallow, brittle ice. There were little islands of an old oiled pavement in the road too, but most of it was mud, now frozen rigid. The frozen mud still bore the toothed impress of great tanks, and a wanderer on the neighboring undulations might have stumbled, in this light, into large, partially filled-in and weed-grown cavities, their banks channeled and beginning to spread into badlands. These pits were such as might have been made by falling meteors, but they were not. They were the scars of gigantic bombs, their rawness already made a little natural by rain, seed, and time. Along the road there were rakish remnants of fence. There was also, just visible, one portion of tangled and multiple barbed wire still erect, behind which was a shelving ditch with small caves, now very quiet and empty, at intervals in its back wall. Otherwise there was no structure or remnant of a structure visible over the dome of the darkling earth, but only, in sheltered hollows, the darker shadows of young trees trying again.

Under the wuthering arch of the high wind a V of wild geese fled south. The rush of their pinions sounded briefly, and the faint, plaintive notes of their expeditionary talk. Then they left a still greater vacancy. There was the smell and expectation of snow, as there is likely to be when the wild geese fly south. From the remote distance, towards the red sky, came faintly the protracted howl and quick yap-yap of a prairie wolf.

North of the road, perhaps a hundred yards, lay the parallel, and deeply intrenched course of a small creek, lined with leafless alders and willows. The creek was already silent under ice. Into the bank above it was dug a sort of cell, with a single opening, like the mouth of a mine tunnel. Within the cell there was a little red of fire, which showed dully through the opening, like a reflection of a deception of the imagination. The light came from the chary burning of four blocks of poorly aged peat, which gave off a petty warmth and much acrid smoke. But the precious remnants of wood, old fenceposts and timbers from the long-deserted dugouts, had to be saved for the real cold, for the time when a man's breath blew white, the moisture in his nostrils stiffened at once when he stepped out, and the expansive blizzards paraded for days over the vast open, swirling and settling and thickening, till the dawn of the cleared day when the sky was thin blue-green and the terrible cold, in which a man could not live for three hours unwarmed, lay over the uniformly drifted swell of the plain.

Around the smoldering peat four men were seated cross-legged. Behind them, traversed by their shadows, was the earth bench, with two old and dirty army blankets, where the owner of the cell slept. In a niche in the opposite wall were a few tin utensils which caught the glint of the coals. The host was rewrapping in a piece of daubed burlap four fine, leather-bound books. He worked slowly and very carefully and at last tied the bundle securely with a piece of grass-woven cord. The other three looked intently upon the process, as if a great significance lay in it. As the host tied the cord he spoke. He was an old man, his long, matted beard and hair gray to nearly white. The shadows made his brows and cheekbones appear gnarled, his eyes and cheeks deeply sunken. His big hands, rough with frost and swollen by rheumatism, were awkward but gentle at their task. He was like a prehistoric priest performing a fateful ceremonial rite. Also his voice had in it a suitable quality of deep, reverent despair, yet perhaps at the moment a sharpness of selfish satisfaction.

"When I perceived what was happening," he said, "I told myself. 'It is the end. I cannot take much; I will take these.' "

"Perhaps I was impractical," he continued. "But for myself. I do not regret, and what do we know of those who will come after us? We are the doddering remnant of a race of mechanical fools. I have saved what I love; the soul of what was good in us is here; perhaps the new ones will make a strong enough beginning not to fall behind when they become clever."

He rose with slow pain and placed the wrapped volumes in the niche with his utensils. The others watched him with the same ritualistic gaze.

"Shakespeare, the Bible, *Moby Dick*, the *Divine Comedy*," one of them said softly. "You might have done worse, much worse."

"You will have a little soul left until you die," said another harshly. "That is more than is true of us. My brain becomes thick, like my hands." He held the big, battered hands, with their black nails, in the glow to be seen.

"I want paper to write on," he said. "And there is none."

The fourth man said nothing. He sat in the shadow farthest from the fire, and sometimes his body jerked in its rags from the cold. Although he was still young, he was sick and coughed often. Writing implied a greater future than he now felt able to consider.

The old man seated himself laboriously and reached out, groaning at the movement, to put another block of peat on the fire. With bowed heads and averted eyes his three guests acknowledged his magnanimity.

"We thank you, Dr. Jenkins, for the reading," said the man who had named the books.

They seemed then to be waiting for something. Dr. Jenkins understood but was loath to comply. In an ordinary moment he would have said nothing. But the words of *The Tempest* which he had been reading, and the religious attention of the three made this an unusual occasion.

"You wish to hear the phonograph," he said grudgingly.

The two middle-aged men stared into the fire, unable to formulate and expose the enormity of their desire.

The young man, however, said anxiously, between suppressed coughs, "Oh, please," like an excited child.

The old man rose again in his difficult way and went to the back of the cell. He returned and placed tenderly upon the packed floor, where the firelight might fall upon it, an old portable phonograph in a black case. He smoothed the top with his hand and then opened it. The lovely green-felt-covered disk became visible.

"I have been using thorns as needles," he said. "But tonight, because we have a musician among us—he bent his head to the young man, almost invisible in the shadow—"I will use a steel needle. There are only three left."

The two middle-aged men stared at him in speechless adoration. The one with the big hands, who wanted to write, moved his lips, but the whisper was not audible.

"Oh, don't!" cried the young man, as if he were hurt. "The thorns will do beautifully."

"No," the old man said. "I have become accustomed to the thorns, but they are not really good. For you, my young friend, we will have good music tonight."

"After all," he added generously, and beginning to wind the phonograph, which creaked, "they can't last forever."

"No, nor we," the man who needed to write said harshly. "The needle, by all means."

"Oh, thanks," said the young man. "Thanks," he said again in a low, excited voice, and then stifled his coughing with a bowed head.

"The records, though," said the old man when he had finished winding, "are a different matter. Already they are very worn. I do not play them more than once a week. One, once a week, that is what I allow myself.

"More than a week I cannot stand it; not to hear them," he apologized.

"No, how could you?" cried the young man. "And with them here this."

"A man can stand anything," said the man who wanted to write, in his harsh, antagonistic voice.

"Please, the music," said the young man.

"Only the one," said the old man. "In the long run, we will remember more that way."

He had a dozen records with luxuriant gold and red seals. Even in that light the others could see that the threads of the records were becoming worn. Slowly he read out the titles and the tremendous, dead names of the composers and the artists and the orchestras. The three worked upon the names in their minds, carefully. It was difficult to select from such a wealth what they would at once most like to remember. Finally the man who wanted to write named Gershwin's "New York."

"Oh, no!" cried the sick young man, and then could say nothing more because he had to cough. The others understood him, and the harsh man withdrew his selection and waited for the musician to choose.

The musician begged Dr. Jenkins to read the titles again, very slowly, so that he could remember the sounds. While they were read he lay back against the wall, his eyes closed, his thin horny hand pulling at his light beard, and listened to the voices and the orchestras and the single instruments in his mind.

When the reading was done he spoke despairingly: " I have forgotten," he complained. "I cannot hear them clearly."

"There are things missing," he explained.

"I know," said Dr. Jenkins. "I thought that I knew all of Shelley by heart. I should have brought Shelley."

"That's more soul than we can use," said the harsh man. *"Moby Dick* is better."

"By God, we can understand that," he emphasized.

The Doctor nodded.

"Still," said the man who had admired the books, "we need the absolute if we are to keep a grasp on anything."

"Anything but these sticks and peat clods and rabbit snares," he said bitterly.

"Shelley desired an ultimate absolute," said the harsh man. "It's too much," he said. "It's no good; no earthly good."

The musician selected a Debussy nocturne. The others considered and approved. They rose to their knees to watch the Doctor prepare for the playing, so that they appeared to be actually in an attitude of worship. The peat glow showed the thinness of their bearded faces, and the deep lines in them, and revealed the condition of their garments. The other two continued to kneel as the old man carefully lowered the needle onto the spinning disk, but the musician suddenly drew back against the wall again, with his knees up, and buried his face in his hands.

At the first notes of the piano the listeners were startled. They stared at each other. Even the musician lifted his head in amazement but then quickly bowed it again, strainingly as if he were suffering from a pain he might not be able to endure. They were all listening deeply, without movement. The wet, blue-green notes tinkled forth from the old machine and were individual, delectable presences in the cell. The individual, delectable presences swept into a sudden tide of unbearably beautiful dissonance and then continued fully the swelling and ebbing of that tide, the dissonant inpourings, and the resolutions, and the diminishments, and the little, quiet wavelets of interlude lapping between. Every sound was piercing and singularly sweet. In all the men except the musician there occurred rapid sequences of tragically heightened recollection. He heard nothing but what was there. At the final, whispering disappearance, but moving quietly so that the others would not hear him and look at him, he let his head fall back in agony, as if it were drawn there by the hair, and clenched the fingers of one hand over his teeth. He sat that way while the others were silent and until they began to breathe again normally. His drawn-up legs were trembling violently.

Quickly Dr. Jenkins lifted the needle off, to save it and not spoil the recollection with scraping. When he had stopped the whirling of the sacred disk he courteously left the phonograph open and by the fire, in sight.

The others, however, understood. The musician rose last, but then abruptly, and went quickly out at the door without saying anything. The others stopped at the door and gave their thanks in low voices. The Doctor nodded magnificently.

"Come again," he invited, "in a week. We will have the 'New York.' "

When the two had gone together, out towards the rimed road, he stood in the entrance, peering and listening. At first there was only the resonant boom of the wind overhead, and then far over the dome of the dead, dark plain the wolf cry lamenting. In the rifts of clouds the Doctor saw four stars flying. It impressed the Doctor that one of them had just been obscured by the beginning of a flying cloud at the very moment he heard what he had been listening for, a sound of suppressed coughing. It was not near by, however. He believed that down against the pale alders he could see the moving shadow.

With nervous hands he lowered the piece of canvas which served as his door and pegged it at the bottom. Then quickly and quietly, looking at the piece of canvas frequently, he slipped the records into the case, snapped the lid shut, and carried the phonograph to his couch. There, pausing often to stare at the canvas and listen, he dug earth from the wall and disclosed a piece of board. Behind this there was a deep hole in the wall, into which he put the phonograph. After a moment's consideration he went over and reached down his bundle of books and inserted it also. Then, guardedly, he once more sealed up the hole with the board and the earth. He also changed his blankets and the grass-stuffed sack which served as a pillow, so that he could lie facing the entrance. After carefully placing two more blocks of peat upon the fire he stood for a long time watching the stretched canvas, but it seemed to billow naturally with the first gusts of a lowering wind. At last he prayed, and got in under his blankets, and closed his smoke-smarting eyes. On the inside of the bed, next the wall, he could feel with his hand the comfortable piece of lead pipe.

For Discussion

1. Why is the portable phonograph the central symbol in the story? What exactly does it represent?
2. This story depicts the world that might remain after a nuclear war. What descriptive devices does the author use to give the story a wasteland atmosphere?
3. If the characters are indeed "a doddering remnant of a race of mechanical fools," who is responsible for this fact: the men themselves? the government?

4. Evaluate Dr. Jenkin's control of the phonograph in terms of "the common good."
5. How is the final paragraph important to an understanding of the story? What aspects of the "walk softly and carry a big stick" idea are there?

For Comparison

1. This story deals with a wasteland that is in part the product of man's greed. What aspects of that wasteland are also a part of the scene described by Davis in "Overpopulated America"?
2. In "Last Speech to the Court" Vanzetti says "Never / in our full life could we hope to do such work / for tolerance; for justice, for man's understanding of man, as we do by accident." To what extent is the meaning found in these lines exemplified in this story?

For Composition

1. My evaluation of Dr. Jenkins.
2. I would (would not) want to live through nuclear war.
3. Man can (cannot) begin again.

ALBERT CAMUS

THE GUEST

The schoolmaster was watching the two men climb toward him. One was on horseback, the other on foot. They had not yet tackled the abrupt rise leading to the schoolhouse built on the hillside. They were toiling onward, making slow progress in the snow, among the stones, on the vast expanse of the high, deserted plateau. From time to time the horse stumbled. He could not be heard yet but the breath issuing from his nostrils could be seen. The schoolmaster calculated that it would take them a half hour to get onto the hill. It was cold; he went back into the school to get a sweater.

He crossed the empty, frigid classroom. On the blackboard the four rivers of France, drawn with four different colored chalks, had been flowing toward their estuaries for the past three days. Snow had suddenly fallen in mid-October after eight months of drought without the transition of rain, and the twenty pupils, more or less, who lived in the villages scattered over the plateau had stopped coming. With fair weather they would return. Daru now heated only the single room that was his lodging, adjoining the classroom. One of the windows faced, like the classroom windows, the south. On that side the school was a few kilometers from the point where the plateau began to slope toward the south. In clear weather the purple mass of the mountain range where the gap opened onto the desert could be seen.

Somewhat warmed, Daru returned to the window from which he had first noticed the two men. They were no longer visible. Hence they must have tackled the rise. The sky was not so dark, for the snow had stopped falling during the night. The morning had dawned with a dirty light which had scarcely become brighter as the ceiling of clouds lifted. At two in the afternoon it seemed as if the day were merely beginning. But still this was better than those three days when the thick snow was falling amidst unbroken darkness with little gusts of wind that rattled the double door of the classroom. Then Daru had spent long hours in his room, leaving it only to go to the shed and feed the chickens or get some coal. Fortunately the delivery truck from Tadjid, the nearest village to the north, had brought his supplies two days before the blizzard. It would return in forty-eight hours.

Besides, he had enough to resist a siege, for the little room was cluttered with bags of wheat that the administration had left as a supply to distribute to those of his pupils whose families had suffered from the drought. Actually they had all been victims because they were all poor. Every day Daru would distribute a ration to the children. They had missed it, he knew, during these bad days. Possibly one of the fathers or big brothers would come this afternoon and he could supply them with grain. It was just a matter of carrying them over to the next harvest. Now shiploads of wheat were arriving from France and the worst was over. But it would be hard to forget that poverty, that army of ragged ghosts wandering in the sunlight, the plateaus burned to a cinder month after month, the earth shriveled up little by little, literally scorched, every stone bursting into dust under one's foot. The sheep had died then by thousands, and even a few men, here and there, sometimes without anyone's knowing.

In contrast with such poverty, he who lived almost like a monk, in his remote schoolhouse, had felt like a lord with his whitewashed walls, his narrow couch, his unpainted shelves, his well, and his weekly provisioning with water and food. And suddenly this snow, without warning, without the foretaste of rain. This is the way the region was, cruel to live in, even without men, who didn't help matters either. But Daru had been born here. Everywhere else, he felt exiled.

He went out and stepped forward on the terrace in front of the school-house. The two men were now halfway up the slope. He recognized the horseman to be Balducci, the old gendarme he had known for a long time. Balducci was holding at the end of a rope an Arab walking behind him with hands bound and head lowered. The gendarme waved a greeting to which Daru did not reply, lost as he was in contemplation of the Arab dressed in a faded blue *jellaba*, his feet in sandals but covered with socks of heavy raw wool, his head crowned with a narrow, short *chèche*. Balducci was holding back his horse in order not to hurt the Arab, and the group was advancing slowly.

Within earshot, Balducci shouted, "One hour to do the three kilometers from El Ameur!" Daru did not answer. Short and square in his thick sweater, he watched them climb. Not once had the Arab raised his head. "Hello," said Daru when they got up onto the terrace. "Come in and warm up." Balducci painfully got down from his horse without letting go of the rope. He smiled at the schoolmaster from under his bristling mustache. His little dark eyes, deepset under a tanned forehead, and his mouth surrounded with wrinkles made him look attentive and studious. Daru took the bridle, led the horse to the shed, and came back to the two men who were now waiting for him in the school. He led them into his room. "I am going to heat up the classroom," he said. "We'll be more comfortable there."

When he entered the room again, Balducci was on the couch. He had undone the rope tying him to the Arab, who had squatted near the stove. His hands still bound, the *chèche* pushed back on his head, the Arab was looking toward the window. At first Daru noticed only his huge lips, fat, smooth, almost Negroid; yet his nose was straight, his eyes dark and full of fever. The *chèche* uncovered an obstinate forehead and, under the weathered skin now rather discolored by the cold, the whole face had a restless and rebellious look. "Go into the other room," said the schoolmaster, "and I'll make you some mint tea." "Thanks," Balducci said. "What a chore! How I long for retirement." And addressing his prisoner in Arabic, he said, "Come on, you." The Arab got up and, slowly, holding his bound wrists in front of him, went into the classroom.

With the tea, Daru brought a chair. But Balducci was already sitting in state at the nearest pupil's desk, and the Arab had squatted against the teacher's platform facing the stove, which stood between the desk and the window. When he held out the glass of tea to the prisoner, Daru hesitated at the sight of his bound hands. "He might perhaps be untied." "Sure," said Balducci. "That was for the trip." He started to get to his feet. But Daru, setting the glass on the floor, had knelt beside the Arab. Without saying anything, the Arab watched him with his feverish eyes. Once his hands were free, he rubbed his swollen wrists against each other, took the glass of tea and sucked up the burning liquid in swift little sips.

"Good," said Daru. "And where are you headed?"

Balducci withdrew his mustache from the tea. "Here, son."

"Odd pupils! And you're spending the night?"

"No. I'm going back to El Ameur. And you will deliver this fellow to Tinguit. He is expected at police headquarters."

Balducci was looking at Daru with a friendly little smile.

"What's this story?" asked the schoolmaster. "Are you pulling my leg?"

"No, son. Those are the orders."

"The orders? I'm not . . ." Daru hesitated, not wanting to hurt the old Corsican. "I mean, that's not my job."

"What! What's the meaning of that? In wartime people do all kinds of jobs."

"Then I'll wait for the declaration of war!"

Balducci nodded. "O.K. But the orders exist and they concern you too. Things are bubbling, it appears. There is talk of a forth-coming revolt. We are mobilized, in a way."

Daru still had his obstinate look.

"Listen, son," Balducci said. "I like you and you've got to understand. There's only a dozen of us at El Ameur to patrol the whole territory of a small department and I must be back in a hurry. He couldn't be kept there. His village was beginning to stir; they wanted to take him back. You must take him to Tinguit tomorrow before the day is over. Twenty kilometers shouldn't faze a husky fellow like you. After that, all will be over. You'll come back to your pupils and your comfortable life."

Behind the wall the horse could be heard snorting and pawing the earth. Daru was looking out the window. Decidedly the weather was clearing and the light was increasing over the snowy plateau. When all the snow was melted, the sun would take over again and once more would burn the fields of stone. For days still, the unchanging sky would shed its dry light on the solitary expanse where nothing had any connection with man.

"After all," he said, turning around toward Balducci, "what did he do?" And, before the gendarme had opened his mouth, he asked, "Does he speak French?"

"No, not a word. We had been looking for him for a month, but they were hiding him. He killed his cousin."

"Is he against us?"

"I don't think so. But you can never be sure."

"Why did he kill?"

"A family squabble, I think. One owed grain to the other, it seems. It's not at all clear. In short, he killed his cousin with a billhook. You know, like a sheep, *kreezk*!"

Balducci made the gesture of drawing a blade across his throat, and the Arab, his attention attracted, watched him with a sort of anxiety. Daru felt a sudden wrath against the man, against all men with their rotten spite, their tireless hates, their blood lust.

But the kettle was singing on the stove. He served Balducci more tea, hesitated, then served the Arab again, who drank avidly a second time. His raised arms made the *jellaba* fall open, and the schoolmaster saw his thin, muscular chest.

"Thanks, son," Balducci said. "And now I'm off."

He got up and went toward the Arab, taking a small rope from his pocket.

"What are you doing?" Daru asked dryly.

Balducci, disconcerted, showed him the rope.

"Don't bother."

The old gendarme hesitated. "It's up to you. Of course, you are armed?"

"I have my shotgun."

"Where?"

"In the trunk."

"You ought to have it near your bed."

"Why? I have nothing to fear."

"You're crazy, son. If there's an uprising, no one is safe; we're all in the same boat."

"I'll defend myself. I'll have time to see them coming."

Balducci began to laugh, then suddenly the mustache covered the white teeth. "You'll have time? O.K. That's just what I was saying. You always have been a little cracked. That's why I like you; my son was like that."

At the same time he took out his revolver and put it on the desk. "Keep it; I don't need two weapons from here to El Ameur."

The revolver shone against the black paint of the table. When the gendarme turned toward him, the schoolmaster caught his smell of leather and horseflesh.

"Listen, Balducci," Daru said suddenly, "all this disgusts me, beginning with your fellow here. But I won't hand him over. Fight, yes, if I have to. But not that."

The old gendarme stood in front of him and looked at him severely.

"You're being a fool," he said slowly. "I don't like it either. You don't get used to putting a rope on a man even after years of it, and you're even ashamed—yes, ashamed. But you can't let them have their way."

"I won't hand him over," Daru said again.

"It's an order, son, and I repeat it."

"That's right. Repeat to them what I've said to you: I won't hand him over."

Balducci made a visible effort to reflect. He looked at the Arab and at Daru. At last he decided.

"No, I won't tell them anything. If you want to drop us, go ahead; I'll not denounce you. I have an order to deliver the prisoner and I'm doing so. And now you'll just sign this paper for me."

"There's no need. I'll not deny that you left him with me."

"Don't be mean with me. I know you'll tell the truth. You're from around these parts and you are a man. But you must sign; that's the rule."

Daru opened his drawer, took out a little square bottle of purple ink, the red wooden penholder with the "sergeant-major" pen he used for models of handwriting, and signed. The gendarme carefully folded the paper and put it into his wallet. Then he moved toward the door.

"I'll see you off," Daru said.

"No," said Balducci. "There's no use being polite. You insulted me."

He looked at the Arab, motionless in the same spot, sniffed peevishly, and turned away toward the door. "Good-by, son," he said. The door slammed behind him. His footsteps were muffled by the snow. The horse stirred on the other side of the wall and several chickens fluttered in fright. A moment later Balducci reappeared outside the window leading the horse by the bridle. He walked toward the little rise without turning around and disappeared from sight with the horse following him.

Daru walked back toward the prisoner, who, without stirring, never took his eyes off him. "Wait," the schoolmaster said in Arabic and went toward the bedroom. As he was going through the door, he had a second thought, went to the desk, took the revolver, and stuck it in his pocket. Then, without looking back, he went into his room.

For some time he lay on his couch watching the sky gradually close over, listening to the silence. It was this silence that had seemed painful to him during the first days here, after the war. He had requested a post in the little town at the base of the foothills separating the upper plateaus from the desert. There rocky walls, green and black to the north, pink and lavender to the south, marked the frontier of eternal summer. He had been named to a post farther north, on the plateau itself. In the beginning, the solitude and the silence had been hard for him on these wastelands peopled only by stones. Occasionally, furrows suggested cultivation, but they had been dug to uncover a certain kind of stone good for building. The only plowing here was to harvest rocks. Elsewhere a thin layer of soil accumulated in the hollows would be scraped out to enrich paltry village gardens. This is the way it was: bare rock covered three quarters of the region. Towns sprang up, flourished, then disappeared; men came by, loved one another or fought bitterly, then died. No one in this desert, neither he nor his guest, mattered. And yet, outside this desert neither of them, Daru knew, could have really lived.

When he got up, no noise came from the classroom. He was amazed at the unmixed joy he derived from the mere thought that the Arab might have fled and that he would be alone with no decision to make. But the prisoner was there. He had merely stretched out between the stove and the desk and he was staring at the ceiling. In that position, his thick lips were particularly noticeable, giving him a pouting look. "Come," said Daru. The Arab got up and followed him. In the bedroom the schoolmaster pointed to a chair near the table under the window. The Arab sat down without ceasing to watch Daru.

Are you hungry?"

"Yes," the prisoner said.

Daru set the table for two. He took flour and oil, shaped a cake in a frying pan, and lighted the little stove that functioned on bottled gas. While the cake was cooking, he went out to the shed to get cheese, eggs, dates, and condensed milk. When the cake was done he set it on the window sill to cool, heated some condensed milk diluted with water, and beat up the eggs into an omelette. In one of his motions he bumped into the revolver stuck in his right pocket. He set the bowl down, went into the classroom, and put the revolver in his desk drawer. When he came back to the room, night was falling. He put on the light and served the Arab. "Eat," he said. The Arab took a piece of the cake, lifted it eagerly to his mouth, and stopped short.

"And you?" he asked.

"After you. I'll eat too."

The thick lips opened slightly. The Arab hesitated, then bit into the cake determinedly.

The meal over, the Arab looked at the schoolmaster. "Are you the judge?"

"No, I'm simply keeping you until tomorrow."

"Why do you eat with me?"

"I'm hungry."

The Arab fell silent. Daru got up and went out. He brought back a camp cot from the shed and set it up between the table and the stove, at right angles to his own bed. From a large suitcase which, upright in a corner, served as a shelf for papers, he took two blankets and arranged them on the cot. Then he stopped, felt useless, and sat down on his bed.

There was nothing more to do or to get ready. He had to look at this man. He looked at him therefore, trying to imagine his face bursting with rage. He couldn't do so. He could see nothing but the dark yet shining eyes and the animal mouth.

"Why did you kill him?" he asked in a voice whose hostile tone surprised him.

The Arab looked away. "He ran away. I ran after him."

He raised his eyes to Daru again and they were full of a sort of woeful interrogation, "Now what will they do to me?"

"Are you afraid?"

The Arab stiffened, turning his eyes away.

"Are you sorry?"

The Arab stared at him openmouthed. Obviously he did not understand. Daru's annoyance was growing. At the same time he felt awkward and self-conscious with his big body wedged between the two beds.

"Lie down there," he said impatiently. "That's your bed."

The Arab didn't move. He cried out, "Tell me!"

The schoolmaster looked at him.

"Is the gendarme coming back tomorrow?"

"I don't know."

"Are you coming with us?"

"I don't know. Why?"

The prisoner got up and stretched out on top of the blankets, his feet toward the window. The light from the electric bulb shone straight into his eyes and he closed them at once.

"Why?" Daru repeated, standing beside the bed.

The Arab opened his eyes under the blinding light and looked at him, trying not to blink. "Come with us," he said.

In the middle of the night, Daru was still not asleep. He had gone to bed after undressing completely; he generally slept naked. But when he suddenly realized that he had nothing on, he wondered. He felt vulnerable and the temptation came to him to put his clothes back on. Then he shrugged his shoulders; after all, he wasn't a child and, if it came to that, he could break his adversary in two. From his bed, he could observe him lying on his back, still motionless, his eyes closed under the harsh light. When Daru turned out the light, the darkness seemed to congeal all of a sudden. Little by little, the night came back to life in the window where the starless sky was stirring gently. The schoolmaster soon made out the body lying at his feet. The Arab was still motionless but his eyes seemed open. A faint wind was prowling about the schoolhouse. Perhaps it would drive away the clouds and the sun would reappear.

During the night the wind increased. The hens fluttered a little and then were silent. The Arab turned over on his side with his back to Daru, who thought he heard him moan. Then he listened for his guest's breathing, which had become heavier and more regular. He listened to that breathing so close to him and mused without being able to go to sleep. In the room where he had been sleeping alone for a year, this presence bothered him. But it bothered him also because it imposed on him a sort of brotherhood he refused to accept in the present circumstances; yet he was familiar with it. Men who share the same rooms, soldiers or prisoners, develop a strange alliance as if, having cast off their armor with their clothing, they fraternized every evening, over and above their differences, in the ancient community of dream and fatigue. But Daru shook himself; he didn't like such musings, and it was essential for him to sleep.

A little later, however, when the Arab stirred slightly, the schoolmaster was still not asleep. When the prisoner made a second move, he stiffened, on the alert. The Arab was lifting himself slowly on his arms with almost the motion of a sleepwalker. Seated upright in bed, he waited motionless without turning his head toward Daru, as if he were listening attentively. Daru did not stir; it had just occurred to him that the revolver was still in the drawer of his desk. It was better to act at once. Yet he continued to observe the prisoner, who, with the same slithery motion, put his feet on the ground, waited again, then stood up slowly. Daru was about to call out to him when the Arab began to walk, in a quite natural but extraordinarily silent way. He was heading toward the door at the end of the room that opened into the shed. He lifted the latch with precaution and went out, pushing the door behind him but without shutting it.

Daru had not stirred. "He is running away," he merely thought. "Good riddance!" Yet he listened attentively. The hens were not fluttering; the guest must be on the plateau. A faint sound of water reached him, and he didn't know what it was until the Arab again stood framed in the doorway, closed the door carefully, and came back to bed without a sound. Then Daru turned his back on him and fell asleep. Still later he seemed, from the depths of his sleep, to hear furtive steps around the schoolhouse. "I'm dreaming! I'm dreaming!" he repeated to himself. And he went on sleeping.

When he awoke, the sky was clear; the loose window let in a cold, pure air. The Arab was asleep, hunched up under the blankets now, his mouth open, utterly relaxed. But when Daru shook him he started dreadfully, staring at Daru with wild eyes as if he had never seen him and with such a frightened expression that the schoolmaster stepped back. "Don't be afraid. It is I. You must eat." The Arab nodded his head and said yes. Calm had returned to his face, but his expression was vacant and listless.

The coffee was ready. They drank it seated together on the cot as they munched their pieces of the cake. Then Daru led the Arab under the shed and showed him the faucet where he washed. He went back into the room, folded the blankets on the cot, made his own bed, and put the room in order. Then he went through the classroom and out onto the terrace. The sun was already rising in the blue sky; a soft, bright light enveloped the deserted plateau. On the ridge the snow was melting in spots. The stones were about to reappear. Crouched on the edge of the plateau, the schoolmaster looked at the deserted expanse. He thought of Balducci. He had hurt him, for he had sent him off as though he didn't want to be associated with him. He could still hear the gendarme's farewell and, without knowing why, he felt strangely empty and vulnerable.

At that moment, from the other side of the schoolhouse, the prisoner coughed. Daru listened to him almost despite himself and then, furious, threw a pebble that whistled through the air before sinking into the snow. That man's stupid crime revolted him, but to hand him over was contrary to honor; just thinking of it made him boil with humiliation. He simultaneously cursed his own people who had sent him this Arab and the Arab who had dared to kill and not managed to get away. Daru got up, walked in a circle on the terrace, waited motionless, and then went back into the schoolhouse.

The Arab, leaning over the cement floor of the shed, was washing his teeth with two fingers. Daru looked at him and said, "Come." He went back into the room ahead of the prisoner. He slipped a hunting jacket on over his sweater and put on walking shoes. Standing, he waited until the Arab had put on his *chèche* and sandals. They went into the classroom, and the schoolmaster pointed to the exit saying, "Go ahead." The fellow didn't budge. "I'm coming," said Daru. The Arab went out. Daru went back into the room and made a package with pieces of rusk, dates, and sugar in it. In the classroom, before going out, he hesitated a second in front of his desk, then crossed the threshold and locked the door. "That's the way," he said. He started toward the east, followed by the prisoner. But a short distance from the schoolhouse he thought he heard a slight sound behind him. He retraced his steps and examined the surroundings of the house; there was no one there. The Arab watched him without seeming to understand. "Come on," said Daru.

They walked for an hour and rested beside a sharp needle of limestone. The snow was melting faster and faster and the sun was drinking up the puddles just as quickly, rapidly cleaning the plateau, which gradually dried and vibrated like the air itself. When they resumed walking, the ground rang under their feet. From time to time a bird rent the space in front of them with a joyful cry. Daru felt a sort of rapture before the vast familiar expanse, now almost entirely yellow under its dome of blue sky. They walked an hour more, descending toward the south. They reached a sort of flattened elevation made up of crumbly rocks. From there on, the plateau sloped down—eastward toward a low plain on which could be made out a few spindly trees, and to the south toward outcroppings of rock that gave the landscape a chaotic look.

Daru surveyed the two directions. Not a man could be seen. He turned toward the Arab, who was looking at him blankly. Daru offered the package to him. "Take it," he said. "There are dates, bread, and sugar. You can hold out for two days. Here are a thousand francs too."

The Arab took the package and the money but kept his full hands at chest level as if he didn't know what to do with what was being given him.

"Now look," the schoolmaster said as he pointed in the direction of the east, "there's the way to Tinguit. You have a two-hour walk. At Tinguit are the administration and the police. They are expecting you."

The Arab looked toward the east, still holding the package and the money against his chest. Daru took his elbow and turned him rather roughly toward the south. At the foot of the elevation on which they stood could be seen a faint path. "That's the trail across the plateau. In a day's walk from here you'll find pasturelands and the first nomads. They'll take you in and shelter you according to their law."

The Arab had now turned toward Daru, and a sort of panic was visible in his expression. "Listen," he said.

Daru shook his head. "No, be quiet. Now I'm leaving you." He turned his back on him, took two long steps in the direction of the school, looked hesitantly at the motionless Arab, and started off again. For a few minutes he heard nothing but his own step resounding on the cold ground, and he did not turn his head. A moment later, however, he turned around. The Arab was still there on the edge of the hill, his arms hanging now, and he was looking at the schoolmaster. Daru felt something rise in his throat. But he swore with impatience, waved vaguely, and started off again. He had already gone a distance when he again stopped and looked. There was no longer anyone on the hill.

Daru hesitated. The sun was now rather high in the sky and beginning to beat down on his head. The schoolmaster retraced his steps, at first somewhat uncertainly, then with decision. When he reached the little hill, he was bathed in sweat. He climbed it as fast as he could and stopped, out of breath, on the top. The rock fields to the south stood out sharply against the blue sky, but on the plain to the east a steamy heat was rising. And in that slight haze, Daru, with heavy heart, made out the Arab walking slowly on the road to prison.

A little later, standing before the window of the classroom, the schoolmaster was watching the clear light bathing the whole surface of the plateau. Behind him on the blackboard, among the winding French rivers, sprawled the clumsily chalked up words he had just read: "You handed over our brother. You will pay for this." Daru looked at the sky, the plateau, and, beyond, the invisible lands stretching all the way to the sea. In this vast landscape he had loved so much, he was alone.

For Discussion

1. What is Camus trying to suggest by entitling his story "The Guest"?
2. Does Daru have a responsibility to accept the prisoner?
3. Is Daru shirking his responsibility to the state when he decides to let his prisoner go? Does he let him go to fulfill an obligation to himself rather than to the state?
4. What responsibility is placed upon the Arab by Daru's act? What aspect of freedom is a part of that responsibility?
5. What would you have done had you been in the Arab's place?

For Comparison

1. MacLeish ("Brave New World") suggests that small men no longer dare great deeds. Is Daru a small man? Would MacLeish approve of what Daru did?
2. What similarities and differences can you find in the situations of Bonaparte ("Guests of the Nation") and Daru? Which of the two is the more responsible?

For Composition

1. Daru was (was not) being responsible.
2. Free choice brings responsibility.
3. The Arab's decision.

Frank O'Connor

GUESTS OF THE NATION

I

At dusk the big Englishman, Belcher, would shift his long legs out of the ashes and say "Well, chums, what about it?" and Noble or me would say "All right, chum" (for we had picked up some of their curious expressions), and the little Englishman, Hawkins, would light the lamp and bring out the cards. Sometimes Jeremiah Donovan would come up and supervise the game and get excited over Hawkins's cards, which he always played badly, and shout at him as if he was one of our own "Ah, you divil, you, why didn't you play the tray?"

But ordinarily Jeremiah was a sober and contented poor devil like the big Englishman, Belcher, and was looked up to only because he was a fair hand at documents, though he was slow enough even with them. He wore a small cloth hat and big gaiters over his long pants, and you seldom saw him with his hands out of his pockets. He reddened when you talked to him, tilting from toe to heel and back, and looking down all the time at his big farmer's feet. Noble and me used to make fun of his broad accent, because we were from the town.

I couldn't at the time see the point of me and Noble guarding Belcher and Hawkins at all, for it was my belief that you could have planted that pair down anywhere from this to Claregalway and they'd have taken root there like a native weed. I never in my short experience seen two men to take to the country as they did.

They were handed on to us by the Second Battalion when the search for them became too hot, and Noble and myself, being young, took over with a natural feeling of responsibility, but Hawkins made us look like fools when he showed that he knew the country better than we did.

"You're the bloke they calls Bonaparte," he says to me. "Mary Brigid O'Connell told me to ask you what you done with the pair of her brother's socks you borrowed."

For it seemed, as they explained it, that the Second used to have little evenings, and some of the girls of the neighborhood turned in, and, seeing they were such decent chaps, our fellows couldn't leave the two Englishmen out of them. Hawkins learned to dance "The Walls of Limerick," "The Siege of Ennis," and "The Waves of Tory" as well as any of them, though, naturally, we couldn't return the compliment, because our lads at that time did not dance foreign dances on principle.

From *More Stories by Frank O'Connor*. Published 1954 by Alfred A. Knopf, Inc. Reprinted by permission of the publisher.

So whatever privileges Belcher and Hawkins had with the Second they just naturally took with us, and after the first day or two we gave up all pretense of keeping a close eye on them. Not that they could have got far, for they had accents you could cut with a knife and wore khaki tunics and overcoats with civilian pants and boots. But it's my belief that they never had any idea of escaping and were quite content to be where they were.

It was a treat to see how Belcher got off with the old woman of the house where we were staying. She was a great warrant to scold, and cranky even with us, but before ever she had a chance of giving our guests, as I may call them, a lick of her tongue, Belcher had made her his friend for life. She was breaking sticks, and Belcher, who hadn't been more than ten minutes in the house, jumped up from his seat and went over to her.

"Allow me, madam," he says, smiling his queer little smile, "please allow me"; and he takes the bloody hatchet. She was struck too paralytic to speak, and after that, Belcher would be at her heels, carrying a bucket, a basket, or a load of turf, as the case might be. As Noble said, he got into looking before she leapt, and hot water, or any little thing she wanted, Belcher would have it ready for her. For such a huge man (and though I am five foot ten myself I had to look up at him) he had an uncommon shortness—or should I say lack?—of speech. It took us some time to get used to him, walking in and out, like a ghost, without a word. Especially because Hawkins talked enough for a platoon, it was strange to hear big Belcher with his toes in the ashes come out with a solitary "Excuse me, chum," or "That's right, chum." His one and only passion was cards, and I will say for him that he was a good cardplayer. He could have fleeced myself and Noble, but whatever we lost to him Hawkins lost to us, and Hawkins played with the money Belcher gave him.

Hawkins lost to us because he had too much old gab, and we probably lost to Belcher for the same reason. Hawkins and Noble would spit at one another about religion into the early hours of the morning, and Hawkins worried the soul out of Noble, whose brother was a priest, with a string of questions that would puzzle a cardinal. To make it worse, even in treating of holy subjects, Hawkins had a deplorable tongue. I never in all my career met a man who could mix such a variety of cursing and bad language into an argument. He was a terrible man, and a fright to argue. He never did a stroke of work, and when he had no one else to talk to, he got stuck in the old woman.

He met his match in her, for one day when he tried to get her to complain profanely of the drought, she gave him a great come-down by blaming it entirely on Jupiter Pluvius (a deity neither Hawkins nor I had ever heard of, though Noble said that among the pagans it was believed that he had something to do with the rain). Another day he was swearing at the capitalists for starting the German war when the old lady laid down her iron, puckered up her little crab's mouth, and said: "Mr. Hawkins, you can say what you like about the war, and think you'll deceive me because I'm only a simple poor countrywoman, but I know what started the war. It was the Italian Count that stole the heathen divinity out of the temple in Japan. Believe me, Mr. Hawkins, nothing but sorrow and want can follow the people that disturb the hidden powers."

A queer old girl, all right.

II

We had our tea one evening, and Hawkins lit the lamp and we all sat into cards. Jeremiah Donovan came in too, and sat down and watched us for a while, and it suddenly struck me that he had no great love for the two Englishmen. It came as a great surprise to me, because I hadn't noticed anything about him before.

Late in the evening a really terrible argument blew up between Hawkins and Noble, about capitalists and priests and love of your country.

"The capitalists," says Hawkins with an angry gulp, "pays the priests to tell you about the next world so as you won't notice what the bastards are up to in this."

"Nonsense, man!" says Noble, losing his temper. "Before ever a capitalist was thought of, people believed in the next world."

Hawkins stood up as though he was preaching a sermon.

"Oh, they did, did they?" he says with a sneer. "They believed all the things you believe, isn't that what you mean? And you believe that God created Adam, and Adam created Shem, and Shem created Jehoshophat. You believe all that silly old fairytale about Eve and Eden and the apple. Well, listen to me, chum. If you're entitled to hold a silly belief like that, I'm entitled to hold my silly belief—which is that the first thing your God created was a bleeding capitalist, with morality and Rolls-Royce complete. Am I right, chum?" he says to Belcher.

"You're right, chum," says Belcher with his amused smile, and got up from the table to stretch his long legs into the fire and stroke his moustache. So, seeing that Jeremiah Donovan was going, and that there was no knowing when the argument about religion would be over, I went out with him. We strolled down to the village together, and then he stopped and started blushing and mumbling and saying I ought to be behind, keeping guard on the prisoners. I didn't like the tone he took with me, and anyway I was bored with life in the cottage, so I replied by asking him what the hell we wanted guarding them at all for. I told him I'd talked it over with Noble, and that we'd both rather be out with a fighting column.

"What use are those fellows to us?" says I.

He looked at me in surprise and said: "I thought you knew we were keeping them as hostages."

"Hostages?" I said.

"The enemy have prisoners belonging to us," he says, "and now they're talking of shooting them. If they shoot our prisoners, we'll shoot theirs."

"Shoot them?" I said.

"What else did you think we were keeping them for?" he says.

"Wasn't it very unforeseen of you not to warn Noble and myself of that in the beginning?" I said.

"How was it?" says he. "You might have known it."

"We couldn't know it, Jeremiah Donovan," says I. "How could we when they were on our hands so long?"

"The enemy have our prisoners as long and longer," says he.

"That's not the same thing at all," says I.

"What difference is there?" says he.

I couldn't tell him, because I knew he wouldn't understand. If it was only an old dog that was going to the vet's, you'd try and not get too fond of him, but Jeremiah Donovan wasn't a man that would ever be in danger of that.

"And when is this thing going to be decided?" says I.

"We might hear tonight," he says. "Or tomorrow or the next day at latest. So if it's only hanging round here that's a trouble to you, you'll be free soon enough."

It wasn't the hanging round that was a trouble to me at all by this time. I had worse things to worry about. When I got back to the cottage the argument was still on. Hawkins was holding forth in his best style, maintaining that there was no next world, and Noble was maintaining that there was; but I could see that Hawkins had had the best of it.

"Do you know what, chum?" he was saying with a saucy smile. "I think you're just as big a bleeding unbeliever as I am. You say you believe in the next world, and you know just as much about the next world as I do, which is sweet damn-all. What's heaven? You don't know. Where's heaven? You don't know. You know sweet damn-all! I ask you again, do they wear wings?"

"Very well, then," says Noble, "they do. Is that enough for you? They do wear wings."

"Where do they get them, then? Who makes them? Have they a factory for wings? Have they a sort of store where you hands in your chit and takes your bleeding wings?"

"You're an impossible man to argue with," says Noble. "Now, listen to me—" And they were off again.

It was long after midnight when we locked up and went to bed. As I blew out the candle I told Noble what Jeremiah Donovan was after telling me. Noble took it very quietly. When we'd been in bed about an hour he asked me did I think we ought to tell the Englishmen. I didn't think we should, because it was more than likely that the English wouldn't shoot our men, and even if they did, the brigade officers, who were always up and down with the Second Battalion and knew the Englishmen well, wouldn't be likely to want them plugged. "I think so too," says Noble. "It would be great cruelty to put the wind up them now."

"It was very unforeseen of Jeremiah Donovan anyhow," says I.

It was next morning that we found it so hard to face Belcher and Hawkins. We went about the house all day scarcely saying a word. Belcher didn't seem to notice; he was stretched into the ashes as usual, with his usual look of waiting in quietness for something unforeseen to happen, but Hawkins noticed and put it down to Noble's being beaten in the argument of the night before.

"Why can't you take a discussion in the proper spirit?" he says severely. "You and your Adam and Eve! I'm a Communist, that's what I am. Communist or anarchist, it all comes to much the same thing." And for hours he went round the house, muttering when the fit took him. "Adam and Eve! Adam and Eve! Nothing better to do with their time than picking bleeding apples!"

III

I don't know how we got through that day, but I was very glad when it was over, the tea things were cleared away, and Belcher said in his peaceable way: "Well, chums, what about it?" We sat round the table and Hawkins took out the cards, and just then I heard Jeremiah Donovan's footstep on the path and a dark presentiment crossed my mind. I rose from the table and caught him before he reached the door.

"What do you want?" I asked.

"I want those two soldier friends of yours," he says, getting red.

"Is that the way, Jeremiah Donovan?" I asked.

"That's the way. There were four of our lads shot this morning, one of them a boy of sixteen."

"That's bad," I said.

At that moment Noble followed me out, and the three of us walked down the path together, talking in whispers. Feeney, the local intelligence officer, was standing by the gate.

"What are you going to do about it?" I asked Jeremiah Donovan.

"I want you and Noble to get them out; tell them they're being shifted again; that'll be the quietest way."

"Leave me out of that," says Noble under his breath.

Jeremiah Donovan looks at him hard.

"All right," he says. "You and Feeney get a few tools from the shed and dig a hole by the far end of the bog. Bonaparte and myself will be after you. Don't let anyone see you with the tools. I wouldn't like it to go beyond ourselves."

We saw Feeney and Noble go round to the shed and went in ourselves. I left Jeremiah Donovan to do the explanations. He told them that he had orders to send them back to the Second Battalion. Hawkins let out a mouthful of curses, and you could see that though Belcher didn't say anything, he was a bit upset too. The old woman was for having them stay in spite of us, and she didn't stop advising them until Jeremiah Donovan lost his temper and turned on her. He had a nasty temper, I noticed. It was pitch-dark in the cottage by this time, but no one thought of lighting the lamp, and in the darkness the two Englishmen fetched their topcoats and said good-bye to the old woman.

"Just as a man makes a home of a bleeding place, some bastard at headquarters thinks you're too cushy and shunts you off," says Hawkins, shaking her hand.

"A thousand thanks, madam," says Belcher. "A thousand thanks for everything"—as though he'd made it up.

We went round to the back of the house and down towards the bog. It was only then that Jeremiah Donovan told them. He was shaking with excitement.

"There were four of our fellows shot in Cork this morning and now you're to be shot as a reprisal."

"What are you talking about?" snaps Hawkins. "It's bad enough being mucked about as we are without having to put up with your funny jokes."

"It isn't a joke," says Donovan. "I'm sorry, Hawkins, but it's true," and begins on the usual rigmarole about duty and how unpleasant it is.

I never noticed that people who talk a lot about duty find it much of a trouble to them.

"Oh, cut it out!" says Hawkins.

"Ask Bonaparte," says Donovan, seeing that Hawkins isn't taking him seriously. "Isn't it true, Bonaparte?"

"It is," I say, and Hawkins stops.

"Ah, for Christ's sake, chum!"

"I mean it, chum," I say.

"You don't sound as if you meant it."

"If he doesn't mean it, I do," says Donovan, working himself up.

"What have you against me, Jeremiah Donovan?"

"I never said I had anything against you. But why did your people take out four of our prisoners and shoot them in cold blood?"

He took Hawkins by the arm and dragged him on, but it was impossible to make him understand that we were in earnest. I had the Smith and Wesson in my pocket and I kept fingering it and wondering what I'd do if they put up a fight for it or ran, and wishing to God they'd do one or the other. I knew if they did run for it, that I'd never fire on them. Hawkins wanted to know was Noble in it, and when we said yes, he asked us why Noble wanted to plug him. Why did any of us want to plug him? What had he done to us? Weren't we all chums? Didn't we understand him and didn't he understand us? Did we imagine for an instant that he'd shoot us for all the so-and-so officers in the so-and-so British Army?

By this time we'd reached the bog, and I was so sick I couldn't even answer him. We walked along the edge of it in the darkness, and every now and then Hawkins would call a halt and begin all over again, as if he was wound up, about our being chums, and I knew that nothing but the sight of the grave would convince him that we had to do it. And all the time I was hoping that something would happen; that they'd run for it or that Noble would take over the responsibility from me. I had the feeling that it was worse on Noble than on me.

IV

At last we saw the lantern in the distance and made towards it. Noble was carrying it, and Feeney was standing somewhere in the darkness behind him, and the picture of them so still and silent in the bogland brought it home to me that we were in earnest, and banished the last bit of hope I had.

Belcher, on recognizing Noble, said: "Hallo, chum," in his quiet way, but Hawkins flew at him at once, and the argument began all over again, only this time Noble had nothing to say for himself and stood with his head down, holding the lantern between his legs.

It was Jeremiah Donovan who did the answering. For the twentieth time, as though it was haunting his mind, Hawkins asked if anybody thought he'd shoot Noble.

"Yes, you would," says Jeremiah Donovan.

"No, I wouldn't, damn you!"

"You would, because you'd know you'd be shot for not doing it."

"I wouldn't, not if I was to be shot twenty times over. I wouldn't shoot a pal. And Belcher wouldn't—isn't that right, Belcher?"

"That's right, chum," Belcher said, but more by way of answering the question than of joining in the argument. Belcher sounded as though whatever unforeseen thing he'd always been waiting for had come at last.

"Anyway, who says Noble would be shot if I wasn't? What do you think I'd do if I was in his place, out in the middle of a blasted bog?"

"What would you do?" asks Donovan.

"I'd go with him wherever he was going, of course. Share my last bob with him and stick by him through thick and thin. No one can ever say of me that I let down a pal."

"We had enough of this," says Jeremiah Donovan, cocking his revolver. "Is there any message you want to send?"

"No, there isn't."

"Do you want to say your prayers?"

Hawkins came out with a cold-blooded remark that even shocked me and turned on Noble again.

"Listen to me, Noble," he says. "You and me are chums. You can't come over to my side, so I'll come over to your side. That show you I mean what I say? Give me a rifle and I'll go along with you and the other lads."

Nobody answered him. We knew that was no way out.

"Hear what I'm saying?" he says. "I'm through with it. I'm a deserter or anything else you like. I don't believe in your stuff, but it's no worse than mine. That satisfy you?"

Noble raised his head, but Donovan began to speak and he lowered it again without replying.

"For the last time, have you any messages to send?" says Donovan in a cold, excited sort of voice.

"Shut up, Donovan! You don't understand me, but these lads do. They're not the sort to make a pal and kill a pal. They're not the tools of any capitalist."

I alone of the crowd saw Donovan raise his Webley to the back of Hawkins's neck, and as he did so I shut my eyes and tried to pray. Hawkins had begun to say something else when Donovan fired, and as I opened my eyes at the bang, I saw Hawkins stagger at the knees and lie out flat at Noble's feet, slowly and as quiet as a kid falling asleep, with the lantern-light on his lean legs and bright farmer's boots. We all stood very still, watching him settle out in the last agony.

Then Belcher took out a handkerchief and began to tie it about his own eyes (in our excitement we'd forgotten to do the same for Hawkins), and, seeing it wasn't big enough, turned and asked for the loan of mine. I gave it to him and he knotted the two together and pointed with his foot at Hawkins.

"He's not quite dead," he says. "Better give him another."

Sure enough, Hawkins's left knee is beginning to rise. I bend down and put my gun to his head; then, recollecting myself, I get up again. Belcher understands what's in my mind.

"Give him his first," he says. "I don't mind. Poor bastard, we don't know what's happening to him now."

I knelt and fired. By this time I didn't seem to know what I was doing.

Belcher, who was fumbling a bit awkwardly with the handkerchiefs, came out with a laugh as he heard the shot. It was the first time I heard him laugh and it sent a shudder down my back; it sounded so unnatural.

"Poor bugger!" he said quietly. "And last night he was so curious about it all. It's very queer, chums, I always think. Now he knows as much about it as they'll ever let him know, and last night he was all in the dark."

Donovan helped him to tie the handkerchiefs about his eyes. "Thanks, chum," he said. Donovan asked if there were any messages he wanted sent.

"No, chum," he says. "Not for me. If any of you would like to write to Hawkins's mother, you'll find a letter from her in his pocket. He and his mother were great chums. But my missus left me eight years ago. Went away with another fellow and took the kid with her. I like the feeling of a home, as you may have noticed, but I couldn't start again after that."

It was an extraordinary thing, but in those few minutes Belcher said more than in all the weeks before. It was just as if the sound of the shot had started a flood of talk in him and he could go on the whole night like that, quite happily, talking about himself. We stood round like fools now that he couldn't see us any longer. Donovan looked at Noble, and Noble shook his head. Then Donovan raised his Webley, and at that moment Belcher gives his queer laugh again. He may have thought we were talking about him, or perhaps he noticed the same thing I'd noticed and couldn't understand it.

"Excuse me, chums," he says. "I feel I'm talking the hell of a lot, and so silly, about my being so handy about a house and things like that. But this thing came on me suddenly. You'll forgive me, I'm sure."

"You don't want to say a prayer?" asked Donovan.

"No chum," he says. "I don't think it would help. I'm ready, and you boys want to get it over."

"You understand that we're only doing our duty?" says Donovan.

Belcher's head was raised like a blind man's, so that you could only see his chin and the tip of his nose in the lantern-light.

"I never could make out what duty was myself," he said. "I think you're all good lads, if that's what you mean. I'm not complaining."

Noble, just as if he couldn't bear any more of it, raised his fist at Donovan, and in a flash Donovan raised his gun and fired. The big man went over like a sack of meal, and this time there was no need of a second shot.

I don't remember much about the burying, but that it was worse than all the rest because we had to carry them to the grave. It was all mad lonely with nothing but a patch of lantern-light between ourselves and the dark, and birds hooting and screeching all round, disturbed by the guns. Noble went through Hawkins's belongings to find the letter from his mother, and then joined his hands together. He did the same with Belcher. Then, when we'd filled in the grave, we separated from Jeremiah Donovan and Feeney and took our tools back to the shed. All the way we didn't speak a word. The kitchen was dark and cold as we'd left it, and the old woman was sitting over the hearth, saying her beads. We walked past her into the room, and Noble struck a match to light the lamp. She rose quietly and came to the doorway with all her cantankerousness gone.

"What did ye do with them?" she asked in a whisper, and Noble started so that the match went out in his hand.

"What's that?" he asked without turning round.

"I heard ye," she said.

"What did you hear?" asked Noble.

"I heard ye. Do ye think I didn't hear ye, putting the spade back in the houseen?"

Noble struck another match and this time the lamp lit for him.

"Was that what ye did to them?" she asked.

Then, by God, in the very doorway, she fell on her knees and began praying, and after looking at her for a minute or two Noble did the same by the fireplace. I pushed my way out past her and left them at it. I stood at the door, watching the stars and listening to the shrieking of the birds dying out over the bogs. It is so strange what you feel at times like that you can't describe it. Noble says he saw everything ten times the size, as though there were nothing in the whole world but that little patch of bog with the two Englishmen stiffening into it, but with me it was as if the patch of bog where the Englishmen were was a million miles away, and even Noble and the old woman, mumbling behind me, and the birds and the bloody stars were all far away and I was somehow very small and very lost and lonely like a child astray in the snow. And anything that happened me afterwards, I never felt the same about again.

For Discussion

1. How does each of the Irish soldiers view the prisoners?
2. Did the Irish soldiers bring the situation on themselves by treating the men as guests rather than prisoners?
3. Bonaparte was fulfilling his responsibility to the state, but was he fulfilling his obligations to himself? What about his personal convictions?
4. What happens when an individual's conscience conflicts with demands

of the state? Suggest situations in which this might occur. What
should the person do? Which side takes precedence—personal conscience or state?

For Comparison

1. How would Thomas Jefferson, at least as he is described by MacLeish
   ("Brave New World"), react to Bonaparte?
2. What role would Bonaparte play if he were transposed to the scene
   and situation in "The Portable Phonograph"? What would be his attitude toward Jenkins? Toward the phonograph?

For Composition

1. Personal conscience versus demands of state.
2. Bonaparte was (was not) being responsible.
3. The unnatural hostilities of war.

ARCHIBALD MACLEISH

BRAVE NEW WORLD

But you, Thomas Jefferson,
You could not lie so still,
You could not bear the weight of stone
On the quiet hill,

You could not keep your green grown peace
Nor hold your folded hand
If you could see your new world now,
Your new sweet land.

There was a time, Tom Jefferson,
When freedom made free men.
The new found earth and the new freed mind
Were brothers then.

There was a time when tyrants feared
The new world of the free.
Now freedom is afraid and shrieks
At tyranny.

Words have not changed their sense so soon
Nor tyranny grown new.
The truths you held, Tom Jefferson,
Will still hold true.

What's changed is freedom in this age.
What great men dared to choose
Small men now dare neither win
Nor lose.

You, Thomas Jefferson,
You could not lie so still,
You could not bear the weight of stone
On your green hill,

You could not hold your angry tongue
If you could see how bold
The old stale bitter world plays new—
And the new world old.

For Discussion

1. Why does MacLeish address Thomas Jefferson? What persons representative of contemporary government might he have addressed?
2. What happened to man's freedom according to the poet? How is it possible that freedom might become afraid?
3. Why do small men now not dare what great men once dared? Is it impossible to have any more great men in America?
4. Who is responsible for the situation described? Is there anything that you as an individual can do to correct it?

For Comparison

1. Basing your ideas solely on the characterization of Jefferson in this poem, suggest what you think his attitude might be toward McKay's narrator in "The White City."
2. Does the concept that MacLeish holds of Jefferson refute the one projected by Commager in "The Declaration Is for Today"? How might some of Jefferson's opinions be different if he were alive today?

For Composition

1. What Thomas Jefferson would do today.
2. Tyranny versus freedom.
3. The greatest need in America today.

CARL SANDBURG

FOUR PRELUDES ON PLAYTHINGS OF THE WIND

"The past is a bucket of ashes."

1

The woman named Tomorrow
sits with a hairpin in her teeth
and takes her time
and does her hair the way she wants it
and fastens at last the last braid and coil
and puts the hairpin where it belongs
and turns and drawls: Well, what of it?
My grandmother, Yesterday, is gone.
What of it? Let the dead be dead.

2

The doors were cedar
and the panels strips of gold
and the girls were golden girls
and the panels read and the girls chanted:
    We are the greatest city,
    the greatest nation:
    nothing like us ever was.
The doors are twisted on broken hinges.
Sheets of rain swish through on the wind
    where the golden girls ran and the panels read:
    We are the greatest city,
    the greatest nation,
    nothing like us ever was.

3

It has happened before.
Strong men put up a city and got
    a nation together,
And paid singers to sing and women
    to warble: We are the greatest city,
        the greatest nation,
        nothing like us ever was.
And while the singers sang
and the strong men listened
and paid the singers well
and felt good about it all,
        there were rats and lizards who listened
        . . . and the only listeners left now
        . . . are . . . the rats . . . and the lizards.

And there are black crows
crying, "Caw, caw,"
bringing mud and sticks
building a nest
        over the words carved
        on the doors where the panels were cedar
        and the strips on the panels were gold
        and the golden girls came singing:
            We are the greatest city,
            the greatest nation:
            nothing like us ever was.

The only singers now are crows crying, "Caw, caw,"
And the sheets of rain whine in the wind and doorways.
And the only listeners now are . . . the rats . . . and the lizards.

4

The feet of the rats
scribble on the doorsills;
the hieroglyphs of the rat footprints
chatter the pedigrees of the rats
and babble of the blood
and gabble of the breed
of the grandfathers and the great-grandfathers
of the rats.

And the wind shifts
and the dust on a doorsill shifts
and even the writing of the rat footprints
tells us nothing, nothing at all
about the greatest city, the greatest nation
where the strong men listened
and the women warbled: Nothing like us ever was.

For Discussion

1. Is the action of the woman in the first stanza responsible? What aspects of contemporary society might she represent?
2. What specific reasons can you list for the collapse of the "greatest nation" that ever was? How closely do your descriptions fit scenes in current American life?
3. What are some of the rats and lizards that sneak in at night to destroy the nation?
4. What action must a nation take to prevent itself from being destroyed in the manner described in this poem?

For Comparison

1. What advice given in D. H. Lawrence's "The Spirit of Place" might have prevented the kind of situation described by Sandburg?
2. Are Sandburg and Jeffers ("Shine, Perishing Republic") expressing the same criticism of American society? Does Sandburg's poem indicate that good and evil always exist together?

For Composition

1. Destructive forces in government.
2. Irresponsibility in government.
3. Excessive national pride can be destructive.

ROBINSON JEFFERS

SHINE, PERISHING REPUBLIC

While this America settles in the mould of its
    vulgarity, heavily thickening to empire,
And protest, only a bubble in the molten mass, pops
    and sighs out, and the mass hardens,

I sadly smiling remember that the flower fades to
    make fruit, the fruit rots to make earth.
Out of the mother; and through the spring exultances,
    ripeness and decadence; and home to the mother.

You making haste haste on decay: not blameworthy;
    life is good, be it stubbornly long or suddenly
A mortal splendor: Meteors are not needed less than
    mountains: shine, perishing republic.

But for my children, I would have them keep their
    distance from the thickening center; corruption
Never has been compulsory, when the cities lie at the
    monster's feet there are left the mountains.

And boys, be in nothing so moderate as in love of
    man, a clever servant, insufferable master.
There is the trap that catches noblest spirits, that
    caught—they say—God, when he walked on earth.

For Discussion

1. Who is responsible for the condition of the republic as it is described by Jeffers?
2. Should man keep his "distance from the thickening center"? Is this a responsible attitude?
3. Is Jeffers suggesting that country life ("the mountains") are better places than the cities? Do you agree? Why? Why not?
4. The poet seems to suggest that "ripeness and decadence" always exist together. Is this true? Must there always be evil as well as good?
5. What is Jeffers alluding to in the last two lines? What is the trap?

For Comparison

1. Is Daru's ("The Guest") retreat to the mountain similar to what Jeffers recommends in this poem?
2. What ideas in this poem give support to the central thesis in Davis's essay "Overpopulated America"?

For Composition

1. Protest does (does not) accomplish good.
2. Goodness and evil in America.
3. Youth's relationship to corruption in society.

CLAUDE MCKAY

THE WHITE CITY

I will not toy with it nor bend an inch.
Deep in the secret chambers of my heart
I muse my life-long hate, and without flinch
I bear it nobly as I live my part.
My being would be a skeleton, a shell,
If this dark Passion that fills my every mood,
And makes my heaven in the white world's hell,
Did not forever feed me vital blood.
I see the mighty city through a mist—
The strident trains that speed the goaded mass,
The poles and spires and towers vapor-kissed,
The fortressed port through which the great ships pass,
The tides, the wharves, the dens I contemplate,
Are sweet like wanton loves because I hate.

For Discussion

1. What is the meaning of the first line of this poem? What specifically is the "it"?
2. The poem obviously deals with racial tensions in the city. What are some of those tensions? How might the state have acted to have prevented them from existing?
3. Discuss this poem in terms of the hostilities felt by a Black person toward what is typically called "The American dream." How important is it that the object of attack in the poem is "the white city"? Why not the white farm, for instance?

For Comparison

1. How might McKay talk back to Commager ("The Declaration Is for Today!")? How would Commager answer?
2. McKay feels alienated from the American dream and so does Vanzetti ("Last Speech to the Court"). What lines in Vanzetti's poem would have particular meaning to McKay?

For Composition

1. Hate in the ghetto.
2. The lost dream of American equality.
3. State responsibility in racial issues.

MARIANNE MOORE

IN DISTRUST OF MERITS

Strengthened to live, strengthened to die for
    medals and position victories?
They're fighting, fighting, fighting the blind
    man who thinks he sees, —
who cannot see that the enslaver is
enslaved; the hater, harmed. O shining O
        firm star, O tumultuous
            ocean lashed till small things go
        as they will, the mountainous
            wave makes us who look, know

depth. Lost at sea before they fought! O
        star of David, star of Bethlehem,
O black imperial lion
        of the Lord—emblem
of a risen world—be joined at last, be
joined. There is hate's crown beneath which all is
            death; there's love's without which none
        is king; the blessed deeds bless
        the halo. As contagion
            of sickness makes sickness,

contagion of trust can make trust. They're
        fighting in deserts and caves, one by
one, in battalions and squadrons;
        they're fighting that I
may yet recover from the disease, My
Self, some have it lightly, some will die. "Man's
            wolf to man" and we devour
                ourselves. The enemy could not
            have made a greater breach in our
                defenses. One pilot-

---

ing a blind man can escape him, but
   Job disheartened by false comfort knew
that nothing can be so defeating
   as a blind man who
can see. O alive who are dead, who are
proud not to see, O small dust of the earth
   that walks so arrogantly,
         trust begets power and faith is
      an affectionate thing. We
         vow, we make this promise

to the fighting—it's a promise—"We'll
   never hate black, white, red, yellow, Jew,
Gentile, Untouchable." We are
   not competent to
make our vows. With set jaw they are fighting,
fighting, fighting,—some we love whom we know,
      some we love but know not—that
         hearts may feel and not be numb.
      It cures me; or am I what
         I can't believe in? Some

in snow, some on crags, some in quicksands,
   little by little, much by much, they
are fighting fighting fighting that where
   there was death there may
be life. "When a man is prey to anger,
he is moved by outside things; when he holds
      his ground in patience patience
         patience, that is action or
      beauty," the soldier's defense
         and hardest armor for

the fight. The world's an orphans' home. Shall
   we never have peace without sorrow?
without pleas of the dying for
   help that won't come? O
quiet form upon the dust, I cannot
look and yet I must. If these great patient
      dyings—all these agonies
         and woundbearings and bloodshed—
      can teach us how to live, these
         dyings were not wasted.

Hate-hardened heart, O heart of iron,
   iron is iron till it is rust.
There never was a war that was

>   not inward; I must
> fight till I have conquered in myself what
> causes war, but I would not believe it.
>   I inwardly did nothing.
>   O Iscariotlike crime!
>   Beauty is everlasting
>   and dust is for a time.

For Discussion

1. Do you agree with Moore that man's greatest enemy is himself and that man is indeed "wolf to man"?
2. Why does the poet constantly make reference to a blind man? What accusation is she making?
3. Is the dream that " 'We'll / never hate black, white, red, yellow, Jew, Gentile, Untouchable' " possible in the present century?
4. Moore concludes that we must look at the dyings and learn from them how to live. Do you agree with her that this is one of the lessons that we must learn from war? Is it the only one? What others do you recognize?

For Comparison

1. Moore says that man is his own worst enemy, and Commager ("The Declaration Is for Today") makes much issue of the fact that all men are created equal. Is it important that we see this type of equality as extending beyond national boundaries? Would Commager agree with Moore that real peace is little more than a dream?
2. In what way do both Daru ("The Guest") and Bonaparte ("Guests of the Nation") give evidence of Moore's statement that "the enslaver is / enslaved"? What types of limitations are placed upon government by its wars, prisons, police departments, etc.?

For Composition

1. We will (will not) always have war.
2. The good that can come from war.
3. War is never justified.

WILFRED OWEN

MENTAL CASES

Who are these? Why sit they here in twilight?
Wherefore rock they, purgatorial shadows,
Drooping tongues from jaws that slob their relish,
Baring teeth that leer like skulls' tongues wicked?
Stroke on stroke of pain, — but what slow panic,
Gouged these chasms round their fretted sockets?
Ever from their hair and through their hand palms
Misery swelters. Surely we have perished
Sleeping, and walk hell; but who these hellish?

— These are men whose minds the Dead have ravished.
Memory fingers in their hair of murders,
Multitudinous murders they once witnessed.
Wading sloughs of flesh these helpless wander,
Treading blood from lungs that had loved laughter.
Always they must see these things and hear them,
Batter of guns and shatter of flying muscles,
Carnage incomparable and human squander
Rucked too thick for these men's extrication.

Therefore still their eyeballs shrink tormented
Back into their brains, because on their sense
Sunlight seems a bloodsmear; night comes blood-black;
Dawn breaks open like a wound that bleeds afresh
— Thus their heads wear this hilarious, hideous,
Awful falseness of set-smiling corpses.
— Thus their hands are plucking at each other;
Picking at the rope-knots of their scourging;
Snatching after us who smote them, brother,
Pawing us who dealt them war and madness.

For Discussion

1. What sort of society is Owen depicting in this poem?
2. Who is responsible for the condition of the society? Is Owen attempting to place blame on the men involved in war or on the men who control government and direct the affairs of war? Which do you feel

is the most responsible, or is there an equal amount of responsibility?
3. Is killing during a time of war an actual murder, or do you feel Owen's terminology is too harsh?
4. What meanings are implied in the word *brother* in the next to the last line of the poem?

For Comparison

1. Do you feel that Bonaparte ("Guests of the Nation") will eventually become one of the mental cases described by Owen? What might prevent this from happening?
2. Will the individual cases of mental despair and insanity described by Owen eventually lead to the total collapse of our civilization as described by Sandburg ("Four Preludes on Playthings of the Wind")?

For Composition

1. How war affects soldiers.
2. Killing during war is (is not) murder.
3. The responsibility for war.

W. H. AUDEN

THE UNKNOWN CITIZEN

(To JS/07/M/378 This Marble Monument Is Erected by the State)

He was found by the Bureau of Statistics to be
One against whom there was no official complaint,
And all the reports on his conduct agree
That, in the modern sense of an old-fashioned word, he was a saint,
For in everything he did he served the Greater Community.
Except for the War till the day he retired
He worked in a factory and never got fired,
But satisfied his employers, Fudge Motors Inc.
Yet he wasn't a scab or odd in his views,
For his Union reports that he paid his dues,
(Our report on his Union shows it was sound)
And our Social Psychology workers found
That he was popular with his mates and liked a drink.

The Press are convinced that he bought a paper every day
And that his reactions to advertisements were normal in every way.
Policies taken out in his name prove that he was fully insured,
And his Health-card shows he was once in hospital but left it cured.
Both Producers Research and High-Grade Living declare
He was fully sensible to the advantages of the Installment Plan
And had everything necessary to Modern Man,
A phonograph, a radio, a car and a frigidaire.
Our researchers into Public Opinion are content
That he held the proper opinions for the time of year;
When there was peace, he was for peace; when there was war, he went.
He was married and added five children to the population,
Which our Eugenist says was the right number for a parent of his generation,
And our teachers report that he never interfered with their education.
Was he free? Was he happy? The question is absurd:
Had anything been wrong, we certainly should have heard.

For Discussion

1. Is the citizen described by Auden in this poem a good citizen? What are some of his good points? His bad ones?
2. If he was so perfect a person, why was he described as "unknown"?
3. To what extent does this citizen represent the Establishment so often criticized by the young of our generation? Is their criticism valid?
4. The citizen worked for Fudge Motors, a name suggesting some type of improper or illegal business. Is he in any way responsible for what goes on at work?
5. In what way can a citizen "serve the Greater Community" for the wrong reasons?

For Comparison

1. Is the unknown citizen in this poem the same type of person as the speaker in e. e. cummings' poem? Do they both hold the same basic philosophy of citizenship? Specify as nearly as you can that philosophy.
2. Does the unknown citizen evidence the type of freedom described in Lawrence's essay? Would Lawrence enjoy knowing such a person as the one described by Auden?

For Composition

1. Conformity makes for good citizenship.
2. Blind conformity is a weakness in society.
3. The unknown citizen was (was not) happy with life.

---

e. e. cummings

next to of course god

"next to of course god america i
love you land of the pilgrims' and so forth oh
say can you see by the dawn's early my
country 'tis of centuries come and go
and are no more what of it we should worry
in every language even deafanddumb
thy sons acclaim your glorious name by gorry
by jingo by gee by gosh by gum
why talk of beauty what could be more beautiful than these heroic happy dead
who rushed like lions to the roaring slaughter
they did not stop to think they died instead
then shall the voice of liberty be mute?"

He spoke. And drank rapidly a glass of water

For Discussion

1. What type of person is the narrator in this poem? Do you feel he is
   sincere in this attitude? Is he responsible?
2. This poem is in part a criticism of an almost ritualistic loyalty to
   America without thinking about what such loyalty means. Is there
   a danger that the loyalty taught in the early school years may be in-
   correctly focused? Do you feel a deep-seated loyalty to America?
   Why? Why not?
3. What aspects of American life other than war are being criticized by
   cummings?
4. What meaning does the title of the poem contribute?

For Comparison

1. How much of the ritualistic admiration for America that is expressed in this poem might also have been a part of the background for the characters in "The Portable Phonograph"? Which character can you picture most readily here reciting this litany?
2. How would McKay's narrator ("The White City") relate to this poem? See if you can structure a poem somewhat similar in style to this one which McKay's narrator might recite.

For Composition

1. Patriotic for the wrong reasons.
2. America is (is not) beautiful.
3. A real reason for loyalty.

BARTOLOMEO VANZETTI

LAST SPEECH TO THE COURT

I have talk a great deal of myself
but I even forgot to name Sacco.
Sacco too is a worker,
from his boyhood a skilled worker, lover of work,
with a good job and pay,
a bank account, a good and lovely wife,
two beautiful children and a neat little home
at the verge of a wood, near a brook.

Sacco is a heart, a faith, a character, a man;
a man, lover of nature, and mankind;
a man who gave all, who sacrifice all
to the cause of liberty and to his love for mankind:
money, rest, mundane ambition,
his own wife, his children, himself
and his own life.

From *Letters of Sacco and Vanzetti* edited by Marion Denman Frankfurter and Gardner Jackson. Copyright 1928, renewed 1956 by The Viking Press, Inc. Reprinted by permission of The Viking Press, Inc.

Sacco has never dreamt to steal, never to assassinate.
He and I have never brought a morsel
of bread to our mouths, from our childhood to today
which has not been gained by the sweat of our brows.
Never . . .

Oh, yes, I may be more witful, as some have put it;
I am a better babbler than he is, but many, many times
in hearing his heartful voice ringing a faith sublime,
in considering his supreme sacrifice, remembering his heroism,

I felt small at the presence of his greatness
and found myself compelled to fight back
from my eyes the tears,
and quanch my heart
trobling to my throat to not weep before him:
this man called thief and assassin and doomed.

But Sacco's name will live in the hearts of the people
and in their gratitude when Katzmann's bones
and yours will be dispersed by time;
when your name, his name, your laws, institutions,
and your false god are but a dim rememoring
of a cursed past in which man was wolf
to the man . . .

If it had not been for these thing
I might have live out my life
talking at street corners to scorning men.
I might have die, unmarked, unknown, a failure.
Now we are not a failure.
This is our career and our triumph. Never
in our full life could we hope to do such work
for tolerance; for justice, for man's understanding
of man, as we do by accident.

Our words, our lives, our pains—nothing!
The taking of our lives—lives of a good shoemaker and
    a poor fishpeddler—
all! That last moment belongs to us—
that agony is our triumph.

For Discussion

1. Nicola Sacco and Bartolomeo Vanzetti were defendants in a famous
   murder trial that rocked the world in the 1920s. Both were finally con-

victed of the crime which they—and half the world with them—maintained they did not commit. What, then, does Vanzetti mean when he says, "Now we are not a failure. / This is our career and our triumph"?
2. Many people felt that Sacco and Vanzetti were executed for their somewhat anarchistic and radical beliefs. How does Vanzetti's speech support this feeling?
3. How responsible is man to see law and justice done? Did Sacco have a right to sacrifice all—"his own wife, his children, himself"?

For Comparison

1. What would be Vanzetti's reaction to cummings' poem, "next to of course god"? How would he react particularly to the reference to the "heroic happy dead/who rushed like lions to the roaring slaughter"?
2. Compare the life lived and described by Vanzetti with that of the unknown citizen discussed in Auden's poem. Which type of life is the most fulfilled? Examine the two in light of the next-to-last line of Auden's poem.

For Composition

1. Justice always demands responsibility.
2. Living for what you believe is sometimes dangerous.
3. I am not free to jeopardize another for my beliefs.

Index of Authors and Titles